The Japanization of British Industry

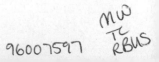

Human Resource Management in Action

Series Editor: Brian Towers

The Japanization of British Industry

New Developments in the 1990s

NICK OLIVER AND
BARRY WILKINSON

Copyright © Nick Oliver and Barry Wilkinson, 1988, 1992

The right of Nick Oliver and Barry Wilkinson to be identified as author of
this work has been asserted in accordance with the
Copyright, Designs and Patents Act 1988.

First published 1988
Second edition published in 1992
Reprinted 1993, 1997

Blackwell Publishers Ltd
108 Cowley Road, Oxford OX4 1JF, UK

Blackwell Publishers Inc.
238 Main Street, Cambridge, Massachusetts 02142, USA

British Library Cataloguing in Publication Data
A CIP catalogue record for this book is available from the British Library

Library of Congress Cataloging in Publication Data
Oliver, Nick
The Japanization of British industry / Nick Oliver and Barry Wilkinson —
2nd ed.   p. cm.
Includes bibliographical references and index.
ISBN 0–631–18676–X (pbk)
1. Corporations, Japanese—Great Britain. 2. Great Britain—Industries.
I. Wilkinson, Barry. II. Title.
HD2845.043   1992
338.8'8952041—dc20

Typeset in 11 on 13pt Plantin by Best-set Typesetter Ltd, Hong Kong
Printed and bound in Great Britain by Athenæum Press Ltd, Gateshead, Tyne & Wear

This book is printed on acid-free paper

Contents

Figures

Tables

Foreword

Something started to go wrong with the British economy soon after the Great Exhibition of 1851 – as the economic historians keep reminding us. Of course it was only relative, with the Americans, Germans and Japanese beginning to take on the pioneering British.

Now the USA is, at best, in transition and may have gone into long-term decline. The German *Wirtschaftswunder* is less of a miracle than it once was but is still impressive and provides an example much closer to home in economic and cultural terms for the UK to try to emulate. However, it is the Japanese who are the most beguiling.

There is much to awake and maintain Western interest in the Japanese in their homeland. What is not widely understood, in historical terms, is that Japan was a rising economic power in the last quarter of the nineteenth century, with industries that provided a platform for the defeat of Russia in 1905–6 and the ability to contain the combined, overwhelming strength of the Allies for the long duration of the Second World War.

These formed the roots of the spectacular successes of Japanese firms from the 1960s to the 1990s. Japan, as Oliver and Wilkinson remind us, is now the richest nation in the world, producing over 10 per cent of world GDP in 1987, compared with a figure of only 2 per cent twenty years earlier. Japanese motor cycles, cameras, videos, watches, calculators, microwaves, hi fi, and televisions dominate world markets almost to the extinction of the competition. Small and medium-sized Japanese automobiles have flooded the world's roads, and Japanese car producers are now even beginning to worry luxury car makers in Germany, Italy and the UK. Oliver and Wilkinson tell us that, at home, the Japanese are prodigious savers and investors, putting aside more than a third of all incomes and investing above 30 per cent – significantly ahead of Germany and the USA, with the UK lagging far behind with savings and investment ratios of only 17.6 per cent and 19.9 per cent respectively.

This stunning performance has attracted admiration. 'The great and the good' have dutifully made the trip to Japan to study business methods – much as they did to the United States in the post-war years. It has also attracted some fear: at the 1991 TUC conference in Glasgow, MSF moved a motion that was carried overwhelmingly, stating that Japanese companies had 'brought an alien approach to trade union organization' in the form of single-union agreements.

Another reaction has been emulation, not least in the UK. This book uses case studies of three Japanese companies ('K-Electric', Komatsu and Nissan) and the evidence of two surveys (in 1987 and 1991) to assess the impact of the Japanese presence in the UK upon British household names such as Lucas and Rover, as well as on the less well-known 'Southern Components' – a light engineering company in the south of England. This 'Japanization' process is also examined in terms of the major US inward investors – Ford and IBM.

The authors find that an emulation process is widespread, although it has never been total even in those companies that have sought to 'Japanize' themselves. Further, although the process has generally been successful in terms of human relations, productivity and corporate goals, this success is now less evident than it was in the 1980s, as a result of the expected cultural 'obstacles to Japanization'. Even so, despite this flatter achievement curve, the 'imperative to change is still fixed in the minds of British managers.'

The detailed, carefully assembled evidence in the book constitutes timely information for current policy debates in cabinet, boardroom and the factory, and should not be muddled by medieval schoolmen criticisms of the precision to be attached to the actual term 'Japanization'. Oliver and Wilkinson have written a book – now in its second, revised edition – that is required reading for those with faith in the emulation route to commercial success, providing, as it does, the lessons of case studies to digest, learn from, or even reject. It should also be looked at by those fearing for British traditions: in this respect, the evidence may or may not be comforting. But whatever the book does, let it be understood that it has a critical theme: the capacity of the economy to provide us all with good jobs and hence the economic foundations of satisfactory lives.

Brian Towers
Strathclyde Business School

Acknowledgements

In producing the 1988 version of this book we incurred many debts, especially to all those who gave generously of their time to talk to us about their experiences of the changes currently taking place in manufacturing industry, not just in Britain but across the world.

The material in this book reflects the ideas of many people. Most directly involved are those who have been in and around the Cardiff Business School over the last few years – as colleagues, as students, as visitors. The input of these people has been valuable in many ways and taken many forms, from engaging in debates that have helped us in the refining of ideas, and suggesting interesting and relevant reading to, in many cases, working with us on joint projects. Although to mention anyone in particular is to guarantee the omission of someone important, we would like to extend our appreciation to Mike Bresnen, Annette Davies, Rick Delbridge, Simon Gleave, John Hassard, Jonathon Lewis, Jim Lowe, Jon Morris, Ken Khi Pang, Graham Sewell, Steve Sloan, Richard Spiridion, Paul Stewart, Rhys Thomas and Pete Turnbull.

Additionally, we extend our gratitude to Niki Jacobs for her work on the 1991 survey and to the staff of the Aberconway library, in particular the late Joyce Brown, for keeping us well supplied with up-to-date information about contemporary developments. Thanks also to Mair Price, Nona Pritchard and Heather Rowlands, who all provided secretarial support, and to Eric Stenton for his efforts as desk-editor.

Any errors, omissions and misrepresentations are, of course, our own.

Nick Oliver
Barry Wilkinson
Cardiff
July 1992

Introduction

The idea for *The Japanization of British Industry* originally came as a theme for a conference, organized by the authors, that was held at Cardiff Business School, Cardiff, Wales, in 1987. We borrowed the term 'Japanization' from an article by Peter Turnbull that appeared in the *Industrial Relations Journal* in 1986. Turnbull used the term to refer to organizational changes that Lucas Electrical, suppliers of components to the motor industry, were then in the process of implementing. These changes were described as 'Japanization' largely because they were based on methods of production used by many large Japanese corporations. What was particularly interesting about Turnbull's article was his suggestion that the changes in manufacturing methods were creating pressures for changes in the *social* arrangements of production.

This observation was consistent with those that we had made ourselves during visits to other UK companies that were attempting to use Japanese-style production methods. It suggested that the attempts that many Western companies were making to emulate Japanese industrial practices – particularly manufacturing techniques – carried wider social and political implications than was commonly realized, and this prompted us to explore the area further.

At the time, we used the expression 'Japanization' as an umbrella term to refer to the process by which some aspects of UK industry appeared to be converging towards a Japanese-style model of management practice. This process encompassed two strands – the emulation of Japanese manufacturing methods by Western manufacturers and also the increasing volume of Japanese direct manufacturing investment in Western economies.

At the beginning of 1987, we put out a call for papers for a conference entitled 'The Japanization of British Industry'. The call brought forward 30 papers on the subject. At the conference, which was held in September 1987, many ideas crystallized, and in this book we have drawn widely on material that was presented there. Additional material for *The Japanization of British Industry* came from surveys, from interviews with managers, trade unionists and public office holders, from the endeavours of our postgraduate students, and from published sources. The evidence at the time suggested that British industry was undergoing a fundamental transformation, the nature of which was neatly captured by the term Japanization.

The Japanization of British Industry was published in 1988, and the range of responses with which it was greeted probably said as much about the spread of opinions in the field as it did about the book itself. Thus, when Blackwell Publishers wished to reprint the book in 1990, it seemed sensible to treat it as a second edition, and incorporate some of the developments of recent years, rather than to issue it as a straight reprint.

As things have turned out, the book is rather more than just a second edition. Although a significant proportion of the material that appears here also appeared in the 1988 version of the book, we have added the findings of a second survey, conducted in 1991, included two new cases, and completely updated and revised the rest of the material.

About the Book

As with the 1988 book, we have endeavoured to make this version of relevance and accessible to practitioners as well as academics. We have tried to make each chapter more or less self-contained, so that the book can be 'dipped into' and still make sense.

Chapter 1 deals with the background to the current interest in Japanese industrial practices, and discusses the 'Japanization debate'. Chapter 2 presents a review of the industrial practices found in Japan itself. This chapter is useful for referral in order to make comparisons and contrasts between the Japanese and British situations; one thing that emerges from it is the apparent 'fit' between manufacturing practice, personnel and industrial relations practice, and wider economic and political conditions, and it is this fit that is the subject of exploration in chapter 3. There we suggest that Japanese production methods are based on the successful management of high-dependency relationships. Put simply, because Japanese industrial practice places the organization in a situation of high dependency on its constituents – trade unions, suppliers, customers and so on – senior management must find ways of living with these high-dependency relations.

Chapters 4 to 9 discuss the experiences of both UK companies and Japanese companies in the UK. Chapter 4 is a set of short case studies of five Western companies operating in the UK that are designed to give a 'feel' for what attempts at emulation entail. Chapters 5, 6, and 7 take a systematic look at the broader evidence for the emulation of Japanese methods, looking at manufacturing methods, personnel practices and buyer–supplier relations respectively, and detailing progress (and problems) with the various elements of the package. Chapter 8 presents the cases of three Japanese manufacturers, and chapter 9 looks more broadly at the experiences of Japanese manufacturers in the UK.

Chapters 5, 6, 7 and 9 draw on evidence from the authors' own surveys of the extent of adoption and use of Japanese-style manufacturing and personnel practices, and this is supported by other survey, case study and anecdotal evidence.

Chapter 10 considers the implications of Japanization for trade unions, demonstrating how fundamental union adjustment is likely to be. Also described is the union response to date, which, it seems, has been largely a defensive one, in the context of trade union decline.

Finally, in chapter 11, we draw together the evidence and arguments in order to address the policy questions raised by the 'Japanization' process. We conclude then with a discussion of the likely consequences of Japanization for the individuals and institutions involved in British industry.

1
Western Interest in Japan

During the late 1970s and the 1980s the world woke up to Japan's remarkable economic success story. The secret of this success has been ascribed to many things, different explanations coming in and out of vogue at different times. These include culture (Pascale and Athos 1982; Morishima 1982), collaboration between government and industry coupled with 'unfair' trading practices (Wolf 1985; James 1989), strategic marketing (Dace 1987; Wong, Saunders and Doyle 1987), manufacturing methods (Schonberger 1982; 1986; Womack, Jones and Roos 1990), prowess at manufacturing systems engineering (Parnaby 1987a), personnel practices (Pucik 1985), management accounting (Hiromoto 1988) and Japan's position as a late developer (Dore 1973a and b).

The contribution of the Japanese economy to world GDP grew from just 2 per cent to over 10 per cent between 1967 and 1987 (Okumura 1989), and in the 1990s Japan is moving ahead of the United States as the wealthiest nation in the world. In 1991 Japan's per capita income had reached US$23,570 compared with the United States' US$21,653 (*Chicago Tribune*, 16 June 1991). Even *endaka* – the steep rise of the Yen forced on Japan by the world's other major economic powers since 1984 – appears not to have hampered Japan's export competitiveness, but rather to have boosted its determination to remain one of the most efficient and competitive nations in the world. Japan's US$45 billion trade surplus in 1984 had risen to over US$100 billion by 1989, corporate profitability was up 30 per cent, and one report by Fuji Bank claimed that Japanese factories had reduced the break-even point for the profitability of their exports from Y210 to the dollar in 1985 to Y114 in 1988 (*Financial Times*, 20 May 1989).

Table 1.1 Japanese share of world markets (1986)

Product	Percentage share
35 mm cameras	84
Video recorders	84
Watches	82
Calculators	77
Microwave ovens	71
Motorcycles	55
Colour televisions	53

Source: Adapted from BBC/OU 1986a

The Japanese Management 'Industry'

Although, as indicated above, different explanations for Japan's industrial success have been put forward at different times, it is the prowess of the Japanese as manufacturers of high-quality, low-cost goods that has dominated Western perceptions and interest in Japanese industrial affairs since the early 1980s. Table 1.1 demonstrates the extent of Japanese penetration of world markets by the mid-1980s.

In addition to these figures on market share, by the mid-1980s anecdotal evidence of significant productivity differentials between Japanese and Western industries was accumulating, as table 1.2 demonstrates.

Figures such as those in table 1.2 demonstrating an apparent competitive advantage of Japanese firms over Western firms with comparable operations reinforced the idea that the Japanese were doing something right, and that Western industry had much to gain by emulating their practices.

When we wrote the first edition of *The Japanization of British Industry* in late 1987 and early 1988 there was a sense of urgency, almost of evangelism, amongst many Western companies about their attempts to emulate Japanese practice. As the 1980s drew to a close this enthusiasm appeared to be on the decline, as the difficulty in implementing these practices began to be appreciated. In 1990 and 1991 interest in Japanese business ideas appears to be reviving again,

Table 1.2 Japanese and Western business performance in the electro-mechanical components industry

Performance indicator	Japan	Western
Sales per employee per annum	$150 K	$85 K
Stock turnover ratio	15	5
Ratio indirect : direct labour	1 : 2	3 : 2
Lead-times (development & manufacture)	50%	100%

Source: Adapted from Parnaby 1987b

following the publication of the influential book *The Machine that Changed the World* (Womack, Jones and Roos 1990).

The Machine that Changed the World was the culmination of the International Motor Vehicle Programme, a five-year research project into productivity and management practices in the world motor industry. The programme set out, amongst other things, to compare systematically the productivity and quality of different car producers around the world and to relate this to management practice. The main finding was that one model of production organization, for which the researchers coined the term 'lean production', was systematically related to superior productivity and quality. The study indicated that lean production was the dominant form of production used by vehicle producers in Japan, but that the methods were apparently transferable to locations outside Japan. Figures 1.1 and 1.2 show the differentials in productivity and quality between groups of car producers around the world.

When comparing the productivity of car plants in different regions of the world, some substantial differences are apparent. Figure 1.1 shows the length of time taken to assemble a standard vehicle by six groups of producers: by those in Japan itself (J/J), by Japanese-owned car plants in America (J/NA), by American-owned car plants in the USA (US/NA), by American-owned and Japanese-owned plants in Europe (US&J/E), by European-owned plants in Europe (E/E) and by plants in countries that have begun manufacturing vehicles relatively recently (NIC). This last group includes countries such as Mexico, Brazil and Taiwan. For each region, the figures for the best and worst performers are given, along with the weighted average for that region.

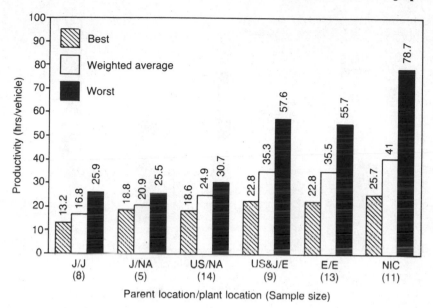

Source: IMVP World Assembly Plant Survey

Note: Volume producers include the American 'big three'; Fiat, PSA, Renault and Volkswagen in Europe; and all of the companies from Japan.

J/J = Japanese-owned plants in Japan.
J/NA = Japanese-owned plants in North America, including joint venture plants with American firms.
US/NA = American-owned plants in North America.
US&J/E = American- and Japanese-owned plants in Europe.
E/E = European-owned plants in Europe.
NIC = Plants in newly industrializing countries: Mexico, Brazil, Taiwan and Korea.

Figure 1.1 Assembly plant productivity

The figures for Japan (J/J) and Europe (E/E) are based on eight car plants in Japan and 13 plants in Europe, and refer to the hours of actual working effort taken to assemble a car of equivalent specifications in terms of size, options and content. The figures thus reflect genuine *productivity* differences, and not simply differences in the size and complexity of vehicles manufactured in different parts of the world. The figures refer to a Ford Escort to Ford Sierra class of vehicle.

On average, it takes 16.8 hours to assemble a standard vehicle of this class in Japan. The average for car plants in Europe is more than *double* this at 35.5 hours. The best Japanese plant takes 13.2 hours of effort to assemble a car; the worst European plant takes 55.7 hours.

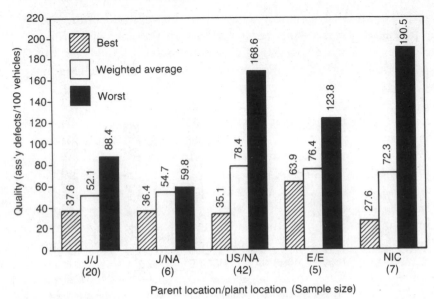

Figure 1.2   Assembly plant quality

Note: Quality is expressed as the number of defects per 100 cars traceable to the assembly plant, as reported by owners in the first three months of use. The reports only include cars sold in the United States.

Source: *IMVP World Assembly Plant Survey*, utilizing a special tabulation of defects by assembly plant provided by J. D. Power and Associates

It is easy to imagine that the high productivity figures of the Japanese plants must come at the cost of product quality, following the logic that if the cars are put together so quickly then they must contain more assembly defects than cars built more slowly. Paradoxically, the reverse is the case, as figure 1.2, which shows vehicle quality region-by-region, demonstrates.

Figure 1.2 shows the numbers of defects per 100 vehicles from the groups of producers described in figure 1.1. The figures refer only to those defects that can occur at the assembly stage, and therefore ignore features such as engine and transmission performance and reliability. It is features such as the fit and finish of body panels, interior fittings and trim, quality of paint finish, electrical connections and so on that are covered by figure 1.2. Focusing on Japan and Europe again, another substantial gap is apparent. On average, there are 52.1 assembly defects per 100 vehicles coming out of the Japanese plants, compared with 76.4 in the case of Europe. These figures are corroborated by a recent *Which?* survey. Of the top ten most reliable cars in the one- to two-year-old age bracket four were Japanese. Of the top ten cars in the three- to five-year-old bracket six were Japanese (*Which?* 1989).

The net effect of figures such as these has been threefold. First, they have reinforced Western awareness of Japanese manufacturing methods. Second, they have spread an alarmist message about the size of the productivity and quality differentials in the vehicle industry, but with the implication that such differentials are replicated elsewhere. Third, they have sent a message of hope to those wishing to adopt lean production methods outside Japan, because the productivity and quality of Japanese transplants in North America come close to equalling those of Japanese plants in Japan itself.

Western interest in Japanese production methods, whether expressed in the form of attempts at emulation by Western companies, or inspired by the management practices used by Japanese manufacturers operating in the West, thus seems set to continue into the 1990s. However, even a casual perusal of the field reveals that there is a wide variety of perspectives on the phenomenon, and in the section that follows we try to map some of these out. The focus in this section is primarily on Japanese production methods, in particular just-in-time (JIT) production, although, where appropriate, other elements of Japanese practice will also be considered.

Perspectives on Japanese Practice

Japanese production methods have been viewed from a variety of perspectives, the three main ones being the technological, the social–political and the ideological, each of which is reviewed below.

The technological/rational perspective

Early proponents of this view were Voss and Robinson (1987), who described 23 practices (from flexible working to *kanban* materials control), all of which they classified as 'elements' of JIT. Voss and Robinson's work is described in some detail in chapter 5. From this perspective, JIT is used as an umbrella term to refer to a package of techniques. The criteria for the inclusion of techniques in this package are rarely articulated, but centre on custom and practice. This view of JIT amalgamates the commonly espoused ends of JIT (such as continuous improvement, inventory reduction) with the means used to achieve them (smoothed build rates, set-up reduction). From this viewpoint, the successful implementation of JIT is seen primarily as a technical problem, requiring enhanced responsiveness and particularly precise coordination of the resources involved in the production process.

The work of Womack, Jones and Roos (1990) on lean production also fits into this perspective, although conceptually and empirically this work is considerably more advanced than that of Voss and Robinson. Lean production is seen as a package, an interrelated and mutually supportive set of manufacturing practices capable of delivering Japanese levels of manufacturing performance anywhere in the world, if implemented correctly. Other examples of work that predominantly lies within this perspective include Schonberger 1982; 1986; Goldratt and Cox 1984; Aggarwal 1985; Potts 1986; Parnaby 1987a; Ingersoll Engineers 1986; and Macbeth 1987.

The social–political perspective

The second perspective on Japanese methods has focused on its social and political dimensions. This perspective covers a diversity of views. One recognizable position is held by those whose predominant approach to Japanese methods is from a critical social science perspective (Turnbull 1986; 1988; Crowther and Garrahan 1988; Dickens and Savage 1988; Briggs 1988; Holloway 1987; Fucini and Fucini 1990; Garrahan and Stewart 1992). The predominant argument of this group is that Japanese manufacturing methods lead to work intensification, and that the social relations of production that surround them rely on the assertion of managerial prerogatives to the detriment of the workforce, which is even further subordinated than it was under previous manufacturing regimes. From this perspective, the new management techniques are seen as the latest weapon in the corporate arsenal and should be treated (and resisted) as such by those faced by their introduction.

A second recognizable group of authors writing with a social–political perspective adopts what might be termed a socio-technical systems perspective (Dohse, Ulrich and Malsch 1986; Sayer 1986; Oliver and Wilkinson 1988; Wilkinson and Oliver 1989; Oliver 1990; Oliver and Davies 1990; Kenney and Florida 1988). This group also includes those who have noted some of the difficulties inherent in implementing these techniques and who have commented on the ways in which the methods may fail, be circumvented or be adapted to local circumstances (Smith 1988; Black and Ackers 1988; Trevor and Christie 1988; Hague 1989; Klein 1989; Radford 1989; Dawson and Webb 1990).

Philosophical/ideological perspective

A third recognizable perspective on Japanese methods, and JIT in particular, is as a set of beliefs that provide those who subscribe to them with a distinct world-view – in the same way as a faith or religion provides a set of principles that guide action in (and interpretation of) the world. One of the earliest proponents of this perspective was Graham (1988), who has explored the manner in which the dialogue about Japanese management methods is shaped and used by those with vested interests in the area. Pollert (1988) has adopted a similar line of analysis of the related phenomenon of the 'flexible firm'. More recently, this line of analysis has been taken up by Oliver (1990), who has used Kuhn's ideas on scientific revolutions to explore how traditional production philosophies have been displaced by the 'new' approach. One strand to Graham's argument is that many of the elements in the 'Japanese' manufacturing package have been sought by manufacturing managers for years. However, their apparently 'Japanese' identity links them to competitiveness, and therefore legitimates their introduction. In support of this, Graham has analysed the results of a survey by Voss (1987), which examines the extent to which British companies are currently using, implementing or planning to introduce the elements of Japanese-style production management techniques. Noting that flexible working comes top of this list in terms of its prevalence as a Japanese technique in use in the UK, Graham concludes:

> The most striking point about the results of this survey is that the JIT techniques which are being most widely considered are not in themselves novel. Manufacturing managers have recognized the inefficiencies caused by task specialization which exist in both craft and

Taylorist manufacturing systems and have sought to remove or reduce demarcation, without this being seen as a copying of practice in Japan. (Graham 1988, p. 76)

Ford's 'After Japan' programme of productivity improvement of the early 1980s is one example of this, involving 'a process of giving publicity to the need to face up to the competition', but nonetheless involving many changes to existing practices at all levels in the company (Ackroyd et al. 1988).

A second strand to this perspective concerns the 'shaping' of ideas about Japanese manufacturing methods. Writing specifically about JIT, Graham argues that those groups with a significant stake in the manufacturing status quo have succeeded in diluting JIT principles in order to protect their interests. Citing computer software houses, hardware suppliers and management consultants as groups who have interests in promoting centralized computer-based scheduling systems such as MRP, he concludes:

> The result of this political shaping is that most of the actual claimed implementations of JIT techniques in the West are too superficial to claim to represent a new production paradigm. (Graham 1988, p. 73)

Having examined some of the perspectives on Japanese manufacturing methods, we shall now briefly consider 'Japanization' as a concept and review the debate over the term's usefulness and legitimacy.

The Japanization Debate

The Japanization debate is a story with many sub-plots. The picture is complicated because the term 'Japanization' is just one of a number of labels current in the late 1980s and early 1990s attached to models developed and promoted by various movements in management thinking that purport to explain changes in the way in which Western industry organizes and manages its production processes. In addition to the 'Japanese' model – or Western perceptions of it – there are several others, such as those of 'flexible specialization' (Piore and Sabel 1984), 'the flexible firm' (Atkinson 1987) and the 'excellence movement' (Peters and Waterman 1982), all of which encompass clusters of management practices that apparently share many elements in common. Other 'movements' focusing on particular aspects of management have sought to develop models encapsulating the rise of new practices in specific areas. For example, with respect to the management of labour, there is currently heated debate about the rise of 'human resource management' (HRM). There is controversy about whether HRM actually exists in practice; about what it involves; about its desirability; and about the extent to which HRM is displacing traditional approaches. Although somewhat more specialized, such debates clearly have implications for the Japanization debate.

There is no doubt that the use of labels such as 'Japanization' or 'flexible specialization' to describe contemporary changes can be problematical. At the more critical end of the spectrum Dickens and Savage (1988) have described Japanization as a 'chaotic conception' and a 'bad abstraction':

> A bad abstraction arbitrarily divides the indivisible and/or lumps together the unrelated and the inessential, thereby 'carving up' the object of study with little or no regard for its structure or form. (Dickens and Savage 1988, p. 61)

Writing about the related flexibility debate, Pollert (1988) identifies further dangers inherent in the careless use of labels:

> Most of the flexibility literature tends to be either prescriptive, or assumes there is a 'new' trend, which it then proceeds to describe and generalize. There has been no discussion on the origins of the term, to unravel its many connotations, to question what is indeed 'new' and to set this against the ideological processes which have unleashed it. Such a situation has political dangers: it defines the agenda of debate, assumes a radical break with the past, conflates and obscures contradictory processes within the organization of work, and by asserting a sea-change of management strategy and employment structure, fuses description, prediction and prescription towards a self-fulfilling prophecy. (Pollert 1988, pp. 42f.)

Our own initial use of the term 'Japanization', as described in the Introduction, was simply as a short-hand term that captured what we perceived to be a move by Western manufacturing industry towards a particular configuration of manufacturing, personnel and buyer–supplier practices. In the mid-1980s these practices were found in their highest concentration among the major Japanese corporations in Japan itself. However, the practices, or at least their functional equivalents, were also found in some Western companies, Peters and Waterman's 'excellent' companies being particularly pure examples.

Our argument in 1987 was essentially that production systems that are run according to 'Japanese' principles such as just-in-time and total quality (described in chapter 2) create the need for particular sets of social relations – both within and between organizations – centred on the production process. This idea was consistent with Turnbull's early observation that the success of Japanese-style production techniques was:

> dependent on a social organization for the production process intended to make the workers feel obliged to contribute to the economic performance of the enterprise and to identify with its competitive success. (Turnbull 1986, p. 203)

Many UK firms professed to be emulating Japanese manufacturing methods. Our thesis was that the adoption of these methods would force them to adopt other aspects of the 'Japanese' package, in terms of personnel practices, relations with suppliers, and so on. This did not necessarily mean that *exactly* the same practices as those found in Japan – for example lifetime employment, seniority-based payments systems and enterprise unions – would be adopted. To use the example of employee relations, the argument was rather that Japanese manufacturing systems created the need for certain core conditions – for instance, a flexible workforce that was willing and able to take responsibility for matters such as quality control and local problem-solving and was *unlikely* to make use of the inherent fragility of the production system as a bargaining counter. In environments outside Japan, such core conditions could be created and sustained in ways that were different from those found in Japan, but that were *functionally equivalent*. Our tacit assumption was – and still is – that it is legitimate to describe this process as 'Japanization'.

Objections to 'Japanization'

There are two broad threads to objections to the term 'Japanization'. One is based on theoretical premises, the other on empirical ones. Different commentators generally object on different premises, and objections fall into five broad types, each of which is described below.

(1) 'There's no such thing as *Japanese* management.' This objection is typically articulated by those who have (or claim to have) some knowledge of industrial conditions in Japan. Their argument is that, upon close examination, a significant variety of management practices are discernible within Japan itself, and therefore to assume that there is a 'Japanese' model that Western companies are attempting to emulate is fundamentally flawed. Whilst there is clearly some truth in the observation that different Japanese companies operate in different ways – as Cusumano (1986) demonstrates in the cases of Nissan and Toyota – studies such as the International Motor Vehicle Programme, by demonstrating clear differences in management practice (and results) across different car-producing regions, clearly call this into question. A sub-set of this school of opinion regards the term as racist on the grounds that it implies a homogeneity of Japanese practice not actually found in reality. Wood (1992) has provided a recent overview of this argument.

(2) 'Describing the process of change as "Japanization" obscures the real process.' This position is typically held by those on the Left, who claim that labelling the process of change as 'Japanization' redraws the political map in an 'inappropriate' way, by suggesting competition between nations rather than between labour and capital, thereby obscuring fundamental conflicts between management and workers. From this position, decribing the process of change as 'Japanization' draws attention away from the fact that the new techniques represent another set of *management* strategies. The key interest of those writing from this perspective is in issues of power and control under the new relations. Examples include Pollert (1988) and Garrahan and Stewart (1992).

(3) 'The world is more complicated than that.' Those who hold this position may or may not agree that change is taking place, but if they accept that it is, they dispute that a simple convergence towards the

'Japanese' model is involved. This position rests on the idea that industrial change is complex, piecemeal and a response to a variety of technological, social, political and economic pressures. Its advocates typically view the change process at the level of the political economy, not at the level of the firm, and seek evidence in structural changes at this macro level. Elger (1990) has provided one of the most comprehensive reviews in this area. His argument is that:

> Specific technical changes in manufacturing during the 1980s have not served as simple levers of managerial power in the production process, but neither have they been fully assimilated into existing patterns of work organization and industrial relations. Rather they have been coupled with and have sometimes given a distinct twist to modest and incremental moves . . . [W]hilst labels such as Fordism, neo-Fordism, post-Fordism, Japanization, or even Toyotism or Fujitsuism, have served to highlight the potential significance of contemporary changes, they have also served to short-circuit analysis of the patterns of shifting, contradictory and contested social relations involved, both at the level of the social organization of the immediate production process, and in relation to the wider political economy. (Elger 1990, pp. 94f.)

Other commentators writing in this vein include McKenna (1988) and Williams, Williams and Haslam (1989).

(4) 'Nothing has changed.' Writers on the Left, such as MacInnes (1987; 1988) and Batstone (1988), argue that the evidence, particularly in the sphere of industrial relations, suggests that there is more continuity than change in industrial practice. Moreover they argue that, where change is occurring (for example in areas such as levels of unionization), it is better explained by structural shifts in the economy (such as a move towards service industries and a reduction in the average size of firms) than by management strategies. Marginson (1989) has produced a similar argument based on the findings of the *Workplace Industrial Relations Survey*.

(5) 'Things may be changing, but not towards the Japanese model.' This camp has support from academic and practitioner communities. Those writing from a managerial perspective have their own variation of this particular theme, which frequently finds expression in the view that, while changes may be taking place, such change has little or nothing to do with the Japanese example. Rather, recent develop-

ments are occurring as a consequence of local (Western) managers applying common sense and the principles of 'good management'. Thus Andy Barr, describing Rover's 'Working With Pride' programme of the late 1980s, commented:

> I suppose at the end of the day many of the things we are doing with employees come out as something similar to what the Japanese do. But ours is mainly a structured programme – it's nothing to do with culture. It's structured in such a way that it's a programme we want to become a way of life – and 'Working with Pride' is a way of life. (BBC 1988)

Academic objections to the term 'Japanization' from this perspective frequently stem from a rather literal interpretation of Japanese methods. Usually commentators focus on one or two of the labour relations practices in Japan – for example lifetime employment, seniority pay systems or enterprise unions. On finding little evidence of these exact practices in UK firms, the conclusion is drawn that the Japanization process is not occurring. Examples of this view include Marchington and Parker (1988) and McKenna (1988).

Toward a Typology of Japanization

In an attempt to begin the task of bringing more precision to the term 'Japanization', Ackroyd et al. (1988) have described three types of process, which they have labelled 'direct', 'mediated' and 'full' or 'permeated' Japanization. *Direct* Japanization refers to Japanese companies setting up operations – particularly manufacturing operations – in the UK, and the effects that this is having on the wider British industrial situation. Ackroyd et al. divide *mediated* Japanization into two sub-categories, labelled mediated Japanization I and mediated Japanization II. The former covers the attempts of British companies to emulate Japanese practice, or at least Western perceptions, correct or otherwise, of Japanese practice. In contrast, Ackroyd et al.'s 'mediated Japanization II' refers to what might be considered the *hidden agenda* behind Western companies' use of Japanese practice, which relates to the association between Japan and international competitiveness. By emphasizing that new production methods and working practices are linked to those of Japan and hence to competitiveness, management instils an imperative likely to legitimate change in the eyes of those who will be affected by it. This is essentially the view put forward by Graham (1988) that was described above.

Finally, Ackroyd et al. argue that *full* or *permeated* Japanization would be evidenced by Britain developing strategies similar to those of Japan in terms of investment patterns and strategic marketing in the international trade arena. In emphasizing these elements of the Japanese industrial situation, they ascribe much of Japan's remarkable economic success to the country's economic structures, and therefore argue that comparisons between Britain and Japan relating to their alleged convergence should be made at this level. These ideas are further explored in chapter 2.

The authors see Japanization as a fundamental process of change because it entails a whole set of assumptions about, and demands on, the 'constituents' upon whom an organization's activities impinge – not just labour but also trade unions, suppliers and other actors in the broader polity of Britain. Those organizations failing to take account of the social and political dimensions of Japanization are unlikely to make the transformation. Instead, their plans will be blocked by resistance from trade unions and middle managers, and hampered by supplier inability and unpreparedness to meet its demands. Japanization is not simply a matter of implementing total quality control and just-in-time (JIT) production processes – it entails the adoption of particular work practices and personnel and industrial relations systems as well, and the whole package of change is most likely to succeed where the organization has some degree of control over its external environment.

The term 'Japanization' grates with some people, as the criticisms of the term reviewed in this chapter indicate. Such criticisms notwithstanding, we continue to consider it an appropriate short-hand expression to describe the gamut of changes – many of them admittedly piecemeal – currently taking place across British industry. Some Western companies *have* successfully adopted Japanese manufacturing methods, and our own previous work and, more recently, that undertaken as part of the International Motor Vehicle Programme (MacDuffie 1991) suggest that these methods are most successful when embedded in an appropriate set of *social* relations. These may be created by practices such as those found in Japan itself, or by Western versions that perform the same function. After all, as we shall show in the chapter that follows, many so-called Japanese manufacturing practices were originally borrowed from the

West by Japan. The important point here is that Japanese industry dramatically refined and developed these practices in an environment very different from that of traditional Western industry and demonstrated their practical effects. The West is importing (or reimporting) the system, and this raises intriguing questions about the transfer process. For this reason we would still argue that 'Japanization' is a legitimate label to apply to the process.

2

Japanese Industrial Practice

The aim of this chapter is to describe industrial conditions in Japan under the categories of manufacturing methods; organizational structures and systems; personnel practices; and environmental factors – supplier relations, unions, and the economic and political context. We would argue that a proper understanding of Japan's economic success must take all these factors into account.

Manufacturing Methods

Although many manufacturing practices are currently being labelled as 'Japanese', one theme that runs through most of these practices is the central significance of quality, and the control of processes in order to achieve this. Particularly striking is how considerations of quality are linked not just to customer satisfaction but to the efficiency of the production process itself. This contrasts with the traditional Western view, in which the maintenance of high quality standards has been construed as adding cost to a product. In Japan, maintenance of high standards of quality is seen to result in a net reduction in costs, for reasons that we shall explore shortly. First, however, we shall consider one of the key elements of the Japanese production process, namely total or company-wide quality control.

Total quality control

In common with many of the ideas in vogue in contemporary management literature, the total quality concept (also referred to as company-wide quality control) is frequently assumed to be Japanese in origin. In fact, the idea may be traced to an American, J. M. Juran, a specialist in quality control who was invited to Japan in 1954 by a branch of JUSE (the Japanese Union of Scientists and Engineers). Juran's philosophy was that quality control should be conducted as an integral part of management control, in contrast with the traditional situation in which responsibility for product quality was vested in the hands of a quality control department, which acted as a 'policeman' to production. Between 1955 and 1960, these ideas spawned the company-wide quality control movement (Ishikawa 1984).

Juran and other American quality control experts, such as Deming and Feigenbaum, were peddling these ideas in Europe and America at this time, but they were largely ignored in the West. Schonberger (1982) suggests that the take-up of these ideas in Japan can be explained by two factors. First, resource scarcity in Japan created stronger pressure for the elimination of waste caused by the production of bad output in the form of scrap or products requiring rectification work. Secondly, in Japan the dysfunctions of specialization in organizations – in particular the lack of concern or sense of responsibility for any area other than one's own – do not fit into the culture (Schonberger 1982). This, Schonberger suggests, has led to responsibility for quality remaining in its 'natural' place, namely where production is performed. In contrast, the traditional 'policing' role of Western quality control departments is the legacy of highly segregated, specialized organizational forms based on scientific management principles.

In the West, the expression 'quality control' has traditionally had the connotation of inspectors standing at the end of production lines monitoring the production workers. The total quality concept is antithetical to this – it 'despecializes the inspection function' (Palmer and Allen 1989) – and it is worth spelling out in some detail exactly what the phenomenon encompasses. The first point to note is the broad conception of control applicable in this context, which has elements of both local responsibility and centralized direction. Within the context of company-wide quality control, control has been described as:

A process for delegating responsibility and authority for a management activity while retaining the means of ensuring satisfactory results. (Feigenbaum 1983, p. 10)

A second point concerns the use of the term 'quality'. Although many authors emphasize the traditional view of quality as 'conformity to a specification', a wider definition, and one that underpins the total quality concept, is one of fitness for purpose. One such conception is provided by Feigenbaum (1983, p. 7) who defines quality as:

> The total composite product and service characteristics of marketing, engineering, manufacture and maintenance through which the product and service in use will meet the expectation of the customer.

Notable in this definition of quality is the emphasis on the meeting of customer needs and expectations – a distinctive feature of total quality organizations. This customer orientation typically extends inside the organization as well, with individuals and departments having internal 'customers' whose requirements they have an obligation to meet. Although it is the major Japanese corporations that are generally associated with total quality control principles, some Western companies have applied these principles for many years. Notable are the 'excellent' American companies (Peters and Waterman 1982), many of which also carry the title 'total quality' organizations. The key philosophy behind total quality control has been summarized by Feigenbaum (1983) as a management approach 'which regards the quality of products and services as a primary business strategy and a fundamental determinant for business health, growth and economic viability.' Quality, in this sense, does not necessarily mean the 'best' in the way in which one thinks of, say, Rolls-Royce cars. It rather means best for particular customer requirements, these requirements being determined by the use to which the product is put and the price at which it is sold. Total quality control thus comprises the systems that:

> enable marketing, engineering, production and service at the most economical levels which allow for full customer satisfaction. (Feigenbaum 1983, p. 7)

These aims imply a tightly integrated organization, efficient in its use of resources so that it is price-competitive, but simultaneously flexible enough to respond to customer requirements. The types of organizational structures and control mechanisms required to meet these performance criteria have as yet attracted little attention from organizational researchers, although Peters and Waterman (1982) and Kanter (1985) have put forward some preliminary ideas and popularized the issue. Schonberger's (1982) view is that total quality control is a 'fundamental production function', along with many other Japanese manufacturing methods, such as quality control circles (utilizing elementary problem-solving and statistical techniques), just-in-time production, and tight in-process controls. In Japan these methods are both supported by, and in turn foster, the philosophy of *kaizen* or 'continuous improvement'. We shall now briefly describe each of these practices.

Quality circles

Quality circles are a significant component of the total quality control concept. The quality circle movement in Japan started in 1962 with the publication of *Genba-To-QC* (*Quality Control for the Foremen*), and it was in that year that the first quality control circles were set up in various factories (Ishikawa 1984). Quality circles are small groups, usually of between five and ten people, who meet voluntarily to try to improve quality and productivity in their work areas. The leaders of quality control circles in Japan are typically foremen, assistant foremen or team leaders, although this role may be performed by shopfloor workers. JUSE has defined a quality circle as:

> A small group to voluntarily perform quality control activities within the workshop to which they belong. This small group with every member participating to the full carries on continuously, as part of company-wide quality control activities, self-development and mutual development, control and improvement within the workshop utilizing quality control techniques. (Fortune and Oliver 1986, p. 24)

In Japan, quality circle members are trained in the use of simple statistical analysis and problem-solving techniques. The 'seven statistical tools' typically employed by circles are Pareto analysis, cause and effect (fishbone) diagrams, stratification, tally cards, histograms, scatter diagrams and Shewhart control charts. In 1981 there were claimed to be 130,000 quality circles registered with JUSE, with a total membership of over one million people (Wolf 1985).

Although quality circles were the first Japanese manufacturing practices really to attract the attention of the West in the late 1970s and early 1980s, Schonberger (1982) suggests that their significance in Japan itself has been overrated. In support of this, he claims that many Japanese companies had enviable reputations for high-quality products before they introduced quality circles, and that circles are not universally popular among the leading Japanese companies. He further argues that workers and foremen are in a position to solve only approximately 15 per cent of quality problems, their impact being most significant in addressing 'the trivial many' – in other words, relatively minor difficulties.

Claims have also been made for the significance of quality circles in the context of motivation. Here it is suggested that quality circles are a 'participative mechanism' creating shopfloor involvement and leading to (among other things) job satisfaction, good management–employer relations, increased commitment, improved morale and opportunities for 'self-actualization' (Yap 1984; Ishikawa 1984). From a critical perspective, writers such as Briggs (1988) have pointed to the pressure that workers may be put under to take part in such activities. Describing quality circles as another 'instrument of management' in the employers' arsenal of 'coercive techniques', Briggs cites Kamata's (1983) account of quality circles at Toyota, alleging that weekly postings of employee suggestion rates pressure workers into participating in the scheme.

In-process controls

Of the techniques used by the Japanese to assist in the control of production processes, statistical process control (SPC) received much attention in the West during the 1980s and has now been assimilated into the routine operating procedures of many companies. The fundamental principles on which SPC is based are relatively simple, although the statistics themselves are less accessible. The principle of SPC is that products emerging from any production process exhibit two sorts of variation. The first is variation that is inherent in a process and that – assuming that the process is capable of reliably producing products to the drawing specification – ought not to create any product that is out of tolerance. This is sometimes referred to as 'natural' or 'unassigned' variation, because it occurs naturally in the process without a specific, recognizable cause. The second type of variation is unnatural or assigned variation. This is variation due to a specific cause, for example excessive wear on a tool, or a machine that is out of adjustment. Uncorrected, this type of variation will cause products to fall outside specified tolerance.

SPC involves first working out the extent of a process's natural variation, and then regularly sampling the process's output. The samples are used to chart the behaviour of a production process, and hence to detect trends that indicate that a machine is starting to produce output that falls outside its 'natural' variability, although such output may still be within design tolerances. Elementary probability theory is used to help the operator to decide when a trend is serious enough for the process to be shut down and reset. Importantly, however, the information is used to trigger corrective action – for example a machine reset – *before* the process actually generates products that fall outside design tolerances and hence generate scrap or rework costs.

SPC thus involves operators periodically sampling their own production, not with a view to accepting it or rejecting it, but in order to produce a chart of how the process itself is behaving. In addition to reducing scrap and rework costs, minimizing variation in components can significantly improve the performance of products. A senior quality manager from an international car manufacturer described to one of the authors how, although the same automatic gearbox was manufactured in North America and Japan using identical plant, the Japanese units were consistently more reliable and smoother in operation, simply because the Japanese controlled their processes better, thereby achieving less variation in the components used to build the gearbox. It was not that more non-conforming components were being fitted to the North American gearbox, simply that variation per se (even within the specified tolerances) affected performance.

Just-in-time production

As the name suggests, just-in-time (JIT) systems of production are those in which goods are produced just in time to be used. The principle underpinning JIT has been described as follows:

> The JIT idea is simple: produce and deliver finished goods just in time to be sold, sub-assemblies just in time to be assembled into finished goods, fabricated parts just in time to go into the sub-assemblies and purchased materials just in time to be transformed into fabricated parts. (Schonberger 1982, p. 16)

A little more provocatively, the goal of JIT has been described in the following terms:

To produce instantaneously, with perfect quality and minimum waste. (Bicheno 1987, p. 192)

[JIT] completely tailors a manufacturing strategy to the needs of a market and produces mixed products in exactly the order required. (Parnaby 1987c)

There are a number of critical elements to JIT production. Given that, ideally, products are produced at a rate perfectly matched to market demand, at least one of two conditions is implied if production is to be performed at the last minute. Either demand is uniform – or at least predictable – and so plans can be made in advance, or the production process itself must be inherently very responsive. The latter condition is obviously necessary if production is to take place at the last minute and be profitable. The goal of perfect quality requires tight control of the production process itself, as illustrated in the preceding section on statistical process control.

Minimizing waste typically involves removing any non-value-added operations from the process. At Toyota, there is a distinction between *muda*, *mura* and *muri*, all of which are terms used to describe elements to be eliminated as far as possible. *Muda* is waste, of which there are seven types: rework or repairs; overproduction (causing stock accumulations); inventory (excess stock); unnecessary motions by workers or machines; too much quality (overspecification); idle time; and double handling in the conveyance of materials. *Mura* refers to the unevenness that occurs when production schedules or volumes are irregular. *Mura* automatically results in *muda*, because workers and machines will be working below capacity for part of the time. *Muri* means overburden – when machines or workers are pushed beyond their capacity. Again, the result of *muri* is inevitably *muda*.

In the early days, just-in-time systems of production were sometimes considered synonymous with *kanban* systems of production. In fact, *kanban* represents one particular aspect of Toyota's just-in-time production system. Under the *kanban* system, materials are moved between the various stages of the production process in purpose-built containers. At Toyota every component has its own special container designed to hold a precise (and usually fairly small) number of those components. There are two cards for each container. These cards are known as *kanban*, and it is from them that the system derives its name. The cards initiate production and accompany the materials as they pass through the factory. This arrangement serves to limit the amount of stock in a system: if there is no container with a *kanban* attached, then no components will be produced. A container with no *kanban* attached is ignored. The amount of stock in the system can thus be varied by altering the number of cards in the system. In this way materials are 'pulled' through the system on a daily basis according to the demands of final assembly, rather than 'pushed' through by an inflexible production plan. As well as reducing inventory, an efficient *kanban* system reduces production lead-times by improving the processing vs non-processing time ratio.

Recently, Japanese companies have been developing 'electronic *kanban*', and on-line ordering of parts is being gradually introduced. At Hino Motors, the automation of the just-in-time system has helped to enable the manufacture of 1,900 different types of trucks, with 700 engine types, on the same production lines. Trucks are assembled one at a time (the previous minimum lot size was five) and lead-time has been reduced to five days. Hino's in-process stocks average four-and-a-half days' production, though about one-third of this at any one moment is in transit from suppliers or to customers. The Managing Director has remarked that the 'congested roads around Tokyo are our most important warehouse' (*Financial Times*, 20 May 1989).

At Toyota, to create the stability necessary for production to take place (successfully) at the last minute, production schedules are 'smoothed' over a monthly period. A forecast for the month's production of finished vehicles is made, and the total required number of each component is calculated. This is then divided by the number of operating days in the month – say 20 – and that becomes the daily base-line target for each production unit. *Kanban* orders thus function primarily to 'fine tune' the system around this base line (Sugimoro et al. 1977; Monden 1981a; 1981b; Burbidge 1982).

Requirements are modified as the month goes on, according to whether orders are conforming to the forecast or not. There is little published evidence of Toyota's system having to cope with significant periods of slack demand; Kamata's account of life at Toyota suggests that manning levels are such that overtime is an integral part of the system if output is to meet forecasts. Increases in demand are met by even more overtime. A just-in-time system, *kanban*-controlled or otherwise, is not limited simply to the operations of a particular plant or even a particular company, but may stretch back from final assemblers to their suppliers, to their suppliers' suppliers and so on.

There are various accounts of the origins of JIT practice. Schonberger (1982) suggests that the concept was first applied in the late 1950s or early 1960s in the Japanese shipbuilding industry, and followed an over-expansion of the Japanese steel industry. Because of excess capacity, shipbuilders were able to get steel delivered virtually on demand and, as a consequence, dropped their stocks down from about one month's requirements to three days'. The idea spread to other businesses, and was applied to the holding of stocks between the different manufacturing operations within companies, as well as to bought-in supplies. Another suggested explanation for the development of JIT in Japan centres on the country's economic circumstances. Operating from a small, geographically isolated, nation with little in the way of natural resources and with scarce land space, Japanese manufacturers were at a relative disadvantage compared with some of their Western competitors. JIT evolved as a response to these resource constraints (Sugimoro et al. 1977).

Voss (1987) claims that JIT originated at Toyota. According to this account, Toyota began experimenting with a range of new approaches to manufacturing management, including the just-in-time concept, as early as 1948, and by 1954–5 JIT was being extended backwards to suppliers and forwards to the sales department, which was asked to take the lead in production planning. The effort was headed by Taiichi Ohno, who at the time was General Manager of the machine works. The fundamental idea, based on the American 'supermarket system' (Aoki 1987), was that the people at the end of a particular process would take only those parts that they needed for their work. At the same time, the people at the beginning of the process would replace only the parts that had been taken. *Kanban* signs were introduced in the early 1960s, and used by those at the end of a process to communicate the names and numbers of parts needed. The just-in-time and *kanban* systems were diffused throughout Toyota's factories, and on to many suppliers, during the 1950s and 1960s (Cusumano 1986). Attention to JIT methods by other Japanese companies was spurred on by the oil shock of the early 1970s. By the mid-1970s the 'Toyota production system', as it was known, had attracted widespread attention within Japan, and other Japanese companies began to emulate it. JIT systems diffused rapidly in Japan during the late 1970s and early 1980s.

For a JIT system to work effectively, a number of conditions must be met. Indeed, some of the benefits of this system of production may be attributable to companies being forced to create these conditions, as will be described shortly. The Japanese use of *kanban* as a control system for JIT has largely been confined to mass produced components, especially in the vehicle industry, where production layout is based on flow-lines.

The conditions necessary for JIT, whether *kanban*-controlled or not, to work effectively are: swift machine set-ups (Burbidge 1982; Schonberger 1982); simple unidirectional material flow, typically achieved by line layouts or group technology and the product form of organization (Burbidge 1982); and total quality control (Schonberger 1982).

If materials are to be produced 'just in time', then a capability to produce relatively small batches is necessary. The problem with very small batches is that one is likely to run up against cost constraints that may make them uneconomical. Typically, a compromise is reached by calculating the batch size that will give the lowest unit cost. This is achieved by balancing the economies of large batches, due to the fact that set-up costs are spread over many units, against the costs of large batches, which result from having large amounts of capital tied up in inventories. For example, fitting a machine with the appropriate tools and then setting it up, running off trial pieces and readjusting it may take several hours, creating a pressure for a long production run to justify the time expended. However, a significant part of Japan's success with JIT systems has stemmed from Japanese determination not to accept set-up times as given, but to devote effort to reducing set-up times in order to approach a (theoretical) economic batch size of one. For instance, as part of its move to just-in-time, Toyota managed to cut times for the changeover of dies in its stamping shops from as much as ten hours to 165 seconds. The performance of each individual and team, task-by-task, on every changeover, is displayed on bar charts on notice boards, helping to sustain pressure to keep reducing the changeover time (*Financial Times*, 20 May 1989). Table 2.1 shows set-up times at Toyota compared with those typically found in Western companies.

Historically, Western manufacturers have regarded set-up times as given elements in the economic batch size equation. JIT challenges the basic premises of the cost curves in such equations by bringing set-up time – and hence cost – down. Typical strategies for reducing set-up times are machine standardization, pre-kitting, the development of special tools and intensive training of operators.

A second requirement for the successful use of a JIT system is that there should be a relatively simple workflow. Burbidge (1982)

Table 2.1 Set-up times for heavy power presses

	Toyota	*USA*	*Sweden*	*W. Germany*
Set-up time (hours)	0.2	6.0	4.0	4.0
Set-ups per day	3.0	1.0	–	0.5
Lot size (days' use)	1.0	10.0	31.0	–

Source: Burbidge 1982

comments that all successful applications of the *kanban* system have been achieved where operations are organized on a product, as opposed to a process, basis. In factories organized on a process or functional basis, people and machines are grouped according to the function that they perform. Thus in, say, an engineering factory laid out on such a basis, one would probably find lathes grouped together in one area, milling machines in another and so forth. In a factory organized on a product basis, people would be grouped around the products that they produced (output-based groupings) rather than around the functions that they performed (input-based groupings). 'Families' of machines, dedicated to the production of specific, and usually similar, products are characteristic of the product form of organization. Examples are group technology and cellular production, which we shall discuss in more detail shortly. In concerns that are organized on a process or functional basis the JIT system does not work so well, as materials may have to revisit a work station a number of times.

The complexity of the workflow is one among a multiplicity of reasons for stock accumulation, and it is probably because of this that JIT is sometimes seen as a 'tool-box' of techniques; different elements of the package address different aspects of stock accumulation. Stocks may be split into three types: raw materials and bought-in parts, work-in-progress, and finished goods. And there are also three different causes of stock accumulation: uncertainty, inflexibility and complexity.

Stocks of raw materials and bought-in parts are typically held as insurance against disruption to the supply chain, to protect production against late delivery or non-delivery of materials, or the delivery of materials not up to specification. Quality assured supplies delivered just in time address this problem, although acquiring them demands particularly close and cooperative relationships with supplying companies. If such a supply system is to adhere to the popular conception of its function by providing just what customers want exactly when they want it (in the absence of stocks), then the efforts of all the sub-units in the production system must be *precisely* synchronized.

Accumulated work-in-progress also stems from (assumed) inflexibilities in the manufacturing process. The 'economic order quantity' (EOQ) concept takes set-up times as given, then derives a batch size that balances the 'fixed' cost of a set-up with the stockholding costs generated by long production runs.

Finally, work-in-progress may increase where production is complex; as the range of products to be scheduled through the various processes rises, work piles up at bottlenecks (Goldratt and Cox 1984). It is this issue that cellular manufacture addresses. Under JIT, the emphasis is on maintaining a steady *flow* of materials through a succession of value-adding operations. Materials that are stationary as they await their turn to enter the next stage in the system accumulate cost (because of the resources tied up in them), but gain no value.

A third, and crucial, aspect of JIT production is the aforementioned condition of total quality control. As JIT systems run with virtually no margin for error, it is essential that the various upstream work stations deliver to their downstream counterparts goods that are not only on time and in the right quantity but are also of the right quality. For this reason, it is suggested that JIT systems will only work effectively within the wider context of total quality control. This relationship between quality and JIT production is not a one-way dependency of the latter on the former. As we shall see later, JIT not only requires total quality control, it is also one device by which total quality may be realized. The two production philosophies that respectively underlie JIT and the traditional Western approach (sometimes referred to as 'just-in-case' (JIC)) are summarized in table 2.2.

Of course, to describe JIC and JIT as 'philosophies' or 'regimes' could be misleading, to the extent that it implies an internal coherence that does not necessarily exist in reality. They are best viewed as ideal types rather than manufacturing systems that are found in practice. This is particularly the case with JIC, which is not so much a coherent strategy as traditional Western custom and practice.

One theme that particularly stands out from table 2.2 is that under the JIT regime the focus lies very much on the performance of the

Table 2.2   Orientations of JIC and JIT

Issue	Just-in-case	Just-in-time
Official goal	Maximum efficiency.	Maximum efficiency.
Stocks	Integral part of system.	Wasteful – to be eliminated.
Lead-times	Taken as given and built into PPC routines.	Reduced to render small batches economical.
Batch sizes	Taken as given, and EOQ calculated accordingly.	Lot size of one is the target.
Production planning & control	Variety of means. MRP models existing system and optimizes within it. Informal 'pull' for hot orders.	Centralized forecasts in conjunction with local pull control.
Trigger to production	Algorithmically derived schedules. Hot lists. Maintenance of sub-unit efficiencies.	Imminent needs of downstream unit via *kanban* cards.
Quality	Acceptable quality level. Emphasis on error detection.	Zero defects. Error prevention.
Performance measures	Financial measures. Machine utilization. Standard hours. Variance: standard.	Evolving. Flow. Value-added. Non-financial.
Performance focus	Sub-unit efficiency.	System/organization efficiency.
Organizational design	Input-based. Functional.	Output-based. Product.
Suppliers	Multiple. Distant. Independent.	Single/dual sourcing. Supplier as extension.

Source: Oliver 1991

system as a whole (Goldratt and Cox 1984). Under the traditional Western approach there is an underlying assumption that maximizing the efficiencies of the individual components leads to the optimal performance of the system as a whole. JIT implicitly confronts this assumption.

Williams, Williams and Haslam (1989) argue that a reduction in inventory levels of 90 per cent typically produces benefits of the following magnitudes: a 15–40 per cent reduction in the cost of sales; a 90 per cent reduction in production lead-time; a 50 per cent reduction in manufacturing space; and a 75–90 per cent improvement in quality.

In terms of the effects of JIT, a number of beneficial outcomes have been posited to follow from just-in-time methods of production. The most common ones are a more efficient use of working capital, a reduction in lead-times, improvements in quality and reductions in waste. JIT permits more efficient utilization of working capital essentially by reducing the levels of inventories and stocks. Materials lying around in this form add cost (for example interest charges on the capital thus tied up), but not value, to a product. By reducing stocks, capital can be released and may be used more productively elsewhere. A second strength of JIT, albeit an indirect one, is that the necessary reduction in machine set-up times permits a reduction in batch sizes. As batch size is a major determinant of lead-time, just-in-time systems can permit greater responsiveness to customer demands – assuming that the system stretches all the way up the supply chain. Switches in demand can be accommodated by 'pull' systems of production control better than under highly centralized 'push' systems, although it should be recalled that *kanban* is essentially a fine-tuning device, used in combination with smoothed production schedules. According to Toyota, demand variations of about 10 per cent can be handled by the *kanban* system. Production smoothing or 'schedule stabilization' at Toyota refers to both production volume and the variety or 'mix' of product types. The company strives to keep schedule variations to within 10 per cent from month to month and day to day, a process called *heijunka*. The stability thus brought to the production environment is crucial to the efficient operation of a JIT system. In the case of greater fluctuations, either the number of *kanban* (and the amount of material) in the system must be increased, or adjustments to the production process must be made. For example, more overtime working may be demanded, temporary workers may be taken on (or laid off), or production lines may be rearranged (Monden 1983). Such demands carry obvious implications for personnel policy, which we will explore later in this chapter.

The flexibility of the JIT system (within the limits indicated above) may provide a company with a crucial competitive advantage where market environments are unstable, and where there is a premium on customized goods or short lead-times. Finally, JIT systems can encourage quality and minimize waste, because of the greater visibility that the small amount of stock in the system bestows upon the production process. Machine or human errors are rapidly detected, simply because the components at one stage are quickly used in the next. Thus sources of problems tend to be quickly detected, and the problems corrected before expensive scrap or rework costs are incurred. The practice of line stop or *jidoka* is central to this process. *Jidoka* is a term used at Toyota and means 'to make the equipment or operation stop whenever an abnormal or defective condition arises' (Sugimoro et al. 1977, p. 557). It refers to the practice of giving operators the power to stop a production line if they detect a problem that is impairing the product. If something is wrong, the line will quickly be stopped and the problem corrected at source. Under this system the 'insurance policies' of buffer stocks, reserve staff and so on (which allow part of a process to go wrong without total disaster striking) are construed as obstacles to improvement. By permitting one to live with a problem, such spare resources remove the imperative to correct it.

The visibility of production status characteristic of JIT/total quality control systems is typically reinforced by visual controls. *Andon* boards (panels with lights that show at a glance the current status of work operations), and regularly updated graphs, charts and tables displaying team and individual productivity and quality performances are all found in the typical Japanese factory. Even the casual observer can see immediately if production is proceeding normally or not. For instance, at a consumer electronics factory in Japan recently visited by one of the authors, one form of 'visible control' (a term used by managers) was a set of electronic display boards above work stations. The boards indicated, in real time, the number of components that should have been produced at any particular moment according to the day's schedule, together with the number that had been produced and the extent of any disparity between the two figures. The system was 'fool proofed', because the numbers on the board changed only in response to a final electronic quality check on the component. At a glance, managers (or anyone else) could see which teams faced problems, so that corrective action could be taken. This carried the added advantage that work teams ahead of schedule – performing above expectations – were also noticed. In the latter case, 'waste' was implied, and this could be addressed, for instance, by speeding up the line or taking a worker out of the team.

Visibility can, then, provide a springboard for *kaizen*, or continuous improvement, to which we shall now turn our attention.

Kaizen

For many commentators, *kaizen* is *the* distinguishing feature between Japanese and Western organizations, and the belief in the possibility and desirability of continuous improvement has been held out as underpinning Japanese production methods. Kolm (1985, p. 237) has argued that the emphasis on continuous improvement derives from Buddhism, because:

> the idea of perfection . . . is far more present in this way of thinking than in that of the West. It is associated with a pessimism which is typically Buddhist and which is grounded on the fact that one knows one will never get there – in contrast to the optimism of the Westerner who can reach his goal because he is happy with less.

One of the results of the application of the 'idea of linear progress, without any limit to possible improvement', which is 'inherent in Buddhism', is that:

> A Western factory normally sets itself a quality goal for example, 95 per cent of the items produced free of defects – and it is satisfied if it arrives at that goal. This never happens for a Japanese company: the objective is always 100 per cent perfection, one can therefore always achieve an improvement over the actual situation, one can always make progress, and they attempt to do so. In terms of the theory of rational choice, the Japanese producer is a devotee of maximization, not of 'satisficing'. (Kolm 1985, p. 237)

Eliminating waste in Japanese companies through *kaizen* involves an attempt to harness the mental as well as the manual skills of shopfloor workers. Individuals are encouraged to make suggestions – through quality circles, suggestion schemes and so on – as to how savings can be made. Such participation is not mandatory, though Kamata (1983) comments that at Toyota, failure to make suggestions will result in criticism and may mean smaller bonuses. Appraisals that affect wages (described below) may also encourage a high degree of participation.

The improvements sought through *kaizen* include maximum

utilization of labour through the elimination of unnecessary movements and idle time. Discussing a Kawasaki plant, Schonberger (1982) describes how green, amber and red lights indicate how smoothly the line is running. Green indicates that all workers are within cycle times, red that the line has stopped, amber that there are some problems. Management like to see amber lights, because 'it means we are really busting ass.' If there are no amber lights, the line pace is increased or workers removed from the line. Such measures mean that *kaizen* is built into the system on a day-to-day basis. Where improvements are incorporated into the job and the task redesigned, it is then standardized. At Toyota, each operator must be able to perform a standard repeatable sequence of operations based on a given *takt* time (the time taken to produce a component or vehicle) with a specified quantity of parts to work on. This is recorded on paper and displayed at the work site as a visual control. The standard then acts as a benchmark for further improvements.

According to Rehder (1990, p. 97), the effect is as follows:

> ... in traditional organizations ... the workers banded together to control their work pace through the group's control of 'rate busters' and by keeping their know-how about improvements they developed on the shopfloor from management. This control provided the workers with a cushion when management attempted to speed up the work process. The informal work group of traditional organizations had now been largely brought under management's control.

Work organization

A flexible production system, achieved in the absence of stock to take up fluctuations in demand, clearly requires a flexible and responsive workforce. Team working or cellular manufacture, adjuncts of just-in-time production systems, are frequently found. Cellular manufacture contributes towards the advantages sought through JIT because it simplifies workflow, hence permitting reductions in work-in-progress and improving throughput (Edwards 1974; Burbidge 1979). The basic idea behind cellular manufacture, which according to Graham (1988) derives originally from the Soviet Union in the 1950s, is to group machines by family rather than by function. That is, the machines necessary for the production of a 'family' of components are grouped together so that machine tooling can be made specific to those components and so that production flows are simple and components do not have to follow tortuous routes through different functional areas around the factory. An added advantage is that responsibility for sub-standard components is more easily identified as 'ownership', for a product, or a set of operations upon a product, tends to be concentrated within cells or teams rather than dispersed among a range of different functional groups. If this device is used in tandem with a just-in-time system, errors quickly surface – if things go wrong, feedback from the next cell or 'customer' is immediate.

In the Toyota production system the flexibility of labour to meet fluctuations in demand is termed *shojinka*. There are two key methods by which such flexibility is attained: a particular type of machine layout, and the use of multi-skilled workers. The machine layout used in Toyota's flexible workshops is based on U-shaped assembly lines, and is represented in figure 2.1.

According to Monden (1983) this layout enables the range of jobs for which each worker is responsible to be widened or narrowed very easily. A worker in the enclosed area can theoretically tend two (or more) machines, and is also well positioned to assist others who may be falling behind or who are having difficulty with their work. Thus the balancing of the various operations on the line can be achieved via the flexibility of labour deployment, rather than by having

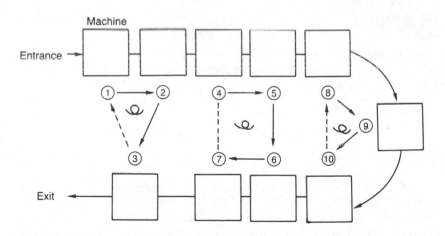

Numbered discs represent worker operations

Source: Monden 1983, p. 101 © Toyota Production System, Institute of Industrial Engineers, 25 Technology Park, Atlanta Norcross, Georgia 30091, USA

Figure 2.1 U-shaped production lines at Toyota

buffers to accommodate fluctuations in work rate at the various stations along the line.

This arrangement presupposes that the workers possess the necessary skills, which is where the requirement of multi-skilling is of importance. At Toyota multi-skilling is developed by a high degree of job rotation, with workers sometimes being rotated through different jobs several times a day. Sayer (1986) recounts how one Toyota worker performed 35 different production jobs and walked six miles in one day. This job rotation, and the relatively high degree of 'ownership' and responsibility that the system confers on teams of workers, have led some commentators (Sugimoro et al. 1977; Monden 1983) to describe it as a 'respect-for-human' system. However, Kamata (1983), whose book *Japan in the Passing Lane* is an autobiographical account of life in one of Toyota's factories, presents a picture of an intense, gruelling work experience. Describing his reason for producing the book he writes:

> I wanted to show the inhumanity of it all – not only its inhumanity but also the unquestioning adherence to such a system. Is the prosperity of a modern, industrial society worth such a cost, such a cruel compulsion of robot-like work? (Kamata 1983)

That Japanese production systems place considerable demands on workers is not disputed; the effect on worker experience, however, is. Domingo (1985, p. 22), for instance, argues that the Toyota system 'requires an almost military discipline' and that it 'indefinitely simulates a crisis so that management and workers are always on their toes', a view shared by Slaughter (1987), who describes the system as 'management-by-stress'. Domingo (1985, p. 22) goes on to state that:

> . . . the tension generated . . . is a positive tension and seldom results in any counter-productive fear or anxiety . . . every working day [is] a challenge, a victory to achieve rather than merely a boring expanse of time.

Domingo suggests that the culture and values of the Japanese people predispose them to enjoying work under such a regime, and this argument would be supported by Turpin (1991), who comments that 'persistence' and the 'will to endure' (*gambare*), together with other Confucian values, are instilled in Japanese children early in their lives. He comments further:

After graduation, the neophyte employee merges with the rest of the group to form a team for whom *gambare* is a permanent slogan. In plants such as the Mazda works in Hiroshima, children's drawings with *gambare* slogans can be seen on the walls, to remind their fathers to work hard and diligently.

Turpin cites a survey of 3,600 Japanese and 400 European executives that asked 'what is your favourite word in life?' For the Europeans 'love', 'family' and 'fun' topped the list, for the Japanese 'effort', 'persistence', and 'thank you'.

Teamwork – a central characteristic of Japanese work organization – is similarly subject to controversy as to its effects on work experience and the quality of working life of the Japanese worker. Clearly, working in a team may offer advantages over the isolation of the traditional production line, but with teamwork may also go strong peer pressures. For instance, if one member of a team is absent, late for work, or lacking in diligence, the rest of the team, in the absence of 'cover' from spare labour, suffers, and has to work harder to make up the shortfall, or to work overtime to meet targets. Some Japanese companies actively remind employees of how fellow team members are hurt by absenteeism (Rehder 1990), and public displays of individual performances, for instance in terms of quality, absenteeism and so on, may serve to increase the pressure on individual workers.

Traditions of teamwork and collective responsibility were maintained in Japanese organizations despite the advent of Taylorism in the early part of this century. Littler (1982) describes how Taylorism became popular in Japan in the 1920s and 1930s but, unlike in the US and the UK, did not result in a rigid separation of planning and execution of tasks, nor in social fragmentation. Rather, although some aspects of job analysis and work procedures were adopted, they were modified and diluted in order to leave work teams with their internal flexibility intact, and the foreman retained most production planning responsibilities rather than surrendering them to a separate planning department. Littler attributes this preservation of teamwork and foreman responsibilities to the historical political strength of the *oyakata* (the internal sub-contractors common in the late nineteenth and early twentieth centuries who employed teams of workers). This strength meant that the sub-contractor was not destroyed, as in Britain, but incorporated into the company structure. Hence, over the last two or three decades, when Japan adopted the manufacturing techniques described in this section, it found itself already with the basis of the concomitant work organization.

Organizational Structures and Systems

In this section we review three aspects of the structures and systems of the major Japanese corporations, and examine how they differ from the arrangements found in the West.

Management accounting

Hiromoto (1988) has argued that Japanese accounting systems reinforce a top-to-bottom commitment to product and process innovation. He contrasts this with the situation in the West, where accounting practice has typically been dominated by considerations concerning the stewardship of assets and external reporting requirements (Johnson and Kaplan 1987). Although Japanese companies have similar requirements, the argument is that the Japanese do not let these accounting procedures dominate their management control systems. Thus there is a more direct link between management accounting practices and corporate goals.

Hiromoto argues that in Japan this permits an overriding commitment to market-driven management, in which cost estimates of new products are derived from a competitive market price, rather than historical cost data. Products are designed and built for a price that will meet with market success – irrespective of whether the price is supported by current manufacturing practice – and accounting procedures take account of this. An example from the product development system of the motor vehicle manufacturers Daihatsu illustrates this process at work, and also provides a general illustration of how structures and systems can drive or impede improvement activities.

At Daihatsu the product development process lasts three years. A product or project (cross-functional) manager is responsible for new vehicles from planning through to sales. During the development process, input from all the functions is sought on attributes such as the performance levels and features that the car should possess. On this basis, a development plan is formulated. Then comes cost estimation, but this is *not* just a case of turning the design over to the accountancy function to arrive at a figure based on existing engineering standards. A target selling price (based on market acceptability) and target profit margins are established; the difference between the two is the *allowable cost* per car (in practice far below what can be achieved). Production costs on the basis of current capability (assuming no innovation) are also calculated. A compromise between the two is sought and this becomes the goal towards which everyone works. The system thus works to *force* improvement (Hiromoto 1988). An additional aspect of this model is a heavy use of non-financial measures.

The organization of R&D activities

Until recently one of the popular stereotypes of Japanese companies represented them as organizations that were competent at manufacturing but poor at innovation. In the car industry, findings from the IMVP have increasingly called this stereotype into question. Womack, Jones and Roos (1990) describe what they call the process of 'lean design', as found in the Japanese vehicle industry. The central figure in this is the *shusa*, or 'large-project leader'. Unlike officials with cross-functional roles in many Western companies, the holder of this position has considerable power. The *shusa* assembles a team of people that is assigned to a development project for its full duration. These people will be from different functions, but their allegiance is unquestionably to the project leader. At an early stage in the project, the system forces the team to confront the difficult trade-offs that it will need to make during the development process. In this environment, it is unsurprising that ideas such as 'design for manufacture', in which quality is *designed* into the product at the outset by ensuring ease of manufacture, can thrive.

Table 2.3 shows the comparative performance of Japanese and Western vehicle producers across a range of product development activity measures.

Indices of innovation show similar patterns. In the mid-1980s the US vehicle industry was spending about $7,000 million on R&D, compared with approximately $5,500 million on the part of the Japanese and $5,000 million in the case of the European vehicle industries. Yet the number of patents per year being filed by the Japanese producers was much greater – about 2,300 compared with 1,750 and 1,400 on the part of the US and European producers respectively (Womack, Jones and Roos 1990).

Organizational structures

As we shall see in chapter 5, when Western companies emulate Japanese systems, they often claim to be moving towards relatively

Table 2.3   Japanese product development performance

	Japanese producers	*American producers*	*European producers*
Average engineering hours per new car (millions)	1.7	3.1	2.9
Average development time per new car (months)	46.2	60.4	57.7
Number of employees in the project team	485	903	904
Return to normal productivity after new model (months)	4	5	12

Source: Adapted from Womack, Jones and Roos 1990

flat, simple organizational structures. However, more systematic examination of the organizational structures found in Japan itself suggests that the Japanese firm is actually more (formally) hierarchical and bureaucratic than its Western counterpart. This is demonstrated by one of the most rigorous pieces of work in this area, carried out by Lincoln and Kalleburg (1990). Using a series of measures, many drawn from the Aston programme of research (Pugh and Hickson 1976), they compared 100 matched firms from Japan and the US covering 8,000 employees. The results of this comparison are shown in table 2.4.

Lincoln and Kalleburg's objective measures broadly confirmed many of the popular stereotypes of Japanese management systems, in particular demonstrating higher flexibility of production systems and lower specialization than in the West. Relatively high levels of employee activity in quality circles and company welfare provision were also revealed. However, the Japanese firms were clearly more bureaucratic in some ways. They had more hierarchical levels than their Western counterparts and significantly greater formality of activities. The Japanese firms also showed higher *formal* centralization of decision-making, although *in practice* it appears that many decisions are actually made at lower levels in the Japanese firms than in their Western counterparts. The taller hierarchies in the Japanese organizations clearly contradict some stereotypical models of Japanese-style organization, and constitute a subject worthy of careful scrutiny in the future.

Table 2.4 Organizational structures in Japan and the West

	US mean	Japan mean
Workflow rigidity	High	Low
Specialization	High	Low
Hierarchical levels	4.9	5.5
Formalization	Low	High
Formal centralization (levels vary from 1–6)	4.66	4.99
De facto centralization	4.36	3.82
Proportion in quality circles	27%	95%
Welfare provision (% of practices present out of 9)	58%	74%

Source: Lincoln and Kalleburg 1990

Personnel Practices

It is the employment and personnel practices of the major Japanese corporations that have, at least until recently, when attention has shifted to 'hard' manufacturing systems, most captured the attention of Western observers. Here the arguments rest on a line of reasoning that links the success of the Japanese in world markets to 'progressive' personnel policies, such as single-status terms and conditions, consultative management styles, lifetime employment guarantees, and company-based welfare schemes. These are held to generate the commitment and loyalty so lacking in Western organizations. This section details these practices under the categories of employment contracts; selection, induction and training; payment and reward systems; and consultation and communication.

Employment contracts

Perhaps the most widely publicized aspects of personnel management in Japan are the provision of lifetime employment and company-based welfare. These are frequently, if erroneously, presented as stemming directly from Japanese Confucianism and the feudal legacy (Morishima 1982; Nakane 1973), and are often held to create a high degree of commitment and loyalty to the organization.

The origin of lifetime employment provision has been traced back to the days of the *zaibatsu* – the huge family-owned and family-controlled conglomerates that dominated Japanese industry until the 1930s – when youths would join firms as apprentices and eventually rise into the ranks of management (Sethi, Namiki and Swanson 1984). Littler (1982) describes how the system emerged during the incorporation of the *oyakata* (sub-contractors) into giant corporations in the late nineteenth and early twentieth centuries. Apart from encouraging company loyalty, it is argued that a lifetime commitment to employees reduces labour mobility between firms and increases the potential for mobility within firms – these advantages being reinforced by a seniority pay and promotion system (described below). The mutual commitment characteristic of the system means that employees are more likely to be treated as 'assets' than 'costs', and employers are hence more willing to train and develop their human resources at their own expense.

The feudal legacy argument must, however, be read carefully, for the evidence does not suggest that lifetime employment is necessarily a culturally determined institution. Dore (1973b) shows that, although the ideology of loyalty to one feudal lord was used to underpin the system, restrictions on the mobility of the workforce represented a conscious managerial strategy designed to cope with an acute shortage of skilled labour following the Japanese decision to industrialize in 1867. Morishima (1982) adds that lifetime employment was also encouraged by the military – both for planned production for war, and for the preparation of workers for army life.

Further qualifications regarding the significance of the institution of lifetime employment are raised by the following considerations. First, the retirement age for the majority of Japanese is 55 (Franko 1983), though eligibility for welfare pensions does not begin until the age of 60. Pensions tend to be meagre, and the 1980 census in Japan indicated that over 80 per cent of Japanese men over 60 were still in the labour force, while 45 per cent of males over 65 were still economically active (Sethi, Namiki and Swanson 1984). Second, women are virtually excluded from the system. Third, the system is made viable by companies surrounding themselves with 'layers' of temporary workers (Littler 1982) – an important point that will be elaborated in a section on 'the dual economy' below. And finally, lifetime employment is not a legal or contractual obligation, but rather a matter of company policy.

Despite the last qualification, employers have normally been able to fulfil their commitment to lifetime employment, especially since the policy has mainly been restricted to very large corporations that can re-deploy labour in other organizational branches when necessary. However, in the late 1980s the strong Yen, anti-dumping laws in the US and Europe, and competitive pressure from other East Asian newly industrialized countries led to slowed growth in many businesses and to redundancies in the steel, coal and shipbuilding industries. The official unemployment rate, at 3.2 per cent in 1987, had reached a post-war high, and in the same year most Japanese unions accepted the lowest pay rise in 28 years. This was just over 3 per cent in the steel, automobile and electronics industries (*Financial Times*, 10 April 1987).

Since then, the Japanese economy has picked up, with official unemployment falling to 2.0 per cent in 1991 (*Japan Times*, 31 July 1991), and a record 2.57 million workers (from a total workforce of 61.59 million) changing jobs in the year to February 1991. Almost four-fifths of these changes were voluntary ones (*Japan Times*, 26 July 1991).

The other aspect of the Japanese employment contract associated with company loyalty in popular literature is company-based welfare provision. In schemes characterized as paternalistic, many Japanese companies offer a range of benefits that Hirschmeier and Yui (1981) divide into three categories: assistance in cases of sickness, accident or death; educational benefits for employees; and facilities to foster loyalty and community spirit, such as subsidized housing, holiday homes and company shops and schools. Dore (1973a) contrasts Hitachi's expenditure on welfare, at 8.5 per cent of labour costs, with that of the median British firm, at 2.5 per cent.

As with lifetime employment, the context of the emergence of corporate welfarism is crucial. Again, it emerged as a conscious managerial initiative, rapidly diffusing through Japanese industry in the 1920s and 1930s as a control strategy intended to head off radical trade unionism. Littler (1982, p. 155) describes how employers at the time:

> saw paternalism as a panacea for all the ills of industrial capitalism and specifically as an alternative to Western-type class struggle . . . this managerial strategy received active support from the Japanese government.

Company welfarism fosters employee dependency on the company, which is often increased by subsidized leisure activities that pervade non-working hours.

Paternalism is seen as desirable and potentially transferable by many in the West (Pascale and Athos 1982). Others are cynical; Briggs (1988), for instance, comments that 'the very advantages the large organizations offer their workers can become chains', and Kamata (1983, p. 57), describing Toyota, provides an illustration of this:

> Approximately 4,000 workers have supposedly bought houses built with the help of [company] loans, and in a very real sense these young married men are tied to the company – that is, to the assembly line – by their loan repayments until the day they retire.

Selection, induction and training

Vogel (1980) suggests that 'in initially hiring employees, the company aims to be as merciless as possible in order to select people of quality.' Obviously, in view of the expectation that (core) employees will remain with the firm until retirement, recruitment and selection constitute a careful process. The vast majority of recruits are taken straight from college, people who have worked elsewhere generally being avoided. In any case, there is enormous competition among school-leavers and graduates to enter the large corporations as core workers – educational performance being the key to entry (Ouchi 1981). The major corporations recruit directly from the educational institutions with the best reputations, which in turn recruit from the best high schools, and so on down the educational system. Consequently there is strong competition to gain admission even to the best kindergartens, and cramming classes for four- to five-year-olds are common (Ouchi 1981).

Close attention is also given to hiring new employees who will fit into the company culture. Careful screening ensures that candidates likely to endorse the company's values and philosophy are selected, and 'moderate views' and a 'balanced personality' are a prerequisite. Radical views or an inability to 'get along with others' result in rejection, regardless of ability and potential (Robbins 1983), and Pucik (1985) claims that private investigators are routinely used to check on candidates' backgrounds, as well as those of families, neighbours and friends.

Because recruitment is straight from college, employers seek potential as opposed to specific skills, job training being provided on entry. Immediately before job training, however, there is a period of induction that typically begins with an entrance ceremony. The induction programme, which lasts on average about ten days (Naylor 1984), may involve group residence, team activities, physical exercise, and instruction in the history, philosophy and mottoes of the firm, and a spokesman for the new entrants may read a speech pledging the intake's best efforts. The aim is 'to make each employee realize that he is a member of the organization' (Hirschmeier and Yui 1981).

Following induction, employees are typically further socialized in an initial training programme, sometimes lasting as long as six months, the main purpose of which is to familiarize them with the organization. Azumi (1969) suggests a similarity in this training to that given in religious orders or military schools, and some companies since the 1960s have sent entrants to the army or to Zen temples for periods of 'character building' (Ishida 1977). Training and socialization continue throughout employees' careers, and typically are provided on-the-job and involve frequent rotation. This experience encourages an acceptance of flexibility and prepares employees for promotion by giving them generalist, rather than specialist, skills (Clegg 1986).

Payment and reward systems

The Japanese are well known for their seniority-based pay systems. These emerged at the same time as lifetime employment when the *oyakata* were incorporated into the *zaibatsu* (Littler 1982). The *nenko joretsu* wage system meant basically that length of service and age played a more important role in determining wages than job performance or competence. It has been suggested that the system provides the advantages of encouraging skill development, diminishing internal competition (Sethi, Namiki and Swanson 1984), and reducing labour turnover (Dickens and Savage 1988). Monden (1983) points out how the system functions by assigning a wage to an individual on the basis of age rather than job grade. He suggests that this facilitates the development of multi-functional workers by eliminating territorial arguments along the dividing lines between grades.

Most Japanese corporations retain a seniority element in their wages system, but with recent changes, such as the increased cost of labour, slowed economic growth and an ageing population, most have also actively considered its elimination, or at least dilution, in favour of performance-determined pay (Japan Institute of Labour 1984). Today, individual competition between employees for higher pay and for promotion is reported to be high (Pucik 1985; Robbins 1983; Moore 1987). In fact, according to a Ministry of Labour survey in 1989 (reported in Endo 1991), around 80 per cent of Japanese firms that employ over 1,000 people use personal assessment systems in consideration of individuals' pay and promotion. The *satei* system, as it is known in Japan, influences both the rate of promotion and the level of monthly pay, and it applies to blue-collar as well as white-collar workers (excluding temporary staff). The annual (or sometimes twice-yearly) assessment is based on objective measures of past performance, but also on subjective assessments by the worker's immediate supervisor relating to factors such as eagerness, attitude to the work group, and potential ability to perform jobs more effectively. According to Endo (1991), the effects of the system include intense individual competition for high *satei* scores, an acceptance of managerial prerogatives, under-reporting of working hours, and workers refusing to apply for their full paid holiday entitlement. Yamamoto (1990) comments that at one large Japanese corporation supervisors are encouraged to designate workers who refuse to do overtime without offering a reason, or who ask other workers about their salary raise, or who show great interest in occupational diseases, as 'problematic persons' or 'troublemakers'.

Japanese companies, however, appear to achieve teamwork at the same time as individual competition. The provision of team-building training is obviously one factor (Hirschmeier and Yui 1981); so is the typical organization of employees into teams with group responsibilities for tasks (Littler 1982). Nonetheless, individual competition and teamwork appear to be contradictory notions. Ouchi (1981) suggests that this dilemma is resolved by frequent rotation of managers, which may prevent the formation of 'too cosy' relationships, and by the practice of including teamwork ability and quality of relations with subordinates in personal assessments.

It is appropriate here to mention briefly a few other aspects of systems of motivation. Total quality management places pressure on work group supervisors to meet quality and output targets, and, with responsibility for maintenance and quality control typically delegated to the work group, there is less opportunity to blame failure on anyone else, or to 'hide' productivity problems in other ways. Publicly displayed output target and feedback systems also increase the pressure to perform – any problems are visible to the whole factory. Briggs (1988) suggests that high effort is forthcoming for fear of 'loss of face' or shame – a view supported by Kamata (1983). Certainly such systems heighten the visibility of behaviour and hence increase the possibility of errors or misbehaviour, accidental or otherwise, being found out.

By all accounts, employees in Japan are extremely hard workers, and the above descriptions of employment contracts, selection, induction, personal assessment and work organization may give some clues as to the sources of motivation. Assumptions that motivation is related to work satisfaction deriving from the 'Japanese management style' have, however, been questioned in empirical investigations. For example, Lincoln and Kalleburg (1990), in a comparative analysis of work attitudes in the US and Japan, observed that commitment was higher in Japan, but satisfaction was lower, as table 2.5 illustrates.

They concluded that:

> ... the indisputable discipline and compliance of the Japanese workforce are rooted not in individual workers' feelings of commitment to and identification with firms, but rather in management, work group and community pressures. (Lincoln and Kalleburg 1990, p. 72)

Hofstede (1980) suggests that many Japanese employees feel pressured at work, and Cooper's (1987) research places Japanese executives in a high position in an international league table of stress. Briggs (1988) explains this high degree of stress in terms of the culturally embedded concept of *gaman* – a resigned acceptance of hardship without pain. The importance of a Japanese proclivity to accept hardship (as with a proclivity to work in groups and to feel a sense of obligation to one's peers) in explaining levels of motivation is difficult to assess, but it may be a relevant factor. What is clear is that, particularly in the absence of strong and independent trade union representation, the personnel management practices described

Table 2.5 Job satisfaction: US vs Japan

	Positive (%)	Undecided (%)	Negative (%)
US sample	34.0	61.4	4.5
Japanese sample	17.8	66.4	15.9

Source: Lincoln and Kalleburg 1990

above are likely to foster a sense of shared destiny between employer and employee – a condition that we shall argue is a necessary prerequisite for the Japanese manufacturing regime to operate successfully.

Working time

Recent reports circulating in the West have alleged the rise of a new generation of fun-seeking *shinjinrui*, or 'new human beings' (*Chicago Tribune*, 16 June 1991). However, working hours in Japan actually increased after the first oil shock in 1974–5. Ministry of Labour statistics showed that in 1987 the number of hours worked annually by an average Japanese employee exceeded those of average workers in the United States and Britain by more than 200 and those of average workers in West Germany and France by over 500 (see table 2.6). These official figures would imply that the Japanese work roughly one to three months more per year than their Western counterparts. The Japanese government's figures are similar to those obtained by the International Labour Organization in 1988 (ILO 1989).

According to Morioka (1990), the figure for Japan in table 2.6 is likely to be an underestimate of real Japanese working hours. The first reason for this is that the figures do not include small-scale establishments of under 30 employees, in which 57 per cent of the Japanese labour force is employed. A 1986 Ministry of Labour survey indicated that employees in these companies worked 100 hours per year more than the average for those in companies employing 30 people or more. Secondly, because the figures in table 2.6

Table 2.6 International comparison of annual working hours per person in manufacturing industry (1987)

Country	Total annual hours	Overtime hours
Japan	2,168	224
United States	1,947	192
Britain	1,949	177
West Germany	1,642	78
France	1,645	–

Source: Labour Standards Bureau, Ministry of Labour; cited in Kawahito 1991

were compiled from information solicited from companies, unrecorded overtime, for which the employees received no payment – known in Japan as 'service overtime' – is not included. Figures from the government's Statistics Bureau, compiled from questionnaires distributed directly to households, show that in 1987 average Japanese working hours per employee per year were around 2,400. Morioka's estimate for Japanese men is at least 2,600 hours per year, excluding work-related study, small group activities such as involvement in quality circles, socializing with co-workers or clients, and commuting (which is twice as time-consuming as in the US and Europe) – all of which can place heavy demands on time. Morioka's (1990, p. 66) conclusion is that:

> almost all of the active waking hours of working-age males are spent working for their companies . . . This fact puts almost the entire burden of housework and the raising of children on the women. As a result, most women have no choice but to maintain the household full-time for their workaholic husbands or, if they do seek employment, to work on a part-time basis.

Kawahito (1991, p. 154) implies that 'overwork' is the result of peer pressures, visibility of performance and the *satei* personal assessment system:

> Contribution to the company by working long hours is a determining factor in the success of an employee's career. Those who do not work overtime or do take their paid vacation time are given negative performance evaluations. If the negative assessments continue, promotions are delayed and salaries remain low.

In Japan there is an organization, made up mainly of lawyers, doctors and academics, known as the 'National Defense Counsel for Victims of *Karoshi*'. *Karoshi* means 'death from overwork'. The organization attempts to record cases of such deaths systematically, and represents the families of victims in claims for compensation against employers. Proving that a stress-related illness, such as cardiovascular or cerebrovascular damage, is due to work overload is difficult, and only 81 out of 830 compensation claims submitted in 1988 were successful (Vehata 1991). This is despite the fact that a recent Japanese government study estimated that one in eight Japanese workers who die between the ages of 30 and 64 is a *karoshi* victim (*Chicago Tribune*, 16 June 1991). Hiroshi Kawahito, Secretary

General of the Defense Council, links *karoshi* to extreme Japanese nationalism, and described in a recent interview with one of the authors his fear that the Japanese are still fighting a war: 'Soldiers don't die, but many workers die in this war.'

After attempting (unsuccessfully) to persuade the Japanese trade union movement to take up the campaign to reduce the incidence of *karoshi*, the National Defense Counsel has turned its attention to publicizing its claims among overseas governments, employers' associations and trade unions, in the hope that this will lead to official international protests that Japan is competing unfairly because of labour exploitation.

Consultation and communication

The Japanese decision-making process is frequently referred to as decision-making by consensus, or *ringisei*. Literally translated this means a 'system of reverential enquiry about a superior's intentions' (Sethi, Namiki and Swanson 1984). This process, most widely used amongst lower to middle managers, involves circulating documents to concerned members of an organization to gain their approval for a proposal in advance of its implementation. Typically, the process consists of four stages: proposal, circulation, approval and record. Although final decisions have to be approved at the appropriate level of authority, the process means that subordinates, right down to the level of the work team, are likely to have had the opportunity to have their views heard and perhaps to have had some influence. The process is slow, but when action is taken, any potential resistance to change should (ideally) already have been overcome and collective commitment have been given.

Supporting this system, is the frequent use of face-to-face communication in the Japanese corporation. This occurs not only within the work team, but through managers spending large amounts of time on the shopfloor (White and Trevor 1983), and through the use in some organizations of open plan offices in which all behaviour and actions – even telephone conversations – are visible and audible. The steel company NKK, for instance, uses a 'touching desk' system held to encourage a 'group task force' mentality. Here, apart from that of the general manager or department head, who sits on a raised dais (but is still entirely visible), the managers' desks literally touch each other (Mitchell and Larson 1987). Such devices encourage communication that is informal and extensive, and they may help to explain the popular stereotype of the Japanese white-collar worker who works extremely long hours and who socializes with peers and superiors at the end of the working day. While systems of consultation and communication in large Japanese corporations are regarded positively by some authors (for instance Pascale and Athos 1982), criticisms on the grounds of invasion of privacy and pressures for conformity are also occasionally made. That they are not necessarily culturally specific to Japan, however, is witnessed by the fact that at least some Western organizations, such as IBM, have successfully implemented similar systems (Peters and Waterman 1982).

A final comment, to which we will return later in the book, is worth making initially here. Despite the fact that many date back to earlier parts of the twentieth century, the personnel practices that we have just described appear to 'fit' the manufacturing practices outlined above. Yet the manufacturing practices themselves emerged only in the 1960s. The question is raised, therefore, as to whether the personnel practices were a prerequisite for success with Japanese manufacturing practices. The fit also appears to apply with regard to the third element of the Japanese 'package' – the economic and political context – to which attention will now be turned.

Wider Social, Political and Economic Conditions

Enterprise unions

Unlike Britain's unions, based on occupations and crafts, Japan's unions are predominantly enterprise-based. Over 90 per cent of union members belong to enterprise unions, and the great majority of unions exist in large-scale public and private enterprises employing more than 500 workers. The smaller the enterprise, the less likely is union representation; and those enterprises employing less than 100 workers are approximately 95 per cent non-union. Until recently, there were three main national federations: the Domei and Churitsuroren, covering the private sector, and the Sohyo, comprising public sector unions. In 1987 Sohyo and Domei merged to form a single national trade union centre, New Rengo, representing 7.8 million members (Salmon 1991). However, these organizations are only loosely based and relatively powerless – the enterprise-level union is more or less financially autonomous and self-supporting

(Moore 1987). In 1980 it was estimated that there were 71,780 unions in Japan, with a total membership of 12.3 million. Approximately two-thirds of these were in the private sector, and more than half were confined to the large corporations (*Anglo-Japanese Economic Institute Review*, Bulletin 217, 1980). The unionization rate declined slightly in the 1980s, and by June 1990 membership was down to 12.2 million, representing 25.9 per cent of the total workforce (Miyano 1990).

Japanese unions in their modern form developed only after the suppression of emergent independent trade unions. During a period in which there was a steep increase in the number of people in the industrial working class, in the late 1910s and early 1920s trade unions, often led by revolutionaries, grew rapidly, and industrial conflict became commonplace. The Japanese government responded with policies aimed at suppressing 'dangerous groups' and 'dangerous thoughts', and with surveillance and spasmodic mass arrests of trade union leaders and members of reformist organizations (Littler 1982). Immediately after the Second World War, Japan's American occupiers encouraged trade unions as part of a 'liberalization' programme. According to Kenney and Florida (1988), enterprise unions, which included blue-collar and white-collar workers, were sought by the Japanese Left, which aimed ultimately to transform them into factory soviets. Unions secured contracts that included provisions for worker–management councils with a significant role in enterprise decision-making, including influence over investment and staffing policies; and the axiom 'to each according to his need, from each according to his ability' was pushed forward. However, the communists, who had again emerged as union leaders, were crushed in purges in the 1950s (Morishima 1982). A big turning point was the '100-day dispute' at Nissan in 1953, which was won by management and after which a second moderate union (to become Nissan's present enterprise union) was installed (Cusumano 1986). Lifetime employment and seniority-based pay systems also became more widespread in Japan in the 1950s (Morishima 1982).

The late 1940s and 1950s were a period during which employers went on the offensive against the involvement of worker organizations in issues such as investment and staffing, with the support of the Japanese state. Communist forces were undermined – often by the use of targeted dismissals – and conservative enterprise unions emerged as the norm (Kenney and Florida 1988; Gordon 1985). 'Welfarist' systems, such as lifetime employment and seniority-based wages, which were originally pursued by leftist unions, became 'integrated into the logic of capital accumulation' (Kenney and Florida 1988, p. 127), as large Japanese corporations realized their advantages in terms of worker loyalty.

It would be wrong to suggest that radical trade union influence was completely wiped out in Japan in the 1940s and 1950s. Apart from the legacy of welfarism, for which they were, in part, responsible, some enterprise unions continued to have an influence over the day-to-day running of businesses. Tabata (1989) documents the case of Japan's second largest car manufacturer, which managed to eliminate local union influence and establish full managerial prerogatives over labour deployment, overtime work and so on only in the 1980s. However, he concludes (p. 28) that 'all enterprise-based unions in Japan . . . seem to be showing the same tendency, with their functions on the wane.'

Hence, today, the enterprise union is the most ubiquitous unit negotiating on behalf of labour in Japanese industry. Whitehill and Takezawa (1986) suggest that unions' close identification with their companies weakens their ability to defend the interests of their members. Indeed, it is not unusual for supervisors and middle managers also to be union representatives; the union can function as a career route into more senior management positions. Moore (1987) estimates that around one in six business executives will have been a union leader. Taiichi Ohno, the main architect and promoter of JIT at Toyota, himself served as union president at the company. Cusumano (1986) suggests that this enabled Toyota to put in place the working arrangements to support JIT in a way that eluded other Japanese vehicle assemblers.

Trade union offices are typically provided by the company on the factory site. As unions are enterprise-based, rather than based on occupations or trades, there is reduced scope for demarcation disputes, greatly facilitating acceptance of change and flexible labour deployment within the company. Enterprise unions, together with practices such as seniority-based payment systems and the bestowing of lifetime employment on recruits, serve to increase employees' identification with their companies, and restrict mobility of labour between firms.

A close relationship between enterprise union and company may be cemented by what Yamamoto (1990) calls 'informal organizations'. In a case study of 'T-Electric' (a pseudonym for a Japanese company with over 60,000 employees) Yamamoto describes the Ohgi Kai

('Folding Fan Society'), an informal organization made up mainly of supervisors. About 40 per cent of members of the society are active in the company union. The Ohgi Kai's three main aims are 'corporate growth and stable industrial relations', 'making the workplace cheerful', and the encouragement of 'well-cultured, mature human beings'. The society's endeavours are directed towards maintaining 'order in the workplace' and keeping the workplace free of 'troublemakers' or 'problematic persons'. Members are given instructions on how they should identify troublemakers in their roles as union members and supervisors. Descriptions of potential troublemakers include:

> A person [who] is interested in, and is eager to deal with, problems on the shopfloor, and political, social and economic problems.
> At the time raises in salary are given, a person [who] goes around the shopfloor, asking other people how much they got.
> A person [who] has become better versed in the shop regulations and other regulations . . . trying to take all the available paid holidays and/or all the monthly physiological leave allowed.
> A person [who] is very particular about the staffing level, and, should there be any vacancy, persistently demands that it be filled.
> A person who shows great interest in occupational diseases.
> A person [who] has begun to discuss wages and other labour conditions at the company consciously in comparison with those at other companies.

Yamamoto lists 41 such 'diagnostic check-points', and comments that Ohgi Kai members, who constitute around one in 30 of the workforce, are willing to 'tail' suspect workers outside working hours in order to discover whether they have involvements with leftist organizations. Identified 'problematic persons' are informally pressured into either mending their ways or leaving the company.

Nakane (1973) argues that the result of company-based union organization in Japan is a culture with vertical social divisions along enterprise lines, rather than the characteristic British horizontal social divisions based on occupation or class – a perspective that suggests that Japanese society is more egalitarian. However, given our discussion of the emergence of enterprise unions and their characteristics, this argument may be difficult to sustain, and in any case horizontal divisions are evident in Japan when taking into account temporary workers or workers in small firms, who are not covered by enterprise unions. This is the phenomenon to which we shall now turn attention.

The dual economy

Until the mid-1980s Western observers tended to focus on the more attractive aspects of the Japanese industrial system, particularly its seemingly progressive personnel practices. However, when one extends the analysis to the economy as a whole, it may be seen that the benefits enjoyed by industrial workers apply to only a minority of the working population. In short, the dual economy in Japan is very marked, and there are substantial differences in the benefits enjoyed by those on the periphery and those enjoyed by core workers. This extends both across and within enterprises. We shall consider two elements here: first, the use of core and peripheral workers within the major enterprises, and secondly the use of sub-contracting companies in the economy as a whole.

Estimates of how many workers in Japan actually enjoy lifetime employment vary considerably. Sethi, Namiki and Swanson (1984) estimate that 35 to 40 per cent of the total workforce enjoy lifetime employment, with 40 to 60 per cent of the employees in the large corporations covered by this system. Other commentators have suggested that the proportion of the total workforce with lifetime employment may be as low as 10 per cent (Kendall 1984). Of those workers outside the lifetime employment system, two distinct types may be discerned: workers mobile between firms who did not join the company immediately after leaving full-time education, and peripheral workers. Included in this latter category are part-time workers, and temporary workers such as seasonal or sub-contracted workers. Halliday and McCormack (1973) refer to these as 'nothing but an industrial reserve army of Japan, obliged to work under less than satisfactory conditions, laid off when business becomes dull.' Women are considerably over-represented in this latter category; they are less likely to be granted lifetime employment. The differential between female and male wages is around 15 per cent for the 16–20 age group, rising to around 50 per cent at age 35. The figures are unsurprising, given the exclusion of women from 'core' occupations and seniority wages (Kenney and Florida 1988).

Working life for the workers on the periphery can be an unattractive proposition, as Kamata's (1983) autobiographical account of the life of temporary workers on the production lines at Toyota illustrates. As we mentioned earlier, the dominant images are of a relentless work rate, along with compulsory overtime and institutionalization in the form of dormitory accommodation. In the foreword to Kamata's (1983) book Dore suggests that Kamata's experience at Toyota may have been exceptional and unrepresentative of Japanese working life, but given that Toyota has been held up in the West as an example of good Japanese practice, the account is of significance. Indeed, what we have termed 'Japanization' has been referred to elsewhere as 'Toyotism'. In the area of manufacturing methods in particular, when people talk about Japanese methods they are often specifically referring to the Toyota production system.

The second element of the dual economy involves the widespread use of sub-contracting by the major corporations. Kendall (1984) has likened the major Japanese corporations to sharks that swim around the Japanese economy surrounded by pilot fish (the companies to which they sub-contract work). In the motor industry, for example, in 1984 Japan had 11 assemblers employing 155,000 workers. Feeding these assemblers were 7,000 parts manufacturers employing 360,000 workers. Lifetime employment is less likely to exist in these sub-contracting companies, where there are also relatively low wages and poorer working conditions. This situation is illustrated by the figures presented in table 2.7, which describe Japanese manufacturing industry as a whole.

As table 2.7 demonstrates, the differential between the largest and the smallest companies is quite substantial – much higher than in the

Table 2.7 Japanese manufacturing industry wage differentials (1978)

Company size *(No. of workers)*	*Wages (1)**	*Percentage of workforce (2)*
1–9	33.8%}	
10–49	54.8%}	46.6
50–99	60.3%}	
100–499	73.4%}	32.9
500–999	85.5%}	
1,000+	100.0%}	20.5

* As percentage of average wage for worker in company employing 1,000+.
Sources: (1) *Katsuyo Rodo Tokei* (*Labour Statistics Manual*, 1981). (2) *Kojo Tokeihyo* (*Census of Manufacturers*, 1983). Both quoted in Gleave 1987

United States, for instance (Japan Institute of Labour 1984). The significance of this differential is heightened when one considers the proportion of the Japanese labour force working in the small to medium-sized companies; according to table 2.7, almost half work in enterprises of less than 50 people, and nearly 80 per cent work in companies of less than 500 employees. Ministry of Labour statistics from a 1986 survey showed that workers in establishments employing less than 30 employees also suffered by working on average 100 hours per year more than those in establishments employing 30 or more (Morioka 1990). When these figures are considered longitudinally, it appears that the proportion of the labour force employed in small to medium-sized enterprises decreased during the economic upswings of the 1910s, late 1930s and 1960s and increased during the troughs in the 1920s and 1970s. This suggests that the small and medium-scale enterprises have served to absorb fluctuations in the economy (Gleave 1987). This analysis is consistent with that of Kendall (1984), who also argues that in the event of the economy faltering, it will be the extended line of sub-contractors that suffers, rather than the major corporations themselves.

Research in the 1980s suggested that wage and salary differentials between large and small firms were narrowing, and that employment guarantees were being extended to give permanent status to employees in smaller companies (reported in Kenney and Florida 1988). However, Aoki (1987), citing Ministry of Labour statistics, claims that if one compares benefits in kind – bonuses, pensions, lump-sum retirement compensations, and so on – there is evidence of a widening of differentials.

None of this is to say that the major corporations in Japan are necessarily harsh with their suppliers. Indeed, it is interesting to note that buyer–supplier relations in Japan, at least as regards the primary suppliers to the big corporations, are typically of a long-term nature. We shall now examine why this is the case and how it is achieved.

Buyer–supplier relations in Japan

Buyer–supplier relationships in Japan are characterized by longer-term commitment (and the reciprocal obligation that this implies) than their counterparts in the West. Before looking at Japanese practice in detail, it is worth considering the two types of supplier relationship; one based on competition, the other on cooperation.

In a competitive relationship, both buyer and supplier attempt to secure the best deal for themselves, typically at the expense of the other party. The situation may be characterized as a zero-sum game; any gain by one party is at the expense of the other. The advantages stemming from this arrangement centre around the 'survival of the fittest' philosophy, whereby competition keeps everyone on their toes, ensuring the efficient operation of the system as a whole. The drawback of the system is that frequent changes of suppliers may be required, and that the competitive nature of the relationship means that it must constantly be policed. An example of such policing might be heavy goods-inward inspection to ensure that the supplier does not ship below-par goods to the purchaser.

In a cooperative relationship, both parties have a sense of obligation to assist each other and protect the other's interests, at least to some extent. This type of relationship is described as relational or obligational contracting. Relational contracting is very common in Japan, and it has been suggested that this is because Japanese companies and their sub-contractors have a more developed sense of their interdependency than do their equivalents in Britain. An informative example of relational contracting from the Japanese motorcycle industry has been provided by the Boston Consulting Group (1975, quoted in Fortune, 1986). The following features were described as critical elements of this practice: experience-based cost reductions due to the long-term nature of the relationship; raw materials purchase by the final purchaser on behalf of the component makers; integration of planning activities; simplification and standardization of parts design; and sharing of new technology and production methods.

In combination, these elements permit a tightly integrated system of supply and assembly, with a minimum of waste in terms of inventories and inspection activities, all of which add cost, but not value, to a product. Dore (1983) has put forward three reasons why this system has evolved in Japan. The first concerns the financial horizons used by Japanese business, which are long by Western standards. Thus, there is a willingness to forgo short-term gains on price competitiveness in order to maintain a relationship that may bear fruit in the long term. Secondly, the Japanese have a greater sense of obligation to the national interest, and see cooperation with suppliers as one way of discharging this duty. Thirdly, Dore argues, the Japanese feel more comfortable in high-trust situations and therefore automatically seek to avoid low-trust situations, of which competitive purchasing relationships are one manifestation. It should be added, however, that this 'high-trust' relationship could also be described as one of interference and control. The larger purchasing company places 'trust' in its supplier only in the context of a thorough knowledge of the supplier's competences, only after a lengthy probation period, and often only when financial leverage is gained through monopsony or through a direct stakeholding in the firm (Sako 1987).

The potential advantages of 'obligational contracting' are clear. But the question raised is why the Japanese developed *keiretsu* systems (*keiretsu* companies being the smaller firms controlled by the industrial giants), rather than pursuing the policy of vertical integration adopted in many Western countries since the nineteenth century, which theoretically should also lead to a situation where planned integration, standardization, and sharing of technology between different production processes will occur. One answer may be that a *keiretsu* system helps to avoid the worst dysfunctions of bureaucracy typically found in very large organizations and maintains at least a degree of competition. A more obvious explanation, in the context of the above section on the dual economy, is that:

> the *keiretsu* system's birth can be traced to the dual structure of the Japanese economy, that is, the wage gap between large and small and medium-sized companies. The big manufacturers had a large proportion of their parts or even the products themselves made by smaller companies where the wages were low. (Okumura 1990)

Just-in-time production complexes, with close geographical proximity between buyers and suppliers, contribute to the close relations among *keiretsu* groups. The best example of such a complex is Toyota City. In 1980, Toyota controlled ten important subsidiaries and had 220 primary sub-contractors. Some 80 per cent of these had plants within the production complex (Kenney and Florida 1988). In turn, these were served by 5,000 secondary sub-contractors and 30,000 tertiary sub-contractors (Cusumano 1986). Okumura (1990) comments that, as a result, in 1989 'GM's sales amounted to about double those of Toyota, but it has more than 10 times the number of workers.'

Particularly in the motor industry, the contrast between Japanese and traditional Western practice is marked. European motor manufacturers typically source 50–60 per cent of their parts and assemblies from outside suppliers. In Japan, the figure is higher, with Toyota and Nissan buying in 70–75 per cent of their components (Cusumano

1986). As in other industries in Japan, in the motor industry assemblers frequently hold a minority equity stake in their suppliers. *Keiretsu* operate as suppliers' 'clubs', and serve as arenas of information exchange between buyers and suppliers. Contracts are typically long term in nature, and suppliers are given much more responsibility for product development. Unsurprisingly this has taken place within the context of supply bases largely dedicated to particular assemblers, although there is some evidence of a shift to a sharing of suppliers by the assemblers in recent years.

Supplier–purchaser relationships of this nature also permit the use of JIT techniques between buyers and suppliers. Toyota's suppliers typically make several deliveries of components each day, often delivering directly to the factory area where the components will be used (Monden 1981b). Nishiguchi (1989) reports that in Japan automotive suppliers make an average of 7.9 JIT deliveries per day, compared with 0.67 deliveries per day in Europe. Moreover there are 24.0 component failures per 100 vehicles manufactured in Japan, compared with 62.1 in Europe (Nishiguchi 1989). Experience-based cost reductions and continuous improvement (within a framework of a shared understanding of costs) are important features of this model. In these circumstances, high dependability with respect to both delivery and quality is essential, as the disruption resulting from late or poor-quality parts would be both swift and substantial.

'Lean' retailing

Although there is not a coherent model of Japanese retailing as there is of Japanese manufacturing, Toyota, the leading proponent of 'Japanese' production methods, has developed a distinct model of retailing in the car industry, which differs markedly from the traditional Western approach, at least as far as the Western car industry is concerned (Delbridge and Oliver 1991a). Proponents of a pure just-in-time system are very clear that the information upon which build decisions are taken must come from the marketplace. As Taiichi Ohno put it:

> The *information flow* begins in the marketplace reversing the planned mass production flow prevalent since Henry Ford's day . . . (Ohno 1988, p. 3)

In the case of car assembly under a pure JIT system, the information for build should originate in the marketplace and be passed up the chain via the dealer network. In this case, the information that triggers build will be a firm order contract. This information passes to the assembler where it is analysed, 'exploded' and sent to the relevant production facility. It will be received there by those handling the final assembly process and then, as Ohno puts it, 'the information begins its climb up the hill of the production process.' Toyota's strategy is thus to fine tune the factory with the marketplace, in Ohno's words 'grasping precisely the *Now!* needs of the market and in turn reacting instantly.' Ohno continues:

> The Ford system took as its authority forecasts of a necessarily uncertain future based on an analysis of past data and an observation of past trends. *This old-fashioned method no longer applies.* (Ohno 1988, p. 59, with emphasis added)

In the vehicle industry, the inflexibility of a traditional planned mass production system is such that adaptation to market needs is problematical. With this 'push' system the company carries out market research, builds to a production plan, and pushes products onto the marketplace. The clear danger here is the production of goods for which there turns out to be no demand. Under a 'pull' system, the market pulls exactly what it needs from the factory, thus reducing stocks of finished goods. This, according to Ohno, is the theme of the Toyota production system, and the just-in-time production system has developed out of pursuing that goal.

In the case of Toyota in Japan, there are five distribution channels, each of which sells a restricted part of the total Toyota range. The sales staff in each dealership are grouped into teams consisting of seven or eight people, who spend most of their working days selling cars door-to-door. Individual households within the vicinity of a dealership are profiled, and members of the sales team periodically visit each one, ascertaining the needs of the household and its future purchasing intentions. This information is fed back to the assembler to assist in the product planning process. Because of this system, some claim that practically all cars in Japan are made to a specific customer order (Womack, Jones and Roos 1990).

This is not to say that production is not planned or initiated until firm customer orders are received. The factory makes an estimate of the demand expected for different models and establishes a build schedule, which is also passed on to the components suppliers. Then, when specific customer orders come in, the build schedule is adjusted accordingly. This is facilitated by the flexibility inherent in the Japanese just-in-time system. Also, the initial plan tends to be more accurate in Japan than in the West because of the greater degree of feedback from customers. Japanese factories can deliver a customer-ordered car in under two weeks in Japan itself, and the whole distribution system contains less than three weeks of finished stock, all already sold (Womack, Jones and Roos 1990).

Role of government support

An additional factor to be noted in Japan's success lies in the co-operative nature of the relationship between government and business. At the extreme, this relationship has been seen as a national conspiracy and popularized as such by authors such as Wolf (1985). Sethi, Namiki and Swanson suggest that the Japanese government, particularly via the Ministry of International Trade and Industry (MITI), plays an important role in planning and implementing long-term industrial and economic policy. They argue that the Japanese government systematically selects target industries, products and technologies as being of strategic importance and beneficial to the national interest, and promotes them. To achieve this, it uses a combination of economic controls involving the provision of public funds for research and development, capital expansion and export subsidies, and 'administrative guidance' – the shaping of business's behaviour by denying financial assistance to companies that do not cooperate, or placing bureaucratic impediments in their way. The national interest in this sense has been furthered primarily by the creation of internationally competitive export industries. In the 1950s and 1960s shipbuilding, chemicals and synthetic fibres were promoted, and more recently the development of supercomputers, bio-technology and new materials manufacture has been encouraged as part of the programme to shift Japan from the status of 'pursuer' to 'pioneer' (Gow 1989).

Government support is not limited solely to a developmental role. Boyer (1983) has described how industries in decline receive help in shifting resources to stronger sectors of the economy. Such assistance takes a variety of forms; examples are subsidies for retraining and employment benefits, to tide workers over periods of employment adjustments.

While MITI and the Japanese government undoubtedly play a role in guiding Japanese corporations along nationally profitable paths, it would be wrong to assume simple government dominance.

Indeed, as the attention of Japanese corporations since the 1970s has been shifting to higher value-added and R&D-intensive operations (*The Economist*, 2 December 1989), so has the rapidly increasing R&D expenditure come from private rather than public sector funding (Gow 1989). This is demonstrated in table 2.8. The impressive increase in (especially private) R&D spending implies a long-term perspective on economic growth and profitability, a phenomenon to which we shall now turn attention.

Economic structures

A final element in any account of the Japanese economy must be the financing of Japanese industry. From the latter part of the nineteenth century onwards, in fact, the state was heavily involved in industrial policy, a situation that led in the 1920s to a heavy concentration of economic power in the *zaibatsu* with financial as well as manufacturing interests (Ackroyd et al. 1988). After the Second World War, the American occupation of Japan led to the fragmentation of *zaibatsu* into smaller units, but state support of industry was offered through the Bank of Japan and the Industrial Bank of Japan in the form of long-term credit and preferential treatment of firms, as opposed to individuals. Gradually, the network of reciprocal shareholdings, trade-oriented economic activity and banking links was regenerated (Ackroyd et al. 1988; Okumura 1991).

With respect to the role of Japan's economic structures in the country's economic success, there are two basic positions. One view, embodied in the idea of 'Japan Inc.', considers that there is a conspiratorial relationship between government and industry. For example, the cover of Wolf's (1985) book, entitled *The Japanese Conspiracy*,

Table 2.8 Japanese national expenditure on R&D

Year	R&D Expenditure (US$ millions)	Percentage of national income	Percentage from public funding
1970	5,011	1.96	25.2
1975	10,991	2.11	27.5
1980	19,635	2.35	25.8
1985	34,025	3.19	19.4

Source: Science and Technology Agency Japan; cited in Gow 1989

carries the sub-heading 'Their plot to dominate industry world-wide and how to deal with it'. The Japanese Ministry of International Trade and Industry (MITI), it is suggested, plays a key role by systematically identifying particular international markets and encouraging Japanese companies to target them. The alternative view attributes Japan's success to private economic activities, which are influenced, though not dominated, by government policy.

Today, Japan's financial and industrial structure is organized around a small number of business groups, with preferential financial, production, and trade operations within each group. The banks play a 'tutelary' role: for instance, Toyota's three largest shareholders are Mitsui Bank, Sanwa Bank and Tokai Bank; while Nissan's largest shareholder is the Industrial Bank of Japan. The leaders of these large groupings take prominent positions on Japan's four major business associations, which interact closely with MITI and the Ministry of Finance in the development of industrial policies (Orru 1990).

It is not within the scope of this book to explore Japan's economic structures in depth. However, what is critically important is that, by all accounts, financial time horizons in Japan are considerably longer than they are in Britain. Dore (1986) comments that the net effect of the financial structure of Japanese industry is:

> to very much reduce the pressure from shareholders on corporate managers – to reduce it to a degree not easily imagined by those used to thinking of the British or American economic system as a 'normal' or universal form of capitalism. This very much reduces the importance of short-term profits among corporate objectives and permits the development of a managerial culture which makes market shares rather than profits the index through the contemplation of which managers can massage or flagellate their egos. (Dore 1986, p. 71)

In contrast, in the UK companies are limited by a short-term profit horizon due to a high dependency on the stockmarket, this being compounded by the fact that British banks are not inclined to provide long-term, low-interest loans. The fact that the Japanese are greater savers (see table 2.9) is clearly significant here, as it means that the financial institutions have greater funds available for loan.

According to Ackroyd et al. the proportion of British industrial funds contributed by bank loans is the smallest of any highly industrialized country – 6 per cent of total funds, as opposed to 44 per

Table 2.9 Savings and investment ratios in selected countries

		Year			
		1975	1980	1985	1988
Britain	IR	18.4	16.9	17.0	19.9
	SR	17.4	19.1	18.8	17.6
US	IR	16.8	18.6	18.5	17.3
	SR	15.7	17.2	14.1	13.9
Germany	IR	19.8	23.5	19.5	20.4
	SR	22.7	23.3	23.9	26.1
Japan	IR	32.8	32.3	28.4	30.8
	SR	32.7	31.3	32.2	33.7

IR = gross investment ratio
SR = gross savings ratio
Source: Bank of Korea

cent in Japan – and, compared with that of all other industrial nations, British industry has the largest proportion of funds supplied by ploughed back profit. Clearly, long-term strategic planning for production, human resource development and marketing – for which the Japanese are renowned – is greatly facilitated by the close ties between manufacturing and finance capital. Whether moves by British managements to adopt various Japanese methods are hampered by weak manufacturing–finance capital relations is a question to which we shall return later in the book. Suffice it to say here that short-term profit and cost consciousness, to the extent that it dominates British top managements, could work against the risk-taking and long-term organizational development necessary if British companies are seriously intending to reassert themselves as leaders in world markets.

Having examined the key practices and conditions prevalent in Japan, we shall now move on in the next chapter to present a conceptual framework that can by used to explain how these ideas fit together.

3

Theoretical Perspectives

Having described the elements of Japanese industrial practice, we now turn to concepts useful in gaining insight into the dynamics of how these practices operate. Our focus is at the level of the firm. Given the mix of Japanese manufacturing methods, personnel practices, organizational structures and systems, the structure of Japanese industry and indeed the nature of the Japanese economy, how may the interrelations between these factors be understood? What implications do they carry for their emulation in different contexts? And how far do these conditions have to be replicated before Japanese management practices can be implemented successfully in the Western environment?

As stated in chapter 1, the authors' perspective is that the term 'Japanization' is useful as a means of describing the process by which firms adopt a particular set of manufacturing practices together with the necessary organizational supports. What are the mechanisms by which this process occurs? It is this question that this chapter seeks to address.

The theoretical interrelationships among the elements of Japanization must clearly be unpacked if the notion is to be useful analytically and escape the charge of being a 'chaotic conception'. Specifically, is it possible to identify particular clusters of practices that appear to fit together as a 'package', and wider conditions that facilitate the successful operation of this package? The authors' thesis is that Japanese manufacturing methods dramatically increase the *interdependencies* between the actors involved in the whole production process, and that these heightened dependencies demand a whole set of supporting conditions if they are to be managed successfully.

The analysis in this chapter involves, first, a consideration of the areas in which Japanese industry is successful, second, an analysis of the factors apparently responsible for this success, and third, exploration of the social and political consequences of the adoption of these methods. The first area of analysis is illuminating in itself, as it immediately reveals that it is not the success of Japanese industry per se that we are trying to explain, but rather the success of a particular group of Japanese companies. It is really these companies that the West is trying to emulate, not necessarily Japanese industry as a whole. Indeed, Peters and Waterman's best-seller *In Search of Excellence* (1982), which describes 'excellent' (highly successful) American companies, reveals significant parallels between large Japanese manufacturing corporations and some 'excellent' American ones, such as IBM. Interestingly, 50,000 copies of the Japanese translation of *In Search of Excellence* were sold within two days, and 320,000 within six weeks, mainly to Japanese managers, many of whom claimed parallels between their own companies and those described in the book (Ohmac 1983). This raises a significant caveat relating to the term 'Japanization': the production and personnel systems under consideration are not necessarily *specific* to Japan – indeed the Japanese appear to be continuing to look for lessons from the West in the constant refinement of their own systems. Also, a variety of practices, many of which may not be Japanese, can act as the *functional equivalents* to some of the supporting conditions found in Japan itself. Nonetheless, the Japanese have most widely adopted total quality systems, just-in-time philosophies and so on, and it is to Japanese organizations that the West has increasingly looked in recent years for lessons in international competitiveness.

Given that the major Japanese companies are serving as a model for the West, how can their continuing international success be explained? It is clear that it is attributable in large part to two factors: the high quality and the relatively low price of the products that they manufacture. To explain how these requirements (which according to traditional Western thinking are mutually opposed) are met, it is first necessary to consider the production process itself. The central means by which the apparent price/quality paradox is resolved is by viewing quality as 'freedom from waste', which effectively dispels the idea that quality automatically adds cost to a product. The successful Japanese corporations keep their quality up and their costs down through particular production systems and manufacturing methods. The use of total quality principles and in particular JIT production techniques is central here, being the major tactic for meeting these requirements. However, the JIT production system in turn generates an additional set of requirements on the wider organization, implying that its success is dependent on a set of supporting conditions.

The theoretical framework for interpreting the *social* processes involved in Japanization draws on three related sets of ideas. These are Galbraith's (1974) theory of coordination and control in organizations, Marchington's (1979) analysis of power and technology, and Pfeffer's (1981) ideas on power and conflict in organizations.

Power and Dependency

Faced with the problem of coordination and control, what strategies and design alternatives are available to organizations, and what are their implications for power relations? In order to answer these questions, we turn our attention to a theory of organizational design originally put forward by Galbraith (1974).

Organizational design

Galbraith is concerned with the strategies that organizations can use to coordinate and control the people and processes that they comprise. His starting point is the assumption that, for an organization to perform satisfactorily, it must be able to coordinate the activities of its various elements or sub-units – be they individuals, groups, departments or whatever – effectively. In the case of routine activities, organizations typically resort to one of two strategies to accomplish this: rules and procedures to be followed, or goals and targets for the sub-units to meet. Both strategies enable coordinated action to take place without the need for constant (and costly) communication between the various organizational sub-units. However, as there will always be situations not covered by the existing rules and procedures, or occasions when goals and targets cannot be met, decisions on how to handle such exceptional circumstances are referred up an organization's hierarchy until (in theory) they reach a level of competence or authority where a decision can be made in the absence of rules. As situations will always arise for which there are no rules and procedures – for example if there is a sudden switch in demand for a company's product, or a machine failure, or a shortage of parts due to a supplier failing to deliver – organizations must be able to cope with unanticipated contingencies. Pfeffer refers to this as an organization's capacity to cope with uncertainty. According to Galbraith, the critical limiting aspect of an organization's structure is its ability to handle these non-routine, unprogrammed or crisis-type events. It is hence this that determines an organization's capacity to perform.

Uncertainty causes organizations problems because it makes effective coordination dramatically more difficult. Galbraith argues that organizations have basically three options under conditions of uncertainty: to reduce uncertainty; to develop ways of coping with uncertainty – in other words to adapt to their inability to reduce uncertainty; or to accept reduced levels of performance (for example over-runs on cost, delivery and so on). If one of the first two options is not actively adopted, then the third, reduced performance, will happen by default. Thus, if an organization cannot reduce uncertainty by exerting control over the sources of that uncertainty, then its ability to handle uncertain or unpredictable situations becomes a critical determinant of how well the organization as a whole will perform. The sources of uncertainty can be internal (for example the performance of the organization's people and/or processes) or external (such as markets and suppliers). The options open to organizations to cope with uncertainty are represented in figure 3.1.

Faced with uncertainty and unpredictability, and hence (in Galbraith's terms) a need to process information, organizations can follow two basic routes. The first involves reducing the *need* to process information; the second involves increasing the organization's *capacity* to process information. Both assume that, faced with an unforeseen event, organizations have to begin moving information

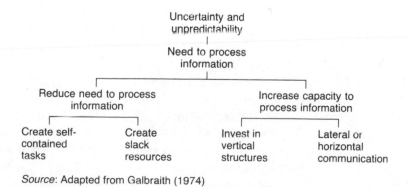

Source: Adapted from Galbraith (1974)

Figure 3.1 Strategies for coping with uncertainty

around internally in order to take appropriate action. An example might be an unexpected machine breakdown: information must be transmitted to the downstream work stations to warn them of the impending delay in the arrival of materials, and to maintenance to get them to come and fix the machine. If the machine is of critical importance to the whole process, alternative arrangements may have to be put into operation to make or obtain the products elsewhere until the machine is up and running again. Similar responses will be necessary in any unanticipated situation – for example if a batch of components is discovered to be faulty, or if personnel are absent or withdraw their labour. An instance of the problems that such events can generate is provided by a company visited by one of the authors. The company, a supplier to the vehicle industry, was having problems meeting delivery dates and was getting three or four 'fire alarm' calls from its customers per day. The image of a fire alarm going off neatly captures the essence of what happens when unanticipated but critical events occur. Galbraith terms the ability to deal effectively with such situations as an organization's *information-processing* ability.

One of the commonest methods of handling uncertainty – and the information-processing needs that it creates – is to reduce the *dependency* between the various elements involved in a production process; Galbraith cites the creation of slack resources and self-contained tasks as means by which this can be achieved, the emphasis typically being on the former.

Slack resources within a production system are an important component in the management of the system, as they mean that the temporary failure of one part of the process is possible without the whole system being disabled. Obvious examples of slack resources are substantial buffer stocks between operations, so that if one part of the process fails to deliver, the whole system does not immediately grind to a halt. Slack resources are important because they temporarily allow the various stages of a process to operate out of synchronization without immediate corrective action being required. They thus also ease the burden of coordination. The production of more goods than is absolutely essential in case some are below standard, the quoting of longer than necessary lead-times to allow scope for hiccups whilst still meeting delivery targets, or the possession of spare machine capacity (and/or extra staff) are further examples of methods of building slack into the system. Goods-inward inspection could also be seen as fulfilling this role of insurance policy – a company is less dependent on the competence and integrity of a supplier if resources are devoted to double-checking.

Strategies such as these carry a price of course. Buffer stocks tie up working capital and can delay the discovery of problems in the production process – it may be days, weeks, or even months before a batch of components is used and discovered to be faulty. Long lead-times may also involve costs, as potential customers go elsewhere to obtain their supplies more swiftly; while extra staff and equipment carry obvious costs too.

A second strategy to reduce the need to move information around an organization is the creation of *self-contained tasks*. To illustrate this point, consider the case of an engineering company engaged in the manufacture of fairly complex products. As was described in chapter 2, one method of laying out a factory is to have it arranged on a process basis; for an engineering works this might involve a bank of milling machines in one area of the factory, a bank of lathes in another, and so on. Each section is typically under the control of a foreman, production superintendent or some similar agent. Batches of components move between processes and have various operations performed on them. Production organized in this way carries the advantages of skill development and specialization that come of having substantial concentrations of people and machines engaged in similar work. If there are (say) 20 people all working lathes, then there is scope for operators to become specialists in particular types of turning jobs.

The drawback of this system is that it is complex, and consequently substantial resources are required to coordinate the efforts of all these functional areas. Factories laid out on this basis are typically characterized by armies of progress chasers trying to urge materials through the factory, and complex vertical structures, with many layers of management, whose job it is to try to control the seething mass below.

An alternative strategy is to make the various operations within a factory more self-contained. This typically involves organizing people and machines around *products* rather than *processes*. In this way 'families' of machines (and people) perform all the work – or at least as much as possible – on particular products. Under this system, workflow is simplified and 'ownership' of the product is pinned down to a restricted set of people. The costs of this strategy lie in the loss of the economies of scale and the specialization that process-based production layouts permit. Current changes at Lucas

Industries, which are described in depth in chapter 4, provide an example of traditional process-based layouts being transformed into ones based around relatively self-contained tasks.

The alternative to reducing the need to process information is to increase the organization's ability to process it. This can be achieved via two devices: investment in vertical structures – the means to move information up and down an organization – and mechanisms of lateral or horizontal communication.

Examples of the first device are elaborate management structures and detailed monitoring to ensure tight control. Typically this results in intensive supervision, with many foremen and first-line supervisors and a high number of vertical levels in management. According to the information-processing view of organizations, these layers of managers and administrators function as a gigantic system of information collection, consolidation and transmission. In a typical hierarchical organization, information about problems climbs up this 'tree', and decisions (and ideally solutions) flow down. For example, if one operation in a manufacturing system experiences a problem with components from another operation, information will flow up the management hierarchy until it reaches a level where an individual has the authority (and theoretically the knowledge) to resolve it – possibly until it reaches a manager whose jurisdiction covers both operations.

The costs of this system are obvious – a high proportion of indirect labour relative to direct labour, with correspondingly high overheads. Moreover, as information has to pass through many hands, decision-making becomes increasingly slow, and the scope for information distortion (accidental or otherwise) increases – the organizational equivalent of 'Chinese whispers'.

Computerized information systems can represent another aspect of the 'vertical information systems' strategy. Certainly information and control systems for JIT represent an issue that has excited considerable debate in recent years. The argument involves the appropriateness of sophisticated computerized systems of production control such as MRP systems for JIT manufacture (Heard 1983; Sonnenburg 1983). Under MRP-type systems, information about what to produce and when is collated at a central point and then 'exploded' into schedules for the various sub-assembly operations. Decisions about corrective actions are taken centrally in the light of actual performance and then conveyed back to the various sub-units. The mechanism by which such systems operate has been described thus:

The emphasis was to pre-define the manufacturing process and then attempt to manage the process with a computer system. This MRP task is accomplished by first quantifying base data such as bills of material, on-hand and on-order balances, and then using a series of logic rules (explosions, planned orders etc.) to present information to manage the process to closer tolerances. (Edwards 1988, p. 46)

This may be contrasted with JIT:

JIT is a dynamic process of improvement while MRP II is a static reaffirmation of accepted ways of doing things. (Edwards 1988, p. 46)

One problem with centralized systems such as MRP is that they require every agent in the production process to be strictly disciplined about feeding updates into the system (Aggarwal 1985). Without such discipline, errors with regard to stock levels, parts availability, and so on begin to accumulate. Because each sub-unit does not know exactly what the others are doing, natural bottlenecks in the production process start to accumulate stock on their upstream side and generate shortages on their downstream side.

The second model of production control utilizes systems where the primary information flow is horizontal rather than vertical. In Galbraith's terms, this is the 'creation of lateral relations'. Thus, information is moved directly across the organization rather than up, across and down, and decisions regarding corrective action in the face of production problems are taken locally rather than centrally. For instance, Toyota's *kanban* system is a horizontal communication system that enables downstream units to communicate their imminent needs for supplies directly to their upstream feeders.

The ultimate control under *kanban* is the 'pull' of final assembly (which in turn is theoretically dictated by the needs of the market). *Kanban* is capable of operating as a local control system that is 'self-adjusting'. Effectively, the system recognizes that the conditions required for MRP to work successfully are difficult to fulfil in practice, and so allows the system to be self-adjusting at the operational level. *Kanban* can be seen as formalizing what frequently occurs by default under the vertical, centralized system, namely informal horizontal information flow in the form of progress chasing and expediting.

Quality circles represent one way in which the hierarchy can be horizontally short-circuited, essentially by bringing problem-solving and decision-making resources to the level at which problems exist, rather than vice versa. Not surprisingly, stiff resistance to quality circles has come not only from the shopfloor and trade unions, but more often from first-line supervisors and middle managers, who have felt threatened by what they see as an erosion of their authority and power (Dale and Hayward 1984; Klein 1984).

Galbraith does point out that there is an alternative to organizations making internal structural responses in order either to reduce the need for information processing or to increase their capacity to process information. This involves reaching out and controlling their environments, thus reducing the incidence of unanticipated events, and hence reducing their information-processing needs. Examples of such strategies include forming cartels, developing positions of market dominance, and so on.

Applying these ideas to just-in-time production systems is revealing. Much in evidence are design characteristics that embrace heavy use of self-contained tasks, backed up by output controls based on intensive performance measurement and a 'customer-driven' ethos. Also present are strategies of horizontal communication – *kanban* being one example, quality circles another. What is particularly striking, however, is the removal of one design strategy in particular – that of slack resources. At a technical level, the removal of slack resources will push organizations towards other coordinating strategies. But at a social level, there are also profound implications endemic in the removal of the 'insurance policy' of slack resources.

Power and dependency relations

The most obvious consequence of removing slack resources – for example, buffer stocks – is to increase dramatically the *dependency* between the various agents involved in the production process. This is significant because Pfeffer (1981) has argued that dependency is a key source of power in an organizational setting:

> The power to control or influence the other resides in control over the things he values, which may range all the way from oil resources to ego support. In short, power resides implicitly in the other's dependence. (Emerson, quoted in Pfeffer 1981, p. 99)

> Power is having something that somebody else wants. (Farney, quoted in Pfeffer 1981, p. 100)

Slack resources are one way of reducing one party's dependency on another, in that they confer a degree of independence or 'loose-coupling' between operations. For example, the Ford Motor Company was able to run down inventories in its UK factories by simultaneously manufacturing the same model in other European countries. These inventories had in part been kept to safeguard production in the event of isolated industrial disputes. With an alternative source of supply secure, the dependency of the company on its British workers was reduced; from the company's point of view, this reduced unions' ability to 'hold it to ransom', because supply was substitutable from elsewhere. Consequently the insurance policy of generous inventories could be dispensed with. This reveals an obvious problem with systems of production (such as JIT) that have little slack. They are very vulnerable to disruption, whether accidental or deliberate, whether due to human beings or machines.

Focusing on human sources of disruption, Marchington (1979) has developed a set of ideas useful in analysing the relationship between the nature of production processes and the dependencies of the parties involved in them, and it is to Marchington's ideas that we now turn.

Marchington applied his theory specifically to the dependencies that particular types of production processes create, arguing that the strategic position of individuals and groups within an organization is determined primarily by the degree of centrality of their relationship to the organization's core activities – in Pfeffer's terms, the extent to which the organization has a high dependency upon them. More specifically, Marchington suggested that the more *pervasive* and *immediate* the impact of any disruption a group could inflict on the manufacturing process, the greater would be the *power capacity* (the ability to exert influence) of the group capable of causing such disruption. 'Disruption' need not mean a total stoppage, but could also refer to problems with the production process due to lack of diligence or skill on the part of the operators, unauthorized absence, reduced turnover, and so on.

Factors outside the production process will also bear on the power capacity of groups within an organization, particularly factors such as labour market conditions, which affect the substitutability of labour. However crucial their role may be in a manufacturing process, those who are expendable for reasons unrelated to that process are unlikely to command a high dependency, and hence a strong bargaining position. Marchington thus argues that three factors are critical to explaining the social and political arrangements surrounding a given production process: the potential *pervasiveness* of a disruption caused by those involved in the process; the likely *immediacy* of a disruption; and the *substitutability* of those involved in the process. When these three simple concepts are applied to an archetypal Japanese production process, a number of important social and political consequences are revealed, and these will be explored below. First, however, the three concepts themselves merit further explanation.

Pervasiveness refers to how far through an organization the effects of a disruption will be felt. Pervasiveness is closely related to the degree of interdependency between the various operations in the process. Where interdependency is high, the effects of a problem at one point are likely to be widely felt at other points. Oil refineries and chemical processing plants provide examples of production systems with high levels of pervasiveness, and this may explain in part the relatively high wages and good conditions found in these industries by, for instance, Blauner (1964) and Woodward (1965). That is, good wages and conditions may represent pre-emptive provisions by management as an insurance against disruptions that would be certain to be costly.

Immediacy refers to the speed with which the effects of a disruption are felt. The newspaper industry provides an example of a production process where disruption causes rapid damage. The unsaleability of yesterday's news has not been overlooked, nor unexploited, by print workers.

Marchington's third critical characteristic of production processes for power and dependency relations, *substitutability*, refers to the resources that contribute to the processes involved. Marchington applies the idea to human resources, but the substitutability of physical resources – materials, machines and so on – will also have an impact on arrangements surrounding and supporting a production process. Taking human resources first, the substitutability principle helps to explain the wage differentials between those with scarce skills – such as computer professionals – and those without them. The heightened dependency of organizations on the former group gives that group a better bargaining position. A strategy of deskilling makes sense in this context. An example of applying the substitutability principle to physical resources would be spreading one's requirements across a number of agencies – not 'putting all one's eggs in one basket', as it were. The tradition of multiple sourcing of components in the UK motor industry in the 1960s and 1970s is an illustration of this. This practice developed in the context of labour unrest within the components industry.

However, applying the substitutability principle can also carry a price. For instance, if a company spreads the risk of failure of a particular supplier by multiple sourcing, then the administrative costs for the bought in part rise substantially, and the company has more suppliers to 'police' in terms of the quality and delivery of parts. Similarly, if workers with scarce skills are made substitutable (and therefore cheaper) through a more extensive division of labour, one cost is likely to be a need for more supervisors, inspectors, and other indirect workers to ensure that production standards are met and work coordinated.

The mechanism that renders pervasiveness, immediacy and substitutability of such critical importance to the arrangements surrounding a production process, we suggest, is to be found in the degree of *dependency* that they create between the operations and agencies involved in that process. High levels of pervasiveness and immediacy and a low level of substitutability imply a high degree of dependency in organizational relationships, and vice versa.

We suggested earlier that dependency carries important implications for power and control – dependency equates with an ability to be influenced or to influence, according to whether one is depending on, or being depended upon by, another party. Technologically, there are obvious steps that can be taken to guard against the breakdown of critically important machines. But what about the people who operate the machines? This takes us on to the final element in the theoretical framework, the conditions under which power is likely to be used, or in the terms used previously, dependency relationships exploited.

Given the existence of dependency, Pfeffer argues that two conditions determine whether or not such dependency finds expression in the exercise of power and, usually, the emergence of conflict. The first condition for the emergence of conflict lies in *goal heterogeneity* – that is the existence of goals that conflict or are inconsistent with one another. The second condition necessary for the emergence of conflict is *resource scarcity*. In situations where there are sufficient resources to satisfy everyone's goals and desires, the fact that some of these goals may be inconsistent is not critical. However, as soon as demands exceed available resources, choices have to be made about the allocation of these resources. Under conditions of resource scarcity, such choices are likely to create winners and losers, generating conflict and hence uncertainty.

From the perspective of the organization as a whole, resource dependency gives various groups within and without the organization the *ability* to exert an influence on it for their own benefit; in combination, goal heterogeneity and resource scarcity can provide the *motivation* to utilize this ability.

The analysis thus far suggests that it is vulnerability to disruption that is the Achilles' heel of JIT production systems. But the issues go further than this. Their emphasis on low stock levels is only one facet, albeit a crucial one, of the whole package of Japanese-style manufacturing practices. Other elements – shopfloor problem-solving, continuous improvement activities, operator responsibility for quality – also serve to heighten the dependency of the employer upon the abilities and cooperation of the workforce.

We have now developed the essence of our model of dependency relations that will guide our interpretation of Japanization. However, two further aspects need to be mentioned. First, it will be clear by now that the characteristics sought of the organization's constituents (particularly suppliers and employees, but, in theory, potentially also customers, governments and other groups) will differ according to the type of production system. Secondly, wider social, political and economic conditions will have a bearing on the state of dependency relations and their outcomes.

Taking constituent characteristics first, a variety of research has shown that different production systems carry different implications for social relations. Woodward (1965), for instance, identified that different administrative structures were required by different production systems, those for small-batch and process production being quite different from those for large-batch and mass production, which in turn were different from those for process industries. Blauner (1964) argued that highly automated production led to more autonomy and control for (and therefore more dependency on) workers. Other theorists (such as Friedman 1977) argued that wider economic and political factors, particularly labour market conditions and the strength of trade unions, also have an importance in determining the labour control strategies employed by a particular organization. In Friedman's terms, the JIT/total quality system perhaps more closely approximates a strategy of 'responsible autonomy' than one of 'direct control' as regards the management of labour.

Briefly, the strategy of direct control entails a rigid division of labour, with tight supervision, whereas responsible autonomy refers to the delegation of authority down the organization. Clearly, a responsible autonomy strategy is closely related to an organizational design based on self-contained tasks (work teams, cells and so on) and also on lateral communication and a customer-oriented ethos. This leads to a requirement for more reliable, flexible, and probably more skilled, workers than in a direct control strategy. Hence responsible autonomy implies a heightened dependency of the organization on its workers, though also a lessened dependency on the agents of direct control, such as supervisors and middle management. However, it should be emphasized here that, as explained elsewhere, operators are given heightened responsibilities only in the context of tight production controls and constant monitoring of performance against targets.

Looking outside the bounds of a single organization, a high dependency on suppliers is implied when a policy of single sourcing is involved. Some organizations are willing to heighten their dependency on suppliers, via long-term contracts for instance, in return for promises – and performance to match – regarding quality, delivery and price. Others prefer to take advantage of the competition between suppliers, constantly playing each off against the others. In the latter case, supplier characteristics are not a cause for concern, only the cost of their goods.

Finally, the organization's social, political and economic environment will affect dependency relations in a multitude of ways. As well as labour market conditions, mentioned above, government policies, the political climate, national cultures, and the competitive situation are all of importance. Besides affecting the choice of production system, such factors can influence levels of dependency. For instance, a slack labour market or a situation of high supplier competition might increase the potential substitutability of constituents. These situations also imply a heightened constituent dependency on the organization. Environmental factors can also influence the probability of overt power utilization – something very likely to lead to conflict. Examples of this might be a strong national culture creating a homogeneous social system (reducing goal heterogeneity, in Pfeffer's terms), a government's economic policy that reduces (or increases) the scarcity of organizational resources, or legislation on industrial action that limits workers' ability to exercise their full power capacity.

Applying the concepts

We argued earlier that being the object of high dependency gives a group the capacity to exert power and influence, while heterogeneity of goals, and resource scarcity, provide it with the motivation to do so. Issues of dependency relations and issues of power in organizations are inextricably intertwined. Thus, as soon as one starts talking about dependency relations, one very quickly enters the realm of influence, control and power relationships, both within and between organizations. When Japanese production methods are considered in terms of this model, it quickly becomes apparent that they entail high interdependencies. This is particularly the case in the practice of total quality management and JIT production, where slack resources are removed virtually altogether from the production process. Their removal drastically increases the interdependencies between those involved in the production process.

The implications of the increased dependencies characteristic of Japanese production systems for power relations within the workplace and between the organization and its external constituents will now be outlined. We shall then examine how the elements of Japanese industrial practice fit together to cope with these heightened dependencies. Finally, we shall comment on the implications of this theory of dependency relations for the uptake of Japanese-style production methods in the West.

Managing high dependencies

Japanese production methods possess a number of features that self-evidently create greater dependency of the organization on its constituents, the prime example being JIT production. To use Marchington's terms, such a system bestows upon those who work in it the capacity to create disruptions that, intentionally or otherwise, are likely to be extremely *pervasive*. With little or nothing in the way of buffer stocks, each operation is entirely dependent on the upstream one to deliver its materials; each must meet the requirements of the next just in time. Hence great importance is attached to sound plant and machinery and in-process controls – the production disruption caused by a machine breakdown, for example, could be considerable. Equally critical is that the suppliers should supply materials on time, and of the right quality. For the same reasons, the effect of production disruption under a JIT system is *immediate*.

With low inventories and buffer stocks, the effect of a failure of supply or of the internal system at any one point will quickly ripple through the whole system.

Other total quality principles also heighten the dependency of organizations on their constituents. In particular, if responsibility for quality control, maintenance and so on is largely vested in the suppliers and production workers themselves (thus eliminating the 'slack resource' of quality control inspectors and other specialist groups) then this gives these constituents extra scope to cause disruption, be it by accident or design. The company's dependency on them to perform their functions conscientiously and effectively is hence increased, as the safety net of the inspectors is removed. Interestingly, Buchanan and Bessant (1985) describe how some British companies prefer to choose information technologies that invest responsibility for production control in the hands of managers rather than production workers.

Turning attention next to *substitutability*, Japanese production systems entail a difficulty in substituting constituents. Suppliers are likely to be persuaded to deliver high-quality goods just in time only in return for long-term contracts, and workers who are multi-skilled, reliable and flexible are not so easy to replace as those who are not. A low level of substitutability, as our model implies, contributes to heightened dependency.

In sum, Japanese systems of production, particularly JIT and total quality control, heighten the dependency of the organization on its agencies or 'constituents', especially employees and supplying companies. This means, as demonstrated by the theories of Pfeffer and Marchington, that the ability of the organization's constituents to exert leverage in their own interests is increased. The obvious implication is that it is imperative that such organizations take steps to counterbalance this by averting the possibility of such power being used. According to Pfeffer, this requires moves towards goal homogeneity, or resource abundance, or equally profound dependencies on both sides – a logic similar to 'mutually assured destruction'.

Japanization, power and dependency

Given that Japanese companies are apparently allowing themselves to be heavily dependent on their suppliers and their own workers, what mechanisms have evolved to prevent these dependencies being exploited? Examination of Japanese practices with respect to personnel strategy and relations with suppliers (described in chapter 2) suggests an answer to this question: the high dependencies of the companies on their constituents appear to be balanced by an equally profound set of dependencies of the constituents on the companies.

In the light of the vulnerability of Japanese production systems to disruption and in the light of the high dependencies of the Japanese organization on its constituents, we suggest that such a system will only work successfully in a situation where organizations have either taken active measures to create the appropriate set of social relations around the production process, or where social, economic and political conditions automatically provide such safeguards. Both these conditions, we argue, exist in Japan. In other words, Japanese success with JIT and total quality management may be seen as a consequence of an effective fit between Japanese production systems and Japanese personnel practices, supplier relations and so on – the whole system being supported by an appropriate set of social, political and economic conditions. In Pfeffer's terms, the dependency of the company on its constituents should be balanced by a dependency of the constituents on the company, goal heterogeneity should be minimized, and the problem of resource scarcity should be eliminated. We shall now examine how each of these is achieved.

Beginning with dependency relations, company-based welfare schemes, seniority-based payment systems and lifetime employment (conditional on remaining with the same company) may all function to generate and sustain employees' dependency on their company. For this reason critics such as Briggs (1988) talk of workers being 'chained' to their companies, and Kamata of workers being 'tied to the company until the day they retire'. The *mutual* dependencies created by such paternalistic practices serve to reduce the likelihood of the exercise of power.

Japanese supplier relations may also serve to heighten the dependencies of suppliers on the buyer organization. This is achieved, for instance, through creating a situation of monopsony or through a direct stakeholding in the supplying firm, either of which gives the corporation financial leverage over the supplier. Hence the dependency of the organization on its suppliers is balanced by a dependency of the supplier on the organization, and in return for long-term contracts, the organization is in a position to exert control over the supplier. As the case studies in chapters 4 and 8 demonstrate, this can mean strong influence over the supplier's cost structure, production process, delivery schedules, and even personnel and industrial relations practices.

Many Japanese practices also function to minimize goal heterogeneity. One example is giving employees long time horizons. Differences in the time horizons employed by organizations and those employed by their members can lead to differences of interest that eclipse those attributable to ownership structure. Even under the theoretically low-conflict conditions of employee ownership of the company, decisions concerning resource allocation frequently 'stick' on the divide between the longer-term interests of the organization as a whole and the generally shorter-term interests of those who are members of it at any one time (Oliver 1987). The aforementioned practices of lifetime employment and seniority-based payment systems may serve to reduce this difference of interest, essentially by increasing the time horizon of people's association with their company, fostering a sense of 'shared destiny'.

Goal heterogeneity stems primarily from two sources. The first is the organization's environment, viewed particularly in terms of other groups to which employees belong, examples being professional associations, trade unions, families, friends, political parties and so on. The second is constituted by the structural divisions of the organization itself, which typically lead to the members of different parts of the business viewing the world in different ways. The typical divide between sales and production, whereby sales desires products as individual as its customers, whilst production seeks long, low-variety product runs, is a classic example of this.

Many Japanese practices function to minimize heterogeneity from both these sources. The practice of recruiting people raw from college, at least for the core workforce, permits people to be more easily socialized into the company philosophy in the course of the intensive training and education programmes through which they are put. In addition, employees' opportunities to encounter goals and values other than those promoted by the company are, as far as possible, minimized. If a core worker marries someone inappropriate or associates with 'unsuitable' groups such as communists or even consumer associations, his 'lifetime' employment is liable to come to an end.

On the other hand, heterogeneity in the context of internal arrangements may be countered by an emphasis on single status (reinforced by everyone wearing the same uniform), internal promotion systems and rotation between different functional areas. Clegg (1986) reports that experience and promotion in Japan are gained from functional moves, and contrasts the generalist career path of a Japanese manager with that of his more specialist British counterpart:

Japanese man: I work for Canon, at present in purchasing.
British equivalent: I'm an engineer, currently with Canon.

Another example of reduction of goal heterogeneity is provided by the Japanese enterprise union. Being enterprise-based and incorporated, rather than craft-based or occupation-based and independent, unions in Japan are far less likely to have goals that are at odds with those of the company; their dependency on the company itself is too great to make that a probability. Moreover, without any craft or occupational divisions, the scope for conflict between unions themselves due to goal heterogeneity is lessened.

With regard to relations with suppliers, goal homogeneity is essential because of the high dependency of the corporation on its suppliers. Such homogeneity may be achieved through long-term 'relational' contracting, interlocking directorships, supplier 'clubs' and so forth. Dore (1986) suggests that these tactics permit the high degree of sub-contracting found in Japan to substitute for vertical integration.

One final factor contributing to goal homogeneity that finds frequent popular expression could be the nationalism for which the Japanese are renowned. Certainly the struggle to rebuild the economy after the Second World War appears to have served to unify and drive those involved in Japanese industry. Loyalty to the company could be one way of expressing loyalty to the nation. It has been suggested, for example, that one of the reasons why multinational organizations in Singapore, including Japanese organizations, have failed to generate the sort of loyalty found in Japan is that loyalty to the *foreign-owned* companies that predominate in Singapore cannot be equated readily with national loyalty (Wilkinson and Leggett 1985). Whether or not the same might apply to Japanese companies setting up in the UK is an interesting question.

Having considered how Japanese practice deals so effectively with dependency relations and goal heterogeneity, we can turn our attention to resource scarcity. The answer to this problem is found largely in the wider social, economic and political conditions in Japan, as identified in the preceding chapter.

The Japanese dual economy means that the security of the core workers is gained partly at the expense of the insecurity of the many who work on temporary contracts in the major companies, or in the smaller sub-contracting companies where conditions are very much poorer, while pay and working conditions for women are on average far worse than those for men. As peaks and troughs in demand are borne primarily by those psychologically, if not physically, outside the boundaries of the major corporations, conflict due to resource scarcity may be avoided within these companies. In other words, the privilege and protection of core workers are provided by 'rings of defence' in the form of peripheral workers. Of course, at the same time, conflict outside the major corporations is also made less likely, because peripheral workers are less likely to be in a position to organize themselves and take action.

Another contribution to resource abundance may be the strategic guidance and support of MITI, coupled with Japanese companies' approach to international marketing. These two factors appear to have stimulated steadily increasing demand for the products of the industrial sectors that they are designed to promote, creating the resources to avoid the condition of resource scarcity that could, in combination with high goal heterogeneity, lead to conflict. The relatively long time horizons of Japanese financial institutions, which give protection against the vagaries of the marketplace, further assist in this process. In sum, Japanese organizations, because of the wider political economy, have found themselves in a situation where sustained growth is possible and therefore where scarcity of resources has been less likely.

Japanese practices in Britain

Having described a conceptual framework with which to think about both the social and technical side of Japanese production methods, we turn to the central questions of this book. Is the Japanization of British industry under way? Can companies in Britain, Japanese or otherwise, cope with the dependencies that the new systems force them to have on their constituents – their workers, trade unions and suppliers? And do the wider social, economic and political conditions support the emergence of the sorts of radical changes implied?

Our basic argument is that Japanization entails the successful management of the conditions generated by 'low-waste' production systems, and as we shall see, any consideration of this implicitly includes considerations of power and control. Japanization, we suggest, is a complex but logically coherent process, with social and political as well as technical dimensions. We suggest that to consider Japanization as simply involving the transferability (or otherwise) of Japanese management practices abroad is insufficient. This downplays the equally important question of how well the various elements of a company's business strategy fit together – for example how well a personnel strategy fits with an organization's manufacturing and marketing strategies and how appropriate these strategies are, given the wider political and economic environment.

Our thesis is that at the heart of the success of the major Japanese corporations lies their ability to manage their internal and external dependencies in a more effective way than the vast majority of their Western counterparts have traditionally been able to do, and that they have been considerably assisted in this by a supportive set of socio-economic conditions. If there is a 'secret' to Japan's success, we suggest that it lies in the synergy generated by a whole system, and not, as some have suggested, in specific parts of that system.

The remainder of this book attempts to elucidate the issues raised above by examining the recent experiences of Western companies operating in Britain in their attempts to emulate Japanese practices (mediated Japanization), and the experiences of Japanese companies themselves operating in Britain. The evidence for this discussion is provided by a set of case studies, followed by survey and other evidence. After examining the specific implications of Japanization for trade unions, and their responses to it, we then draw together the policy implications of our analysis.

4

Case Studies in Emulation

In this chapter we present five self-contained case studies designed to give an impression of what the process of emulation of Japanese practices actually looks and feels like. The first four cases are of Western manufacturers that are attempting to introduce Japanese-style practices, namely Lucas Industries, the Rover Group, Ford UK and 'Southern Components', an engineering firm. The final case study is of IBM, an American-owned organization whose management practices featured extensively in Peters and Waterman's *In Search of Excellence*.

Lucas Industries is a major aerospace, automotive and industrial systems and components group. Faced with radical changes in its major markets, Lucas has embarked on a major programme of change in order to transform its 'total approach to achieving and maintaining world-wide competitiveness' (Lucas Chairman's Review, 1986). Many of these changes are based on Japanese-style manufacturing practices, and Lucas provides a comprehensive example of the process and nature of Japanization.

The second case focuses on the Rover Group – formerly Austin Rover, and before that British Leyland – which has similarly, and in line with the UK automotive industry in general, attempted a fundamental change in its production and personnel practices in response to heightened international competition, particularly from Japan. In some respects, particularly with regard to flexible work practices and team working, Rover is leading the field in Japanization in the British automobile industry. However, it seems that although *in-principle* acceptance of new working practices has been obtained from the workforce, the cultural leap necessary for Japanization poses more difficult problems.

The Ford Motor Company is a particularly interesting case in relation to the adoption of Japanese manufacturing methods, because it represents a firm that historically has had a strong market position (unlike Rover) and also strong unions. The account of events at Ford draws heavily on previous accounts of events at the company by the authors (Wilkinson and Oliver 1990; Oliver and Wilkinson 1992).

With 'Southern Components', the fourth case, we consider the process of Japanization from the perspective of a sub-contracting organization. This company, a sub-contractor to the major car manufacturers in the UK, employs only around 160 people. Its case illustrates the impact of the Japanization of major corporations on supplying companies. Based on information given to the authors by the company's owner–director in 1987 and 1989, the case provides an insight into the way in which relations between core and peripheral firms are evolving in the automotive industry.

The final case, on International Business Machines (IBM), the American-owned manufacturer of computer systems, provides an opportunity for readers to compare the practices of one of Peters and Waterman's 'excellent' companies with those of the flagship Japanese corporations. Although there are differences, the similarities are striking – particularly when considered in the light of the theoretical framework outlined in the previous chapter. This qualifies our use of the term 'Japanization', even though IBM is not typical of Western corporations. What we see as being important here is the fact that *some* Western corporations have successfully operated Japanese-style manufacturing and personnel practices for many years.

Lucas Industries

Lucas Industries is a group of British companies with interests in many countries around the world. Lucas was established in the middle of the nineteenth century and, after initially being a business manufacturing cycle lamps and accessories, moved into products for motor vehicles at the beginning of the twentieth century. Thereafter, the company followed the fortunes of the British motor industry, though it also developed aerospace and other interests, largely pursuing a policy of growth by acquisition. Overseas interests are represented by subsidiaries and shareholdings in foreign businesses. In 1987 Lucas Industries comprised seven companies: Lucas Aerospace, Lucas Industrial Systems, Lucas World Service, CAV, Lucas Electrical, Lucas Girling and Rists. The last four of these all manufacture automotive-type products for applications on cars, trucks and military vehicles. In 1987 Lucas employed 45,565 people in its UK operations, in approximately 120 individual business units; UK sales in this year were £714 million. The group employed 18,001 people in its overseas operations, which generated sales of £905 million.

In 1981 Lucas Industries recorded its first ever loss in over 100 years of trading. As Chairman Sir Godfrey Messervy put it, Lucas had to face up to the fact that its 'overall performance in most of its major markets had become fundamentally uncompetitive' (Vliet 1986). Lucas Electrical was in particular trouble; one of its general managers described its position thus:

> The business, as a lot of UK businesses currently find themselves, was faced with a decline from profitability. Its volume base had gone down, more or less in line with the UK vehicle industry build. Having destroyed the volume base, clearly the whole economics of the business were put into question. That, coupled with an increase in variety led to pretty massive problems in the factory, and it was quite clear some 12–18 months ago that either some very fundamental changes were necessary or the business would inevitably close. (BBC/OU 1986a)

In order to address this problem, Lucas began a radical programme of change to improve its performance. From this point, each individual business unit was required to submit a 'Competitiveness Achievement Plan' (CAP), which is a plan for the achievement of business performance levels comparable with those of the leading international competitor in its area. Business units are not compelled to submit viable CAPs, but those that did not risked being either closed or sold, and by 1986 some 40 had been disposed of. CAPs have been described as a combination of a 'policy of vigorous decentralization with an active programme of measuring up' (Vliet 1986). Lucas business units continue to use CAPs in the early 1990s.

In 1983, Professor John Parnaby joined the Group as Manufacturing Director and began spreading the word about Japanese manufacturing strategy and its relevance to Lucas Industries. Initially this involved presentations, first at company and then divisional level; later an independent company, Systems Engineering Projects, was set up within the Group to provide advice and assistance to business units that needed to make radical changes in order to achieve their CAPs.

Manufacturing practices

A substantial amount has been written about the philosophy behind the changes under way at Lucas (Parnaby and Bignell 1986; Parnaby 1986, 1987a, 1987b, 1987c). Central to the philosophy are the principles of systems engineering, centring on a professional, systematic approach to the design and operation of manufacturing systems, which, it has been suggested, Japanese practice epitomizes:

> The Japanese success is not due to luck or accident but rather it is a consequence of a totally professional approach. There is no single skill or technology which is responsible for Japanese success; on the contrary Japanese engineers and managers apply a total systems approach in which many elements are constantly integrated and applied. They are true manufacturing systems engineers. (Parnaby, 1987a)

In this context, the terms 'systems engineering' and 'integration' are used synonymously. The secret of Japan's success is thus ascribed to:

> ... simple, self-adaptive, and well-integrated manufacturing and business systems which make effective use of people and continually respond to market needs. (Parnaby, 1986)

Although Lucas is borrowing many techniques from the Japanese, its use of these is best understood as one set of elements in a wider strategy. What Lucas describes as the manufacturing systems engineering approach consists of essentially two phases: a target-setting phase and a target achievement phase. The former involves deriving competitive benchmarks and formulating appropriate measures of performance in all areas of the business. Such measures include not only financial ones, but also ones of quality, lead-times, value added and so on. In theory, such measures are derived for all areas of the organization. The second phase involves business re-design activities in order to meet the targets set in the first phase. Diagrammatically the process is represented in figure 4.1.

As figure 4.1 demonstrates, the redesign procedure begins with a performance comparison between a Lucas business unit and the leading competitor in its field. Depending on the size of the competitive gap, and based on an extensive analysis of the current state of the business unit's operations, appropriate purchasing, manufacturing and organizational strategies are developed with a view to

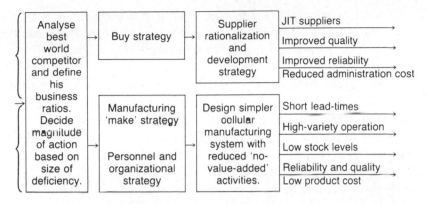

Source: Adapted from Parnaby (1987c)

Figure 4.1 Lucas's systems strategy

achieving the aims outlined on the far right hand side of the diagram. Notable is the emphasis given to supplier rationalization and development. Recognizing that success depends on factors external, as well as internal, to an organization, a member of Lucas Group Training commented:

> Whatever we do inside, getting our design right, our controls right, getting our house in order, unless our suppliers meet our requirements at the right time, we cannot deliver. (BBC/OU 1986a)

It is within this wider strategic framework that Lucas is adopting practices that are recognizably Japanese, such as just-in-time production, the grouping of factory machining processes into product families, total quality control and the like. The emphasis has been very much one of matching a business unit's manufacturing strategy to the needs of the market, within the context of a coherent business strategy. In the case of the automotive side of the business, this has often meant a switch from systems geared to high-volume, low-variety production to systems capable of high variety at low cost and with short lead-times. The principal focus to date has been very much on the (re)design of manufacturing systems, although attention is now turning to the redesign of supporting structures in the wider organization.

One of the main vehicles for change at Lucas has been the task force. Task forces are typically small, multi-disciplinary teams under the control of the local business manager, applying systems engineering principles to develop ways for a business unit to reach the targets in its Competitiveness Achievement Plan. It is task forces that have responsibility for the business redesign activities within the business units.

One of the most visible outcomes of this process has been widespread adoption of cellular manufacturing, sometimes using the Japanese techniques of just-in-time production with *kanban* control. The problems of complexity caused by factory layouts organized on a process basis that have developed incrementally (discussed in chapter 3) are vividly illustrated by Lucas's experience. A member of a task force looking at ignition equipment manufacture within Lucas Electrical describes the manufacturing processes as they were before the redesign exercise:

> The components start life on the one side of the factory, visit the other side of the factory (twice) and then return back to the side they started from for a final process. This comes about because the floor is laid out on a process basis, so if the components have got to visit several of these premises the travel involved is enormous and in this case is three quarters of a mile . . . You've got no control and no ownership of the parts. The inventory on the floor is enormous . . . Not only have you got a problem with the work building up, but you don't necessarily know where it is going anyway. (BBC/OU 1986a)

Using systems engineering techniques, factories that have been laid out on a traditional process basis (for example with banks of lathes in one area, banks of milling machines in another and so on) are now being regrouped into cells, each with its own family of machines. A cell is conceived as a specific collection of resources (people, machines and support services) that are grouped together both organizationally and physically and that have clear and precise targets and objectives to meet. The cells are designed to be as self-contained as possible; methods such as input/output analysis, process flowcharts (to plot information and material flows) and grouping techniques, such as Pareto analysis and volume/variety categories, are all used. In this way, workflows are dramatically simplified, and much clearer 'ownership' of parts established.

Implications for work organization

Turnbull (1986) has characterized the system of cellular production as a series of self-contained mini-factories within a factory. Cell performance is measured in relation to a range of goals – output, quality, lead-time and cash targets. There is a simple structure within the cells; there is a cell leader, 'the father of the team', and below the leader a single-level arrangement comprising manufacturers, manufacturing craftsmen and product assessors. Ultimately, the aim is that these roles will be blended together to permit flexibility within the team. This in turn generates a substantial training and development requirement. As a member of a Lucas Electrical task force commented:

> We are aware that this is going to involve a lot of development of our existing labour force. The employees within these areas have to understand the business . . . For this sort of concept to work everyone must be part of the team. (BBC/OU 1986a)

The systems of just-in-time production that Lucas is also implementing place additional requirements both on production workers and on the management structures that control and coordinate them. A Lucas Electrical task force leader remarks:

> Because of the quality constraints demanded by Kanban, we have to give the right to the operator to shout 'Jidoka!' [Stop the line.] So if we find we have a reject or bad component we don't just keep making it . . . This means that the management structure has to be able to respond to that – otherwise we'd be stopped for two weeks. (BBC/OU 1986a)

The reorganization of the manufacturing processes into production cells not only affects those directly involved with the production process itself. Personnel who have traditionally been based in centralized functional areas, such as production engineering or quality control, are placed in the cells under the control of a cell leader – moves that have not always been welcomed by those involved, as people who were once 'promoted' from the shopfloor are now being asked to return to it. Administrative systems are also undergoing the redesign exercise. What are being sought are:

> natural mixed groupings of people around common information flow routes in order to reduce the number of separate fragmented offices and the size of overhead support . . . In principle it should be possible to run a manufacturing product unit with only three mixed discipline office groups. (Parnaby 1987a)

The introduction of cellular production based on just-in-time principles has involved rigorous analyses of the degree of value added to products operation-by-operation. As far as possible non-value-added activities have been eliminated. In some cases, these value-added analyses have revealed that it is more economical to buy in components rather than to manufacture them on site. Rationalizing the Group's activities has involved redundancies: the number of people employed in the UK by Lucas fell by approximately 8,000 between 1981 and 1986, a fall of 15 per cent (Lucas Industries Annual Report, 1986).

In terms of changes on the shopfloor, there have been experiments with quality circles, though these have met with mixed results. The simplification of workflow and the 'responsible autonomy' that cellular manufacture based on output controls permits will ultimately lead to a flattening of the organizational structure within the business units via a reduction in the number of vertical levels required. Overlaid with these changes, Lucas's 1986 Annual Report declared the aim to be:

> To heighten awareness at Business Unit level of the actions needed to match and beat competitors. This decentralized market awareness and marketing ability has required changes in thinking, attitudes and habits – in other words, moulding a new, dynamic Lucas culture.

Some of the results obtained so far are shown in table 4.1.

Whilst it must be accepted that there have been problems with the introduction of some of the new methods, among many people within the company there has been an enthusiastic response. In the view of a Lucas Electrical general manager:

Table 4.1 Performance improvement at Lucas Industries

	Automotive electronics after 1 year	Automotive electrical after 2 years
Stock reduction	£3 M	80% WIP reduction
Stock turnover ratio	5 (was 4)	13 (was 7)
Manufacturing lead-time	10% of previous	20% of previous
Productivity	Up 35%	Up 25%
Reject level	20% of previous	20% of previous

Source: Adapted from Parnaby 1987a

Most people involved can see the logic in what we're doing . . . it's really simple, Japanese methodology is simple, they like it, they can understand it, and there's tremendous co-operation from the workforce. (BBC/OU 1986a)

Writing from a very different perspective, Turnbull (1986) argues that improvements in quality and productivity have been won at a cost to the Lucas workforce, and that the new production arrangements face a number of potential problems vis à vis the social relations of production. Turnbull has criticized Lucas's changes on the grounds that the new working methods represent work intensification, with little evidence of skill enhancement:

The jobs are just the same as before, you just do more of 'em. And there's no big deal to assigning quality inspection to direct operators – you just stick the components under a feeler gauge several times a day to check things are going OK. (Senior shop steward, Lucas Electrical, quoted in Turnbull 1988)

For Turnbull, one of the most significant elements of the shift to cellular manufacture is the implications for the social relations of production:

The success of module production is dependent on a social organization of the production process intended to make workers feel 'obliged' to contribute to the economic performance of the enterprise and to identify with its competitive success. (Turnbull, 1986)

Conclusions

At the time of writing of the original case study (late 1987), Lucas was still very much in the middle of its programme of change. Consequently, it was difficult to untangle events at the company that were essentially 'management of change' issues from those that were indicative of the success or failure of Japanese techniques per se in the West. Three aspects of what Lucas was doing were of particular relevance to the question of Japanization. The first point was the way in which the company was utilizing specific aspects of Japanese practice as appropriate elements in a total business strategy. Secondly, as figure 4.1 illustrated, there were clear signs that Lucas was increasingly taking account of the 'fit' between manufacturing strategy and other aspects of corporate strategy, such as personnel practices and organizational design, supporting the 'strategic fit' argument presented in chapter 3. Thirdly, the changes at Lucas were attracting a great deal of attention from academics and practitioners alike, and the accounts of these changes demonstrate sharp divisions in views of Japanization. From a managerial or business-efficiency perspective, Japanese techniques were seen as a welcome means of restoring competitiveness and hence ensuring business survival and success. On the other hand, writers such as Turnbull (1986; 1988) viewed these changes in a highly critical way, on the grounds that they led to an intensification of work and a greater concentration of power in the hands of capital.

Lucas's programmes of change have carried on into the 1990s, albeit in a rather piecemeal manner. In late 1988 the Group abandoned centralized pay bargaining for its 14 automotive plants in the Birmingham area (*Industrial Relations Review and Report* 431, 1989). The company continued to shed labour (by 1990 the number of British employees had shrunk to 32,200) and to sell off inadequately profitable sites. Lucas has also entered into a series of joint ventures, a number of them with Japanese autocomponents manufacturers. The company continues to be heavily dependent on the automotive market, with 58 per cent of its sales in 1990 attributable to this sector. Thus, when the vehicle industry took a downturn in 1990 and 1991, Lucas suffered, with 1,800 jobs lost during 1991 (*Financial Times*, 26 March 1991).

The Rover Group

The Rover Group, the UK-based vehicle producer, has developed through a series of mergers and takeovers, spanning many years, involving a number of companies in the UK vehicle industry. This process began in 1952, when Austin and Morris merged to form the British Motor Corporation (BMC). Leyland (commercial vehicles) was acquired in 1961, and in 1966 BMC and Jaguar merged to form one large car and commercial vehicle operation, the British Leyland Motor Corporation. The company was renamed British Leyland in 1975, BL in 1978 and the Rover Group in 1986. In 1988, Rover became a subsidiary of British Aerospace (Economist Intelligence Unit 1990).

During the 1970s and early 1980s, the world vehicle industry faced stagnation. The company's performance slumped as imports increasingly penetrated the British market. In 1981, BL's car production was 347,500, almost half its 1976 figure of 688,000 (*Financial Times*, 31 March 1982). This drop in output, incidentally, was largely responsible for the trouble that Lucas Industries' automotive operations found themselves in during the early 1980s.

Most manufacturers were attempting to adjust to this situation, and many reached the conclusion that collaboration was a suitable strategy. Rover and Honda were no exception. Honda appealed to Rover as a partner because Honda was medium sized and had an outstanding reputation for quality and productivity. Honda was attracted to Rover because of the latter's commitment to high technology, its expertise in suspension systems and its presence in the West European vehicle market (EIU 1990).

At the end of 1979, the two companies signed an agreement, the first fruit of which was the Triumph Acclaim, a Rover-built version of the Honda Accord. Since then, there have been a further three joint vehicles. In 1989, the two companies moved to a more formal relationship with the announcement that Honda was to acquire 20 per cent of the shares in the car operations of the Rover Group, and that Rover would take a similar stake in Honda's UK operations. Joint manufacturing arrangements formed part of this new agreement. In 1989 Honda also announced the establishment of a car plant at Swindon in the UK, in which Rover took a 20 per cent stake.

This case study draws heavily on the detailed work of Smith (1988), Marsden et al (1985) and Bertodo (1989), and describes changes in supplier relations, the production process and working practices, and personnel management and industrial relations. The role of wider contextual factors in the process of change at Rover is also explored.

The Honda–Rover tie-up

Accounts of the outcomes of the Honda–Rover tie-up vary considerably. Rover-based commentators stress the benefits of the alliance for the UK company. For example, Bertodo (1989) argues that Rover has been able to reduce its model cycle to four years or less, compared with the European average of seven to ten years. He describes cross-sourcing of components and ideas between the two companies as 'commonplace', and claims that Rover has learned much from Japanese management practices.

The lessons include a recognition of the power of enterpreneurial, multifunctional teams working in parallel, an erosion of divisions between the different functions and a shift towards greater inter-departmental cooperation. It is further claimed that there has been a shift in management style from one that is directive and controlling to one more geared to 'facilitation, guidance and training of sub-ordinates in a fluid interacting environment' (Bertodo 1989). These changes of emphasis and practice have allowed the company to reduce the product development cycle from six-and-a-half years for the Rover 800 series to four years for the 1989 Rover 200/400 series and three years for the Land Rover Discovery. Management levels have been reduced to four, and management and administrative positions have been cut by 70 per cent. Spans of control have risen accordingly, to between two and three times their previous levels. Defect rates have fallen by between 50 and 70 per cent.

These developments have also extended to the supply base, although the extent to which the driving force here is the Japanese example *in general*, rather than Honda's influence in particular, is unclear. Broadly, and in common with all the other major assemblers, Rover is reducing its supply base to try to develop closer links with more competent suppliers, to engage in joint development pro-grammes and to improve quality and delivery standards to permit a system of just-in-time deliveries to operate.

Honda-inspired or not, these changes have not been without their problems. Some of Rover's suppliers have seen the company's moves towards just-in-time as simply an excuse to pass stockholding costs on to them (Oliver and Wilkinson 1988). Rover in turn describes the process of supplier development as 'slow and laboured, with verbal commitment unmatched by adequate tangible progress' (Bertodo 1989). In-house, the process has also encountered obstacles. Amongst managers, old habits, such as the use of information as a source of power, a reluctance to delegate and a tendency to protect one's territory, have all proved difficult to alter (Bertodo 1989).

Production and working practices

During the 1980s, Vauxhall, Talbot, Ford and British Leyland all endeavoured to introduce flexible working practices as part of an attempt to improve the efficiency of their operations. On the pro-duction line, this meant an attempt to blur distinctions between craft and assembly workers, and in particular to give assemblers responsibilities for machine maintenance and inspection. Marsden et al. (1985) claim that British Leyland went further than the other companies in breaking down demarcations. This was associated with the implementation of the 'Blue Newspaper' in April 1980, which stated that:

> Any employee may be called upon to work in any part of his employing plant and/or to carry out any grade or category of work within the limits of his abilities and experience, with training if necessary.

This replaced 'a mass of restrictive provisions on individual and gang mobility contained in plant level direct and indirect agreements' (Marsden et al. 1985, p. 100), and was associated with a job evaluation scheme condensing around 500 job classifications into five company-wide grades for hourly paid employees. Despite some union resistance, including a refusal to accept the status of the 'Blue Newspaper', implementation of new working practices was achieved in most British Leyland plants by 1983. Marsden et al. report, further, that by 1985 all operators at all British Leyland plants were accepting some responsibility for quality by 'signing off' their work after self inspection, a practice that was rejected by the unions at Ford around the same time during its 'After Japan' campaign.

Most significantly, the changes at British Leyland involved the creation of a team organization, in which the foreman became the 'linchpin' with responsibility for output within his 'zone', and all resources necessary for production within the zone came under the foreman. With little demarcation between the jobs of individual members, rotation of some tasks, and the delegation of some responsibilities for maintenance and quality control to the teams, this was a significant break from past production practices characterized by task fragmentation and specialization of 'support' functions.

Similar changes have been attempted by other car companies, such as Ford's 'area foreman' plan (*Financial Times*, 6 November 1987), described in the case study that follows. The area foreman, as at Rover, is intended to be a shopfloor 'mini-manager' with wide responsibilities for different aspects of production, including assembly, maintenance, inspection, materials handling and janitorial functions. Many of these tasks have traditionally been controlled by specialist foremen, who are likely to find their authority, if not jobs, under threat. Beneath the area foremen are group leaders, who manage multi-skilled semi-autonomous production teams.

Work organization

The introduction of new working practices at British Leyland was achieved after the end of a period of 'worker participation' under Sir Don Ryder and the reassertion of managerial prerogatives under Sir Michael Edwardes. Interestingly, team working had been discussed in various joint committees in the Ryder years (1975–7), but was brought into force only in 1980, after the removal of 'mutuality', a system whereby managers had to agree new practices with shop stewards in advance of their implementation (Marsden et al. 1985). The initiatives in work organization of the 1980s appear to have been related unambiguously to an attempt to break down restrictive practices and improve efficiency – they involved neither the 'worker participation' nor the concern with 'quality of working life' and 'job design' characteristic of the Ryder years, although in some respects the results were similar.

Having reasserted managerial prerogatives and lessened the strength of shop steward organization in its plants, by methods including the reduction of the number of full-time shop stewards from 20 to six in the first few years of the 1980s, the company took various steps to support the changes in production and working practices.

Moves to harmonize pay and conditions of hourly-paid workers were mentioned above. More recently, the company also announced its commitment to similar harmonization for blue-collar and white-collar workers, and Rover's unions expressed their own desire for such a change (Smith 1988). The intention was to remove 'them-and-us' distinctions in order to improve cooperation and motivation.

In line with flexible work practices and enhanced shopfloor responsibilities, Rover announced in 1987 an intention to recruit more educated labour for production line jobs. Smith (1988) has described the means by which Rover at Longbridge has attempted to change the culture of the factory. One such means is the development of an induction programme for new recruits, about 700 of whom passed through the course in early 1987 alone. The induction foundation course lasts one week, and consists of a series of demonstrations, practical exercises, videos, tours and so on. As well as providing an opportunity for the new recruit to be introduced by his supervisor to the specific tasks that he will be undertaking at Rover, the course also explains the company's history and philosophy and stresses the importance of quality. Immediately before the induction, successful applicants spend a Saturday with their families being taken around the Longbridge plant. Smith reports one senior Rover manager as commenting that 'we are not just looking for manual skills and dexterity. We want to know whether their aspirations are the same as the company's.'

In itself, the induction programme is unlikely to be sufficient to create the shared aspirations sought by Rover, but, from early 1986, Rover introduced 'zone briefings' and 'zone circles' to encourage employee involvement and to establish direct communication channels. These developments were in line with the increased use of consultation and direct communication in all the major car firms in Britain in the 1980s.

Zone briefings are a mechanism for direct communication with the workforce, and involve stopping the production line whilst the team foreman provides information on targets, output, performance and related matters. The briefings include plant-wide and company-wide matters as well as matters specific to the zone. Smith reports that, within a year, enthusiasm for zone briefings had considerably waned, many operators, and indeed foremen, seeing them as a waste of time, and welcoming them only insofar as they provided a break from production. The most common complaint related to Smith appeared to be that higher managers tended not to respond, or to respond negatively, to questions and suggestions from workers.

Lack of enthusiasm for zone circles – Rover's version of quality circles – is similarly related by Smith. This is despite serious efforts to ensure their success, including sending around 100 supervisors on a three-day leaders' training course. Twenty-seven circles, each made up of a few volunteers within production zones and headed by zone supervisors, had been established between February 1986 and May 1987, but this was a small number, considering that there were around 10,000 shopfloor workers at Longbridge. In 1987 management at Rover continued to promote the idea of zone circles and to train supervisors in circle leadership skills. The main reason for the failure of zone circles, according to supervisors interviewed by Smith, was the opposition of the unions to an institution that could threaten the role of the shop steward; indeed, stewards were reported as 'getting at' potentially successful circles. Other supervisors reported simple apathy and mistrust, and at least one suggested a lack of commitment from management.

Marsden et al. report that formal union responses to quality circles and other briefing methods have been negative in the context of the other automobile manufacturers that adopted them in the early 1980s – the successes with quality circles at Jaguar (which are discussed in chapter 5) being an exception. As at Rover, the opposition of manual unions has been based on the assumption that the schemes are deliberate attempts to bypass established trade union channels and thereby weaken the unions themselves.

Supplier relations

At the same time as changes were being made to its production system and working practices, as part of the pursuit of 'right first time' and higher quality philosophies, British Leyland attempted to tighten its control over suppliers – including by exerting influence over their industrial relations. It insisted that any wage rises in supplier companies should not be passed on to British Leyland in the form of higher component prices (Marsden et al. 1985). By the mid-1980s, Rover, in common with its competitors, was seeking to move towards just-in-time supplies, having announced intentions to reduce supplies-in-hand from ten days to two days and to take deliveries of high-value components up to four times a day (Smith 1988).

In order to achieve such aims, Rover announced in 1987 its intention to give 'preferred supplier status' to a small number of component suppliers on long-term contracts. Suppliers expressed concern about the future of business with the Rover–Honda ventures, but Rover replied that short-term contracts would be replaced by 'business in perpetuity' with selected companies (*Financial Times*, 30 March 1987). Rover's developments during 1991 in the area of supplier relations are described in some depth in chapter 7.

Contextual factors

Rover has in some respects been at the forefront of the introduction of the 'Japanization' of the car industry, at least as far as work organization is concerned. However, while it appears to have had success in introducing new work practices and production methods, and certainly in making improvements in quality and efficiency, it still has a long way to go. This is particularly the case with regard to the creation of a stable and reliable supplier network necessary for the operation of a fully functioning just-in-time system of production, though important measures are currently under way in this regard. Perhaps more problematic for Rover is the creation of a new company culture accepting of change and willing to give commitment to the institutions aimed at worker involvement. The fact that unions – despite the removal of 'mutuality' in 1980 – have been able to impede the zone circle initiative indicates their continuing independent influence and a failure on the part of the company to bond workers to the company above all else and to give them aspirations identical to those of the company.

Smith comments that the changes introduced by Rover in the mid-to-late 1980s were accepted by the workforce not because of the security that it was given by the company, as may be the case in Japanese companies, but because of the *insecurity* that it faced under the political and economic conditions of the time.

In these circumstances, workers were less likely to give their long-term loyalty to the company, a loyalty that was sought by Rover as part of its package of change. Similarly, under such circumstances, Rover was not in a position to offer long-term employment and premium pay and conditions to a core workforce – the 'political and cultural supports' for loyalty were simply not there. Smith relates the comment of one worker during Rover's induction programme, which brought murmurs of assent and which captures the essence of the limitations to cultural change at Rover: 'my mortgage is with the Halifax, not the Rover Group.'

In 1991, Rover put plans forward to its trade unions in a document entitled 'Rover Tomorrow – The New Deal', the purpose of which was clearly to try to break down divides within the company. The document contained a whole series of proposals, including moves towards single status, the abolition of clocking on, a no-layoffs and redundancies policy, the establishment of a single company council representing all trade unions and employees, with the final resolution of disputes provided by binding arbitration – the equivalent of a no-strike clause. At the time of writing, agreement had still not been reached on this plan, but it gives a clear signal about the direction in which the Rover Group wishes to move.

Ford UK

The Ford Motor Company began manufacturing cars in the UK in 1911. At the time of writing, it has two plants that assemble cars (Dagenham in Essex and Halewood on Merseyside) and a plant that produces light commercial vehicles in Southampton. In addition, it has a number of other UK plants that manufacture engines and vehicle components. Ford of Britain employs approximately 48,000 people in total; while the company has a further four assembly plants in Europe.

The management systems of the Ford Motor Company have historically been seen as the epitome of scientific management principles. This philosophy applies at all levels. At a macro-organizational level, the functional groupings of the company are very strong, so that the route to advancement within the company involves entering a particular function (finance, production, marketing, personnel and so on), staying with that function and being promoted within it. The system is renowned for creating functional 'chimneys' where the understanding of one function by another is typically limited, with relations often being uncooperative and sometimes antagonistic.

This horizontal division of labour is matched by a pronounced vertical division of labour. Historically, very little responsibility or discretion has been given to the shopfloor, engendering an 'I'm not paid to think' mentality. Jobs are rigidly defined, and at the start of the 1980s there were no fewer than 550 job titles on the factory floor, where the emphasis on specialization and a division of labour between functions has led to a fragmentation of responsibilities. The role of production supervisors has been to keep production volumes up, preventing line stops at all costs. The supervisors come largely from the ranks of (unskilled) production workers. Skilled maintenance workers, whose activities are essential to keep the lines running and to deal with breakdowns, come under a specialist section. Responsibility for quality has historically lain with a specialist quality control department, which inspects the vehicles and sends those with defects to a rework area to be rectified. Some plants have a dedicated 'rework line', used purely to rectify defects in the finished vehicles. Finally, the personnel department deals with the vast majority of employee relations matters, such as recruitment, selection, and disciplinary and grievance issues.

Labour relations at Ford have been restless. The multiplicity of job grades has its corollary in the presence of a number of unions representing the interests of different groups of Ford workers. In 1988 there were five main manual unions at Ford UK, a handful of smaller unions and two unions for white-collar workers. Thus, in addition to management/worker divides, there are tensions between skilled and unskilled groups, between different craft groups and between white-collar and blue-collar groups. From 1945 (the year in which unions were first recognized at Ford UK), until the 1960s, management/union negotiations were handled by national union officials. Shop stewards were largely excluded from this forum. Labour unrest during the late 1960s and early 1970s forced a 'pragmatic industrial pluralism' that incorporated shop stewards into the bargaining procedure and was based on the assumption that negotiating agreements with unions was the best method of improving productivity, by ensuring harmonious employee relations (Starkey and McKinlay 1989). At national level, Ford management and the multiple unions represented at Ford agreed common terms and conditions across the company's UK sites in a document known as the 'Blue Book'. Such national agreements did not prevent management/union conflict at plant level, resulting in disruption to production.

Since the late 1970s, Ford world-wide has engaged in a number of initiatives to improve its performance in all areas of its operations. For Ford Europe, one of the key events was a trip to Japan in the late 1970s by its President, who allegedly returned 'in a state of shock' at what he had seen (Starkey and McKinlay 1989). Prior to this, it had been assumed within Ford that the Japanese challenge lay in cheap labour and a protected domestic market, rather than in the way in which the Japanese managed their operations. The most concrete manifestation of this reassessment on the part of Ford was a productivity campaign dubbed 'After Japan'. An important perception lying behind this campaign was the idea that the management style found in Japanese factories was consensual, and drew on the skills and creative abilities of the workforce in working towards company goals. In 1979, Ford began to introduce quality circles, with three objectives in mind: the improvement of productivity; the fostering of greater motivation amongst shopfloor workers; and the provision of a direct communication channel between management and the shopfloor (Starkey and McKinlay 1989).

Ford invested substantial sums of money in the programme, which included training leaders and members of circles in techniques for analysing and solving problems. Plant managers were responsible for circle activities in their plants. There was little consultation with unions or lower levels of management over the introduction of the programme. Some early successes are documented (for example a 2.5 per cent saving in scrap at the Bridgend engine plant), but the campaign soon ran into union resistance, and within two years the unions had withdrawn their support from the programme. The programme was branded a 'resounding failure' in terms of its aims of improving work attitudes and generating cost savings (Guthrie 1987).

Ford management took the view that the programme failed largely due to union bloody-mindedness. However, a major reason for trade union resistance was the way in which the programme was pushed through without consultation. Moreover, unions were concerned that circles were intended to bypass the shop steward system, by encouraging workers to communicate directly with management rather than via the trade union structure. Middle and lower management were also concerned about the introduction of quality circles. Guthrie (1987, p. 30) comments that many supervisors:

> were sceptical of a new 'vogue' management technique, or even felt threatened by their lack of control over quality circles and vulnerable to criticism of the quality and legitimacy of their decisions.

Such sentiments sometimes found expression in an unwillingness to implement circle proposals, aggravating shopfloor cynicism. Although training was provided for shopfloor workers, in some plants the largely immigrant and poorly educated workforces were not well suited to carrying out group discussions with their English supervisors and found problem-solving techniques difficult to grasp. In addition, the average age of the Ford workforce was over 40, making changes in attitudes less likely.

As the 1980s wore on, Ford UK announced its intention of implementing a variety of elements of the Japanese-style management package. JIT and total quality ideas were introduced, both in Ford's own factories and amongst its suppliers. By the mid-1980s, Ford was the acknowledged leader in introducing quality systems into its suppliers' operations. As a high proportion of a modern vehicle comprises bought-in components, the quality of the finished vehicle is crucially determined by the quality of bought-in parts.

During the 1980s Ford Europe developed a tightly integrated production system, involving minimum stock (following JIT principles) and single sourcing or dual sourcing of parts. (Within Ford Europe, many major components are made by the company in one country and then fitted to cars assembled in another.) The economies offered by such a regime are obvious: greater economies of scale at the component manufacturing plants, and reduced costs of stockholding.

Inside its UK plants, Ford has been trying to push through

reforms based on the Japanese model of manufacturing. In 1985, agreement was reached to increase flexibility in working practices. This agreement reduced the number of job classifications on the shopfloor from 550 to 52, permitting some flexibility across skilled grades and giving production workers responsibility for simple maintenance and housekeeping activities. This move was not welcomed by all Ford workers. One assembly line worker commented:

> Flexibility means that every 102 seconds a car comes by, and not only do you have to screw something into the car, but in between you have to tidy up, check your tools, repair things and check you've got enough parts. You do not have a single job any more. If there is no work on the line they move you to where there is work. You are working the whole time. (*Financial Times*, 8 February 1988)

In 1988 Ford sought further reforms in working practices, to extend flexibility further and to introduce team working into its plants. A central component of the team-working concept as proposed by Ford is 'area working'. This scheme is similar to the structure used by Nissan. The aim is to have 'area foremen' responsible, as the title suggests, for a discrete area of the factory and the majority of the functions within it (for example quality control, production and maintenance). This represents a refocusing of the tasks that historically had been taken away from the supervisor and vested in the hands of specialist departments. Under the area foremen will be group leaders, recruited from the shopfloor, who will lead work teams of between eight and ten workers. The group leaders will have responsibility for routine supervisory activities covering work allocation, technical problem-solving and quality. The UK plans are modelled on practices at Ford's Valencia engine plant, where the central maintenance shop has been virtually disbanded and area foremen given responsibility for maintenance (*Financial Times*, 11 February 1988). Other changes sought by Ford were the adoption of a quality statement by each UK plant, the establishment of 'quality discussion groups' (another phrase for quality circles), harmonization of pay and conditions between white-collar and blue-collar workers and the establishment of a single bargaining forum for all workers. Negotiations over these changes were tied up with the 1988 pay deal, and culminated, in February 1988, in an all-out strike by Ford UK's manual workers, largely around the issue of changes in working practices.

The 1988 strike

The 8th of February 1988 saw the start of Ford's first national strike for a decade, after a secret ballot of the workforce produced a rejection of a three-year deal on pay and conditions that took official union leaders and Ford management by surprise. Ironically, both Ford and the unions placed much of the blame for the industrial action on the UK government's recent ballot legislation. Trade union officials had already endorsed the deal, and without the secret ballot of the rank and file members, a strike might well have been averted.

The offer's rejection by shopfloor workers with the support of their stewards was only sanctioned by union leaders after the ballot result, but resistance to it was on three main grounds. First, the deal included a 7 per cent pay rise followed by two further annual increases of 2.5 per cent above the rate of inflation. Given Ford UK's respectable financial performance, workers felt that the company could afford a more substantial rise. Secondly, many workers did not like the idea of being locked into a three-year deal. Finally, the 'strings' – an acceptance of flexible working practices – were considered unacceptable, particularly by skilled workers. One of the skilled craftsmen, who have been particularly critical of the changes introduced since 1985, commented:

> I was taken on as a millwright. I now have to double up as a rigger, welder or plumber. The training is a joke – we had three days learning welding skills . . . Now they want to shove us on the lines when they want. It's not on. (*The Independent*, 9 February 1988)

The changes introduced under the 1985 agreement had been minor compared with those proposed for introduction from 1988, and it appears that it was the proposed changes in working practices, as much as any other factor, that precipitated the 1988 strike. Ford was spurred to make changes in work organization to increase efficiency largely in the face of Japanese competition. For example, the labour content of a Nissan car in 1988 was claimed to be US$550 compared with US$890 for a car from Ford at Halewood (*The Independent*, 11 February 1988).

Ford's two-year agreement in 1985 reduced the number of job classifications from 550 to 52, enabling flexibility across skilled grades, and production worker responsibility for simple maintenance and work station cleaning. Ford's desire was (and still is) for a redesigned production system based on team working, a plan encapsulated in a leaked company document entitled 'The Emerging Vision of Manufacturing Organization in Britain' (*Financial Times*, 20 February 1988).

Flexibility is to be achieved through the further breaking down of demarcations that separate production from maintenance, skilled from unskilled and white collar from blue-collar. Workers will be organized into teams of about ten, team leaders bearing responsibility for organizing the team's tasks, ensuring quality, arranging breaks, and so on. In some cases, skilled maintenance workers will be dispersed from a central maintenance area into the teams, and skilled workers will be expected, where necessary, to carry out some production work. Ford also planned to achieve numerical flexibility through the introduction of temporary workers, but this demand was dropped before the 1988 dispute broke out into a strike.

Ford's planned restructuring involves the elimination of a layer of supervision, with the remaining supervisors becoming area foremen – 'mini-managers' responsible for areas of the shopfloor. Maintenance workers are to report to area foremen rather than to be organized from a central maintenance area. Each UK plant will be expected to adopt a quality statement, and quality discussion groups should be established throughout the company. A harmonization of terms and conditions and a greatly simplified pay structure are also planned to help facilitate flexibility, and, once they are in place, the company is seeking a single bargaining forum for all workers.

Many of the changes planned by Ford for its UK plants are also planned in some of its factories abroad. At its engine chassis plant in Sharonville, Ohio, semi-autonomous work teams are to have responsibility for production scheduling, setting work tasks, establishing criteria for promotion, planning training, and administering a pay structure based on versatility and qualifications. Team leaders are to be elected, and there is to be a single, multi-skilled grade called 'manufacturing technician' (*Financial Times*, 23 March 1988). In Australia, an attempt to impose flexible working and operator responsibility for quality is reported (*Financial Times*, 11 February 1988), and in Belgium and Germany Japanese-style management techniques are being introduced. Belgian trade union officials claimed workers were resentful at being 'forced to become Japanese', and one representative of the German metal workers' union commented:

There is a wide range of opinion concerning Japanese-style management techniques among West German workers, from outright hostility to resigned acceptance . . . but what can we do about it? (*The Times*, 10 February 1988)

Ford UK is not alone in feeling the competition from the Far East. Vauxhall Motors Chairman John Bagshaw claimed that the new Nissan plant at Sunderland enjoyed a cost advantage over Vauxhall's British operations of between £250 and £500 per car (*The Guardian*, 16 December 1986), a discrepancy used to justify sweeping changes in work practices by General Motors' UK outfits. A plant convenor for the TGWU at Vauxhall's Ellesmere Port factory suggested:

All companies, Ford, Austin Rover and Vauxhall, are looking to break down the demarcation lines because we all have to compete with Nissan. I honestly believe, although nobody would ever prove it, that one of the reasons Nissan was allowed here was not to produce employment in the North East but to help get the car workers into line. That is happening now. (*The Independent*, 9 February 1988)

Ford UK can make comparisons not only with its sister plants across the world, but also with its competitors in Britain itself. Here, General Motors, the Rover Group, and most spectacularly Nissan have each introduced Japanese-style working practices that increase the pressure on Ford to make a success of its campaign for change. GM publicly declared its intention to transform its UK operations in the mid-1980s, with Vauxhall Motors Chairman John Bagshaw asserting that:

By the end of this decade we will have to learn to run our plants with far fewer organizational tiers, without clock cards, weekly pay packets, and with far greater job flexibility and overall responsibility right down to the shop floor. (*The Guardian*, 16 December 1986)

The impact of the strike

Ford appeared to be taken by surprise by the 1988 strike and by the strength of opposition to the imposition of new work practices. The effects of the UK strike were substantial and were felt almost instantly. The day after the start of the strike, Ford announced that 2,000 workers were to be laid off at the Transit van plant in Genk, Belgium (*The Independent*, 9 February 1988). On the same day, the

Ford unions claimed that output of Escorts and Orions at Saarlouis in Germany would be halved, and that Escort production at Cologne would be halted the next day. Management denied that the effects would be felt so soon, but within a few days 9,700 workers had been laid off at Genk, Escort and Orion production at Saarlouis had been cut to 1,000 cars per day from 1,350, and 1,500 workers at an axle plant in Düren had been laid off (*The Guardian*, 12 February 1988).

The 1988 strike appears to fit the framework that we introduced in chapter 3. In Ford's case, the production stoppage had *immediate* consequences for the whole of Ford Europe, because stocks were at a minimum. The strike had *pervasive* consequences across Europe because of single sourcing. And *substitutability* was made difficult – for some models impossible – for the same reason. In other words, Ford's move towards just-in-time production had greatly increased the dependency of the company on its employees' goodwill and willingness to work, thereby providing workers with an important bargaining counter. Ironically, it was Japanese-style production integration that gave workers the ability to hit Ford so hard in their resistance to Japanese-style work practices.

In week two of the strike, Ford, by some accounts under instruction from Detroit – though this was denied by Ford UK management (*The Independent*, 17 February 1988) – made concessions acceptable to the workforce, and the dispute was over. The original pay offer was marginally improved to 14 per cent over two years, the demand for a three-year deal was cut to a demand for a two-year deal, and, perhaps most importantly, although the deal incorporated union in-principle agreement to radical changes in work practices, a 'non-imposition' clause meant that all reforms would be introduced only with local agreement (*Financial Times*, 8 February 1988). The managerial prerogative to impose new practices, as under the 1985 agreement, was abandoned, and negotiation and consultation became accepted as a part of the process of change.

The Dundee episode

In October 1987, Ford announced its decision to build a £40-million electronics components plant in Dundee, which would eventually employ around 1,500 workers, and supply Ford assembly plants across Europe. Also announced was a single-union agreement with the AEU. The agreement included provisions for team working, flexibility, and rates of pay in line with those of the Scottish electronics industry (*Financial Times*, 26 March 1988). The deal was to be totally separate from anything signed between Ford and its dozen or so unions in the past, and workers at the plant would be outside Ford UK's 'Blue Book' management–union agreement on wages and conditions. The deal was similar to the new realist single-union agreements signed by Nissan and the AEU and Komatsu and the AEU in 1985, and to other single-union agreements signed by Japanese and Japanizing companies with new realist unions in the late 1980s. Ford was clearly seeking industrial relations arrangements conducive to the flexibility so eagerly sought by the company but resisted, at least by the skilled workers, at its existing plants. The Dundee plant would break the mould of Ford UK's employee relations in a way that would conform with Ford's plans to reorganize work and improve efficiency. Model work practices, perhaps a model for the rest of Ford UK, would now be established in at least one of Ford's British plants.

The announcement of the deal, however, immediately gave rise to an inter-union dispute. The AEU were accused of signing yet another 'sweetheart deal' behind the backs of other unions and of abusing their links with the Scottish Development Agency (*The Guardian*, 31 October 1988). Objections to the deal included the following: first, that Ford's 'Blue Book' agreement should apply to all Ford UK plants; secondly, that the wages and conditions of workers at Dundee should be the same as in all other Ford plants – instead of which Ford wished to pay them less than three-quarters of what it paid equivalent workers elsewhere in the UK (*Financial Times*, 22 April 1988); thirdly, that 1,000 jobs at Ford's electronics factories in Treforest, Enfield and Belfast were claimed to be threatened by the investment (*The Observer*, 27 March 1988); and, finally, that the 'basic trade union principle' that the choice of union was the workers' right, not the company's, was breached (*The Independent*, 2 April 1988). Ford's national joint negotiating committee was reported as threatening to 'black' components coming out of the Dundee factory (*The Times*, 28 March 1988), though officials from several unions, including the TGWU, which voiced the most vociferous criticism, have since vigorously denied that the possibility of a boycott was even discussed (*Financial Times*, 26 March 1988).

As early as the end of October 1987, Ford threatened to withdraw from Dundee if the inter-union dispute continued (*The Guardian*, 31 October 1988), but the formal announcement of its withdrawal in March 1988, only a few weeks after the end of the national strike, surprised most people. Ford's expressed reasons were that a firm guarantee from the unions opposed to the deal, regarding continuity of production and the acceptance of Dundee components across the UK, was not forthcoming (*The Times*, 28 March 1988), and that British unions could not 'guarantee the conditions to make (Dundee) competitive'. A TUC delegation to Detroit (including TUC Secretary General Norman Willis) reassured Ford that the single-union deal with the AEU stood 'in its entirety, without qualification, and with the full endorsement of the TUC' (*The Times*, 26 March 1988). This was not enough for Ford, which demanded 'unanimity of support' from all the unions, one spokesman commenting: 'What authority has the general council (of the TUC) got if not all the unions will give their backing to the agreement?' (*The Times*, 26 March 1988). Ron Todd of the TGWU, and Clive Jenkins and Ken Gill of the MSF union, were continuing to voice opposition to the deal. To quote Ken Gill:

These actions represent a desperate attempt to redefine trade unionism as a management service. The employers – not the employees – will choose the union . . . The Dundee investment is in many ways a test of the quality of national independence, of dignity in the face of corporate arrogance . . . of trade union validity. (*The Independent*, 31 March 1988)

Mrs Thatcher joined in the criticism of the unions opposed to the deal, paying tribute to Gavin Laird, AEU General Secretary, and commenting:

It would be a great advance if the unions could speak with a single voice and they should recognise that many companies that want to invest in Britain would be likelier to do so if there was a single union. (*The Times*, 25 March 1988)

However, given unambiguous TUC support for the deal, it seems likely that Ford's decision to withdraw was heavily influenced by the national strike. In particular, Frank Macher, Ford's Electrical and Electronics Division General Manager, was reported as voicing extreme unease over the leading role played in the strike by Jimmie Airlie, the AEU official who would have overseen the Dundee agreement. Airlie had also expressed a preference for Dundee to be covered by the 'Blue Book' (*Financial Times*, 26 March 1988). In

August 1988, it was reported that the electronics plant would be built in Spain (*The Guardian*, 6 August 1988).

As Ford entered the 1990s this pattern persisted. Attempts to push through changes in work practices and organization continue, as do instances of industrial unrest. In 1990 the Halewood plant on Merseyside was shut down for seven weeks due to a stoppage by skilled workers over Ford's failure to sort out problems with the pay structure; and this stoppage coincided with the build up to the launch of the new Escort. Ford claimed that 39,500 vehicles were lost as a consequence of the dispute and in early 1991 it set a deadline to improve efficiency at the plant. One element of this included demands for the implementation of outstanding agreements on the reduction of demarcations, job progression on merit, more flexible shifts and 'bell-to-bell' working (*Guardian*, 20 May 1991). This dispute affected other Ford plants, including the Bridgend engine plant, and in early 1990 Ford cancelled a £225-million investment there, redirecting it to Cologne and claiming that the unreliability of supplies from its British plants was an important factor in its decision (*Financial Times*, 10 April 1990).

Despite these attempts at reform, the performance of Ford's UK plants lags behind those of its other European factories, let alone those of its Japanese competitors, as table 4.2 demonstrates.

Performance with respect to vehicle quality largely mirrors that of productivity. Dagenham-produced Fiestas average 62.2 warranty

Table 4.2 Productivity at Ford's European plants

Plant	Vehicles per employee	Hours per car
Saarlouis	42	–
Valencia	38	33 (Fiesta)
Genk	34	40 (Sierra)[†]
Halewood	29	59 (Escort)
Southampton	23	79 (Transit)
Dagenham	22	{57 (Fiesta)
		{67 (Sierra)*[†]

* Sierra production ceased on this site in 1990.
[†] Ford estimates that Nissan UK only requires 26 hours to manufacture a Sierra-sized vehicle.
Source: *Financial Times*, 26 June 1990

repairs per 100 vehicles after a month of service, compared with 28.6 for Fiestas from Ford's Valencia plant.

In 1991 the European car market slumped, with the UK, Ford's major market, particularly badly hit. Ford suffered more than most manufacturers and, in mid-1991, was forced to cut the prices of many of its models by 10 per cent.

'Southern Components'

Southern Components is a small specialist light engineering company, based in southern England. The company manufactures a range of components for the motor industry. Established in the mid-1970s, in 1987 Southern Components employed approximately 100 people. By 1989 this number had risen to 160. The company's major customers are vehicle manufacturers and other component manufacturers who in turn also supply the vehicle manufacturers; output goes to both these sets of customers in approximately equal proportions. The company does not recognize a union, although about 20 per cent of the workforce are members of the TGWU. There are no restrictions on working practices – skill levels are the only constraint on flexible working. There is a Works Committee, elected by compulsory voting. The majority of jobs in the factory are semi-skilled. Turnover in 1987 was about £2 million per annum; by 1989 this had doubled to over £4 million.

The pressures for change that Southern Components experienced in the mid 1980s originated primarily from the changing demands placed on them by their major customers, particularly the vehicle assemblers. At that time, the most significant changes were reductions in numbers of suppliers to the major vehicle manufacturers; preferred supplier status; improved quality of supplies; and just-in-time deliveries.

Reductions in numbers of suppliers

In recent years, all the vehicle assemblers have reduced the number of their suppliers. There are two main motives behind this: to reduce the amount of administration generated by purchasing activities and to enable closer relationships to develop between suppliers and purchasers. Part of this drive comes from a wish on the part of the major assemblers to push more responsibility for components out to the sub-contractors. Speaking in 1987, Southern Components' Managing Director observed:

> In many cases customers encourage – demand – major changes in suppliers' procedures and major investment in new techniques and hardware, an example being electronic data communication. If the volume of business they place with you isn't large then as a supplier you are not likely to wish to tailor your operations to their needs unless the ideas make sense in their own right . . . and many of them do *not* make sense other than for a specific customer.

Preferred supplier status

'Preferred supplier status' is the title given to a special relationship between a customer and a supplier and bestowed on the latter by the former. A supplier who is granted preferred supplier status receives from its customer a commitment for a particular volume of output or covering a particular period of time. This status also involves customer–supplier cooperation on issues concerning quality systems and product development, and confers a degree of stability on the relationship. In return for this stability, the supplier has to make a commitment to maintain a given price, which is generally negotiated annually. In practice, assemblers rarely change suppliers on the grounds of price; quality or delivery problems are more likely to lead to such moves. For companies such as Southern Components, preferred supplier status altered the rules of the game in terms of winning contracts. Prior to the development of preferred supplier status, contracts were awarded on the basis of price, after which product development, tooling and so on would take place. This often involved substantial investment by the customer in equipment and tooling to be used on the supplier's premises. Such investment then constrained the customer's ability to withdraw, giving the supplier scope to bump up the price without losing the business. However, under preferred supplier status, a supplier's books are open to the assembler, so that the latter is substantially protected against the supplier taking advantage of this situation. Under this arrangement, the supplier is protected against externally generated increases in costs – for example increases in material costs – but not against internally generated ones.

There are also advantages in this system for the supplier. For Southern Components, the benefits of involvement in product development were particularly marked. As suppliers typically understand their own manufacturing processes better than do the designers employed by their customers, participation in the design and development process can create substantial savings in the manufacturing costs of components – Southern Components estimates that it is not unusual for components designed with supplier participation to cost only 75 per cent of equivalents designed without supplier participation.

Quality systems

It is in matters concerning quality assurance, and especially quality systems, that Southern Components is experiencing some of the most marked and dramatic changes. The company's major customers are demanding practices such as self-certification of product quality and stringent quality systems, including the use of techniques such as statistical process control. A standard definition of a quality system is one with 'organized procedures and methods of implementation to ensure the capability of the organization to meet quality requirements' (BS 5750, 1979). For Southern Components, it is the domain of quality systems:

> where they [the assemblers] most penetrate. In many ways this has been positive and constructive but sometimes it leads to quite bizarre situations where the quality assurance systems of, say, Ford and Rover are at variance, and therefore any attempt to incorporate the preferences of one leads to the immediate rejection of the system by the other.

The demand that the company should guarantee its products to be defect-free may have been easy for its customers to make, but it was less straightforward to implement. In the words of the Managing Director, Southern Components was suddenly required to be 'brilliant and accept no failures'. However, the existing products and designs made this difficult to accomplish:

> Faced with a zero defect quality goal and trying hard to achieve it, we found we were trying to squeeze excellence out of poorly designed products. The only way to protect ourselves from being squeezed between the customers' poor designs and their demands for a perfect product was to deliberately attack the design processes and inform the customers that better design could be achieved if suppliers were more involved.

One element in the changes in quality systems that the car companies – particularly Ford – pushed through at Southern Components is statistical process control, the principles of which were described in chapter 2. The company has enjoyed substantial benefits from the use of statistical process control, describing it as 'the best Japanese import'. The use of this technique led to a conscious decision to upgrade the company's recruitment standards requirements, in order to ensure that personnel were capable of employing it. The new requirements, which cannot always be met because of the tight labour market in the region in which the company is based, rule out about 60 per cent of school-leavers, the company's main recruits. There was some resistance to the new technique on the part of the existing staff, 'mainly due to a lack of confidence with sums'.

Just-in-time supply

The final major change that Southern Components has undergone concerns just-in-time manufacture and delivery of products to its customers, and it is this development that has caused the company the most difficulty. Ford was the first company to push for just-in-time deliveries; 'their demands became more demanding' in 1984. Other assemblers do not have such a deliberate policy of just-in-time delivery, but as they have pursued policies of stock reduction and now do not hold more than two or three days' worth of stock, just-in-time happens by default. Although this idea may be satisfactory in principle, in practice it is not without its problems:

> JIT call-off from customers is a fine concept but as a supplier it means that your lead-time in response to changes in demand has got to be quicker than that required by the customer. This is very difficult to achieve. Customers are demanding almost immediate changes in supply – component to component and quantity to quantity.

In line with the traditional approach in British mechanical engineering, past policy has been to make maximum use of machinery and to let work-in-progress stocks take up variations in manufacturing efficiency. As JIT requires the creation of a surplus stock of machinery with perfectly flexible labour and very low set-up times (so that manufacturing can be started up at a moment's notice), a radical reorientation from the traditional approach has been required:

If you read the literature appearing in the management magazines there is a gradual recognition that JIT often works by swapping the 'waste' of excess stocks for the 'waste' of excess machine capacity.

Successful JIT production is obviously dependent on having the raw material available. However, Southern Components has found that it can be very difficult to pass JIT up the line to its own suppliers. The company has a weak supply base, with few suppliers and long lead-times for changes in orders – typically eight to ten weeks, sometimes as long as 14 weeks. Thus it is only when demand is sufficiently stable for it to be predictable, that JIT can be passed on successfully. In the automotive industry, the ultimate supplier is often the British Steel Corporation, which does not, or cannot, apply JIT principles.

A supplier like Southern Components is therefore piggy-in-the-middle, squeezed between giant customers at one end and monopoly suppliers at the other.

Because of this situation, many suppliers are finding that their optimum response is to build for stock – to cope by increasing the quantities of stock that they themselves are holding. Where this is occurring, JIT is essentially achieved by the transference of stock-holding from customer to supplier. One manifestation of this is the fact that Rover and Jaguar have set up warehouses near their factories at Oxford and Coventry respectively, into which suppliers are required to ship goods. The warehousing costs are met entirely by suppliers, and the customers can call off suppliers on a just-in-time basis, whilst ensuring stability of supply. Southern Components again:

JIT has been used as a myth on which to hang the transfer of the responsibility for stockholding to another point in the supply chain – anywhere so long as it does not cost the assemblers money.

1987–1991

Two years on from the original research on which this case was based, the authors revisited Southern Components. At that time (mid-1989) cynicism about the initiatives of the vehicle assemblers was apparent:

Most of the motor industry initiatives have gone dead or stalled over the last couple of years . . . it's hard to think of one that isn't as dead as a dodo.

You very often get (from nearly all of them) something like a policy document which says we're going to have proper auditing of suppliers, quality assurance surveys, regular reviews of A-rated suppliers and all this kind of stuff. But that implies an enormous increase in the volume of activity researching suppliers and an increase in the number of people to do it. But it's always felt as the thing to do when they're not firefighting . . . it's always so easy to postpone.

Despite this perception of a stalling of initiatives on the part of the vehicle assemblers, Southern Components had gone through an extensive internal reorganization, the design for which was shaped by what the Managing Director had seen whilst on a recent visit to Japan. The functional layout had been reorganized into eight flow-lines, each designed to handle a particular family of products. The company already had operator flexibility. Plant flexibility was achieved by a policy of excess machine capacity; technology levels were intentionally kept low, and the elimination of bottlenecks was a high priority. (The Managing Director is an enthusiast for Goldratt and Cox's *The Goal*, copies of which have been widely circulated within the company.) Each of the eight lines is run by a team, and the movement of labour between the teams is minimized in order to force a team that is having difficulties to confront the underlying problem:

We try very hard not to allow transfer of labour between lines . . . If you cover up the imbalance of resources by swapping resources you never find out what the true resource problem implication is. You've got to have a certain amount of a lack of flexibility to force you to solve the problem. If someone on line A doesn't turn up, and you keep substituting from H to A, you'll never find out why that person's not turning up because the problem's solved.

The factory has been designed with a view to making the layout as flexible as possible. Electricity and air are available at all work stations, and few machines are bolted to the ground. This permits easy experimentation with different layouts, and also allows the manufacturing system to be readily 'tuned' to changing circumstances.

Ironically, although these changes were initially precipitated by the demands of the assemblers, Southern Components capabilities have now moved beyond what the assemblers are demanding, to an extent that is now causing some problems:

> We have now got well ahead of them . . . We've now got a very short production lead-time, maximum three or four days. If a product is called off from us let's say monthly or fortnightly on a due date, we would tend only to start it just in time, three or four days before it's due. Now we're getting bollockings from progress chasers – 'you should be half done now' – because they want to see work-in-progress visibility!

International Business Machines (IBM)

Although manufacturing practices based on total quality and just-in-time methods, and personnel systems that encourage company loyalty are characteristic of large Japanese corporations, we have already commented that many of the practices that they use have their roots in Western ideas and experiments. In fact, some Western organizations, atypical as they may be, are remarkably similar in many respects to their Japanese counterparts. One such company is IBM, the subject of this section.

IBM manufactures computer systems for a wide range of applications. In 1986, turnover was $50 billion, and the company employed 400,000 people throughout the world. Drawing largely on data collected by ourselves and Spiridion (1987) from IBM's Havant plant, this case will focus on IBM's personnel and industrial relations practices, which support its total quality philosophy, just-in-time production systems and customer orientation. In order to facilitate comparison between IBM and large Japanese corporations, its practices will be considered under the categories of manufacturing methods; employment contracts; selection, induction and training; payment and reward systems; consultation and communications; and industrial relations.

Manufacturing methods

Ward (1987) reports that the IBM corporation set itself the goal of becoming *the* low-cost producer in its sector in the 1980s. Continuous flow manufacture (CFM) was identified as a key means of achieving this goal. CFM is, to all intents and purposes, identical to just-in-time production. Although the basic strategy was formulated at corporate level, each plant had discretion to develop methods of implementing it to suit its own particular circumstances. The Havant plant developed a set of ten techniques, revolving around eliminating waste, improving manufacturing flexibility (reducing lead-times) and more effective asset utilization. On the manufacturing side, the techniques used to achieve this were reductions in work-in-progress, group technology (self-contained tasks), mixed-mode assembly and *kanban* control. Related to these, was a drive towards zero defects and a philosophy of management by sight – the latter assisted by the simpler workflow conferred by group technology and the reduction in inventories. To support these strategies, greater multi-skilling was demanded to contribute to line balancing, as was 'teamwork through cooperation' across the functional areas of the organization (Ward 1987). Finally, the development of closer supplier integration was embarked upon. Suppliers were viewed as extensions to the whole manufacturing process.

Employment contracts

IBM has a full-employment policy, and can boast that it has never had to lay off any worker from its UK plants, which in the late 1980s employed around 18,000 people. According to Mercer (1987, p. 22), this is achieved through a tight manning policy: '[IBM] largely resources, in manpower terms, to meet the troughs. The peaks are met by its employees working that much harder; sometimes very much harder.' The flexibility gained through devoting huge resources to training and multi-skilling also contributes in this regard: 'Employment security is not . . . the same as job security. Jobs are constantly disappearing in IBM, and their holders are moved on, retrained, to new positions' (Mercer 1987, p. 192). Around 5 per cent of IBM's manpower is permanently committed to internal education, which cost IBM about $600 million in direct costs in 1984 alone. Peach (1983) describes the beneficial outcome to IBM as follows:

> The result of this 'full employment' practice is to engender a feeling of security which in turn generates an acceptance of change. If one's livelihood is not threatened one is more likely to recognize the need for, and so speed, the acceptance of change which in a high technology industry is essential to survival and prosperity.

As in Japanese companies, the full-employment policy is a moral rather than legal or contractual obligation. That IBM has met these obligations to date in the UK is made all the more remarkable by the fact that temporary workers are not employed, though IBM contracts out non-core operations wherever possible. In addition to providing lifetime employment, IBM pays favourable rates compared with other leading companies in the UK and carefully monitors rates in other companies to ensure that it stays ahead of the competition. This pay survey results in salary ranges and pay boundaries; pay for specific individuals is an individual matter, described shortly.

Selection, induction and training

IBM's policy is to choose candidates of the highest intellectual calibre. IBM's wages and reputation allow it to be selective: in 1984 there were 1.3 million applicants world-wide for jobs with IBM. Perhaps overstating the case a little, Mercer (1987, p. 104) claims that 'IBM is able to, and often does, employ as "workers" people who would qualify as directors in many other organizations; and can afford to pay them as such.' Intellectual calibre is judged by educational performance, and also by IBM's own rigorous intelligence tests.

IBM also seeks, according to an IBM personnel development manager, candidates likely to 'fit in' and work as members of a team; their 'acceptability' to existing employees is an important consideration – candidates who will accept IBM's values are sought. Writing of American 'excellent' companies, including IBM, Pascale (1984, p. 62) comments:

> The company subjects candidates for employment to a selection process so rigorous that it often seems designed to discourage individuals rather than encourage them to take the job. By grilling the applicant, telling him or her the bad side as well as the good, and making sure not to oversell, [excellent] companies prod the job applicant to take himself out of contention if he, who presumably knows more about himself than any recruiter, thinks the organization won't fit his style and values.

In 1987, IBM was reported as using the Economic League – an organization that investigates the political and trade union activities of individuals on behalf of companies, for a fee – to screen potential employees, paying it £5,000 in October 1986. IBM admitted its relationship with the Economic League but said that it had brought it to an end. The *Financial Times* (7 July 1987) reported IBM as stating that the vetting procedure was dropped because its own pre-employment procedures were adequate, *not* because of adverse publicity. Another IBM spokesperson commented 'I think it embarrassed us in the sense that the average employee was not aware that this sort of investigation was being carried out' (*Labour Research*, August 1987, p. 18).

Once recruited, IBM employees all go through an induction process, the responsibility for which falls upon the new employee's immediate superior, but which is guided by a formal induction check-list from central personnel. Within four weeks, superior and subordinate must sign and return a form that covers social introductions to colleagues and others, as well as job duties, policies and systems, and so on. Socialization continues with initial training, when new recruits are introduced to the philosophies, traditions and history of the company.

Training goes on throughout an employee's career, due to IBM's emphasis on flexibility, multi-skilling and internal promotion. Promotion to managerial status normally requires a minimum of four years' service, and typically can take up to ten years. It also typically involves job rotation, so that generalists rather than specialists are created, and a comprehensive training in interpersonal skills such as awareness, sensitivity, and appraisal and interview techniques. According to Spiridion (1987, p. 67):

> every manager must have absorbed IBM's strong corporate culture in order to put it to practical use in his dealings with his subordinates, and in order to communicate to his subordinates the values which it embodies.

Interpersonal skills are reinforced with special managerial training every year – in the case of the Havant plant this is for at least five days per year. In common with many Japanese companies, IBM has single-status terms and conditions.

Payment and reward systems

Payment and rewards at IBM are not based on seniority considerations, nor are they a collective matter. Rather, rewards are an individual affair geared to the one-to-one relationship between manager and subordinate. Pay and grading reviews occur every year in the Appraisal and Counselling interview (A&C). This is a detailed, participatory review of the employee's performance against mutually agreed objectives, undertaken by the immediate superior and over-seen by the superior's superior. Fierce competition for promotion occurs in IBM, but this is tempered by the need to display good interpersonal skills and an ability to work in teams. Any problems in these regards would be raised at the A&C. Good performance is also reinforced with symbolic recognition in the form of awards, plaques and trophies, which are presented to departments and work groups for public display.

Motivation is also encouraged by regular, and often public, feed-back of performance. At IBM Havant, for instance, canteens and work areas have performance displays covering output, quality and so on, in the form of graphs and charts. According to one manager, a reading of some of the displays in the work areas could lead to the ready identification of high (and low) performing individuals. Their use, he said, was spontaneously suggested by the workforce. As well as motivating individuals to perform better, public feedback encourages collective effort in the solution of problems. As Spiridion (1987, p. 26) puts it:

> Commitment is measured by one's willingness to contribute to a solution . . . The fact that the problem originates in (say) another department absolves no-one of responsibility for contributing to the solution, provided they are aware of the requirement to do so. Since problems are likely to come to light anyway, because of the public way in which performance measures are communicated, it is probably in the best interest of those who are experiencing difficulties to request assistance 'spontaneously'.

A final comment worth making is that, although Japanese organ-izations appear at first sight to be diametrically opposed to IBM in terms of payment and reward, because of their emphasis on seniority, many are now attempting to place more stress on merit and appraisal in pay determination. Public displays of performance are also commonly found in Japanese organizations.

Consultation and communication

Informal and extensive face-to-face communication at IBM is en-couraged with open plan offices and an 'open door' policy, as well as the frequent use of teamwork. As indicated already, the primary mechanism for direct communication with employees is through the immediate manager of the work area, and this is backed up with a company newspaper, financial updates, notice boards, management information letters and monthly departmental meetings. In addition, a two-yearly internal opinion survey, which has a response rate approaching 100 per cent, covers a whole range of matters with about 100 questions (Bassett 1986).

Leaving aside the survey, upward communication is achieved through the employee's immediate superior, who is expected always to be receptive to expressions of subordinate dissatisfaction and to solve the problem at that level. Managers failing to solve specific grievances are soon discovered, because of IBM's 'Open Door' procedure. According to Tom Watson junior, previously Chief Executive of IBM, the 'Open Door' scheme 'acts as a deterrent to the possible abuse of managerial power' (Mercer 1987, p. 197). Under the procedure, if a grievance is not satisfactorily resolved by their immediate superior, employees may take it to as high a level as they feel necessary. Typically, employees go to the superior's superior. The manager approached must document the complaint formally and investigate it and respond quickly. If a decision is to take longer than two weeks the manager must tell the appellant why. The appellant, if still not satisfied with the outcome, may go higher and higher, theoretically to the chairman of IBM UK or even of IBM world-wide.

IBM has a second formal upward communication programme called 'Speak Up', whereby employees can submit written complaints and suggestions, this time anonymously if required, to the appropriate senior person. Anonymity is built in by channelling the complaint through the Communications Department, which redirects the enquiry to the appropriate manager minus the name of the complainant. The Communications Coordinator then forwards the reply, which must be given in writing within ten days, to the complainant.

Spiridion (1987, p. 60) sums up the effect of these communication systems on management style as follows:

> They impose a considerable pressure upon managers to resolve their subordinates' dissatisfactions *before* they are formally expressed as grievances. In particular Open Door appeals against a manager can potentially reflect adversely on his performance record. Thus, it is in a

manager's interest to act sufficiently flexibly to preserve harmonious relationships with his subordinates.

Industrial relations

'Open Door' deals with many of the sorts of grievances handled by shop stewards in other companies. However, whereas the anonymous 'Speak Up' procedure produces over 1,000 'speak ups' each year, 'Open Door' produces far fewer – only 19 in IBM UK in 1984, for instance. Bassett (1986, p. 169) comments that:

> From the evidence of its opinion surveys, the company acknowledges that some employees neither understand, nor believe in, the system. In particular, they feel that its use may damage their career prospects.

Nonetheless, extensive communication channels, together with careful selection procedures, a consultative management style, premium wage rates and individually negotiated pay, probably account in large part for the difficulties that trade unions have had in attempting to recruit at IBM – gaining recognition at IBM has been described as the trade union equivalent of putting a man on the moon. In 1977, ACAS was asked by several unions to consider a claim for recognition at IBM's Greenock plant in Scotland: ACAS found that 99.2 per cent of respondents to their survey of IBM employees across the UK (which had a 95.2 per cent response rate) were not in unions, and that only 4.9 per cent (8.9 per cent at Greenock) wanted a union to bargain for them (Bassett 1986).

Unions have continued to be frustrated by IBM in the 1980s, seeing the company as a threat to their influence, not just in itself but also because of the example that it sets to its suppliers and 'hi-tech' industry in general. Senior officials of the EETPU, for instance, claim that IBM in Scotland has persuaded electronics companies there to become, or to remain, non-union, establishing a virtual anti-union cartel.

IBM and its environment

As we mentioned earlier, IBM's Havant plant included supplier integration in its improvement programme. Indeed, relations between IBM and its suppliers do in many ways equate with the Japanese model, in that they are characterized by being generally long-term and high-trust in nature, as one would expect given a use of just-in-time supply, and the emphasis that IBM places on the quality of its products. A couple of features are worthy of note: IBM has a policy of not taking more than 15 per cent of the total output of any of its suppliers, in order to avoid any company having such a dependency on it that the cancellation of a contract would put it out of business; and, perhaps to offset any casualness that this might encourage, IBM tends to offer good prices to its suppliers and settles its accounts promptly – within 30 days.

A further aspect of IBM's relationships with its environment concerns its orientation towards its customers. Certainly there is a strong customer-driven ethos about the company (described in Peters and Waterman 1982), but anecdotal evidence suggests that the picture is less clear-cut than this. Because of its sheer size, IBM has traditionally enjoyed market dominance – perhaps, it could be argued, to the extent of exerting some control over its customers. One example of this is in the personal computer market. Although IBM entered the market relatively late, with a product that was regarded by many as not being technically the most sophisticated in its field, the company's sheer 'muscle' made the IBM machine the industry standard. This situation was compounded by IBM's special relationship with industrial and business computer users, many of whom had an 'IBM-only' policy. (IBM's advertising reflected this; one advertisement carried the caption 'No-one ever got fired for buying IBM.') Certainly anecdotes collected whilst carrying out this research cast doubt on the image of IBM as simply the servant of its customers. Comments ranged from a damning 'up-market bovver boys' (from a competitor in the office systems market) to intimations that breaking an IBM-only policy had permitted substantial improvements in computer-assisted production control in a large British engineering company.

Although we do not wish to make any claims as to how far one can extrapolate from such anecdotes, they do suggest that there is an added dimension to how organizations can manage their dependencies – namely, by reaching out and influencing the market itself. In the USA, IBM has been the target of a number of anti-trust (monopoly) actions, and suspicions have been expressed that it owes its position of strength in the computer industry to powerful allies in Washington and Wall Street.

In the late 1980s and early 1990s there were frequent reports in the press of IBM's worsening financial situation. In early 1991,

IBM announced 10,000 job cuts in North America and Europe, but stressed that these would not involve any forced redundancies (*The Guardian*, 29 March 1991). Shortly after this, John Akers, the Chairman of IBM, hit out at what he considered to be the 360,000-strong workforce's lackadaisical attitude:

> I'm sick and tired of visiting plants to hear nothing but great things about quality and cycle time – and then to visit customers who tell me of problems. (*The Guardian*, 30 May 1991)

IBM and Japanization

Bassett (1986, p. 164) describes 'the IBM way' as 'exactly opposite to the Japanese method' on the grounds that IBM's basic philosophy of 'respect for the individual' runs counter to the Japanese practice – imported by Japanese companies in the UK – of 'forging a corporate whole through collectivism'. Yet a comparison of IBM with Japanese companies both in Japan (see chapter 2) and in the UK (see, for example, the cases of Nissan and Komatsu discussed later) reveals some remarkable similarities. There is not sufficient space in this book to explore the full implications of this coincidence, but it is worth remarking that IBM is a Western organization – albeit an exceptional one – that has for many years done many of the things for which the Japanese have recently become famous. Clearly, then, Japanese management practices, or at least many of them, are not culturally specific. The IBM case, of course, also qualifies our use of the concept of 'Japanization'.

Conclusions

The above case studies are intended to provide insights into, and a 'feel' for, the process of Japanization. They are, however, brief descriptions, and we recognize the limitations of case study evidence when one is arguing that a broad change is taking place – the companies described could be exceptional. The next chapter, however, provides broader evidence of the adoption of Japanese-style practices. This is based on our own observations and those of other surveys, supported by case study and other material where appropriate.

5
Manufacturing Practices and UK Companies

In this chapter we examine the experiences of Western companies with operations in the UK as they attempt to emulate aspects of Japanese practice. Unlike the previous chapter, which sought to give a picture of contemporary changes for entire organizations, it looks at the experiences of a number of companies employing specific elements of Japanese practice; the chapter is thus *practice*-based, rather than company-based. Throughout, our analysis is guided by the theoretical conclusion of chapter 3; namely, that Japanese-style industrial organization is characterized by high-dependency relationships, and therefore requires effective strategies for handling such dependency. The results of two surveys of manufacturing companies form the basis of this chapter, one undertaken in 1987, the other in 1991.

The 1987 survey

All the companies in the 1986 *Times 1,000* index that were known to have manufacturing operations were approached and asked to complete a short questionnaire. The questionnaire covered background information on the companies, such as number of employees, date of establishment, number of sites in the UK and so on. In total, 375 companies were approached, of which 66 completed questionnaires. The fields of operation of the participating companies are shown in table 5.1.

The companies varied in size, employing between 300 and 52,000 workers, on between one and 78 different manufacturing sites. Some 72 per cent were unionized; of this 72 per cent, 6 per cent were single union, while the rest had several unions. Approximately half

Table 5.1 Operations of survey companies (1987)

Operations	Number in sample	Percentage of sample
Vehicles and automotive	5	8
Electronics/electrical	10	15
Engineering	9	13
Food/drink/tobacco	8	12
General manufacturing	16	24
Petrochemicals	11	17
Pharmaceuticals	7	11
	(66)	(100)

the sample companies (48 per cent) were British-owned, with a substantial proportion of the others (38 per cent) American-owned.

The 1991 survey

The 1991 survey was designed to replicate the 1987 survey in certain areas and to develop and extend it in others. One of the problems encountered in the analysis of the 1987 data was that many of the concerns involved functioned as holding companies. In their case, evaluation of the status – and success – of management practices was difficult, as answers spanned a variety of operations. Also, the descriptions of company operations given in the *Times 1,000* index were rather vague, reducing the precision with which the questionnaire was targeted.

For these reasons, the sample for the second survey was constructed in a different manner. All UK companies on the 1991 Microstat Extel database that fell within the manufacturing and industrial classifications were extracted and ranked in descending order by value of sales. The aim was to compile a list of manufacturing companies only; thus operations such as retailing, distribution and mineral extraction were excluded (though mineral processing was retained). This process identified 1,470 companies, a high proportion of which also featured in the *Times 1,000* index. (Microstat Extel was used because it was planned to cross reference the management practice data with financial performance data, the results of which are not reported here.) The 1,470 companies were

Table 5.2 Operations of survey companies (1991)

Operations	Number in sample	Percentage of sample
Vehicles and components	7	11
Chemicals	8	12
Consumer goods	6	9
Electronics	11	17
Plastics and rubber	1	2
Capital goods	5	8
Textiles	6	9
Miscellaneous engineering	3	5
Metals and minerals processing	6	9
Miscellaneous manufacturing	11	17
Food	2	3
	(66)	(100)*

* Approximately: discrepancy due to rounding error.

then subjected to a manual sort to eliminate holding-type companies, on the grounds that data gathered from the corporate offices of conglomerates would be too imprecise to be useful. This process reduced the sample to 460 companies, which were each sent a questionnaire and a covering letter explaining the purpose of the study. Of these, 66 were returned completed, a response rate of 14 per cent.

The companies' workforces ranged in size from 85 to 10,754 employees, while the number of manufacturing sites for any given concern varied from one (38 per cent) to 13. Three-quarters of the sample operated on three or fewer sites. The fields of operation of the 1991 survey companies are shown in table 5.2.

Approximately half (56 per cent) of the companies in the 1991 sample had more than one union; 17 per cent had single-union deals, and the remainder (27 per cent) were non-union.

In addition to this survey material, a range of further material is introduced to support and qualify our evidence at appropriate points. We discuss the experiences of the emulators of Japanese industry under the categories of manufacturing and working practices, personnel and industrial relations practices (chapter 6), and buyer–supplier relations (chapter 7).

Table 5.3 Japanese production methods and practices in UK companies (1987)

Practice	Never used (%)	In use (%)	Planned or being implemented (%)
Group working/work teams	10	85	5
Flexible working	2	80	18
Quality circles	27	68	5
Statistical process control	9	67	24
Total quality control	5	60	35
Just-in-time production	36	34	30
N (number in sample) = 64			

Manufacturing and Working Practices

Six sets of production arrangements for which the Japanese are renowned were explored in the 1987 survey. Work organization was included in this discussion – specifically the use of work teams, flexible working and quality circles – due to its role in relation to the production process itself. The information on these elements is presented in table 5.3 in descending order, according to degree of current usage.

In 1987, group working and the use of work teams were the most widely attested of these practices, although the nature of such schemes varied considerably. In the 'purest' instances, group working meant multi-skilled workers operating their own 'mini-factories', with their own financial, output and quality targets to meet. Systems of cellular production, such as those adopted by Lucas (described in chapter 4), constitute examples of this. In other cases, team working may have meant little more than briefings by supervisors and perhaps some job rotation.

In the 1987 survey, flexible working was the practice next most widely used, with 80 per cent of companies claiming some degree of flexibility in working practices. Virtually all those companies not using flexible working at that time were implementing or planning its use.

Quality circles appeared as the next most widely employed

Table 5.4 Dates of introduction of Japanese production methods and practices to UK companies (1987)

	Pre-1942	1943–1947	1948–1952	1953–1957	1958–1962	1963–1967	1968–1972	1973–1977	1978–1982	1983–1987	Median date	Number in sample
Just-in-time production	–	–	–	–	–	–	–	1 (4%)	1 (4%)	26 (93%)	1986	28
Total quality control	4 (9%)	–	–	3 (7%)	2 (4%)	3 (7%)	3 (7%)	2 (4%)	5 (11%)	23 (51%)	1983	45
Statistical process control	–	–	1 (3%)	–	2 (5%)	1 (3%)	2 (5%)	3 (8%)	4 (10%)	26 (67%)	1983	39
Quality circles	–	–	–	–	–	–	–	2 (6%)	14 (39%)	20 (56%)	1983	36
Group technology/work teams	–	–	–	–	1 (3%)	2 (5%)	1 (3%)	5 (14%)	8 (22%)	20 (54%)	1983	37
Flexible working	–	–	–	–	2 (5%)	1 (3%)	7 (19%)	4 (11%)	6 (16%)	17 (46%)	1981	37

practice, with 68 per cent of companies indicating some usage of circles; they were closely followed by statistical process control (67 per cent). There was, however, a striking difference in the status of the two practices. Although about a third of companies were not currently using either practice, 24 per cent were implementing or planning to implement statistical process control as against 5 per cent in the case of quality circles. This suggested that the feverish interest in quality circles that had gripped the management world in the late 1970s and early 1980s had eased off, and that by the late 1980s the primary focus was on production techniques, a picture confirmed by the proportion of companies in 1987 that were planning or implementing statistical process control, total quality control and JIT production.

In the case of these practices, a high proportion of those companies that were not using them at the time of the survey were in the process of planning or implementing them. Total quality control stood out markedly; of the companies not already applying total quality principles, 87 per cent were involved in planning or implementing them.

A wave of change

A further factor that we explored in 1987 was the *timescale* for the development of these practices in the West. We suspected that many of the so-called Japanese techniques had in fact been around for years, but that the advent of the 'Japan' phenomenon had given commentators a new vocabulary with which to describe these practices – the 'old wine in new bottles' syndrome. We asked companies to indicate the date of introduction of each practice, in order to see if there was a 'wave of change' sweeping through British industry. The results of this analysis are presented in tabular form in table 5.4.

As table 5.4 demonstrates, there appeared to be a massive surge in the usage of Japanese methods, particularly in the five years between 1982 and 1987. JIT production appeared to be a particularly recent arrival, with 93 per cent of the companies that claimed to be using it having adopted it only in the period 1983–7, the median date of introduction being 1986. There were a few companies that had introduced some of these practices many years ago – for example four companies had adopted total quality control before 1942. Interestingly, most of these four companies were American-owned and mentioned by Peters and Waterman (1982) in *In Search of Excellence*. The 1987 survey also indicated a flurry of interest in flexible working, group technology and work teams in the 1960s and 1970s. We suspected this to be a reflection of the interest in quality of working life issues shown by many 'progressive' companies during this period. However, the more recent and pronounced development of these practices, we argued, was driven rather by considerations of quality, responsibility and accountability.

Manufacturing practices four years on

The 1991 survey examined some of the same manufacturing practices that the 1987 survey had covered, and also some that it had omitted. The new additions were: operator responsibility for quality; continuous improvement; set-up time reductions; design for manufacture; and *kanban*. Team working was retitled 'cellular manufacture' to try to increase its precision; the term 'flexible working' was dropped on the grounds that it was unduly vague.

The 1991 data exhibited in table 5.5 display some similarities with the 1987 data and some differences. As one would have expected,

Table 5.5   Japanese production methods and practices in UK companies (1991)

Practice	Never used (%)	In use (%)	Planned or being implemented (%)
Operator responsibility for quality	5	77	18
Continuous improvement	8	72	20
JIT production	18	68	14
Quality circles	18	68	14
Set-up time reductions	24	65	11
SPC	15	59	26
Total quality control	8	56	36
Cellular manufacture	43	50	7
Design for manufacture	39	51	10
Kanban materials control	48	42	10
N = 66			

some practices show increased usage. For example, the proportion of companies using or planning to use JIT production was up from 64 per cent in 1987 to 82 per cent in 1991; while the increase in the case of quality circles was from 73 per cent to 82 per cent. Less predictable, however, was an apparent fall in the reported use or intended use of several practices, namely total quality control (down from 95 per cent to 92 per cent) and SPC (down from 91 per cent to 85 per cent). Both these changes are, however, small and could be attributable to changes in the characteristics of the sample between the two surveys; also conceptions of what 'total quality' is and is not may have subtly altered over the years. Significantly, total quality control shows almost no change in terms of the proportion of companies implementing or planning to implement it, suggesting that implementation may be a longer, slower process than originally anticipated. A surprisingly high proportion of companies claim to have programmes of continuous improvement activities. Anecdotal evidence suggests that continuous improvement is one of the most difficult of the 'Japanese' practices to transfer, although degree of use of a technique clearly does not automatically equate with success. In common with observations by Voss and Robinson (1987), reported in table 5.12, the more difficult-to-implement aspects of the package, such as set-up time reductions, *kanban* and cellular production are less in evidence.

When one considers the dates of introduction for these practices reported in the 1991 survey (table 5.6), an interesting contrast with the 1987 results emerges. The median dates of implementation from the later survey indicate much later implementation than had originally appeared to be the case: two years later for JIT, *six* years later for total quality and quality circles, and five years later for SPC. Some of these differences will be attributable to practices that were at the planning stage in the earlier study coming on stream by 1991; others to implementation schemes getting 'stuck', as companies realized that the introduction of the techniques involved was more difficult than had originally been anticipated.

In order to gain a better understanding of the pressures and forces driving these changes, the 1991 survey sought information on the context of change. Womack, Jones and Roos (1990) have observed that moves towards lean production are facilitated by a sense of crisis, and the sample companies seem to bear this out. More than two-thirds of them had experienced a sense of crisis in recent years,

Table 5.6 Dates of introduction of Japanese production methods and practices to UK companies (1991)

	Pre 1957 (%)	1958–1962 (%)	1963–1967 (%)	1968–1972 (%)	1973–1977 (%)	1978–1982 (%)	1983–1987 (%)	1988–1992 (%)	Median date	Number in sample
Total quality control	–	–	–	–	–	6	28	66	1989	36
Kanban materials control	–	–	–	–	–	5	32	63	1989	22
Quality circles	–	–	–	3	–	12	36	49	1989	36
Set-up time reductions	–	–	–	–	4	11	22	63	1989	27
Continuous improvement	–	–	3	–	–	3	26	68	1989	34
Operator responsibility for quality	5	–	2	5	6	7	32	43	1988	44
SPC	3	–	3	–	–	3	41	50	1988	36
JIT production	–	–	–	–	3	3	31	63	1988	39
Cellular manufacture	–	–	–	–	4	–	48	48	1988	25
Design for manufacture	–	–	4	–	–	–	44	52	1988	25

Table 5.7 Crisis and manufacturing reform in UK companies (1991)

	Yes (%)	No (%)
Sense of crisis	68	32
Manufacturing reform	88	12
N = 66		

Table 5.8 Impetus for change in UK companies (1991)

Factor	Percentage reporting
Competitive pressures	25
Cost reduction	17
Inadequate profitability	15
Severe loss/survival	8
Quality improvement	8
External pressure	5
Improved delivery	5
Productivity improvement	4
Increasing volume/market share	3
Other	10
N = 66	(100)

and almost all of these reported programmes of manufacturing reform, as table 5.7 shows.

To gain a fuller impression of the context of change, respondents were asked to indicate what was the single most important impetus for it. Responses to this question are shown in table 5.8.

Table 5.8 demonstrates that, in the overwhelming majority of cases, manufacturing reform was engaged in for 'defensive' reasons – increasing competition, the need to reduce costs, inadequate profitability and so on. Although there are some signs of manufacturing reform being used in a positive, proactive way, it is clear that motives such as the increase of production volume and market share came well down the list in terms of their priority.

Table 5.9 Evaluation of Japanese production methods and practices by UK companies (1987)

Practice	Not successful (%)	Quite–very successful (%)	Highly successful (%)	Mean*
Total quality control	2	65	33	2.98
Flexible working	6	69	25	2.91
Group working/work teams	3	78	19	2.78
Statistical process control	2	82	16	2.60
Just-in-time production	7	87	6	2.50
Quality circles	17	78	5	2.12
N = 45				

* 1 = Not successful   4 = Highly successful

Evaluation of production methods

The companies surveyed in 1987 were asked to evaluate their experiences with each practice, using a simple four-point rating scale. The responses that this generated are presented in descending order of success in table 5.9. Scores for each item ranged from a minimum of one (unsuccessful) to four (highly successful).

As the mean scores in table 5.9 indicate, in 1987 no practices were rated as unsuccessful by a substantial proportion of companies. Total quality control was evaluated most favourably, followed by flexible working and work teams. In the case of quality circles and JIT, however, there was a marked increase in the 'unsuccessful' rating: only 5 per cent of companies rated their experiences with quality circles as highly successful; while with JIT the figure was 6 per cent.

In the 1991 survey, respondents were asked to use the same rating system to gauge the success of the manufacturing practices that they were adopting. The results of this are shown in table 5.10.

The first general point of interest to emerge from table 5.10 is that virtually across the board the practices received a lower rating of success in 1991 than in 1987. However, the *ordering* of the success of the practices remained very similar, as table 5.11 demonstrates.

The one exception to this is cellular manufacture, which showed the highest success rating of all the practices in 1991, markedly higher than its more nebulous equivalent, 'group working', in the

Table 5.10 Evaluation of Japanese production methods and practices by UK companies (1991)

Practice	Not successful (%)	Quite–very successful (%)	Highly successful (%)	Mean
Cellular manufacture	–	66	34	2.97
Operator responsibility for quality	5	77	18	2.72
Design for manufacture	3	88	9	2.56
Continuous improvement	–	92	8	2.55
Set-up time reductions	3	89	8	2.53
Kanban materials control	11	68	21	2.54
Total quality control	9	78	13	2.48
JIT production	5	79	16	2.44
SPC	7	85	9	2.40
Quality circles	8	82	10	2.37
N = 66				

first survey. There are two plausible interpretations of this. First, it might be that, as understanding of these practices has increased, so their outcomes are being appraised in a more critical light than was the case four years ago. Secondly, and less optimistically, the lower ratings of success picked up by the second survey may be indicative of the end of a 'honeymoon' period – a possibility to which we shall return later in the book.

Having considered some of the overall patterns and trends in the use of these methods by British companies, we shall now consider each one in rather more depth.

JIT production and Kanban

The 1987 survey findings concerning the adoption of JIT broadly concurred with those of a survey conducted by Voss and Robinson, also in 1987. From a sample of 132 companies, they found 57 per cent to be implementing or planning to implement some aspects of JIT, a figure close to the 64 per cent recorded by our survey. Voss and Robinson proceeded to explore the nature and extent of the changes taking place under the generic title of 'JIT'. Only a minority of the companies implementing or planning JIT (17 per cent) claimed

Table 5.11 Evaluation of Japanese production methods and practices by UK companies (1987 vs 1991)

Practices	1987	1991
Cellular manufacture	2.78	2.97
Operator responsibility for quality	–	2.72
Design for manufacture	–	2.56
Continuous improvement	–	2.55
Set-up time reductions	–	2.53
Kanban materials control	–	2.54
Total quality control	2.98	2.48
JIT production	2.50	2.44
SPC	2.60	2.40
Quality circles	2.12	2.37

Table 5.12 Aspects of JIT implemented or planned

Flexible workforce	80.0%
Work-in-progress reduction	67.1%
Statistical process control	58.6%
Set-up time reductions	54.3%
Work team quality control	50.0%
Modules or cells	44.3%
Smoothed build rate	25.7%
U-shaped lines	22.9%
Kanban	11.4%
N = 70	

Source: Adapted from Voss and Robinson 1987

to have a major JIT programme; 20 per cent reported that they were using JIT on an experimental basis, and 46 per cent described their use of JIT as essentially consisting of ad hoc modifications to existing systems. The remainder had not taken any concrete action at the time at which the survey was conducted. Considering the use of specific elements of the JIT package, Voss and Robinson identified considerable variation in their degree of usage, as is shown in table 5.12.

A number of items that Voss and Robinson included as aspects of JIT were considered as separate items in their own right in our 1987 survey (for example flexible working, SPC, and work teams), on the grounds that these techniques were frequently implemented independently of any moves towards JIT proper. However, they do also constitute important elements in a JIT system. It was striking that the proportion of companies that had implemented the 'core' techniques of JIT – *kanban*, U-shaped lines, cellular manufacturing and so on – were in the minority. On the basis of this data, Voss and Robinson conclude that 'many companies are implementing individual aspects of JIT rather than the whole concept.' Moreover, they argue that it is the *easy-to-implement* techniques that are being applied, not necessarily the most useful ones. However, despite this partial or piecemeal approach, many companies reported benefits from their use of JIT. Work-in-progress reduction was ranked as the greatest benefit, followed by increased flexibility, reduction in the use of raw materials and improved quality.

Our 1987 evidence pointed to the need for radical shifts in philosophy, at all levels, in organizations adopting JIT. For example, the system of measuring work in standard hours – the number of hours of output at a given (standard) rate of production – creates a pressure for long production runs. If one is frequently performing machine set-ups, then performance according to standard hours will go down. In a number of companies that we visited, the 'standard hours culture' constituted an obstacle to the implementation of JIT.

Performance measurement

Performance measurement is emerging as a crucial, though still poorly understood, issue in the successful use of JIT methods. Criticism of traditional management accounting methods of measuring manufacturing performance has been mounting for some years now, after being identified as 'The Number One Enemy of Productivity' (Goldratt 1983). The basic argument is that Western accountants have developed measures more appropriate for external reporting than for internal control purposes. Moreover, systems of allocating overhead were developed in a context in which labour was a far more significant component of total costs than it now is and was largely governed by piece rates. This led to overhead allocation systems that were based on *rates of activity* in a factory. With increasing capitalization, a far higher proportion of costs are fixed, but activity-based methods of allocating overhead remain (Kaplan 1984). Conventional measures of shopfloor performance, such as standard hours, work against an ethos of small batches with more frequent machine set-ups. Measures of machine utilization push individual work stations towards continuous production, even if doing so simply piles up inventory elsewhere in the system.

Maskell (1989) has suggested seven characteristics of perform-ance measures appropriate to JIT: (1) a direct relation to manu-facturing strategy; (2) a largely non-financial orientation; (3) tailoring to local needs; (4) an ability to change over time as needs change; (5) simplicity and ease of use; (6) a capacity to provide fast feedback to operators and managers; and (7) an ability to foster improvement rather than purely monitor performance. Other commentators, for example Goldratt (1990), argue strongly against the use of non-financial measures, on the grounds that if a company as a whole is judged on financial criteria, local measures must be consistent with this.

On the issue of high fixed costs and overhead recovery methods, a recent addition to the debate is the idea that appropriate performance measures for JIT should be time-based rather than activity-based, focusing on the *rate over time* at which a system generates income (Waldron 1989). The idea that Japanese management accounting better supports continuous improvement activities has also recently been put forward to support arguments for change in Western prac-tice, as was described in chapter 2 (Hiromoto 1988). Changes in the manufacturing practices of a company are thus likely to require corresponding adjustments in accounting practice.

A further source of adjustment problems revolves around the fact that a *kanban* system does not allow a work station to produce just for the purpose of being seen to be busy, but only when the con-tainers, with *kanban* attached, are there to be filled. A team leader from a company using *kanban* visited by one of the authors remarked:

If a guy's been working the old system for 25 years you can't change it in 25 minutes. People want to work. It's difficult to say to a guy: 'Stop. Don't fill up any more. Stop, Stop.' Because he's used to working. And I know everybody says that workers don't want to work, but we've found the reverse. People get very jumpy when there's no work so they try to create work. Now I don't mind them creating work as long as they're sweeping the floor or emptying the bins. What we don't like is creating work when there's an on-cost on the material when it gets shunted down the line. And it's very difficult. Sometimes you have to handcuff some people.

A factory manager from Lucas Electrical provides an impression of how widespread the old philosophy was in his company, indicating that the problem stretched far beyond the shopfloor:

> We've introduced an animal called the material controller whose sole job is to ensure that we don't make stuff that is not required . . . and let's be honest, it wasn't just the foremen. Factory managers, everyone, served the god of output. And we didn't really understand the implications of that. (BBC/OU 1986a)

Set-up time reduction

As we described in chapter 2, one of the essential elements in creating a successful JIT system is to challenge the concept of the 'economic order quantity', reducing the economic batch size to a theoretical figure of one and making the set-up time the variable element. In an established manufacturing operation, this typically involves major changes in procedure in order to get machine set-up time down. Although this was not an issue directly explored in our 1987 survey, it was considered in 1991, and the indications are of both extensive use (65 per cent of companies) and moderate success. Case study evidence is suggestive of variations in the ease with which set-up time reduction is accomplished, and points to the significance of human factors in the process.

One of the success stories, recounted by Lee (1986), concerns set-up time reduction in the production of engine blocks at the Cummins Engine Company. Here the programme of set-up time reduction was embarked on as part of a wider drive towards JIT manufacture. The programme comprised three key elements: a training scheme for all production operators; the provision of immediate support staff on the engine block line; and the establishment of Set-Up Reduction (SUR) action teams. The training programme consisted of about 10 hours of training in JIT concepts and practices, the business environment in which the plant was operating, and methods of recording and analysis. The attendees were then formed into *action* (not simply *study*) teams, with the target of a 50 per cent reduction in set-up time within six months, and a further 25 per cent within 12 months from the start of the programme. The core members of the teams were the two or three operators who were regularly involved in setting up the machine under study, supported by a process engineer, the tool-room supervisor and a maintenance operator. Set-ups were video-recorded and later analysed by each team.

Lee stresses that care was taken to ensure that the recording was carried out openly and became 'the property of the team'. He comments: 'There needs to be an environment that ensures that the team (particularly the shopfloor members) can trust beyond doubt that the video will not be misused in any way.' At Cummins, ideas for improvement in set-up times 'flowed like water' at the early team meetings. These ideas were recorded and documented, and organized into a prioritized action plan; and particular individuals were assigned responsibility for the plan's execution. Meetings continued on a weekly basis until the teams were happy, whereupon another video was made of the set-up. This was done for a number of reasons: to recognize the team's success, to serve as a training aid, and to ensure that the new method became the standard method of working. According to Lee, most of the SUR teams at Cummins met their targets of 75 per cent reductions in set-up times within a few weeks of the team activity commencing.

In contrast to Cummins' experience, an engineering company visited by one of the authors encountered considerable difficulty in attacking set-up times. The company was seeking to reduce set-up times in order to bring batch size down and reduce lead-times and inventories. Resistance to its efforts stemmed from the fact that the machine setters felt threatened by what they perceived to be an intrusion into their territory. At the time of the visit, the company had been trying to get set-up times down for about six months, and the trade unions had withdrawn their support from joint groups overseeing the change process over the issue. Two factors appeared to lie at the heart of the problem. First, the observation and timing activities demanded by a programme of set-up time reduction carried work-study connotations and were therefore resisted. Secondly, the machine setters saw their skills, and indeed the set-up operation, as *their* property; outside interference was not seen as legitimate.

At the time of the visit, agreement had just been reached on a pilot scheme, but only after a lengthy process of negotiation. Management had appealed to 'motherhood' considerations, such as waste reduction, in persuading those involved to accept the project. As one manager said:

> This appeals to the idea that most people recognize that waste is a
> pretty wicked thing . . .'We're just trying to reduce waste here lads' . . .
> there aren't many people who'll say 'No, no I *want* to waste my time,
> I believe it's right I waste my time.' So we hit those sort of things.

The distinction between 'personal' and 'company' property that
this company encountered in attempting to reduce set-up times may
reflect an important difference in the way in which Japanese and
British workers typically view their relations with their companies.
An executive of Sony's Bridgend plant recounted a story with a
similar theme. A senior Japanese manager walking round the plant
noticed how a group of workers had developed a system that enabled
them to do their jobs a little quicker, and hence make up some time
for a rest. Whilst admiring the ingenuity of the system that the
workers had developed, he expressed his regret that the workers
were keeping the benefits of the system to themselves – in the form
of free time – and not sharing the benefits with the company. Such
an attitude clearly has implications for continuous improvement activities in the West, in that continuous improvement requires that
opportunities for savings in time and energy identified by workers
are 'handed over' to the company.

Statistical process control

One could be forgiven for imagining that the introduction of a
statistical technique to assist in-process controls would be relatively
untraumatic. Certainly, SPC carries fewer political implications than
does, for example, the flexible working demanded by JIT, but technically its effects are considerable, and in many cases a dramatic
rethink in production management philosophy has been called for.
An instructive example comes from Ketlon, an engineering firm that
supplies components to the Ford Motor Company. Ketlon first heard
of SPC in 1980, during a presentation by Ford to its major suppliers. Typical comments from Ketlon managers were:

> We were told quite clearly that to survive – the expression Ford used
> was that they were going to be best of the rest after Japan – we had to
> meet these requirements [SPC] head on. (BBC/OU 1986b)

> We were pushed into it, we certainly didn't discover it on our own.
> (BBC/OU 1986b)

As we described in chapter 2, SPC requires studies to be carried out into the 'natural' variation that machines generate in their output. These capability studies turned out to be a shock for many companies. A task force member from Lucas Electrical commented:

> We carried out process capability studies which measure the capability of the plant to meet drawing specification and found that 75 per cent of the plant was incapable of providing components to the drawing. (BBC/OU 1986a)

The factory manager from Ketlon describes a similar reaction:

> SPC highlighted a lot more problems than we knew we had. Every job we looked at we said 'We're not capable, we can't run it, what do?' We were all running round in circles and panicking. As the dust settled, we realized that we couldn't put it in overnight. (BBC/OU 1986b)

Ketlon started introducing SPC on its finishing processes, and gradually worked back up the factory, systematically overhauling and rebuilding its machines so that they were capable of consistently producing components to the required specification. The resources required to do this were of course considerable, but Ketlon was fortunate in having the skilled personnel to enable it to carry out this operation in-house. Rebuilding its machines was only part of the process; also essential was a comprehensive training programme to introduce operators to the principles and philosophy behind SPC. The company is pleased with the results, and says of the pre-SPC days:

> Back in 1978/79, we, like many suppliers, thought we were in control, but in fact we weren't, because quite honestly, we didn't know that we weren't. We were surviving by 100 per cent inspection. (BBC/OU 1986b)

Positive changes for Ketlon include the extra confidence that its staff, and hence its customers, have in its components, but also a change in attitudes. In particular, the traditional rift between the quality department, with its emphasis on conformity to specification, and production, with its emphasis on output, has closed, as production now has the means to control its own processes. In common with Southern Components, whose case was reported in chapter 4,

Ketlon appears to have embraced SPC wholeheartedly, and to extol its virtues. Notable, however, is the fundamental change in philosophy that SPC has generated in the production areas.

Relating this back to the ideas in chapter 3, the introduction of SPC highlights the importance of tackling causes of uncertainty *at source*, rather than evolving strategies to cope with the consequences of an inability to control a process. What is particularly striking is how the disciplined performance measurement demanded by SPC revealed the extent to which Ketlon and Lucas were simply not in control of their manufacturing processes. The effect of this may be less traumatic than that of simply stripping away the protection of buffers, because introducing SPC does not generally precipitate crises. However, its result in terms of exposing problems that companies did not even know existed is similar.

Cellular manufacture and team organization

Work organization at shopfloor level is a difficult topic to discuss in general terms, as different organizations are emulating different aspects of Japanese practice; moreover, the organizations with which we have had direct or indirect contact are all at different stages in the change process. However, most of the emulators appear to be following the well-publicized example of the Toyota production system, and some clear patterns of factory organization are emerging. These practices centre around accountability for (and hence control of) the production process, in order to gain the advantages of reductions in slack resources and/or improvements in performance with respect to costs, quality and lead-time. Actions to achieve these aims take a variety of forms, but central to them all is the creation of accountable units by organizing production on the basis of cells, modules or work teams. In addition to creating greater accountability, these arrangements also provide the simplified workflow necessary for JIT with *kanban* control to work successfully.

One of the most important conditions for the effective functioning of a total quality organization is that its sub-units – and, ultimately, the individuals within those sub-units – should be accountable and responsible for what they do. One mechanism for achieving this is to organize production in such a way that each group has clearly recognizable inputs and outputs. These may be physical, for example raw material as an input and finished product as an output, or non-physical, as in the case of an administrative task involving information-processing. Each unit should be able to define its output, the recipients of that output and the measures of performance used to gauge the standard of that output. Describing IBM's policy in this area, Harrington (1982) writes:

> Everyone has a customer for their output, from the janitor who sweeps my office to Mr Opel [then President of IBM] who directs the business of the corporation in such a way that the IBM customer receives superior products and services, and the stockholders receive a fair return on their investment. If you find someone who does not have a customer for his output, you have to question if there is a need for him in the organization.

For many UK manufacturing companies, achieving this has meant a radical reorganization of plant configuration. In the case of older plants in which production processes have developed incrementally over many years – a line being added here, a new wing there, and so on – what Schonberger (1986) has described as a 'clustered, jumbled' type of factory organization has resulted. This type of organization is characterized by clusters of generic work stations, little organization along product flows and no easily identifiable flow paths.

Our findings with respect to cellular manufacture are consistent with those of other recent studies into the use of cells in the UK. In a study of 235 manufacturing companies undertaken in late 1990, Ingersoll Engineers (1990) found that half claimed to be using some form of cellular manufacture, and that half of them had introduced it since 1987. Improved delivery, responsiveness and inventory figures are the three main objectives cited in moving towards cells, improved quality being a close fourth.

As far as the results of cellular working are concerned, the Ingersoll study reported almost unremittingly good news across a range of performance indicators, with only a tiny minority of companies reporting a detrimental effect (usually just on a handful of measures). Other impacts included a flattening of organizational structure, and, in some companies:

> the need to replace long-serving foremen by other cell supervisors better able to lead the cell team in the new ways of working. (Ingersoll Engineers 1990, p. 25)

In conformity with this, our evidence suggests that a change to cellular manufacture, particularly if carried out as part of a JIT programme, represents a major upheaval in existing practices, both on the shopfloor and in the wider organization. Part of this trauma undoubtedly stems from the fact that such a dramatic reorganization essentially redraws the organizational map – with all that that implies for territories, resources and power relations. As previously centralized departments, such as maintenance and production engineering, are dismantled and their staff are dispersed amongst teams or cells, 'empires' disappear – to the understandable chagrin of their emperors. In a company that was adopting cellular manufacture visited by one of the authors, production engineers were being dispersed out of a centralized production engineering department that 'serviced' the whole production area and into cells, and were being placed under the control of the cell leaders. Many saw this return to the shopfloor from their office-based positions in a centralized function as a demotion.

Other potential 'losers' from this form of organization are factory supervisors and managers. As we argued in chapter 3, organizations with substantial vertical structures comprising many levels of supervisors and managers have adopted a strategy for coordination and control that the Japanese would regard as wasteful. A switch to forms of organization based around the concept of 'responsible autonomy' largely removes the raison d'être for such groups. The whole philosophy on which factory middle management has been based in many British companies is antithetical to the responsible autonomy concept, a problem that presumably lies behind the above comment about foremen in the Ingersoll report. Commenting on the suitability of his existing foremen and supervisors for a factory being redesigned on a cellular basis, a manager at an engineering company that at that time employed 70 to 80 people in factory management roles made the following remark to one of the authors:

> We probably don't need 70 to 80 and we certainly don't need the 70 to 80 we've got . . . we've appointed seven or eight team leaders and to be quite honest we don't like those that are left very much . . . the type of people we employ as foremen just aren't team leader material . . . They are a mix of progress chasers and backside kickers in their current jobs and they just won't have a role.

Cellular manufacture carries implications over and above the simplification of workflow necessitated by JIT techniques. Another major impact relates to the sense of ownership of a product that cellular production makes possible. This is illustrated in table 5.13, which compares product ownership load under cellular organization with that for the same product when production is organized on a process basis. The figures in this table were calculated during a shift to cellular production in a large British engineering company.

Arranging production on a cellular basis can have dramatic effects on the climate within a company. As a manager of a company that had recently adopted cellular manufacture commented to one of the authors:

> [What cellular manufacture] gives you is a fantastic vehicle on which to float other things – continuous improvement, ownership, training – all those things. You *could* just go out and do them now, but it would be bloody hard work and they probably wouldn't work . . . but the cells give the guys the ownership, and get the commitment . . . You can do your training plan, you can do your continuous improvement, you can do your local control . . . anything you want you can do more easily in a cellular environment; but it doesn't achieve very much on its own, other than the simplified workflow . . . We're doing things in cells that we would *never* have negotiated with the whole factory in 20 years.

This quotation demonstrates how organizing production on a team basis can make control of a factory so much easier. It encourages an ethos of 'serving the customer' – whether internal or external – and accountability is greatly heightened.

This regime can open the way for a different type of control of

Table 5.13 Product ownership load before and after cell manufacture

	Before (%)	After (%)
Turning	9	–
Milling, drilling, grinding	38	4
Assembly	12	–
Processes	13	10
Inspection and test	6	–
Other	22	–
Production cell	–	86
	(100)	(100)

worker behaviour on the shopfloor, by 'self-policing'. An example from an engineering firm adopting cellular manufacture in combination with a programme of stock reduction illustrates this. One process within the manufacturing operation, which involves the tapping of threads into an endshield, reveals the impact of these measures. Under the old process layout, an endshield with imperfect threads produced by a particular operator would typically be stored for some time before use (along with the same items produced by other operators). Under the new regime, the low in-process inventories and team-based work organization meant that the fact that an item was defective emerged immediately. As a cell leader described:

> What happens now is that he makes his endshield and passes it on to the next bloke who's got to put the screws in and he says 'You stupid bastard it's got no bloody threads in there'. Straight away a quality fault has arisen. (Oliver, 1990, p. 37)

Combined with a low-stock policy, this system of working ensures that problems are clearly and quickly pinned down to a particular work team – they cannot be hidden. The use of public displays of team performances – frequently employed by total quality organizations – intensifies this visibility and accountability. The whole system creates an imperative to meet output and quality objectives that would be far more difficult to achieve with traditional 'direct control' methods. In a sense, the system can function to create a series of market-type relations between the various groups of workers who operate a production process, and at the same time generate a sense of obligation between workers of the same team.

Fucini and Fucini (1990) describe how the team arrangement at Mazda's Flat Rock plant in the US creates a 'self-regulating attendance system' that relies on peer pressure to discourage tardiness and absenteeism. The 'Big Three' US vehicle producers keep a reserve pool of labour to fill in for absentees. Thus it is the absentee alone (and indirectly the company) who pays for the transgression, not the team as a whole:

> To his fellow workers [the absentee] is the other driver, pulled off to the side of the road for speeding. His problems are not theirs. This is not the case at Mazda. The speeding driver is not ticketed at the side of the road, but in the middle, forcing all traffic to come to a halt. The transgression of one team member creates problems for all team members. When one team member is absent, his team mates will have to

work that much harder to pick up the slack. (Fucini and Fucini 1990, pp. 136f.)

Similar conditions apply to production errors or problems with work rate – if workers are slow or error-prone, their team mates suffer the consequences by having to perform more rectification work, or having to work overtime to meet production quotas.

Shop stewards from the same (multi-union) UK plant described above recognized the challenge that moves towards cellular production would pose for their own position. As one AEU steward commented:

> Let's be honest, all this cellular manufacture is destroying trade unions, that's what it's all about. [In the future] we won't be talking as parochial trade unionists around the table, we'll be speaking solely for the people on this site. I would think our jurisdiction over people in that environment would be of a lesser nature than it is at this point in time . . . without a shadow of a doubt.

Autonomy represents a danger to management too. Autonomous teams or cells may become loyal to themselves at the expense of the company, perhaps deliberately restricting output or 'covering' for members behaving deviantly in the eyes of the company. Such a situation was observed in an American-owned total quality organization operating a production system based on semi-autonomous work groups. In this case, the response by management was to reassert more direct supervision over those cells considered problematic (Wilkinson and Smith 1983).

A third major impact of team organization, alluded to above, is on the number of levels in the management hierarchy. At Ford, Marsden et al. (1985) reported a devolution of responsibility downwards. This pattern is emerging in many companies; the changes at Lucas and Rover that we described in the previous chapter are in many respects similar to those occurring at Ford. At many of Lucas's factories, a drop in the number of management levels from six to three is taking place; while Jaguar has reduced its levels of management from eight to six. Consistent with the theoretical perspective on Japanization described in chapter 3, the move towards self-contained teams, and the related simplification of workflow, are obviating the need for complex management structures to control the production process.

In summary, the shift towards teamwork and cellular manufacture is associated with, and often made problematic by, the dispersal of specialist departments, visibility and accountability in the production process, and a 'flatter' organization structure. In terms of the theoretical concepts of chapter 3, self-contained tasks lead to a simpler workflow, obviating the need for elaborate vertical structures in the factory.

Flexible working

Elimination of waste obviously necessitates flexible working, since it means that human resources should be deployed as required by production demands, reducing another source of inefficiency in resource utilization. Such a change implies a reassertion of managerial prerogatives over labour deployment, and hence is likely to be resisted by trade unions. The ability to control the deployment of labour represents control over a resource essential to the production process, and is therefore a bargaining counter.

Examples of moves towards greater flexibility may be discerned in three basic areas: temporal flexibility; numerical flexibility and functional flexibility. Temporal flexibility generally refers to flexibility in the use of working time. However, a variant scheme that is increasingly emerging is the system of annual hours, whereby personnel are contracted to work so many hours per year, rather than per day or week, thus permitting slack or busy periods to be accommodated without overtime or layoffs. Numerical flexibility refers to the ability of organizations to vary the number of workers that they employ according to demand. There is little new in this – many organizations that experience fluctuations in the demands made upon them have developed a range of labour strategies to cope. Obvious examples are the hotel, catering and retail industries, all of which make substantial use of temporary and part-time workers. As we have seen, Japan's dual economy provides the conditions for numerical flexibility. Finally, functional flexibility refers to an organization's ability to move its people around between different job grades, according to when and where they are needed.

Different sectors of industry appear to favour different forms of flexibility. A report by NEDO (1986) showed that numerical flexibility was used most widely in the service sector, notably in the aforementioned retail and catering industries, being reflected by an increasing number of part-time staff in low-skill jobs used to meet fluctuations in customer flows. In manufacturing industry, flexibility was mainly achieved by the use of overtime and, most significantly, through functional flexibility. The NEDO report also identified a number of constraints on moves towards greater functional flexibility, the most significant being, first, inadequate skill levels and training resources, and secondly, divisions relating to differences in status and union membership.

Clutterbuck (1985) argues that different types of flexibility may be mutually exclusive, in that the more that firms achieve numerical flexibility through the use of supplementary workers of peripheral status, the lower the functional flexibility that they can expect from those workers. This is because companies are less willing to train their peripheral workers for functional flexibility, and because the workers themselves have little motivation to supply it, with the result that, where pools of deskilled peripheral workers exist, 'they confer a one-way flexibility only, and inhibit versatility in response to change.' As a consequence, companies are tending to segment their labour markets, thus locking groups such as part-time or temporary workers into peripheral status, and achieving functional flexibility among the core group.

It is the development of functional flexibility that is of the most immediate significance to the organization of production along 'Japanese' lines, and it is on this aspect of flexibility that the discussion below focuses. What have companies been doing in this area and how have they fared?

In our 1987 survey, about a quarter of the responding companies considered flexible working to be highly successful; only 6 per cent went so far as to indicate that it had been a failure. Anecdotal evidence suggests that it is not flexible working per se that is the problem area for companies, but rather managing the transition from traditional working practices to more flexible systems. In situations where companies are being set up on greenfield sites, flexible working is generally implemented fairly painlessly, as the evidence from Japanese companies described in chapter 9 illustrates. The insistence of many inwardly investing companies on single-union agreements – if any union is recognized at all – represents one way in which the demarcation disputes that can impede functional flexibility may be avoided. This issue is further explored in chapter 10, on trade unions and industrial relations.

A number of companies that have been relatively successful in implementing flexible working are those that have recognized a need to 're-tune' their reward systems to encourage functional flexibility. For example Pirelli, at its Aberdare plant, has introduced a system whereby there are only two grades of direct labour. Production operators begin at a basic (though relatively high) salary, and people receive increments according to the skills that they develop. Skills are grouped into 'skill modules' that operators work through. Attaining the skill level in each module adds several hundred pounds to an operator's annual salary.

However, there is ample evidence that, for many companies on established sites, effecting the change to flexible working has been problematic. Sometimes improvements in flexibility have been achieved by linking them to pay increases, although such moves have met resistance in other companies. As we described in the previous chapter, Ford UK had a national strike in 1988 (for the first time in more than ten years) over a combined pay increase and flexibility plan.

A company visited by one of the authors encountered both political and economic constraints on the introduction of flexible working. As part of the drive to reduce non-value-added operations, skilled machinists were required to sweep up around their own machines and generally engage in more 'housekeeping' tasks, as well as to learn to operate a wider range of machines. At the time of the visit, no modification to reward systems had been made; consequently, 'flexible working' had come to be equated with an increased work load and a reduction in status, without compensation. This particular company had suffered a severe decline in its major markets, and so was in a poor position to make cash offers to smooth the change.

In another company visited, skills constraints provided a further obstacle to flexible working, in addition to the reluctance of some workers to take on extra tasks. As in the case described above, the company lacked a reward system to encourage multi-skilling. The moves towards multi-skilling were taking place in tandem with a gradual reorganization of production from a process basis to a product form based on work teams. The leaders of the teams had addressed the problem of resistance to flexible working by selecting workers in their early 30s, who were young enough to be flexible, but old enough to have plenty of experience. The fact that people in this age group were also likely to have young families and large mortgages (and hence a high dependency on the company) was seen as a further advantage by at least one team leader interviewed. Indeed, while the importance of people's attitudes is continually stressed in the context of many Japanese practices, this is particularly so in the case of flexible working. The emphasis is very apparent in the selection and recruitment practices of Japanese companies operating in Britain, which are analysed in chapter 9, but the point also holds for companies adopting Japanese-style methods.

A quotation from a team leader in a company setting up work teams who was charged with the task of recruiting operators into his team illustrates the features that he was seeking:

> I personally wasn't interested in what they'd done before. Obviously that came into it, but that wasn't what I was after. What I was after was people with the right attitudes . . . as I said to [the assistant personnel manager] 'You could almost forget the job spec. and write attitude' . . . A guy came in for interview and sat down and said 'I've been with the company for 38 years. I'm not the fastest guy in the world and I'm not the best operator in the factory and I never will be the best operator in the factory. But I tell you what – I'll do whatever you want me to do. I'll help you in every way that I can. I'm always here. And I'm never late.' I said 'You've got yourself a job.'

A second constraint on flexible working in the same company concerned the ability of the existing workforce. Historically, the strategy of employing unskilled people (at unskilled wage rates) for unskilled work may have made sense financially, but it had left a troublesome legacy, in that the company had large numbers of employees who could not be moved around. A senior manager commented: 'rationalizing has generally meant rationalizing upwards; we need fewer people, but of higher quality.' The company now includes 'trainability' as a criterion for selection. The account of a team leader bears out this picture; he perceived people to be scared of performing jobs that were unfamiliar to them and combated this by getting people to double up on jobs until the person unfamiliar with the job gained some confidence. Even so, the team leader estimated that only about 50 per cent of his (selected) staff were capable of performing a range of jobs satisfactorily. This meant that even within the team, which consisted of 15 to 20 people, there was an elite who moved between jobs, while the rest were restricted to relatively simple operations.

The Managing Director of the AB electronics group, describing the company's struggle for survival from 1980 onwards, also places a heavy emphasis on the role of attitudes supporting flexibility:

It was obvious that if the company was to survive let alone move ahead a radical change of attitude on the part of both management and employees was going to be necessary. One of the key problems was perceived to be an almost complete lack of trust between the workforce and management. One of the ways that this manifested itself was an almost total lack of flexibility . . . To my mind the greatest obstacle to remove was the 'them and us' syndrome. We had to get across the message that we were all in the same lifeboat and we'd all better bail. (Merrette 1987)

To get this message across, AB adopted a number of tactics: an open communications system, improvements in the working environment – the toilets, canteen and so on – and a single-status policy. Hours of work, holiday entitlements, pensions, sick pay and canteen facilities were all harmonized. In addition, the company adopted a commitment to a training scheme to furnish people with the *ability* to work flexibly. Each of AB's operating units is compelled to spend the equivalent of 2 per cent of its pay-roll on training.

In 1980, AB's main site was at Abercynon in South Wales, where some 3,000 people were employed. The management view was that the site was unprofitable and suffered from poor industrial relations, and that productivity was 'abysmal'. It was here that the company began its programme of change, part of which involved 400 redundancies. The Managing Director regarded AB's initiative at Abercynon as a failure:

We attempted to improve communications, but the shop stewards did everything they could to prevent it. We tried to encourage training schemes to enable people to extend their range of skills, maximize their potential. Again almost total lack of cooperation. We offered profit-sharing schemes, incentive bonuses, harmonization. We failed, we were not able to overcome the entrenched attitudes.

In the light of its lack of success, instead of placing new investment at Abercynon, AB began spinning off new businesses on greenfield sites. These businesses were started from scratch with modern, single-status facilities and only one union in each case. The sites were deliberately kept small (AB regards about 500 employees as optimal) in order to 'foster the family concept' and maintain 'a sense of ownership on the part of the workforce and the management'. The Managing Director continued:

We will never willingly start up another venture with a multiplicity of
unions, and I would make the recommendation to any inward investor
that he should always seek to reach agreement on representation with
one union.

In the company's view, this strategy has been a success, and,
through its new ventures, it has extended it substantially. Some
change at the Abercynon site has occurred, albeit slowly. In 1987,
employment at Abercynon was down to 900.

A factor that frequently appears to obstruct flexible work practices
is the lack of harmonization of terms and conditions. Indeed, it could
be argued that single-status provisions are a prerequisite for total
flexibility in the deployment of labour – at a stroke, they eliminate
the problems of comparability of terms and conditions associated
with different jobs and remove the possibility of union resistance on
these grounds. Typically, a greatly simplified pay structure is also
associated with the introduction of single-status arrangements for the
same reasons (Linn 1986). For instance, at the Bedford van plant 100
job classifications and 30 pay grades were abolished, to be replaced
by nine grades covering both blue-collar and white-collar workers,
allowing complete flexibility within grades (*Financial Times*, 26 June
1987). Rover, as described in chapter 4, undertook a similar simplification in the 1980s and was planning an even more radical one in
the early 1990s.

The links between flexible working practices, appropriate reward
systems, harmonization of employment conditions, and single unions
thus appear to be strong. Attempts to introduce flexible work practices are likely to meet serious problems unless the other factors are
taken into account, a point to which we shall return in due course.

Quality circles

Of all the Japanese-style practices included in our 1987 survey,
quality circles were the least favourably rated, with 17 per cent of
companies considering their quality circle programmes as unsuccessful, and only 5 per cent describing quality circles as 'highly successful'. Although quality circles received a somewhat more positive
evaluation in 1991 than in 1987 (2.37 compared with 2.12), they
were still rated the least successful of all the practices considered in
both surveys. A number of explanations for this are plausible. The
pattern may partly reflect the fact that quality circles were one of the

first elements of Japanese practice to be emulated by British companies, so that there has been more chance for the 'honeymoon effect' to wear off. However, this is not consistent with the apparent rise in their success between 1987 and 1991. It is more likely that quality circles have been seen by many companies as a relatively low-investment innovation and consequently have failed to attract the necessary commitment, being treated merely as 'bolt-on' accessories. Quality circles have received a fair amount of research attention, and we shall consider some of the documented cases here in two important contexts: the motivation of Western companies in setting up such circles, and the reasons for the apparent successes and failures of various circle programmes.

A handbook on quality circles produced by the Department of Trade and Industry's National Quality Campaign outlines three main reasons for introducing quality circles: to bring about improvements in quality and, in so doing, increase job satisfaction and pride in one's work; to improve management–shopfloor communications; and to improve communications between departments by means of systematic analysis revealing problems in different areas. In conformity with this, a reading of the literature on quality circles demonstrates that companies have a wide range of aims and objectives in introducing them. Typically, improvements in quality feature most highly among these objectives, but issues concerning motivation, morale, and industrial relations come a very close second.

Some early experiments with quality circles were claimed to have produced spectacular results, and many of these were widely publicized in the management literature. Two such cases are Rolls-Royce aero-engines and Wedgwood Potteries, both of which initiated circle programmes in 1979–80, the results of which began to be publicized in the early 1980s. Rolls-Royce claimed savings of hundreds of thousands of pounds from its circle programme. Meanwhile, Wedgwood suggested a payback-to-investment ratio of 3:1, in addition to less tangible benefits, such as changes in people's enthusiasm and attitudes towards work (Fletcher 1984). In the mid-1980s quality circles at Jaguar Cars were hailed as an important component in the company's recovery, and there were a string of publications about Jaguar's success with quality circles around this time (*Industrial Relations Review and Report* 277, 1982; Isaac 1984; Egan 1985). It is not our intention to review the extensive literature on quality circles here. Rather, we focus on examples of success and failure, concentrating especially on Jaguar (which, in the mid-1980s, had one of the more successful programmes of quality circles) and Ford, where, in terms of the company's objectives, quality circles failed.

The account of Jaguar's programme that follows is based on research carried out by one of the authors at Jaguar's Radford and Brown's Lane plants in 1984, backed up by other published material.

In 1980, Jaguar was losing £2 million a month on sales of just 14,000 vehicles a year – half the sales volume of 1978. A high proportion of the workforce were on short-time working; and the company was beset by problems of quality and delivery – in the USA, its major market, '1979' cars were a year late in reaching the marketplace (Isaac 1984). The newly appointed Chairman, John Egan, attacked the problem on two main fronts: Jaguar's internal quality management and the quality of its bought-in components. As approximately 65 per cent of a Jaguar car consists of components made by other manufacturers, the performance of the finished vehicle is obviously heavily influenced by the quality of these products. Jaguar addressed this problem by substantially tightening up its contracts with suppliers:

> One of the first facts to become obvious was that 60 per cent of the faults were the responsibility of our supplier body. . . In order to have common purpose with our suppliers, we made them bear the financial pain for replacement parts and the dealer labour costs of faults in the field . . . This seems to have concentrated minds remarkably! Faults which have existed for decades have mysteriously been cured. (Egan 1985)

The second major assault on Jaguar's quality problems entailed a close look at what could be learned from its major competitors, BMW and Mercedes, and the Japanese vehicle producers. In the light of this, the company began adopting a number of Japanese-style practices, under the banner of its 'Pursuit of Perfection' campaign, which began in mid-1980. The key objectives of this programme were to improve in-company communications and involve employees at all levels in problem-solving, to improve product quality and reliability in a measurable way in comparison with the competition, and to reduce operating costs in all areas, particularly production. Jaguar's Manufacturing Director commented: 'We were utterly dedicated to the fact that our number one priority was to improve quality and reliability' (Beasley 1984).

The company took a number of actions. The quality problems afflicting the cars were documented – there were over 150 of them –

and multi-disciplinary task forces were set up to tackle them. The board of directors took on responsibility for the 12 most serious quality problems. Other steps included the measures involving the supply of bought-in parts mentioned above, a reduction in non-value-added activities, such as inspection (the inspection department was cut by 50 per cent), and reductions in inventory. By 1984, inventory turnaround had been lifted from 2–2.5 times to 12 times per year. A comprehensive communications programme was initiated, and a bonus scheme for both hourly-paid and staff employees was introduced, 'rewarding employees for their efforts as part of a team' (Beasley 1984, p. 20).

All these initiatives are worthy of attention in themselves, but it is Jaguar's adoption of the quality circle that is of particular interest to us here. What is striking about Jaguar's quality circles is how they appeared to take root so well – which raises the question of why they were so successful at Jaguar but failed in other contexts.

One important element in the background to Jaguar's remarkable turnaround from near-bankruptcy to solvency and success may lie in the company's links with British Leyland. Management and work-force alike both resented being part of British Leyland – Isaac reports that the company's subordination to British Leyland had 'stifled local pride and taken away workers' sense of their "Jaguari-ness"', a view reinforced during visits to the company by one of the authors. Certainly, many of Jaguar's workers saw themselves as craftsmen, and different from other car workers. The fact they were put on the same pay grades as workers in other BL plants was thus a further source of resentment. Jaguar's trim-makers, who were largely leather workers, were put onto the same grades as trim-workers on British Leyland's Mini line. This situation, coupled with the desperate financial circumstances in which the company found itself, appeared to generate a degree of common purpose, partly due to British Leyland being seen as a 'common enemy' (on which many of the company's problems were blamed) and partly due to the perception on the part of all staff that their backs were against the wall and that 'everyone had to pull together to save the ship from sinking.' Thus, the combination of a product in which there was scope to take pride, a common enemy and a situation of high dependency – to use our terminology from chapter 2 – was important in creating the right environment for the changes that were subsequently made.

Prior to its full-blown efforts to transform its product quality, Jaguar had made some lesser attempts to improve it. In 1977, for example, it had had a programme entitled 'Quality 77', which had a budget to produce posters, run competitions and so on. In 1984, the Radford Plant Manager described events thus:

> We came to the end of 1977, having considered we had done a fair amount of repair to the quality problem . . . so then we said 'What's next?' – and quality circles had just come up on the horizon.

Approximately two years of discussion about the introduction of quality circles took place between management and senior shop stewards, but very little progress was made. The first major breakthrough was a decision to begin making videos for communications purposes. The Radford Plant Manager again:

> We started the first film ourselves called 'The Price of Quality' and it shocked even me to see what was going on. We took some pictures in our repair yards up in Leeds of [faulty] engines lying on the floor – engines out of cars not more than 12 months old, and that really shook me, because I always had a good opinion of the quality of our engines.

This film was shown to shopfloor workers in groups of about 200 at a time. After each showing, a management team would go in and answer questions about the video and the issues that it raised. There were some ribald comments during question time at some of the showings of this video. However, in the case of subsequent videos, questions became more serious, and ribald remarks less and less frequent. Other methods of communication were also developed, including a plant directors' briefing, which is circulated weekly and gives information about the company's performance, especially with respect to quality levels. Since their introduction, communications videos have been shown three times a year, each showing being followed by a question and answer session. By the middle of 1983, the videos were beginning to lose some of their impact. In the words of the Manufacturing Director:

> They became slightly repetitious, always droning on about quality. It got to the stage where people were saying 'Oh, here we go again, more quality.' (Isaac 1984, p. 42)

In order to combat this, the videos began to talk about company affairs more generally: where the money came into Jaguar, and how it was used. The company also tried to link quality to matters of immediate concern to the shopfloor by pointing out that every lost customer 'cost' the company 21 jobs – which helped to make the videos seem relevant again (Fortune and Oliver 1986). Substantial resources, both financial and in terms of management time, were put into the programme. In 1984, the in-house videos cost £6,000 apiece to produce. The professionally produced communications videos used typically cost Jaguar £20,000 each.

As a consequence of these activities, there was a high awareness of the quality problems facing the company, and deep concern about Jaguar's future. It was into this environment that the quality circle idea was introduced in 1980. By 1984, there were 60 circles operating, encompassing some 10 per cent of the workforce. All circles have followed a few basic ground rules. Membership is voluntary; circles have been allowed to grow and develop naturally, with little 'forcing' by management. Trade unions agreed merely to keep a watching brief over their activities, and industrial relations issues are excluded from the agenda of circle meetings. An issue that soon arose was the risk of redundancies if circles came up with ideas that meant that processes could be run with fewer staff. In response, Jaguar provided a 'cast-iron' guarantee that there would be no redundancies as a consequence of circle suggestions; any workers displaced because of them would be re-deployed within the company.

Within the circles, efforts are made to promote their democratic operation. On the minutes, for example, names are in alphabetical order and no job titles or other indicators of status are used. Circle members receive training in problem-solving techniques. Generally foremen or superintendents lead circles, but at the Radford plant there have been instances of hourly-paid employees acting as circle leaders. Deficiency action reports are kept on each issue raised; these are carried forward from meeting to meeting until the problem is resolved to the circle's satisfaction. A group of senior managers allocate an hour per week to reviewing progress with one or two of the circle chairmen, partly to offer assistance if necessary, partly to demonstrate their commitment to what the circles are doing. If circles come up against a block to solving a problem, they are empowered to approach the plant manager about it directly. They also have the power to visit suppliers themselves if there is a persistent problem due to a bought-in part, and this has happened. The Radford Plant Manager described the effect of this on suppliers as follows:

In the beginning it started to frighten them to death . . . bung four circle members in a car and go off for the day and get into the factory where they make the parts. Tell them you're the quality circle and you've come to talk about their rubbish. It doesn't half make a difference. A managing director of a firm gets a load of people knocking on his door. 'Who are you?' 'We are from the quality circle, we fit these parts, and what a load of rubbish they are . . .' Confronted, attacked on their own doorstep, they find difficulty in wriggling out of it.

The results of Jaguar's quality improvement were impressive; in 1983, sales were up to 29,000 (more than double the 1980 figure), although this was undoubtedly helped by a strong dollar and weak pound, boosting Jaguar's vital US sales. Warranty claims had declined by 40 per cent by 1984, and performance, according to Jaguar's own quality index, improved substantially. The quality index is calculated by taking completed cars off the production line and stripping them down. Cars start with 100 points, and points are deducted for each fault found – the number of points varying according to the nature and severity of the fault. In 1980 the average score was 30 – by 1984 it was 70. For engines, by 1984 the score was in the 90s. In the longer term, designing for manufacture is being used as a strategy for quality improvement. For example, the body of the XJ6 was made up of over 560 pieces; the new XJ40 body comprises only 330 pieces (Isaac 1984).

Jaguar's transformation has not been effected totally painlessly. There were about 3,500 redundancies, although by 1985 about 2,500 new jobs had been created. Half the quality department was made redundant when responsibility was handed over to the operators, some of whom felt they were now earning 'blood money' by filling the roles of their redundant colleagues. In addition, there were some cases of operators simply not checking the quality of their own work. After due warnings have been given, this is a sackable offence.

The introduction of quality circles and other total quality techniques has affected the roles of other personnel in the factory. Process engineers voiced complaints about quality circles constantly inundating them with problems – greater shopfloor involvement meant that they incurred more work. Managers and supervisors had no choice but to develop more open styles of management in the face of an opening up of communications within the company in general, although some appeared to be unhappy with the new order. A factor that may have been significant here was the proportion of Jaguar management that had risen through internal promotion. Jaguar has never had a graduate recruitment programme of anything like the magnitude of that of, for example, British Leyland. The commitment of senior management to the changes also seems to have helped in the process. In the early days, shortly after his arrival, John Egan began insisting on involving everyone in quality control. A couple of managers voiced their disagreement with this - in response to which the message went out that any dissenters should make an appointment with Egan to discuss their future with the company. There were no takers.

In contrast to Jaguar, Ford (whose experiences were described in chapter 4) enjoyed rather less success when it introduced quality circles at about the same time, as part of its 'After Japan' campaign. As already noted, the 'After Japan' campaign was a programme of productivity and quality improvement, a major part of which involved the introduction of quality circles to the shopfloor of Ford's European car plants. The company invested substantial sums of money in the programme, which included the training of circle leaders and members in techniques of problem-solving and analysis. Three people were appointed to coordinate the programme at company level, and plant managers were responsible for circle activities in their plants. There was a short pilot project, after which quality circles were launched across all the plants in the UK. Guthrie (1987) suggests that there was little consultation with unions or lower levels of management, as senior management considered quality circles to be 'a minor change for the better'. In the six months or so following their introduction, some successes were documented (for example a 2.5 per cent saving in scrap at the Bridgend engine plant). However, union resistance was mounting, and in 1981 the trade unions withdrew their support from the programme. According to Guthrie's analysis, the programme was a 'resounding failure' in terms of its aims of improving work attitudes and generating net cost savings, for the reasons described in chapter 4.

In 1984, Ford began an attempt to introduce employee involvement amongst its 13,000 white-collar workers in Britain, but this too ran into trouble. At Dagenham, ASTMS demanded the disclosure of the five-year and ten-year business plans for the plant, a written guarantee of no redundancies, a pledge that staff would not be redeployed elsewhere, and agreement that only union members could be staff representatives on steering committees in the involvement scheme (*Financial Times*, 23 February 1985).

In 1987, an ASTMS national report distributed to senior negotiators expressed concern about quality circles on similar grounds to these behind resistance to them at Ford. It alleged that the circles contained only self-appointed or management-selected members, narrowed discussion to a worker's immediate environment, promoted an often false identification with management aims, failed to provide a means for distributing productivity gains due to circle suggestions, and leap-frogged the hierarchy of supervision and management through which commands normally flowed – a matter of obvious concern to ASTMS, as many of its members performed such jobs (*The Guardian*, 10 January 1987).

It is interesting to note that many of the features that distinguish conditions at Jaguar from those at Ford map onto much of the published survey evidence about quality circle success and failure. Dale and Hayward (1984) found that 42 companies out of 67 had experienced failure of parts of their quality circle programmes, and suggested that the failure rate was likely to increase as the programmes grew older. Eighteen of the 67 companies had suspended their programmes completely. In analysing the problems that companies face in running circle programmes, Hill (1986) distinguished between logistical reasons for quality circle failure, such as labour turnover, company restructuring and/or redundancies, and behavioural ones, such as hostility from key groups or lack of commitment. In practice, of course, so-called logistical problems may simply be manifestations of more deep-rooted behavioural problems. To illustrate this, Dale and Hayward's results are considered in tandem with Hill's in table 5.14. It should be noted that the Dale and Hayward figures refer to quality circle *failures*, whilst the Hill figures refer to *problems* faced by circles.

In terms of 'behavioural' rather than 'logistical' problems, it is interesting to note that resistance from middle management and supervisors is seen as a greater problem than trade union resistance. In another study of circles in 22 companies, Dale and Barlow (1984) noted that managerial resistance centred around fears that circles would show up managers' shortcomings as work organizers, and that their control and authority might be encroached upon. Drawing on accounts from the facilitators of quality circle programmes, Dale and Barlow identified the three most important conditions for quality circle success as: the 'unswerving support and commitment of senior, middle and supervisory management'; sustained management recognition and uncompromising support of circles; and the integration

Table 5.14 Problems faced by quality circles

	Dale and Hayward (1984)	*Hill (1986)*
Redundancies/restructuring	21.7% (54)	8.0% (3)
Turnover/loss of QC staff	19.3% (48)	5.0% (2)
Lack of QC leader/manager time	18.1% (45)	13.5% (5)
Lack of cooperation from middle management	18.1% (45)	13.5% (5)
Lack of cooperation from first-line supervisors	13.7% (34)	5.0% (2)
Trade union hostility	2.0% (5)	13.5% (5)

Source: Adapted from Dale and Hayward 1984 and Hill 1986

Table 5.15 'Ownership' of manufacturing reform (1991)

'Owners'	*Percentage reporting*
Chief executive/board	61
Manufacturing function	28
Corporate HQ	5
Interdisciplinary team	4
Other	2
N = 58	(100)

of circle activities with broader policies of employee involvement, training and development.

The majority of companies in our 1991 survey reported that their programmes of manufacturing reform (not just quality circle initiatives) were 'owned' by senior management, which, in theory at least, should facilitate their success (table 5.15).

For a significant minority of companies – approximately one-third – ownership of their programmes of reform was vested in the manufacturing function. Noticeable by their paucity are programmes of reform 'owned' by multi-disciplinary teams, which some commentators have argued are important for successful implementation (Kanter 1985).

When we began our analysis of Japanese-style practices, our feeling was that quality circles, not being central to the production process, were unlikely to have major ramifications when implemented – in contrast to JIT, which carries obvious implications for power relations. In the light of the evidence, two conclusions emerge, which are, in a sense, different sides of the same coin. The first concerns the conditions necessary for successful circle implementation and operation, the second concerns the effects that a circle programme, once implemented, can have on the wider organization. Considering the facilitating conditions first, the contrast between Ford and Jaguar is informative. Partly by force of circumstance, partly by design, Jaguar was successful in creating the conditions for circles to flourish. The company had a strong identity and a product in which the workforce had traditionally taken pride. Meanwhile, the combination of financial crisis and dislike of being part of British Leyland probably functioned to unite groups usually antagonistic to each other. (An indicator of this is how privatization was welcomed by management and workers alike as a means of freeing Jaguar from British Leyland.) The fact that many of the managers had worked their way up through the company by means of internal promotion, rather than entering it as graduates, may also have assisted in this – note the similarity here to Japanese practice. Of course, this is not to say that the community of interests was such that there was no conflict – indeed, there were a number of strikes in 1984 in the first round of pay talks following privatization.

The manner in which Jaguar introduced quality circles is also significant to their success. The comprehensive communications programme ensured that quality was seen as an issue of genuine importance, and not just the slogan of the week. The obvious commitment of top management and its preparedness to give the circles a genuine capacity to attack problems provided further support. Trade union concerns were largely allayed by ensuring that industrial relations issues were excluded from circle affairs; the no-redundancy promise shows an interesting parallel to elements of the Japanese system, and helped to overcome concerns about job losses as a consequence of efficiency gains.

These features contrasted markedly with those present in the case of Ford. There, circles were introduced into an environment of highly adversarial relations, and with little or no consultation of the key interest groups concerned. Given that circles were introduced into such an environment, in such a manner, their failure is unsurprising. Guthrie (1987, p. 31) concludes:

> Quality circles are a feature of a very different management technique
> to that practised by Ford. They can and do lead to improved quality
> of work, if that is what the company is really aiming for. They do not
> allow an autocratic management to get more for less out of an unwilling
> workforce. The unions saw the programme for what, at least in part,
> it was: manipulation.

The evidence from companies' experiences with quality circles thus seems to bear out our argument in chapter 2 that many Japanese-style techniques depend on an appropriate set of supporting conditions if they are to operate successfully. In many ways, the nature of quality circles renders them particularly sensitive to this. Because participation in them is voluntary, and hence seen as something beyond the employment contract, companies using them are particularly dependent on the goodwill and cooperation of their workforces. Given this heightened dependency, we would expect to find successful circle programmes in companies where such cooperation exists, whether by accident or design. The cases of Ford and Jaguar seem to bear this out.

However, since our analysis in 1987, events have moved on apace. By the late 1980s the appreciation of the pound against the dollar had taken its toll on Jaguar's sales in North America, and reports appeared in the press indicating that all was not well in the company. In 1990, Jaguar was taken over by Ford, showing that success with practices such as the use of quality circles does not, of itself, provide protection against superior financial 'muscle'.

As was argued in the conclusion to chapter 2, there are sound theoretical reasons for viewing the new manufacturing and personnel practices as a 'package' or 'socio-technical system'. When the factors that the companies surveyed in 1991 reported as being the major obstacles to change are considered (table 5.16), this situation appears to be confirmed.

Clearly table 5.16 confounds 'management of change' issues with those likely to be encountered when the new systems settle down to a steady state. What is striking from the table is the significance of human factors, the catch-all category of 'existing culture' being the single most frequently cited obstacle to change. Technical constraints

Table 5.16   Obstacles to change in UK companies

	Number of citations as:			
	First obstacle	Second obstacle	Third obstacle	Percentage of total
Existing culture	17	–	–	27
Unions/demarcation	6	3	–	14
Lack of support at senior levels	7	2	–	14
None	8	–	–	13
Attitudes of middle management	4	2	1	11
Attitudes of labour	–	3	2	8
Lack of resources/investment	3	2	–	8
Technical constraints	2	1	–	5
	(47)	(13)	(3)	(100)

and the availability of resources did not appear to be particularly prevalent as obstacles, receiving just 5 and 8 per cent of citations respectively.

The data reported here thus appear to support the idea that the success of the major Japanese corporations *cannot* be readily assigned to any specific set of practices, such as manufacturing methods or personnel policies, in isolation. What appears to be critical is the goodness of fit between a set of business strategies and a set of wider supporting conditions.

In the chapter that follows, we explore this theme further by examining the personnel practices that the UK companies are – or are not – implementing alongside their Japanese-style manufacturing systems.

6

Personnel Practices and UK Companies

At a number of points in our analysis of British companies' attempts to emulate Japanese manufacturing practice, we have touched on the role of appropriate workforce attitudes and a conducive industrial relations climate in the successful operation of these practices. In some cases, the link is very explicit. AB Electronics is one example, in the context of flexible working; while the experiences of Jaguar and Ford illustrate the importance of the right climate within an organization if quality circles are to take root and operate successfully.

Our argument is simple: many Japanese-style manufacturing practices require *willing cooperation*, not mere compliance, on the part of a workforce. Examples of such cooperation include: a willingness to perform a range of tasks; the commitment to engage in activities of continuous improvement; and a preparedness to do what is required to satisfy one's customers – be they internal or external. This implies that if an organization wishes to operate a manufacturing system with these characteristics, an appropriate set of personnel and industrial relations strategies needs to be in place to support it.

Although not necessarily modelled on Japanese personnel practices directly, many of the practices that form part of the currently fashionable 'human resource management' (HRM) movement appear to constitute the functional equivalents of practices found in the major Japanese corporations. Guest (1987) has identified an idealized model of HRM, the core elements of which are summarized in table 6.1.

The pressures driving the apparent rise of HRM are many. Peters and Waterman's *In Search of Excellence* set the stage for the 'excellence movement' and popularized many of the issues; but, as we have seen, in the manufacturing sphere the capacity of Japanese

Table 6.1 Premises of personnel management and HRM

	Personnel management	*HRM*
Time and planning perspective	Short-term, ad hoc, marginal	Long-term, strategic, integrated
Psychological contract	Compliance	Commitment
Control system	External controls	Self-control
Employee relations perspective	Pluralist – collective – low-trust	Unitarist – individual – high-trust
Preferred structures and systems	Bureaucratic – centralized – formal roles	Organic – devolved – flexible roles

Source: Adapted from Guest 1987

companies to produce high-quality goods at (relatively) low cost has given Western industries some formidable benchmarks to aim at.

Despite differences in their philosophical and contextual roots, the functional similarity between HRM principles and *some* Japanese-style practices is quite striking. Characteristic of the HRM package are: (1) an ethos that places a high value on product or service quality; (2) a customer-driven or market-driven ethos (which, in the purest examples, pervades the whole organization through the concept of internal as well as external 'customers'); and (3) intensive and explicit measurement of performance of individuals and units within the organization.

A capacity for flexibility, innovation and continuous improvement is frequently found alongside these attributes. Work is typically structured around work teams, which operate with a degree of autonomy and have clearly recognizable inputs and outputs. In manufacturing organizations, these groups are likely to have responsibility for the quality of their work (traditionally a prerogative of specialist quality control departments) and also for routine maintenance. The performance of the team, and individuals within it, may be evaluated against a range of targets: volume of output, quality of output and financial performance. (Recent reviews of these developments in the manufacturing sector may be found in *Industrial Relations Review and Report* 415, May 1988 and *Incomes Data Services*, Study 419, October 1988.)

The 'excellence' model clearly implies a shift in terms of the demands of organizations upon their employees. In tandem with the distinctive orientation towards product and service quality, is an equally distinctive approach to the management of people, a basket of ideas typically found under the label of 'human resource management'. Guest (1987) argues that HRM not only represents a radically different model from that of 'traditional' personnel management (as shown in table 6.1), but is actually displacing traditional approaches.

Legge (1988) gives four contrasting interpretations of current developments affecting personnel practices in the UK and the management of labour. These are: (1) *the fall of personnel management*, suggesting that recession and structural change during the 1980s have undermined the power of labour, so diminishing the power and position of personnel departments; (2) *the rise of macho management*, suggesting that there is a new breed of tough managers (epitomized by prominent individuals such as Michael Edwardes and Ian McGregor), who feel little need or inclination to negotiate with labour; (3) the concept of *business as before*, which assumes that little has changed; and (4) the notion of *flexible management for flexible firms*, which argues that a new form of industrial organization (the flexible firm or the Japanese model) is emerging, with a commensurate set of personnel practices broadly consistent with those found under the HRM label – IBM and Marks and Spencer frequently being cited as role models.

The HRM label covers a basket of practices, including: single-status terms and conditions; generous welfare benefits; relatively generous wages (or more likely salaries); output-based controls, often driven by extensive performance measurement and appraisal at all organizational levels; single-union or non-union industrial relations; comprehensive internal communications systems; team-based working; and sophisticated employee selection, induction and development programmes.

The extent to which such practices are finding concrete expression has been a topic of some debate in the late 1980s and early 1990s. With this in mind, both our 1987 and 1991 surveys explored the way and degree in which certain personnel practices were being adopted by companies operating in Britain. The criterion for the inclusion of practices was whether they were conducive to the employee relations

Table 6.2   Personnel practices in UK companies (1987)

Practice	Planned or never used (%)	In use (%)	Being implemented (%)
In-company communications	3	89	8
Employee involvement	3	88	9
Single-status facilities	12	80	8
'Staff' benefits at all levels	9	74	17
High security for core workers	32	68	–
Substantial use (10%+) of temporary workers	44	56	–
N (number in sample) = 64			

climate necessary to support Japanese-style manufacturing systems. Thus, Western personnel practices that appeared to perform similar *functions* to those found in Japan were included, even if they did not exist (in precisely the same form) in Japan itself.

The 1987 survey revealed a less dramatic picture than that found in the case of manufacturing practices, though one that is nonetheless interesting in its own right. Table 6.2 shows the status of the six Japanese-style personnel practices that it explored.

A very high proportion of companies (over 70 per cent) reported the use of comprehensive in-company communications, employee involvement schemes, single-status facilities and 'staff' benefits at all levels. Approximately two-thirds claimed to offer high job security to their core workers, and about half reported a substantial use (defined as 10 per cent plus) of staff on temporary contracts.

When the dates of introduction of these practices were analysed, a markedly different pattern was apparent from that for the production methods. Although the incidence of the personnel practices showed a marked upward trend over time, this trend was both less recent and increased less sharply than in the case of manufacturing methods, as table 6.3 demonstrates.

In 1987, the most recent of the personnel practices by median date of introduction was the use of temporary workers, a pattern consistent with national trends at that time. Although table 6.3 indicates a sharp upward trend, it should be noted from table 6.2 that no companies reported that they were in the process of planning or implementing policies based on a substantial use of temporary workers. (The pattern for part-time staff revealed an even lower incidence of usage, and less of an upward trend.) This may be attributable to the fact that the firms surveyed in 1987 were large, 'core' manufacturing companies. The NEDO report on flexibility referred to previously suggested that it was primarily the service sector that was adopting strategies based on numerical flexibility, such as the use of part-time or temporary staff, whereas manufacturing industry was relying more on overtime and functional flexibility; and the 1987 results are consistent with this.

The 1987 survey also showed employee involvement schemes, such as team briefings, to have a median date of introduction of 1983. There was a marked upward trend in the incidence of such schemes in the mid-1980s, probably in line with the increasing interest in teamwork and perhaps quality circles. In-company communications appeared to have a longer pedigree, with a steady increase apparent from the mid-1960s onwards, albeit with a slight dip in the mid-1970s. Similar patterns were discernible in the case of single-status facilities and staff-type benefits for blue-collar workers, although the median date of introduction of these practices was 1977. Of the six practices described here, the provision of 'staff' benefits at all levels in the organization looked set to show the sharpest increase, with 17 per cent of companies at the stage of planning or implementing harmonization policies.

High security of employment for core workers, one of the best-known characteristics of the major Japanese corporations, does not appear to have been a new development in these companies, suggesting that those companies that claimed to offer it had not introduced it in connection with new Japanese-style production methods. Indeed, the pattern was of a decline in the incidence of promises about job security in the period 1983–7.

The equivalent picture in 1991 is shown in table 6.4. We had treated some of the 1987 results on personnel practices with some suspicion, on the grounds that they presented a rather more 'advanced' picture than our experience suggested was the case. This was due to slight ambiguity in the wording of some items in the original survey. For example, it was felt that items such as 'employee involvement', 'in-company communications' and 'high job security' covered such a range of practices that their meaning was open to wide interpretation. For this reason, some modifications were made to the wording of a number of the items, with a view to improving the

Table 6.3 Dates of introduction of personnel practices by UK companies (1987)

	Pre-1942	1943–1947	1948–1952	1953–1957	1958–1962	1963–1967	1968–1972	1973–1977	1978–1982	1983–1987	Median date	Number in sample
10%+ temporary workers	–	–	–	–	–	1 (5%)	–	–	6 (32%)	12 (63%)	1983	19
Employee involvement	1 (2%)	–	–	–	1 (2%)	3 (7%)	5 (12%)	4 (10%)	6 (15%)	21 (51%)	1983	41
In-company communications	3 (7%)	–	1 (2%)	–	1 (2%)	3 (7%)	6 (14%)	4 (10%)	11 (26%)	13 (31%)	1980	42
Single status	1 (3%)	–	1 (3%)	2 (5%)	2 (5%)	3 (8%)	5 (13%)	6 (15%)	9 (23%)	10 (26%)	1977	39
'Staff' benefits	1 (3%)	–	–	–	1 (3%)	4 (12%)	4 (12%)	3 (9%)	10 (29%)	11 (32%)	1977	34
High security of employment	3 (18%)	–	–	–	1 (6%)	1 (6%)	3 (18%)	3 (18%)	5 (29%)	1 (6%)	1973	17

Table 6.4 Personnel practices in UK companies (1991)

Practice	Never used (%)	In use (%)	Planned or being implemented (%)
Team briefings	5	89	6
Use of temporary workers	38	59	3
Single-status facilities	36	49	15
Performance-related pay	28	64	8
Company council	41	58	1
Profit sharing	39	53	8
Performance appraisal	25	48	27
N = 66			

precision of the results. The price of this is some loss of comparability between the two surveys, but we feel that this is offset by a more accurate picture of actual practice in the second survey.

In the 1991 survey, 'team briefings', the replacement item for in-company communications and employee involvement, appeared with equal frequency to its predecessors, with almost all companies already employing the practice. The use of temporary workers showed a slight increase, up from 56 per cent in 1987 to 62 per cent in 1991; while single-status facilities appeared to be rather less popular, being used or planned by 64 per cent of companies in the 1991 survey, compared with 88 per cent in 1987.

The 1991 survey extended the scope of its predecessor by adding a series of questions about practices that, though not necessarily 'Japanese' in origin, seemed to offer some functional equivalents to Japanese practices by tying the fortunes of a workforce, individually or collectively, more closely to those of the company. Thus, we asked about the status of performance appraisal (for blue-collar as well as white-collar workers), performance-related pay, company councils, and profit-sharing schemes. As table 6.5 illustrates, extensive use of all these practices was reported, with performance appraisal apparently attracting the greatest surge of interest.

Our interpretation of the data on personnel practices from the 1987 survey was that many of the sample companies had introduced them for different reasons and under different pressures from those influencing the adoption of Japanese manufacturing practices. The

Table 6.5 Dates of introduction of personnel practices by UK companies (1991)

	Pre- 1957 (%)	1958– 1962 (%)	1963– 1967 (%)	1968– 1972 (%)	1973– 1977 (%)	1978– 1982 (%)	1983– 1987 (%)	1988– 1992 (%)	Median date	Number in sample
Performance appraisal	–	–	–	8	4	4	20	64	1989	25
Single-status facilities	5	5	–	9	–	14	32	35	1987	22
Use of temporary workers	–	–	–	5	9	5	50	31	1987	22
Team briefings	–	–	5	3	–	16	20	56	1987	44
Profit sharing	4	–	–	11	–	7	48	30	1987	27
Performance-related pay	15	4	7	7	7	7	22	30	1986	27
Company council	21	–	4	8	21	8	17	21	1983	24

Table 6.6 Evaluation of personnel/industrial relations practices by UK companies (1987)

Practice	Not successful (%)	Quite–very successful (%)	Highly successful (%)	Mean*
Single-status facilities	–	64	36	3.15
'Staff' benefits for all	–	62	38	3.09
High job security	–	64	36	2.97
Employee involvement	5	76	19	2.76
Substantial use (10%+) of temporary workers	6	80	14	2.69
In-company communications	3	78	19	2.66
N = 45				

*1 = Not successful   4 = Highly successful

earlier dates of introduction of many personnel practices – particularly the slight 'humps' around the late 1960s and early 1970s – suggested changes driven by personnel departments at a time when progressive employment policies were associated with the 'quality of working life' movement.

Evaluation of personnel practices

On the whole, in 1987 personnel practices were evaluated slightly more favourably than manufacturing practices (table 6.6).

Policies concerning the harmonization of employment conditions, such as single-status facilities and staff-type benefits for other grades of workers were the most favourably rated. This may not be surprising given that harmonization is likely to be welcomed by most blue-collar unions. In some cases (for example at Ford), in-company communications were viewed as attempts to bypass shop stewards; this may explain their relatively low rating in the table. Comparison of the 1987 and the 1991 evaluations (shown in table 6.7) shows that, on average, perceptions of the success of personnel practices were generally lower in 1991 than they were in 1987.

The difference between 1987 and 1991 is particularly marked in the case of single status. In relative terms, it is those practices that *in theory* are concerned with creating a 'community of interests' within

Table 6.7   Evaluation of personnel/industrial relations practices by UK companies (1991)

Practice	Not successful (%)	Quite–very successful (%)	Highly successful (%)	Mean
Team briefings	–	80	20	2.80
Single-status facilities	9	68	23	2.74
Use of temporary workers	9	74	17	2.60
Profit sharing	18	64	18	2.44
Performance appraisal	12	74	15	2.35
Company council	9	88	3	2.34
Performance-related pay	17	74	9	2.33
N = 66				

the firm – profit sharing, company councils and performance appraisal and performance-related pay – that receive the lowest ratings.

What both the 1987 and 1991 survey data suggest is that although many changes in manufacturing may be driven by the 'Japanese' model, personnel practices seem to be driven by a plethora of models and forces. Personnel practices such as the harmonization of employment conditions had a longer history in the 1987 survey companies than did the production methods discussed previously. This suggests that their introduction was not necessarily part of a package – a total business strategy – comprising production methods and employment practices.

In order to test this idea, simple statistical (correlational) analyses of the 1987 data were performed to explore how far manufacturing practices were supported by appropriate personnel practices. This was done in two ways. First, correlations (measures of association) were computed between the various *degrees of usage* of each practice. This was done in order to establish whether those companies that made extensive use of, for example, quality circles also tended to be the ones that offered high security of employment. The most striking point about the results of this analysis was the *lack* of association between the use of Japanese-style manufacturing practices and the use of Japanese-style personnel practices. Although there was some evidence of certain practices coming in 'clusters', this was almost entirely confined to clusters of *manufacturing* practices or clusters of *personnel* practices, and rarely involved a mix of both. For example, there were significant correlations between the use of JIT and the use of total quality control, quality circles and group technology or work teams. However, those companies most extensively using JIT did not appear to be those that were using the personnel practices that, from a socio-technical systems perspective, it would appear to be prudent to implement to ensure adequate levels of stability and dependability in such a fragile system. Unsurprisingly, however, those companies that used substantial in-company communication also tended to exhibit greater employee involvement, and also reported greater use of single-status facilities.

To add a slightly different perspective on the issue, the same analysis was performed to see if practices could be grouped together by *date of introduction* rather than by degree of usage. Again, broadly the same pattern emerged; certain practices did tend to bunch together, but relationships between the introduction of JIT and practices likely to be supportive of harmonious industrial relations were conspicuous primarily by their absence. Those practices that did cluster together in this analysis were quality circles, work teams, flexible working and practices concerning involvement, communication, single status and the provision of 'staff' benefits to blue-collar workers. Furthermore, and in conformity with the findings from the NEDO report on flexible working, those companies that reported extensive *functional* flexibility made significantly less use of the numerically flexible labour strategy of employing temporary workers.

Direct communication and single status

Extensive communication systems, employee involvement schemes, and harmonized terms and conditions of service all have relatively long histories in the UK. Our argument is simply that, where appropriate personnel practices do not exist, or where they are inadequate, the introduction of Japanese-style manufacturing practices will be problematic. This was demonstrated previously in relation to Ford's failure with quality circles. In contrast, Jaguar was successful in part because of strong communication and a more genuine involvement on the part of employees. As we saw, the threat perceived by middle managers as arising from the introduction of employee involvement through quality circles, for instance, can lead to the subversion and ultimate failure of such schemes. Similarly, AB Electronics achieved flexible working practices in part by introducing an open communication system, and at the same time a harmonization policy; in addition, this company compelled its operating units to devote substantial resources to training, to ensure that its workforce was capable of flexible working.

On the basis of the case study and anecdotal evidence presented previously, it appears that many of the companies emulating Japanese manufacturing practices face difficulties in introducing them partly because of their existing employee relations climates – as is indicated by the frequent reports of 'them-and-us' attitude problems.

Selection, recruitment and socialization

Unlike Japanese companies newly investing in the UK, the emulators are mostly attempting to impose Japanese-style practices on managers and workforces accustomed to different ways of working; thus established attitudes, values and patterns of behaviour have to be addressed. This is particularly the case where, as in most British manufacturing companies, the changes are sought in the absence of rapid growth, and hence opportunities to adjust the constitution of a labour force. The 1991 survey addressed this issue by asking respondents to identify their main criteria for selecting new workers. Responses to this question are shown in table 6.8.

The table indicates that the 'traditional' selection criteria of previous experience and skills are the ones most frequently cited in connection with the recruitment of blue-collar workers. However, established manufacturers also appear to be shifting their selection criteria towards attributes such as the possession of appropriate attitudes, 'fit' with the desired culture and so on, which rank closely behind more traditional experience-based criteria.

For some companies, attitude appears to be of paramount importance. For example, as we saw in chapter 4, attitudes and characteristics in line with the company's ends are important at Rover, being considered at least as important as technical skills and abilities. The focus on attitudes rather than technical skills is by no means unusual in companies adopting Japanese manufacturing techniques. In the words of a team leader quoted earlier, 'you could almost forget the job spec. and write attitude.'

What is clear is that many emulators are faced with significant adjustment problems. This may take the form of reluctance and cynicism from both middle managers and workers. Hence Smith (1988) reports that, at Rover, zone briefings often degenerated into

Table 6.8 Selection criteria for blue-collar employees in UK companies (1991)

| Attributes | Number of citations as: | | | |
	First criterion	Second criterion	Third criterion	Percentage of total citations
Experience, skills	30	7	1	32
Personality, attitude, cultural 'fit'	9	14	7	25
Numeracy, literacy	8	4	1	11
Dexterity, fitness	7	5	–	10
Qualifications	2	4	–	5
Team-working ability	3	3	1	6
Trainability	1	1	1	2
Communication skills	1	1	–	2
Capacity for shifts	1	1	–	2
Other	2	1	3	5
	(64)	(41)	(14)	(100)

what team leaders saw as 'time-wasting sessions' and production workers as nothing more than a 'welcome break'. The failure of Ford's quality circles suggests the same problem.

Again, the early experiences of Jaguar may be exceptional in this regard. Here, a shift to total quality principles was achieved through serious attention to the re-socialization of workers and managers, with resources directed into a communications programme of significant proportions. Jaguar was also fortunate insofar as it was commonly agreed that the alternative to new working practices was almost certain bankruptcy, and to the extent that there already was a degree of pride in, and identification with, the company's product. More recently, Jaguar's fortunes have been less rosy, and the extent to which genuine change has occurred is debatable, indicating the sheer scale of the task of reorienting a company's culture.

Management–union relations

A final constraining factor on the introduction of Japanese-style manufacturing and working practices by the emulating companies is the existing state of management–union relations. Unions were on the defensive in the 1980s, and this has clearly carried forward into the 1990s, but as chapter 3 demonstrated, the high dependencies that Japanese manufacturing systems create mean that high degrees of cooperation are demanded from all parties. A simple lack of goodwill on the part of a trade union can be sufficient to pose major problems. The existence of any independent and potentially adversarial party constitutes a threat to Japanese-style manufacturing methods, due to the inherent fragility of the system involved. Yet most emulating companies are faced with several independent trade unions whose rationale is the protection and advancement of the interests of particular occupational groups. Our analysis suggests that the full-blown adoption of these manufacturing methods demands the transformation of this situation into one where the union, if a union exists at all, is responsible for the whole of the company's workforce and identifies an association between company success and workers' interests. Because unions in the emulating companies were typically on the defensive during the 1980s, their resistance to the process of change appears to have been at a local, 'covert' level. This subversive activity may continue to be a major impediment in many cases. In addition, as long as the emulating companies merely take advantage of the apparently weak position of trade unions, they risk the possibility of overt resistance and conflict at some point in the future. In the late 1980s, Ford's plans for teamwork faced overt resistance from its manual workers' unions, which were demanding that the company should drop plans for skilled workers to be available to man production lines. By 1991, there were few signs that the company had made significant progress on these schemes.

Conclusions

Many British and established foreign-owned companies in the UK are now committed to major programmes of manufacturing reform following the Japanese model. However, they face substantial obstacles – problems that often relate either to an unawareness of the importance of managing the heightened dependency relations that arise in this context effectively, or perhaps more often to an inability or incapacity to cope with these heightened dependencies. In this chapter, we focused on the consequences of the heightened dependencies of companies on their employees. New communications, pay grading and selection systems are examples of means by which workers may be made more likely to identify with the company; however, the data from the 1991 survey suggest that the creation of a 'community of interests' – or at least a perception of it – may be the most difficult trick to effect. In the chapter that follows, we extend this analysis outside the boundaries of the single organization, and explore changes in the buyer–supplier relationship.

7

Suppliers, Retailers and UK Companies

As we saw in chapter 2, buyer–supplier relationships in Japan are characterized by higher trust, longer-lasting commitments and more obligational demands than their Western equivalents. In 1987, relatively little had been written about the transplantation of the Japanese model of buyer–supplier relations to the West; by 1991, the literature on this topic had burgeoned. We shall review the situation as it appeared from our 1987 survey, compare this with the results of our 1991 survey and then consider recent developments.

The 1987 survey examined three elements of 'Japanese' buyer–supplier relations in the British context: the use of sub-contracting, quality assured supplies and JIT supply, as shown in table 7.1.

As table 7.1 illustrates, the most widely employed practice of those investigated was the contracting out of non-core activities, with 87 per cent of companies reporting that they used sub-contractors. Rather less use was then being made of quality assured and just-in-time supplies. These two practices go very much hand in hand, as it is not feasible to operate the latter in the absence of the former. About a quarter of the sample reported that they were implementing or planning to implement them. These results were consistent with those of Voss and Robinson (1987), who had found that about 50 per cent of companies with JIT programmes had implemented, or were planning to implement, JIT purchasing. The dates of introduction of these practices indicated by the 1987 survey are given in table 7.2.

Buyer–supplier practices presented a similar picture to that given by manufacturing methods in terms of the recency of their introduction. In the 1987 survey, just-in-time supply systems were recent arrivals, with 1986 as their median date of introduction. Quality assured supplies came next, with a median introduction date of 1985, followed by sub-contracting of non-core activities, with a median of 1980 as its date of introduction. Anecdotal evidence from

Table 7.1 Buyer–supplier practices in UK companies (1987)

Practice	Never used (%)	In use (%)	Planned or being implemented (%)
Sub-contracting (non-core)	8	87	5
Quality assured supplies	16	61	23
Just-in-time supplies	31	42	27
N (number in sample) = 64			

visits to companies suggested some problems with these figures. First, in some companies 'non-core' activities involved little more than catering, security and cleaning operations; many organizations have contracted out such activities for years. Of more significance was the increase in the sub-contracting out of parts of the production process according to a value-added analysis of their operations. This manifested itself as the question 'make or buy?' Our impression of the nature of sub-contracting amongst the companies in the 1987 sample was that sub-contracting of the former rather than the latter type was predominant.

In the light of these concerns, the 1991 survey dropped sub-contracting as an item, but added some additional items on supplier development, supplier involvement in design and single sourcing. The status of these practices is shown in table 7.3 and their dates of introduction in table 7.4.

Compared with the 1987 data, those in table 7.3 show increases in the use of both JIT supplies (up 17 per cent) and quality assured supplies (up 22 per cent). Practices indicating close buyer–supplier relations – supplier involvement in design, supplier development activities and single sourcing – all show significant usage, with approximately two-thirds of companies using or planning to use each practice. Two-thirds of companies reported that they had had programmes to reduce their supplier base in recent years, which is consistent with reports of moves towards single sourcing. For the majority of companies, this falls short of the Japanese practice of taking a financial stake in the supplier – slightly less than 20 per cent of companies reported holding a financial stake in their suppliers.

Tables 7.5 and 7.6 show companies' evaluation of their buyer–supplier practices in 1987 and 1991 respectively.

Table 7.2 Dates of introduction of buyer–supplier practices by UK companies (1987)

	Pre-1942	1943–1947	1948–1952	1953–1957	1958–1962	1963–1967	1968–1972	1973–1977	1978–1982	1983–1987	Median date	Number in sample
Just-in-time supplies	1 (4%)	–	1 (4%)	1 (4%)	1 (4%)	1 (4%)	1 (4%)	–	1 (4%)	16 (70%)	1986	23
Quality assured supplies	1 (4%)	–	–	–	–	1 (4%)	1 (4%)	2 (7%)	2 (7%)	20 (74%)	1985	27
Sub-contracting of non-core activities	1 (3%)	–	–	–	–	3 (8%)	2 (6%)	2 (6%)	15 (42%)	13 (36%)	1980	36

Table 7.3   Buyer–supplier practices in UK companies (1991)

Practice	Never used (%)	In use (%)	Planned or being implemented (%)
JIT supplies	28	59	13
QA supplies	5	83	12
Single sourcing	27	65	8
Supplier development	25	68	7
Supplier involvement in design	33	63	4
N = 66			

The least successful practice in both years has been just-in-time supplies (13 per cent unsuccessful in 1987). For JIT supply to operate successfully two conditions have to be met. First, the quality must be right, as there is little or no slack in the system if products are unusable. Secondly, and self-evidently, the goods must arrive on time; with little stock in the system a late delivery can mean disaster. As the levels of complaints about quality assured supplies (5 per cent unsuccessful in 1987, 7 per cent unsuccessful in 1991) are low, it is probably delivery, rather than quality, that has been the problem area.

JIT and QA supplies clearly both demand a new role from the purchasing function. The case of one company visited by the authors that had both moved over to internal JIT production and had contracted out production previously performed in-house is instructive. In making these changes, the company had run into trouble; buyers had not yet adapted to the new situation, and this was reflected in numerous problems on the shopfloor. Many of the sub-contracts were felt to be unsatisfactory, and much of the blame for this was put on the purchasing department:

> Everyone is twitching about stuff coming in from outside . . . unfortunately we've gone off half-cocked – on the supply side especially . . . In the buying office you need people who not only have an input into what they're buying, but also into what we're producing as well.

Table 7.4 Dates of introduction of buyer–supplier practices by UK companies (1991)

	Pre-1957 (%)	1958–1962 (%)	1963–1967 (%)	1968–1972 (%)	1973–1977 (%)	1978–1982 (%)	1983–1987 (%)	1988–1992 (%)	Median date	Number in sample
JIT supplies	–	–	–	–	–	6	36	58	1989	33
QA supplies	3	3	–	3	3	8	29	51.	1988	38
Single sourcing	–	–	–	–	5	–	24	71	1989	21
Supplier development	–	–	4	4	–	4	32	56	1989	28
Supplier involvement in design	4	–	8	4	–	12	21	51	1988	24

Table 7.5 Evaluation of buyer–supplier practices by UK companies (1987)

Practice	Not successful (%)	Quite–very successful (%)	Highly successful (%)	Mean*
Sub-contracting	–	83	17	2.69
QA supplies	5	84	11	2.41
Just-in-time supplies	13	74	13	2.29
N = 64				

*1 = Not successful 4 = Highly successful

Table 7.6 Evaluation of buyer–supplier practices by UK companies (1991)

Practice	Not successful (%)	Quite–very successful (%)	Highly successful (%)	Mean
QA supplies	7	80	13	2.55
Supplier development	5	81	14	2.52
Supplier involvement in design	7	83	10	2.49
Single sourcing	5	88	7	2.35
JIT supplies	2	93	5	2.30
N = 66				

Product quality and buyer–supplier relations

One firm that led the way in the mid-to-late 1980s in terms of changing the nature of its relationships with its suppliers was the Ford Motor Company. In the company's words:

> To improve the quality of bought-out parts, Ford is reducing its supply base, changing the emphasis on quality assurances and encouraging a greater supplier involvement in the product ... which helps build a long-term relationship with Ford. (Ford Motor Company 1984)

As about 50 per cent of the parts that go into a Ford car are manufactured by outside suppliers, the quality of these parts will obviously have a crucial bearing on the performance of the finished product. In its 1984 'Durability, Quality and Reliability' report, Ford declared its intention to reduce the number of its suppliers by 33 per cent and to source its components:

> . . . only from those with a proven quality track record who can show they have the necessary control systems in existence consistently to produce components to specification. As the number of suppliers is reduced, it is only those prepared to make the effort *and honour the trust placed in them* [our emphasis] who will obtain an increasing share of the Ford business.

Prior to recent changes, Ford operated a scheme of supplier quality assurance for many years. This scheme was used to survey and check the adequacy of the control systems that the suppliers were using. The emphasis has now shifted much more to *self-certification* by the supplier, whereby suppliers are held totally responsible for the quality of their products: they become more involved in their design, and are held accountable for their performance once fitted to completed vehicles. Ford has been the UK leader in supplier development, with its well-known Q101 quality manual of the early 1980s (of which 40,000 copies were printed) clearly spelling out the expectations that it had of its suppliers. Throughout the 1980s Ford laid on substantial training programmes for its suppliers in techniques such as statistical process control, although in 1987 suppliers were charged £250 per day for such training. Many other companies have copied Ford's Q101 programme; some have even simply photocopied pages from it, removed the Ford logos, and included it in their quality documentation to suppliers. In the late 1980s Q101 was superseded by Q1, which represented an even more exacting standard for suppliers to meet.

Other buyers, particularly in the motor industry, have followed Ford's lead with extensive programmes of supplier development. In 1991, Rover published its 'Supplier Business Specification RG 2000', which states that:

> In addition to requiring supplier accreditation to BS5750 . . . Rover Group will be assessing suppliers' attitudes towards employees and the philosophy of total quality. We also want to understand how our suppliers determine their corporate strategy and organize their businesses to best satisfy customers' requirements. Equally important is

the need for the Rover Group and its suppliers to continuously review our businesses with regard to management, planning, and cost reduction to ensure long term growth and the ability to invest in the future. The publication of RG 2000 is an acknowledgement by Rover Group that we need to form close lasting partnerships with suppliers to maintain successful, competitive businesses into the next century. (Rover Group Purchasing 1991, p. 3)

Clearly the behaviour of Ford and Rover towards their suppliers bears some resemblance to elements of Japanese buyer–supplier relationships. From the suppliers' point of view, though, their marriage with Ford has been undertaken under some pressure. The fact that all the motor manufacturers have been reducing their numbers of suppliers has created a degree of competition among the latter that has certainly assisted the assemblers in getting their requirements accepted and implemented. This development applies not only to relatively small suppliers, but also to suppliers who may themselves be large multinational companies. For example, in 1984, Pirelli (which supplies tyres and seat suspension to the motor industry) invested heavily in sophisticated computerized quality information systems, partly because of pressure from Ford to do so (Oliver 1986). Rover's recent documentation indicates that as buyer–supplier relations move forward towards 'partnerships' – a phrase used more often by the assemblers than by the suppliers – more and more of the suppliers' internal operations are likely to come under the scrutiny of their customers.

The suppliers that we have talked to certainly seem to see the changes as having been more or less forced on them, although, once implemented, the advantages of practices such as SPC have not gone unnoticed by the suppliers themselves. Southern Components regards SPC as the 'best Japanese import', a sentiment echoed by managers at Ketlon Ltd.

How far these changes represent a genuine mirroring of Japanese buyer–supplier relationships is difficult to ascertain. As far as quality assurance is concerned, a case could be made for suggesting that there are signs of closer, more cooperative relationships emerging. When we turn to JIT supply, a slightly different picture is apparent.

JIT supply

As we saw in chapter 1, just-in-time supply is widely used between customers and suppliers in Japan, and as the case of Southern

Components illustrates, is a practice that is increasingly being adopted by many UK-based companies. However, the theoretical framework outlined in chapter 3 suggests that simply removing the 'safety nets' of buffer stocks, goods-inward inspection and so on carries a price in terms of increased dependency of the buyer on the supplier, particularly when combined with purchasing policies based on a restricted set of suppliers. This has led some commentators to question the wisdom of adopting these techniques in the UK. For example Ramsey (1985) has argued that:

> The combination of minimal safety stocks and single-sourcing is perfectly rational and desirable for Japanese purchasing departments, but highly risky for their UK counterparts. Adopting Japanese purchasing techniques without first creating conditions in the UK economy comparable to those in Japan appears foolhardy . . . single sourcing plus a just-in-time stockholding policy looks suspiciously like a recipe for disaster.

In support of this, Ramsey compares the number of working days lost through industrial stoppages in Japan and the UK in the period 1978–82. In the UK, 532 working days were lost per thousand employees. The equivalent figure for the same period in Japan was 23. The results from both our surveys of the adoption of Japanese practices in the UK certainly provide some confirmation of Ramsey's view, with JIT supply being rated as one of the relatively less successful Japanese 'imports'. Consistent with this, quality assured supplies are rated highly relative to other supplier-related practices, but relatively low compared with manufacturing practices. Other evidence also suggests that JIT supply has aggravated the effects of disruption in the motor industry. In October 1986, for example, 12,000 people were laid off at Austin Rover due to industrial action at Lucas Electrical's Cannock plant. According to newspaper reports, part of the reason for the speed and severity of the disruption was Rover's adoption of JIT supply arrangements. When the staff at Lucas went on strike, Rover only had a few days' worth of components in stock, and so production was swiftly halted (*The Guardian*, 9 October 1986). The case of Ford of Europe, described in chapter 4, illustrated how the company's employment of single sourcing combined with minimal stockholding led to swift and pervasive stoppages when Ford UK employees went on strike. As was argued in chapter 3, if companies are to run high-dependency systems successfully, appropriate strategies must be adopted to ensure that the system as a whole is not vulnerable to disruption – due to late deliveries, inadequate quality and so on. The motor industry is probably furthest down this road so far, and so it is useful to consider developments in this sector.

One of the first features to bear in mind when considering buyer–supplier relationships in the motor business is the unequal balance of power within the industry – more specifically, the economic muscle of the major assemblers over their suppliers gives them an ability to push through changes in supplier practices. Discussing JIT supply in the American car industry, Main (1984) comments:

> . . . the auto companies are forcing suppliers to 'eat inventory' – in other words much of the inventory still exists, but instead of being in the manufacturers' warehouses it has been pushed out to suppliers. A mere shifting of inventory, of course, will largely defeat the goals of just-in-time. Over the long run the suppliers will find a way to get manufacturers to pay for it.

This situation contrasts with the high-trust, long-term nature of relational contracting as practised in Japan. The question that this raises is whether UK companies are enacting strategies that will, in the longer term, enable them genuinely to emulate Japanese buyer–supplier relationships, or whether they are removing the slack from the system (or forcing it onto someone else) without taking steps to live with the increased dependency that results. Our evidence suggests that their policies represent a mix of both approaches.

The example of Southern Components, in chapter 4, indicates that as far as JIT supply is concerned, it appears that the larger motor manufacturers are indeed forcing their suppliers to 'eat inventory'. To recount a comment from the Managing Director of one automotive supplier:

> JIT has been used as a myth on which to hang the transfer of the responsibility for stockholding to another point in the supply chain as long as it ain't the blooming car companies . . . Basically most people who have achieved it have done it by switching it to some other poor sod.

One factor that seems often to be overlooked (and which the Southern Components case clearly illustrates) is that, to work effectively, JIT requires a certain stability of demand; if suppliers know some time in advance the types and quantities of products required, then these can be made to order. In the face of uncertain customer demand for the final product, and a determination on the part of the car companies not to build for stock, JIT looks a potentially precarious undertaking. In chapter 2, we showed how Toyota's JIT system is in fact dependent on some predictability of demand, and the 'smoothing' of production over a monthly period.

In terms of the UK experience thus far, our evidence suggests that this 'smoothing' is not occurring, at least as far as certain manufacturers in the motor industry are concerned. This may be because some companies face a much more uncertain market than do companies such as Toyota. Without a stable market position, there are real problems in creating the conditions of relative stability and certainty necessary for a JIT system of supply to work effectively. The response of some vehicle assemblers has been to try to 'force' the marketplace, an issue taken up later in this chapter, in the section on JIT and retailing.

A second problem that many British companies face when implementing JIT supply is one of geographical dispersion. This has obvious disadvantages when JIT supply is in use, as transport time is yet another source of lag – and sometimes uncertainty – in a production system. As was mentioned in chapter 4, the spread of JIT supply is one of the factors causing Lucas to locate an increasing proportion of its production abroad, close to those areas where car production is most concentrated.

Again, the motor industry in the UK provides instructive examples of adaptive strategies. Given a geographical dispersion of component suppliers, a desire to minimize stockholding and at the same time a need for high security of supplies, both Rover and Jaguar have built warehouses close to their factories, to which their suppliers deliver components, and from which they themselves withdraw supplies as and when required. The advantage of this system to the vehicle assemblers is that the stock remains the property of the supplier (and hence is held at the supplier's expense) until it is withdrawn. Moreover, while the stock is in the warehouse, the supplier is charged rent for the warehouse space that it is occupying.

In the case of Rover, this operation is sub-contracted out to British Road Services. BRS has a storage depot a mile from Rover's Cowley plant and the firm takes responsibility for storage, selection and delivery of components. Twenty BRS employees are based at Cowley itself, moving components right up to the assembly lines (Turnbull 1988).

The buyer–supplier relationship and the related questions of purchasing strategy and transportation policy all become issues in the face of the implementation of JIT. A central question here concerns the spatial concentration of supplier operations around the main assembly plant(s) that they feed. Much has been made of the geographical concentration of manufacturing facilities in Japan; indeed, it has been suggested that Toyota has enjoyed a degree of success with JIT that Nissan has never been able to emulate because of the former's location in a relatively rural area – which gradually developed into Toyota City (Cusumano 1986). More recently, *travelling time*, rather than absolute *distance* between buyers and suppliers, has been identified as the crucial determinant of success with JIT at the inter-firm level. In the US, 75 per cent of Honda's suppliers are located within 150 miles of the Marysville, Ohio, plant; yet it has been argued that 'you can do JIT from anywhere within the US as long as you give the supplier a stable schedule' (Abraham, Holt and Kathawala 1990).

A further, and largely neglected, aspect to the location question concerns transportation strategy. Monden (1983) has described the 'milk round' that Toyota's suppliers in Japan operate, whereby delivery trucks pick up materials from a number of suppliers, hence spreading the cost of small, frequent deliveries. Suppliers are in charge of the transportation of the product (Smith 1990). Current practice in the UK is not wholly consistent with this. Ford UK has recently taken control of the transportation of components to its factories and now collects materials ex-works; and we have already described the Rover Group's 'distribution centres', both operated by independent contractors to whom suppliers deliver components.

Further up the supply chain

Most analyses of the spread of Japanese-style methods have focused on the activities of the major corporations and, relatedly, their links with their first-tier suppliers. This section reports the findings of a study into the relations between a first-tier automotive supplier and *its own* suppliers, written up by Thomas and Oliver (1991). The study used some measures in common with both our 1987 and 1991 surveys and thus gives an impression of the spread of Japanese methods up the supply chain.

Table 7.7 shows, in percentage terms, the extent to which suppliers were using the practices of total quality, statistical process control, JIT production, and JIT delivery and quality assurance of

Table 7.7 Status of practices in second-tier and third-tier suppliers

Practice	Never used (%)	In use (%)	Planned or being implemented (%)
Total quality	5	82	13
Statistical process control	3	73	24
JIT production	31	59	10
JIT delivery of supplies	48	48	4
QA supplies	0	89	11

Source: Thomas and Oliver 1991

supplies (that is, JIT delivery and quality assurance of parts that the suppliers were themselves buying in).

Table 7.7 indicates that in the late 1980s, when the study was undertaken, Japanese-style methods were passing up the supply chain. Indeed, some practices – for example total quality – show a higher reported incidence than in our 1991 survey. The most likely explanation of this is that the Thomas and Oliver study focused on the automotive industry, where, along with the electronics industry, the take-up of these methods is likely to be strongest. Anecdotal evidence suggests that the take-up outside this sphere is much more patchy. Table 7.8 shows the evaluation of these practices by the sample of companies.

Total quality ideas have clearly spread a considerable distance up the supply chain, with 95 per cent of suppliers using or planning to use this approach. Anecdotal evidence suggests that few companies have gone so far as to eliminate a separate quality control department, but a shift away from post-production inspection to preventive measures is clearly apparent. The vast majority of respondents gauged their total quality programmes to be successful.

All the suppliers using SPC reported success with the technique, although it was not rated as highly as total quality. Perhaps because SPC represents a clearly definable procedure rather than a philosophy, its success or failure is less ambiguous. Comments from respondents indicated a certain ambivalence towards the practice, and there were indications in some cases of a misunderstanding of the philosophy behind it. One supplier reported 'reduced returns but increased internal rejection rates', indicating a failure to solve underlying

Table 7.8 Evaluation of practices by second-tier and third-tier suppliers

Practice	Not successful (%)	Quite successful (%)	Very–highly successful (%)
Total quality	4	12	84
Statistical process control	0	44	56
JIT production	28	50	22
JIT delivery of supplies	29	43	28
QA supplies	0	11	89

Source: Thomas and Oliver 1991

process capability problems. Another felt that his customers over-rated the significance of SPC: 'in our trade SPC is in many cases not applicable because the parts undergo various follow-up operations – the finished part only shows the final result.' This implies that customers failed to understand the suppliers' manufacturing processes when setting their SPC requirements.

JIT production provoked the strongest response from suppliers, with the Managing Director of a small presswork company describing it as 'Japanese Induced Terror'. More than two-thirds of respondents were using or planning to use JIT, but mixed results were apparent in terms of its success. Comments made by the suppliers are indicative of why this should be. Stability of demand schedules was identified as one problem. As one supplier commented:

> JIT . . . is limited to large volume items with regular steady schedules, where suppliers are literally on the doorstep. To make it more successful the whole philosophy of Japanese working practices must be adopted. (Thomas and Oliver 1991, p. 612)

Several comments suggested that the relative weakness of small suppliers feeding large customers was 'corrupting' the principles of JIT: 'The burden of stockholding is in effect transferred from customer to supplier.' Some 83 per cent of respondents reported an increase in their administrative burden, largely due to the requirement for more frequent deliveries of smaller quantities.

There was less evidence of major changes on the upstream side of the suppliers. Approximately half of the respondents reported that they had never tried JIT supply, with a significant proportion of those that had reporting it to be unsuccessful. As one remarked:

> JIT has reduced both finished stocks and work-in-progress, but causes constant delivery problems from our raw materials suppliers and increased cost of sub-contract for small batches. (Thomas and Oliver 1991, p. 612)

The relative size of the suppliers vis à vis *their* suppliers demonstrates that there is a political dimension to the problem; where a supplier is small relative to *its* supplier, it may be unable to exert the pressure needed to force through JIT deliveries. For the smaller suppliers, the successful use of JIT seemed to be associated with companies that produced small quantities of non-standard items and that were able to draw off material 'just in time' from a stockist. In these cases, the suppliers' supplier was clearly not integrated into a JIT manufacturing system. JIT supply was apparently seen as the suppliers' problem; no respondents indicated that they had received any encouragement from their customers to adopt JIT deliveries of their supplies. In some cases, this led to suppliers being caught in the middle, between demands from their customers for JIT call-off of products and the inflexibility of their own suppliers. As the Managing Director of a small engineering firm remarked: 'JIT is causing havoc – schedules are not covering the lead-time for material.'

Of all the practices, quality assured supply was the most widely used, with all suppliers claiming to be either using it or planning to use it. The practice of receiving quality assured supplies was rated very favourably, with no reports of failure. However, despite this generally positive response to QA supply on the upstream side, there were some grumbles about the demands for QA supply that the suppliers themselves were receiving from their customers. A recurrent complaint was the inconsistencies in requirements for quality systems between different customers. As one supplier remarked:

> The inconsistent approach leading to different requirements by major customers can be costly. Acceptance of BS 5750 approvals in place of customers' insistence on their own SQA activities would improve efficiency. (Thomas and Oliver 1991, p. 613)

The emphasis that customer companies placed on quality was reflected in the degree of 'encouragement' received by suppliers to adopt particular practices, as table 7.9 shows.

The emphasis on quality is clear from the 'encouragement' to adopt total quality, quality assured supplies and SPC. Practices likely to ease the suppliers' costs (JIT production and JIT supplies) are not ignored but receive significantly less attention. It is therefore somewhat surprising that only a minority of these second-tier and third-tier suppliers report an increase in stockholdings as a consequence of moves towards JIT by their customers, as table 7.10 demonstrates.

The overall pattern demonstrates a general *decrease* in stocks. The fact that the vast majority of suppliers report either a reduction or no change in stocks suggests either that the effect of JIT demands at the customer end is not filtering this far up the supply chain (at least in a significant way), or that the suppliers are taking steps to improve

Table 7.9 Encouragement from customers to adopt Japanese-style practices

Practice	Received no encouragement (%)	Some encouragement (%)	A great deal of encouragement (%)
Total quality	4	58	38
QA supplies	7	55	38
SPC	7	68	25
JIT production	31	58	11
JIT supplies	63	33	4

Source: Thomas and Oliver 1991

Table 7.10 Effects on stockholding by suppliers

Type of stock	Reducing (%)	No change (%)	Increasing (%)
Raw materials	59	36	5
Work-in-progress	38	45	17
Finished goods	55	28	17

Source: Thomas and Oliver 1991

their manufacturing processes so that they can respond to JIT call-off without having to hold stocks themselves. Considering the apparent problems with JIT delivery, it is incongruous that 59 per cent of suppliers report their raw materials stocks to be falling. It may be that even if supplies are not being provided just in time, then at least deliveries are required to be more frequent and of smaller quantities. Alternatively, the fall in stock levels may be a testament to how 'buffered' the system was prior to recent developments.

The Thomas and Oliver study also investigated who the suppliers perceived to be the main winners and losers in the moves towards the Japanese model of manufacturing, as shown in table 7.11.

No respondents considered all parties to be losers as a consequence of the new regime. However, the main beneficiaries were seen to be the customers rather than the suppliers themselves, and the general picture is of the benefits lessening the further one moves away from the final customer.

Some five years into the Supplier Development Programme initiated by the first-tier supplier, and a year after this survey was conducted, there were still perceived to be problems on the supply side of the operations of the company studied by Thomas and Oliver. Components continued to be designed in-house and the drawings passed out to the suppliers; component manufacturability and standardization frequently suffered as a result. Many suppliers did not have the guaranteed levels of business necessary to justify investment in improved methods of manufacturing. Moreover, the supplier base was too large for the development programme to have sufficient depth or focus. Purchasing continued to be carried out in the traditional manner, with purchasing decisions based largely on price.

In January 1990, a programme entitled 'Strategic Sourcing' was

Table 7.11 Supplier perceptions of the main beneficiaries of Japanese manufacturing methods

The customers	35%
All parties	24%
One or two customers	11%
The suppliers	24%
Suppliers' suppliers	6%
No-one	0%

Source: Thomas and Oliver 1991

started with the aim of significantly reducing the manufacturing cost of bought-in parts, by working much more closely with suppliers. The term 'co-makership' was introduced to describe this new supplier relationship. The aims of the programme included a further reduction in the supplier base (to a maximum of one or two suppliers per product category) and the development of much closer working relationships with suppliers.

The Strategic Sourcing programme contains a number of elements. First, the supplier is heavily integrated into the design process – in some cases, design based on performance specifications will be outsourced to the supplier. The intention of this is to reduce the incidence of non-conformance by combining the product performance knowledge of the customer engineer with the process performance knowledge of the supplier, in order to achieve a more manufacturable design. Secondly, it is planned to provide cost models agreed between the company and its suppliers, in the hope that cost can become a design variable that both parties can minimize jointly. Thirdly, through improving coordination between the company's designers and the supplier, it is hoped to reduce the number of 'specials' required, by increasing the proportion of standard parts and the degree of commonality between components. The aim is, in this way, to reduce the variety of items that have to be ordered, stored, received, issued, audited and carried on systems and drawings.

The new programme contains provision for added security for suppliers in the form of long-term (five-year+) contracts. These contracts contain 'divorce' clauses for contract termination at 18 months' notice. It is hoped that this will give suppliers the confidence to invest in training and equipment and engage in other developmental and improvement activities.

Thus far, the feedback from the suppliers has been largely positive, although some responded with severe doubts that the proposed changes would actually occur. A few indicated that they preferred an 'arm's length' relationship, and would terminate their business with the company rather than be part of the Strategic Sourcing programme.

JIT: Retailing Implications

The material on Japanese manufacturing methods and supplier relations clearly indicates the system-wide implications of practices such as just-in-time; and JIT has been described as an 'economy-wide discipline and control system' (Swyngedouw 1991). Thus, these methods have implications for the downstream, market end of the supply chain as well as for the supply side.

However, the effects of such developments at the retail end of the supply chain have been largely ignored. This oversight is curious, as the desire to eradicate 'waste' and ensure a rapid throughput of goods should be greatest at the retail level, where finished goods represent the highest-value stocks in the whole system. The inherently market-driven nature of JIT suggests that the market–producer relationship is of at least as great importance as relations between producers and suppliers. Yet again, some of the most instructive examples come from the motor industry. We saw in chapter 2 how Toyota manages the retailing side of its operations; here, we draw on recent research into vehicle retailing in the UK (Delbridge and Oliver 1991a) to examine developments in this sphere.

In the United Kingdom, car retailers typically deal directly with vehicle assemblers, although some foreign manufacturers sell through importing agencies that are not necessarily directly owned. Delbridge and Oliver (1991a) report that vehicle dealers typically characterize this relationship as one in which the production operations dictate to the sales operations what they will receive. As a dealer in French-produced cars put it:

> What happens is that France basically say to the UK, 'there's your allocation, that's what we're going to build for you in June' . . . Basically it's a lump that France have told them they are getting and they split it up – that's the way it's done. (Delbridge and Oliver 1991a, p. 22)

The onus is then on the sales operation staff to split their allotment from the factory for distribution to the dealers. This usually involves the assembler's zone manager attending annual sales allocation meetings with individual dealers, with numbers of cars that he or she must off-load on each of them. The totals are calculated by the assembler on the basis of historic performance in the market and specific market share aspirations for the following 12 months. In addition, the model split is usually based on historic model performance. In most cases, there is little scope for negotiation in the setting of each dealer's annual sales target.

At their annual meeting the assembler's representative and the dealer engage in a process of 'horse trading'. In the words of one dealer,

> It's not always possible that you get exactly what you want – you end up taking cars you don't want and if you don't take cars you don't want, you don't get the cars you do want. So it's a bit of a play-off situation. (Delbridge and Oliver 1991a, p. 22)

After the 'head-to-head bargaining' of the annual allocation, the year's sales objectives are set and typically the monthly model mix will also be decided. As the year progresses, the anticipated models are set to exact specification for the monthly allocation. This process is generally an opportunity for the dealer to have an influence on what he or she is to receive. As long as enough time is given to production, the specification of each model, for example colour and options, is the prerogative of the dealer. The specification must usually be communicated to the factory two months before build is scheduled. Delivery takes between six and ten weeks once the derivative has been decided. Order–delivery cycles for the retailers covered by the Delbridge and Oliver study are summarized in table 7.12.

The fact that the yearly sales allocation is based on two elements – historic performance and assembler's market share aspirations – can lead to problems at the dealer level. The dealer has prior knowledge of what will be delivered and must seek to sell that. Whether the dealer will be able to sell a car before actually receiving delivery of it depends on the type of vehicle and the level of demand. With one German luxury car dealer the number of pre-sold vehicles was greater than 90 per cent, and with the other one interviewed it was over 60 per cent. At the volume end of the market, the number of vehicles arriving 'with customers' names on them' was typically only 5 per cent, although the dealer in British cars reported a 90 per cent pre-sold level for some newer models.

Generally, then, volume car dealers are left with around 95 per cent of their monthly allocation as stock. At the other extreme, luxury car dealers may be left with no unsold vehicles by the time that they take delivery. However, if they have the opportunity, they will seek some stock cars for 'impulse purchase'.

Most dealers have a period of subsidized stocking before they become liable for the full price of the car. The exact arrangements for this vary between assemblers, but typically a dealer in the volume market will have 180 days before the vehicle is 'compulsorily

Table 7.12 Pre-selling, lead-times and customer wait times in UK vehicle industry

	Percentage pre-sold (1)	Order–delivery cycle (2)	Acceptable customer wait time (3)
German specialist producer 1	90+	8 weeks	12 weeks+
German specialist producer 2	60+	8 weeks	12 weeks+
German volume producer	–	6–10 weeks	–
American-owned volume producer 1	5	8–10 weeks	2 weeks
American-owned volume producer 2	5–10	6–8 weeks	2 weeks
UK-owned volume producer	10–90*	6–8 weeks	4 weeks
French volume producer	5	10 weeks	2 weeks
Toyota (in Japan)**	95+	3 weeks	–

* Varies between models
** Womack, Jones and Roos 1990
(1) Percentage of cars sold to a specific end customer by time of delivery.
(2) The time between the retailer stating the exact specification required and delivery.
(3) Dealer's perception of how long a customer would typically wait for the delivery of a car made to his or her exact specification.
Source: Delbridge and Oliver 1991a

adopted'. During that period the dealer pays an interest charge on each car. There were cases of the dealer having to pay the full price of the vehicle, less tax and VAT, on delivery or after 45–60 days. Compulsory adoption means that the dealer must buy the car. The dealer in British-built cars did have the opportunity to send some unsold vehicles back to the manufacturer, but accepting them was something that the assembler was 'very reticent to do!' In all cases, the dealer had to pay the assembler in full immediately the vehicle was sold to the end customer.

Some of the dealers that were questioned had never actually heard of just-in-time manufacturing, while others were far more aware of the developments taking place in the car factories themselves. The system was not seen as beneficial by those dealers aware of its practical implications. As the dealer in French-built cars put it:

I think most of the manufacturers, if they are running just-in-time, they don't give a toss whether their cars are just-in-time as long as their sheet metal and components are just-in-time so that their costs are kept down. Once they've produced the vehicles basically it's all down to the dealers . . . if they're at all involved in just-in-time it's not to our advancement, it's to their own. (Delbridge and Oliver 1991a, p. 25)

While the system was seen as having been implemented for the benefit of the assemblers, it had occasioned supply problems for the dealers, and this was typically the impact of just-in-time felt at the dealer level. A dealer in volume cars from an American-owned producer explained:

Every manufacturer at times has problems with component suppliers falling short and there's nothing much they can do. Most of them carry fairly low reserve stocks these days and I think the situation has got worse with the move to just-in-time. I mean we are continually getting electronic mail, we get a weekly order-build summary, and every week there's some specific model that says, 'sorry, production is ceased due to unavailability of parts' . . . My feeling is that it's due to them squeezing the stocks out and then not having enough to cover their backs but they always come up with a different reason. There's the factory view and then there's the dealer's view. (Delbridge and Oliver 1991a, p. 25)

Certainly, there was no evidence of a move to extend the just-in-time supply chain through the dealer to the marketplace. A dealer in volume cars put it succinctly:

We don't have a JIT system with the manufacturer. We're a million miles from it. (Delbridge and Oliver 1991a, p. 26)

Delbridge and Oliver found little evidence that the changes taking place at the assembler and supply chain levels of the vehicle industry were being mirrored at the dealer–market interface. The effects of JIT, to the extent that there were any, were felt by the dealers to be detrimental.

The allocation process between the assemblers and the dealers still bears the hallmarks of the traditional planned mass production system – to the dealers it appears that the production function of the assembler decides what they will receive and hence must sell.

Certainly, there is evidence that the assemblers' production plans are based on historical sales performance. The assertion that each car leaving the factory had a customer's name on it was described as 'poppycock'. The assemblers' make-to-order claims pertain to *dealer orders*, which the assemblers themselves play a major role in quantifying.

Many of the dealers clearly felt that the manufacturer dictated what vehicles they would receive. When a demand/supply mismatch occurs, the vehicle assemblers sometimes revert to 'forcing' the market, by a variety of means. These include providing dealers with bonuses and incentives for moving particular models, and sometimes pressure on dealers to register unsold vehicles as demonstration cars. By means of special deals with rental companies, or even with the fleets that the producers themselves use, new cars are registered and then almost immediately disposed of through vehicle auctions. In one example given, the production company's employees changed their cars as often as once a month if sales dropped off. Such moves may protect market share figures in the short term, but can be devastating to the residual value of the vehicles, something which in the longer term can clearly damage sales. These are the costs of producing to a pre-planned schedule rather than in response to market demand. The three German producers, who all use good residual value as a selling point, strictly controlled the prices at which dealers offered their cars.

There is thus little evidence that the European vehicle industry is any more market-driven than it was before the imitation of Japanese manufacturing practices.

Conclusions

This chapter has demonstrated how the adoption of Japanese-style methods has implications that stretch beyond the boundaries of any single organization. In the last four years, this realization has found expression in an increasing volume of research into the buyer–supplier relationship and, most recently, in an awareness of the need also to consider the downstream, retailing end of the supplier chain.

Having examined the use of Japanese-style methods by UK companies, we now move on to look at the activities of the Japanese companies themselves as they set up operations in the West.

8

Cases: Three Japanese Companies in the UK

This chapter examines the practices, policies and experiences of Japanese-owned manufacturing companies that have set up operations in Britain. Although it is the process of emulation of Japanese practices that is central to our interests – since if it were only Japanese companies investing in Britain that were using Japanese-style methods, change could hardly be considered fundamental or widespread – we suggest that the activities of Japanese companies in the UK are highly significant. This is in part because Japanese investment in the UK has grown rapidly in importance, and also because the activities of these firms heighten the visibility of Japanese practice to British companies, many of which regard them as a direct threat to their own competitiveness and a model to be followed.

The cases of three Japanese companies are presented in this chapter. First, we consider Nissan, which represents one of the larger and better-established Japanese operations located in the UK to date. We then consider Komatsu, which like Nissan chose the North East as its location. Under the banner of the 'Japanese tripod' of 'teamwork, quality consciousness and flexibility', these two companies appear to be enjoying success in implementing many Japanese-style practices. Thirdly, we consider 'K-Electric', a pseudonym for a company that produces electronic consumer goods.

Nissan Motor Manufacturing (UK)

Nissan's new plant in Sunderland is especially important in our discussion of Japanization, as it represented, until the recent arrival of Toyota, the biggest commitment of a Japanese company to manufacturing in the UK. It is also of interest because, unlike Rover and Ford (described in chapter 4) and other car manufacturers already established in Britain, Nissan has started from 'scratch', with no traditions of trade union organization or established shop-floor custom and practice, and has hence been able to experiment from the beginning with a system of its choosing. It may, thus, represent a pointer for the future.

Nissan announced in 1981 that it was making a feasibility study into the possibility of setting up an operation in the UK, and in 1984 the decision to construct a UK manufacturing facility was made public. With extensive media coverage, Mrs Thatcher opened the Nissan plant formally in September 1986. The £350-million investment in an area of industrial decay and high unemployment was welcomed with few murmurs of dissent: around 3,000 manufacturing jobs in a prestige company with a long-term commitment were to be created by 1992. The Washington New Town Development Corporation had attracted the company to the North East in the face of competition from many other local authorities across Britain. In December 1987 Nissan announced plans to produce, on the same site, a high-volume small hatchback car in addition to the Bluebird, and this was already being produced in 1991. The output target was doubled to 200,000 cars per year by 1992, with an additional 1,400 jobs to be created. By the late 1990s, Nissan expects output to reach 400,000 cars per year (Hove et al. 1990). The total investment in Sunderland, which is to be the largest to be made in Europe by any Japanese company apart from Toyota, is now around £610 million.

Finally, in 1989 Nissan announced plans to spend £31 million on design and development facilities in Sunderland and Bedfordshire. This is an important project that may help to quell criticisms of Japanese investment on the grounds that it generates only low-skilled jobs.

The present case study draws mainly on work by Tabata (1989), Crowther and Garrahan (1988) – who refer to Nissan as 'the most complete example of Japanization in Britain' – Garrahan and Stewart (1992), and *The Road to Nissan* (1987) by Peter Wickens, Nissan's Director of Personnel. The case examines developments at the Nissan plant under three categories: production and working practices; personnel practices and industrial relations; and supplier relations. It then comments on the wider implications of Nissan's decision to set up production in the UK. First, however, it is worth describing Nissan's activities in Japan itself, and the context of the company's globalization strategy.

Competition, rationalization and globalization

In 1974 Nissan held 30.8 per cent of the Japanese automobile market, compared with Toyota's 40.4 per cent. After that time, and particularly in the early 1980s, the gap between the two companies widened. By 1985, Nissan's 24.8 per cent compared with Toyota's 42.8 per cent. Tabata (1989) attributes the increasing disparity in large part to Toyota's superior efficiency, achieved as the Toyota Production System took hold and spread through the company during the 1970s. In contrast, at Nissan, attempts at rationalization were resisted by the enterprise union.

Nissan's enterprise union was formed in 1953, following a protracted dispute led by the previous radical trade union organization (Cusumano 1986). The new management–union relationship was one of mutual cooperation. However, as Yasuhiro Ishizuna, a manager in Nissan's Business Research Department, puts it:

> Unfortunately for Nissan, at some point that labour–management cooperation resulted in a blurring of the respective roles which each side was supposed to play. For example, the labour union gradually came to have a say in personnel matters and other issues which were the prerogative of management. In addition, union-related activities and meetings were openly held during working hours and were tacitly tolerated by the company. (Ishizuna 1990, p. 10)

Tabata (1989) comments that the 'amicable industrial relations . . . began to undergo an ordeal' following the first oil crisis of 1973, when competition between the assemblers became intense, in part because of growing US–Japan trade frictions. Prior to this, the Nissan enterprise union, in a period when growth was relatively easy, was allowed to develop a role in day-to-day management, and the situation continued into the 1980s. In more detail, production plans and operating schedules – including the number of automobiles to be produced, manning levels, work allocation, holiday schedules, and overtime work – could be put into effect only with the union's consent. Union consent was also needed before worker transfers or 'loans' could be effected. The union was densely organized at plant level, and senior shop stewards effectively retained the right of veto over management's operating decisions.

In 1977 Nissan introduced a productivity campaign referred to as the '3-P Movement' ('productivity', 'participation' and 'prosperity'), with the aims of reducing production costs and boosting productivity. The union, however, resisted rationalization, and in 1982 announced a refusal to collaborate with the 3-P Movement (Tabata 1989). Interestingly, at the same time, Nissan's union was opposing international projects in the belief that jobs would be 'exported' to overseas locations (Ishizuna 1990).

During 1985 and 1986, Nissan's crisis of competitiveness intensified, and the company recorded an operating loss for the first half of 1986 – the first red ink experienced by the company since being listed on the stock exchange in 1951. According to Ishizuna (1990, p. 11),

> the sense of crisis felt by the individual employee proved to be one of the strongest forces driving the company's transformation . . . Already changes were underway at the grass-roots level throughout the company, and virtually overnight they were accelerated into a concerted drive to transform the corporate culture.

The new culture included a new style of labour relations, with the transformation of the union leadership following criticisms by members, and the firm establishment of management prerogatives. The union agreed that during working hours union activities could only be undertaken with management's permission, and the proportion of full-time officials was reduced from one in 250 workers to one in 500. A comprehensive agreement signed in 1986 expressly stipulated management prerogatives – the union had given up any right to involvement in operating decisions.

In this context, rationalization went ahead, with campaigns to reduce production times and eliminate waste. Tabata documents a reduction in manning by 20 to 30 per cent on many production lines in 1986, and a 'phenomenal' increase in working hours. Further, in 1987 the pay and promotion system was linked directly to performance – foremen (team leaders responsible for between 10 and 20 workers) were given one-year contracts and could be demoted if performance was not considered satisfactory.

As we shall see below, Nissan has probably learned many lessons from the above experiences, and took steps from the beginning to ensure cooperative labour relations and strong managerial prerogatives at its UK plant.

Nissan controlled around 6 per cent of world-wide vehicle sales in 1988 – approximately 2.8 million units. It intends to expand this figure to 4.8 million, or 8 per cent of anticipated global demand, by the year 2000. The plan is to produce 60 per cent in Japan and 40 per cent overseas.

Production and working practices

It was Wickens (1985; 1987) who identified the 'Japanese tripod' of working practices, comprising teamwork, quality consciousness and flexibility, that Nissan intended to introduce to the UK. In its system, supervisors, as work team leaders, are central to the production process, having, according to Wickens, 'responsibility for everything that happens in their area', and almost representing, he goes on, 'a return to the old-style foreman before the specialists took away and diminished many of his tasks'. Supervisors act as mini-managers of their areas, and team leaders are taught every function of their team in considerable detail. Supervisors typically attend courses on leadership, problem-solving, organization, communication and quality. Job flexibility and the delegation of responsibility for inspection and minor maintenance are made feasible by the use of only two job titles for manual workers, with no grade numbers and no job specifications. Manual workers are classified simply as 'manufacturing staff' or 'manufacturing technicians'. There are daily work-area meetings at the beginning of each shift. The content of these meetings often concerns quality issues, but matters such as schedules, work distribution, training and social events are also raised. Wickens (1987) reports that most of the discussion concerns matters of relevance to the team's daily work, and only occasionally is there 'a great message from on high'. In addition, Nissan encourages *kaizen* teams, with the aim, according to the company, of trying to:

> involve every individual in finding better ways of doing his or her job. It means continually seeking to find small improvements in quality, productivity, ease of working or simply making a better work environment.

Ninety per cent of all changes in the body shop are claimed to have been suggested by employees, and in the manufacturing area up to 50 *kaizen* teams may be working at any one time.

At the end of the assembly process, there is a vehicle evaluation system (VEST), which provides information on defects expressed numerically. The causes of defects can be traced back to particular work teams and thence to individual workers, who may be awarded daily or weekly scores for their quality performance (Garrahan and Stewart 1992). Quality control is enhanced by a 'neighbour-check system', described by Nissan managers as a system for 'employee peer surveillance' (Garrahan and Stewart 1992). The area for the repair of faulty finished vehicles is kept deliberately small to force any rectification to be carried out in the area where the fault originally arose.

Work at Nissan is intense. On its application forms the company states:

> All applicants should consider the following points:
>
> • The pace of work will be dictated by a moving production line and will be very demanding.
> • Work assignments will be carefully defined and will be repetitive.
> • Protective clothing will be necessary for some jobs.
> • You may be moved on to a new operation or transferred into a different department at very short notice. (Wickens 1987, p. 176)

The flexibility demanded by the company extends to working hours – Crowther and Garrahan (1988) report that in 1987 Nissan was working a 47-hour production week, of which eight hours were compulsory overtime. The intensity appears to have been too much for some of Nissan's recruits, who were given widespread media attention in May 1987. *The Daily Telegraph* (6 May 1987), for instance, listed the following shopfloor complaints, some of them made anonymously 'for fear of victimization': production lines moved so fast that men had to work unpaid before shifts began and during breaks, to fulfil targets; pay was stopped when men were off sick because supervisors did not believe them; overtime was imposed with minimal notice. The Tyne Divisional Organizer of the single union recognized at the plant, the AEU, described a 'certain disillusion' among some of the workforce and said that he hoped that the media reports would drive workers to join his union. A Nissan spokesman said 'In my own experience I have never seen anything but people who are dedicated to their work.' Garrahan and Stewart (1992, p. 68) argue that this is not surprising, since:

> The reasons for employee apathy towards the union are obvious and it is well to acknowledge them. It is accurate to say the union plays no part in anything that goes on at Nissan presently because it has no

really independent role . . . The union itself is not even allowed to communicate with workers about recruitment.

Nissan responded quickly to the media attention, which included workers being interviewed on television. The local *Evening Chronicle* (6 May 1987), for instance, reported a Nissan spokesman as saying that work in the car industry can be 'fast, competitive and tough', but that Nissan's lines moved more slowly than those in other car factories because of quality considerations. It was further argued that the company's working practices, including overtime at short notice, were made plain to all potential employees during the selection process. In subsequent comments, Nissan stated that it had cut absenteeism to 3 per cent and that labour turnover stood at around 4 per cent – both remarkably low figures for the UK motor industry (*Financial Times*, 8 May 1987; 18 June 1987). At the time of the 1987 TUC conference, where the AEU–Nissan single-union deal was on the agenda, Nissan made a lengthy statement claiming that it had used the best of Japanese and British strengths to create a 'harmonious and productive working environment' (*The Guardian*, 8 September 1987).

A recent study of work experience at Nissan found that many workers did indeed find the work pace gruelling, but also that there were some positive feelings inspired by the 'togetherness' of team working. Garrahan and Stewart (1992) conclude that Nissan workers are engaging in a rational choice by accepting tough industrial work in exchange for employment in 'a good family firm'. Despite such a rational choice, for Garrahan and Stewart (1992) the picture of working life at Nissan is one of 'self-subordination' for Nissan's workers, under a 'new regime of subordination'. With a divergence of views characteristic of this area, where Peter Wickens (1987) sees 'quality, flexibility and teamwork' Garrahan and Stewart see 'control, exploitation and surveillance'.

Personnel practices and industrial relations

Wickens (1985) argues that Nissan's success depends on emphasizing a commitment to quality when recruiting, training and motivating people at all levels in the company. The selection process is described as 'tough', and Nissan seeks employees willing to be flexible and capable of teamwork. Bassett (1986, p. 151) states that 'Nissan could winnow out those applicants who possessed the quality it wanted – a positive, constructive attitude towards the company, reducing the risk of conflict from selection onwards.' Certainly Nissan could be choosy: male unemployment in the Sunderland area in 1986 was around 30 per cent. The application forms for the first manual jobs were distributed through job centres – approximately 20,000 of them were requested in response to advertising. These application forms covered seven sides of paper; the fact that this would probably put off the less enthusiastic was seen as an advantage. About 11,500 application forms were returned completed, a response rate of 57.5 per cent. The applicants were initially narrowed down to 1,900, largely on the basis of their answers to a simple questionnaire included in the application form. This number was further honed down by a series of aptitude, numerical, fluency and mechanical comprehension tests, reducing the number of candidates to 1,100. The next stage consisted of a series of tests of practical skills:

> At all times we were looking for their attitude and approach to problems, and this was further reinforced by a general discussion involving candidates and supervisors. (Wickens 1987, p. 178)

At this stage, a total of 500 jobs was on offer (*The Guardian*, 8 September 1987). By 1989, Nissan employed 900 workers, with an average age in the mid-20s.

Nissan spends at least six hours selecting, testing and interviewing each new member of its manufacturing staff, all applicants going through the same procedure as that described for the original applicants. Practical tests and general discussions take place before interviews conducted by supervisors; the supervisors make the final decision as to whether to select someone for their particular teams, and it is the supervisors who are responsible for the annual appraisal that determines the individual worker's level of pay. New employees are given a one-day induction course, followed by on-the-job instruction – for example, a minimum of 1,500 job cycles under the supervision of the team leader.

The company takes on some workers on five-month fixed-term contracts to enable it to meet peak demands. The contract includes one month's training, and part-timers are paid at the same rate as full-timers. The best performers are selected to join the full-time workforce. Nissan's use of temporary workers for the assembly of cars, which gives more security to the core workforce and contributes further to flexibility, is the first instance of this practice being employed in the UK motor industry since the 1940s (*Financial Times*, 16 February 1987).

As already indicated, the work team is an important mechanism of motivation and, by implication, control, at Nissan. It is difficult to assess its success, though Nissan's Personnel Director has described how some work sections, at the initiative of workers, make public displays of attendance lists. He further comments:

> Sometimes they come up with things like that, but we don't go around saying everybody has got to do it . . . The whole philosophy is to try to create the atmosphere where that sort of thing is possible, but not to insist on it. (*Financial Times*, 19 August 1987)

An equally important communication channel at Nissan is the Company Council. Representatives of all groups of employees – manual and non-manual – sit on this body, which has three main roles. These roles are as a consultative forum, as the final decision-making body in the in-house grievance procedure, and, in sessions entirely separate from its usual (quarterly) meetings, as an institution for the negotiation of pay and conditions. Its agreements are ratified by the full-time AEU official overseeing the negotiations (Wickens 1987). The council's chairman and secretary are specially appointed managers, while workforce representatives are elected from different sections of the plant. The company has the right to object to the nomination of any candidate that it feels might impede the smooth working of the consultation system (Crowther and Garrahan 1988).

McFadden and Towler (1987) have criticized the Nissan consultation system on the grounds that it weakens trade union power and influence: daily work-area meetings led by the team foreman eliminate the traditional role of the shop steward as conveyer of information to a particular locality; and the Company Council, made up of members who do not have to belong to a trade union, 'has the effect of portraying the trade unions as troublemakers when they raise valid and legitimate issues with the company.' Figures ranging from 10 per cent to 30 per cent have been cited regarding union membership at Nissan.

The single-union agreement signed between Nissan and the AEU in 1985 – prior to the commencement of production proper – does not forbid strikes, but does make them unlikely and is in most respects similar to other single-union deals signed by Japanese and Japanizing companies in the 1980s, discussed in detail in chapters 9 and 10. Specifically, the Company Council is the primary forum for collective bargaining – the union only becomes involved at later stages, in the event of failure to reach agreement, and the deal stipulates union support of productivity goals and flexible working practices (Crowther and Garrahan 1988). Wickens (1985) argues that the Nissan deal 'owes more to the work of British and American companies than to agreements reached between Nissan and the Japan Auto Workers' Union'. Its effect, nonetheless, is to reduce the likelihood of industrial action and thereby provide the industrial relations stability necessary for a just-in-time system of production. Further, it firmly stipulates managerial prerogatives over operating schedules and labour deployment.

Garrahan and Stewart (1992) make the following comments on the Nissan–AEU agreement:

> The AEU [is] secondary to the . . . company council which is the real forum for 'involvement'. Half the members of the company council are management nominees, therefore the role of the union is dependent on patronage by the company. There is no sense in which an independent union operates within Nissan. The company council delivers participation without power, whilst the union achieves recognition but is marginalised from any participation in procedures.

Nissan's view of the union situation is rather different from the one expressed above. The Personnel Director describes the process of union recognition as follows:

> The Nissan decision to recognize the AEU came not from any assessment of the political tendencies of the unions, their numerical strength in the region or who would give us the best deal, but from our judgement as to which union our employees were likely to join . . . A number of commentators have suggested other motives, laying particular emphasis on the supposed national moderation of the AEU as opposed to the TGWU. But all such tendencies are transitory and to base a decision on such a factor would lead us down the wrong path. There simply was no ulterior motive in the Nissan decision. (Wickens 1987, p. 137)

Industrial relations at Nissan and other Japanese and Japanizing companies will be taken up again in later chapters. However, in discussing its links with suppliers, we shall see how Nissan's influence over industrial relations may go beyond the confines of its own plant.

Supplier relations

When Nissan decided to move to the region, Sunderland Borough Council parcelled off an area of land three times the size needed for Nissan's own factory, giving the company 'unfettered control over its immediate production environment'. Nissan has since begun to attract to this site sub-contractors that are prepared to enter long-term trading relationships with the company – Ikeda–Hoover, which supplies seats and headliners, being one of the first. Because of the factory's close physical proximity to its suppliers, parts deliveries can, of course, be made more nearly 'just in time' for Nissan's production needs. This is one sign that Nissan intends to develop its supplier relations in a similar manner to those that it enjoys in Japan. Another is that Nissan has taken an 80 per cent equity shareholding in a recently formed joint company with Yamatu Kogyo Ltd. The company is located in Sunderland and supplies small body pressings. This 80 per cent stake is, of course, exceptional – Nissan's policy is reported as being to gain 20 per cent holdings in its supply companies, since it considers this sufficient to gain some financial leverage over them. Crowther and Garrahan (1988) describe Nissan as developing a 'spatially concentrated production process', and suggest that such spatial concentration is a key element of Japanization. This is consistent with our argument in chapter 3, as it represents one aspect of heightened dependency relations between organizations and their suppliers.

According to McFadden and Towler (1987), Nissan's policy is to keep stocks to a level representing seven hours of production needs, and to attract 'trading partners' capable of delivering components every two hours. Further, a heavy reliance on Nissan is preferred, as is the acceptance of a 20 per cent Nissan stake in the supplying company (compare above). The Deputy Managing Director of Nissan UK has argued that British suppliers should adopt the policy of 'negative pricing' – reducing sale prices by continually raising productivity by double-digit figures every year; he has added that such a culture may take several years to take root (*Financial Times*, 8 May 1987).

Gaining a long-term trading partnership with Nissan is not easy. Nissan looks in detail at the supplier's cost structure, quality control procedures, material stocks and purchasing policies. In addition, industrial relations, work practices, trade union structure and strike record are examined. McFadden and Towler comment that this means that many workers in supplier companies could be subject to the same type of industrial practices as exist at the Nissan plant itself.

Wider considerations

As well as having a 'knock-on' effect through the British components sector, Nissan's practices are clearly providing a lead for the rest of the British car industry, which is rapidly attempting to adopt many of them and often justifying doing so on the grounds of competition from Nissan. As described in the case studies of Rover and Ford, British manufacturers have been attempting changes along the same lines for the past several years, but the pressures for change are now more explicit and more immediate.

Occasionally, existing car manufacturers have voiced fears of Nissan swamping the UK market, but overall Nissan has received wide public support, particularly insofar as it is generating jobs in an unemployment blackspot. Garrahan and Stewart (1992) point out, however, that Nissan has been a recipient as well as provider of public goods – it has received free media exposure (mostly good news) and free public relations ('Far East Rescues North East' was a typical headline), as well as around £120 million of regional aid and selective financial assistance.

As readers may have observed both in this case and in the case of Lucas Industries, two distinct and sharply contrasting perspectives on Japanization are apparent – one that is generally positive about the process, another that is critical. The premises from which this divergence of views arises raise important issues about the adoption of Japanese-style practices in the UK, and we shall return to these later in the book.

Komatsu (UK)

The Japanese firm of Komatsu was founded in 1921 as a manufacturer of machine-tools and mining equipment. Today it is the second largest manufacturer of earthmoving and construction equipment in the world, the largest being Caterpillar. Komatsu (UK) was set up in Birtley, in north east England, in 1986, the fifth Komatsu manufacturing operation to be established outside Japan. The company has set up other operations in Brazil (in 1975), Mexico

(1976), Indonesia (1982) and the USA (1985). The force behind this off-shore investment has been a desire to be closer to markets, and hence more responsive to them. In the case of the European investment, a further benefit is the avoidance of trade friction and the competitive disadvantages conferred by a strong Yen (*Industrial Relations Review and Report*, 5 May 1987).

Komatsu UK's operations were established in a factory that had been vacated by its major competitor, Caterpillar, in 1984. The company received a grant of 15 per cent of approved capital expenditure (*Industrial Relations Review and Report*, 5 May 1987), conditional on an undertaking to ensure 60 per cent local content in the final product. In late 1987, the company employed 200 people; it was anticipated that this would rise to about 270. The company planned to produce 2,400 earthmoving vehicles per year at Birtley, for a sales area comprising Europe and North Africa. This case study will consider Komatsu's activities and experiences in three distinct areas: the production process, personnel practices and industrial relations, and supplier relations.

The production process

The average skill level of shopfloor workers at Komatsu is between semi-skilled and skilled. Manufacturing practices include total quality control, and voluntary quality circles are encouraged. There is a U-shaped manufacturing and assembly line, and an above average degree of automation (Gleave 1987).

Loyalty and commitment to the company were put to the test in the task of getting the production process under way and running smoothly. In the early days, production workers had to work seven days a week, and the strain began to tell. A number voiced concerns that the company was asking too much of them – particularly in terms of expecting that it should come before family life. (Interestingly, in Japan the term 'my homeism' is sometimes used to describe a weak orientation towards the company.) Of course, any company that is starting up production is likely to make substantial demands on its workforce – hence the effect of Komatsu being Japanese is confounded with Komatsu also being a company setting up operations in a new location. One production worker commented:

> We realize that the company has got to succeed for everybody's good,
> but to what extent do you take it? Speaking for myself, my family

comes first. Obviously without the company I wouldn't have a job, so I'll do my best, but I'll draw the line in certain areas. (BBC 1987)

One issue that caused problems was that of tea-breaks. Initially, the company insisted that there should be 'bell-to-bell' working, which for the production workers meant a four-hour stint in the morning without a break until lunchtime. The afternoon also comprised a four-hour block, again without a break. Meanwhile, workers were expected to come in early (and unpaid) for a team briefing before production commenced. The emphasis on bell-to-bell working is regarded by some as the secret of Japan's success. As a production supervisor commented,

All that the British worker has got to do to work to the Japanese system is to work during the time he is paid . . . once the British worker has done that he has fulfilled the Japanese system. (BBC 1987)

The issue of tea-breaks was raised at the company's Advisory Council, and was resolved by the installation of beverage machines adjacent to the production lines. However, an initially uncompromising position by the company caused some cynicism about the allegedly consensual nature of the Advisory Council's decision-making processes.

By mid-1987, one quality circle had been set up voluntarily by personnel in the paint shop. The circle met regularly for approximately an hour after production had finished for the day. The members were not paid extra for the time spent at these meetings.

Personnel practices and industrial relations

Recruitment for Komatsu was handled largely by local job centres and the Professional and Executive Register. There were 3,000 applicants for the first 70 production line jobs. An initial screening reduced these to 200, all of whom were under 35 and few of whom had any history of trade union activism. The applicants were put through a rigorous selection procedure, involving pencil-and-paper psychological tests. The company selected recruits on the basis of appropriate attitudes – particularly ones supportive of teamwork and flexibility – rather than because they possessed the basic skills or experience necessary for the production process.

The induction period for new recruits at Komatsu spans ten

weeks, and begins with an initial half-day programme. Thereafter, they undergo five formal and five informal induction sessions. In addition, some supervisors have been sent to Japan for four weeks of specialist training. On joining Komatsu, every worker receives a copy of the company handbook. This is a glossy ring-bound folder, which is filled up with professionally produced handouts as the employees move through their induction procedure. When complete, the handbook is over 75 pages long, and contains items such as background information on the company, company philosophy (particularly with respect to quality control), terms and conditions of employment, details of the agreement with the recognized trade union and so on.

There is a comprehensive performance review and appraisal system, which covers everyone within the company. The Komatsu handbook states that:

> The company's policy is to match individual development with that of the company . . . Komatsu UK's policy is to help staff develop their own careers in order to help the company grow.

The methods of performance analysis were devised by managers and supervisors in workshop sessions during February and March 1987. There are two elements to this system. Performance review is recorded on a standard 18-item form; the superior of the person being assessed makes a rating on each item. The breadth of the characteristics covered by this process is striking. Items include not only the more conventional ones, such as job knowledge, quality of work, work rate and reliability, but also others, such as flexibility, adaptability to change, determination, teamwork, personal contact skills and activities 'beyond the contract'. The second element in the system, that of appraisal, is completed jointly by the person being assessed and the reviewer, and considers the former's strengths, weaknesses, future work preferences and development needs.

Initially, it was planned that the performance analysis would be carried out quarterly, with merit pay adjustments twice a year – however six-monthly reviews and annual merit pay adjustments were considered to be more realistic, and this system is currently operating, although the reviews may be reduced further, to once a year (*Industrial Relations Review and Report*, 5 May 1987).

The AEU has sole negotiating rights at the site. Single-union recognition was agreed before the set-up decision was announced officially at the end of December 1985. The company chose the AEU on the grounds that it was the most appropriate body, given the combination of engineering, technical and supervisory staff in the plant. The fact that the AEU divisional organizer had experience in negotiating start-up deals in the North East – in particular with Nissan – is also said to have given the AEU an advantage over the General and Municipal Workers' Union, the GMB. The union represents all full-time staff up to and including supervisors. Under the terms of the agreement all employees enjoy conditions of employment of the same status. This includes a common pension scheme, sick pay from the first day of illness, free medical cover and a free uniform. All employees are required to wear the same uniform (and perform morning exercises) to emphasize the single-status nature of the company, a situation that slightly rankles some of the managerial staff:

> I spent 20–30 years of people telling me that when you get promoted and when you move on you take the overalls off and put a white coat or a suit on. And for 20 years I dreamed about the day I would go to work with a tie on and polished shoes and a suit . . . that had to go out of the window here. (BBC 1987)

In the event of an industrial dispute that cannot be resolved internally, the agreement with the AEU permits reference to ACAS for conciliation. If the issue is still unresolved:

> both parties may agree to refer the dispute to an independent arbitrator who will determine positively in favour of one side or the other . . . Both parties agree to accept the decision of the arbitrator.
>
> There will be no industrial action of any kind while an issue is in procedure or the subject of conciliation and arbitration. In the unlikely event of total exhaustion of the above procedure without resolution, no industrial action will be taken without a full, secret, audited ballot of all affected employees. (Komatsu/AEU agreement)

There is a comprehensive clause in the agreement concerning the use of manpower. The union accepts 'complete flexibility and mobility of employees', that 'changes in processes and practices will be introduced to increase competitiveness and that these will improve productivity and affect manning levels', and that 'manning levels will be determined by the company using appropriate industrial engineering and manpower planning techniques.' Union membership (which Komatsu agreed to encourage) stands at about 50 per cent of all those eligible for membership and at 70 per cent of those from the production areas.

Although the AEU has a presence at Komatsu and membership is encouraged by the company, the main institution for collective representation is the Advisory Council. This body consists of elected representatives from each area of the company (an area typically consisting of about 30 people), a president (normally the Managing Director), a secretary (who is both a member of management and a management appointee) and the Union Divisional Organizer. The Komatsu handbook describes the role of the Advisory Council as follows:

> The Advisory Council is not a 'talking shop' without muscle, neither is it a traditional 'Works Council' where managers and employee representatives sit and glare at each other from entrenched positions. It exists to share information, pool ideas, represent staff and company interests and come to agreed conclusions. It cannot dictate to Komatsu UK what policy will be, but it can and will influence the company's future direction in the mutual interest of Komatsu UK and Komatsu UK employees.

An example of the operation of the Council is provided by the first annual pay review, which took place in March 1987. The Council was presented with information on the company's performance in its first year and on movements in the cost of living and in earnings in comparable industries, and on the basis of this information made a recommendation to management for a 5 per cent increase in basic pay. This was granted, and so no real negotiations over pay took place (Gleave 1987).

Relations with suppliers

In Japan, Komatsu sends its engineers into its suppliers' factories to improve their production methods in order to get costs (and hence prices) down. In the UK, the detailed approach of the Japanese to negotiations with would-be suppliers led to some hard bargaining, as suppliers disagreed with Komatsu's estimates of appropriate costs. In the words of one potential supplier to Komatsu:

> We have to disagree with their estimates of how long it will take us to produce in our own factory, based on their experiences of how long it

takes them in their factories in Japan . . . It is making us turn our thinking inside out and upside down – we're looking at everything from new angles – trying to think in Japanese terms, really. (BBC 1987)

The process involved in the negotiations over contracts was also unfamiliar to Komatsu's would-be suppliers. One commented on the 'Japanese ability to go into minute detail and not make a decision until everything has been gone through in detail'. The Manager of Curl Engineering, a medium-sized engineering company pursuing a contract to supply cab doors to Komatsu, commented:

> Komatsu first turned up in February. It was six months before we got an indication that there might be an order. We had three or four meetings a week during that period.

With the contract awarded, this pattern continued. Curl Engineering again:

> The Japanese tend to camp out on your doorstep. We've got English firms that we see once or twice a year . . . it's nothing for the Japanese to turn up two, three or four times a day.

Supplied parts are an obvious pressure point in the situation, as Komatsu has an obligation to meet the 60 per cent local content ruling. To achieve this whilst maintaining cost and quality targets has not been easy, and early production was dogged with problems with supplied parts being delivered late and not being up to scratch in terms of quality.

Conclusions

From his study of Komatsu, Gleave (1987) concludes that, in general, the firm appears to have been quite successful in its first two years of UK operations. Labour turnover and absenteeism are low, and all major targets (such as reaching the 60 per cent local content level) have been met. Describing Komatsu's personnel practices, Gleave notes the latitude that has been given to the UK Personnel Director in this area, and summarizes the system that has emerged as a 'unionized human resources system'. A comment from the

Personnel Director himself provides a thought-provoking conclusion to the Komatsu story so far:

> This is not a case of just going and working for a foreign company. This is a case of assisting a foreign company to have a base in the UK which will in fact revolutionize the attitudes in British industry. If it doesn't then I don't believe we [the British] have an industrial future.

1987–1991

By 1991, employment at Komatsu's Birtley plant stood at 450, compared with the 1987 target of 270. The local content of Komatsu's products is about 70 per cent (*Financial Times*, 22 April 1991); and about 80 per cent of production is exported. Union membership at the plant remained fairly static between 1986 and 1989, at about 50 per cent. Komatsu claims that the single-union agreement is working 'very well indeed' and says that it makes 'tremendous efforts' to encourage new employees to join the union (*Industrial Relations Review and Report* 453, 1989).

The Advisory Council has remained the sole forum for issues of a collective bargaining type within the company, the annual pay review being the item that consumes the most time and attention. The Council has not yet failed to reach consensus, although the 1989 pay agreement was 'achieved with some difficulty' (*Industrial Relations Review and Report* 453, 1989). Although the Council is a major vehicle for communication, it is backed up by a team briefing system, which involves team leaders briefing their work groups (typically comprising seven to ten employees) at the start of work. The performance analysis scheme has been retained, and is judged as successful. The company operates a merit pay scheme, which can pay up to 6 per cent of salary.

At the end of 1989 there were some 13 quality circles at Komatsu, covering 19 per cent of all employees (*Industrial Relations Review and Report* 453, 1989)

'K-Electric'

K-Electric is one of Japan's largest corporations, and its UK plant was established approximately ten years ago as part of the Japanese parent company's strategy of setting up transplant factories within its major world markets. The plant was previously British-owned and was reopened by K-Electric, with much of the same, 're-recruited' workforce, after being closed for several months. K-Electric (UK) supplies the European market, and it has sister plants in Japan, Singapore, Mexico and the United States. Production at K-Electric, in line with market demand, has increased rapidly and consistently through the 1980s and into the early 1990s. The factory, which now employs over 700 people, is basically an assembly plant; the direct–indirect labour ratio is around 3.5:1, 70 per cent of the direct labour and 50 per cent of the indirect labour being provided by women. Around 50 to 70 people work on temporary contracts, the number varying to meet seasonal changes in demand. Only five Japanese nationals are engaged in the plant. One of these is the Assistant Managing Director, but the Managing Director and all other directors are British. Close contact is, however, maintained with the head office in Japan, and most managers have spent time in Japan as part of their training and development.

The following account is based on case study work undertaken by Graham Sewell (now of the School of Management, UMIST), together with Barry Wilkinson, in 1989 and 1990.

Production and materials control

The three main production sections at K-Electric, each of which is headed by a Section Manager, are: 'machining', where printed circuit boards (PCBs) are prepared and some components inserted using automatic machines; 'panels', where more components are manually inserted onto the PCBs on production lines; and 'assembly', which includes sub-assembly of some components, as well as final assembly. There is a final test facility within the assembly section. Certain high-value components are bought in, some from Japan, but K-Electric is in the process of establishing its own production facilities for some of these.

Since taking the plant over, K-Electric has gradually moved towards just-in-time production and supply. Work-in-progress has been reduced from a six-week to a three-day average, and many components are now delivered to the factory one or two days before they are used. K-Electric tries to develop its suppliers' abilities and has rationalized the number that it deals with, so that many parts are now single-sourced. However, the company faces difficulties in improving the JIT supply situation because of continuing inadequacies on the part of local suppliers and because of the complex logistics involved in sourcing parts from overseas, including Japan.

Materials procurement is closely integrated with production and sales. A production, sales and inventory plan (PSI) is produced and revised on a monthly basis, and looks forward 12 months. The accuracy of the PSI depends on the accuracy of sales information, and K-Electric goes to great lengths to ensure that distributors' orders are both accurate and firm. A production schedule is derived from the PSI (using a micro-computer) and this indicates a line-by-line loading on a daily basis for the following month, together with procurement requirements. After detailed production meetings, the company is then committed three months forward on labour and materials. We will describe later how the Labour Hours Analysis and Work Study are used to fine tune labour utilization.

Productivity and quality improvements are sought constantly through an improvement programme. This is based on weekly meetings of team leaders, each of whom is expected to produce one 'measured' suggestion every week. These suggestions should originate from, or at least be tried out in, discussions with team members. They are then processed by the Facilities Engineering Department. Within a few days of the weekly meeting, team leaders are told what action will be taken, and if the idea is not pursued, Facilities Engineering is obliged to give an explanation. This information is relayed by the team leader back to team members. Those suggestions for improvements that are accepted and successfully acted upon are often publicly displayed on notice boards in prominent positions around the factory.

In recent years, many improvements have been made; most of them are small but, added together, they are significant. Over a two-and-a-half-year period between 1987 and 1990, the following improvements were attributed to the programme:

- reduction of work-in-progress by 35 per cent
- cutting of internal lead-times
- reduction of standard times by 15 per cent
- saving of 11 per cent of floor space
- saving of 57 team members (i.e. 57 more workers would have had to be employed otherwise)

More generally, productivity and quality have been maintained, as we shall see below, by very careful and constant monitoring of performance and by taking action immediately any problem comes to light. Production levels and quality are the responsibility of the production department, and team leaders (and ultimately team members) are held accountable for any problems within their control that occur.

Working practices

Team leaders have extensive responsibilities, including member selection, on-the-job training and appraisal. A typical 'team' is made up of around 40 members. The leader is also involved in the details of production scheduling, and is responsible for labour deployment, meeting production targets, and maintaining a high level of quality. Each leader is responsible to a 'customer' (often internal), and the leader's job is frequently defined in terms of 'meeting my customer's requirements'. Similarly, each production manager has a customer, for example, in the form of the final assembly section production manager.

Production managers, and most of the team leaders, have been internally promoted from operator level and have wide and detailed knowledge of shopfloor operations. Typically, like most managers at K-Electric, they work long hours, and several remarked that when there are periods of high demand they can find themselves on duty from 7am to 9.30pm for several months at a time. Operators' working time varies between around 34 and 46 hours per week according to shifts in seasonal demand during the year. But, because of a deliberately tight staffing policy, they are often required to do overtime of between two and four hours per day.

Complete flexibility of labour deployment within the whole factory is possible in theory. In practice, operators work mostly within their sections, and again most tend to remain within their teams. Many operators are trained in more than one skill, gaining recognition for their achievements in the form of a higher pay grade. They mostly continue to work within their own teams, but are sometimes switched between teams in the case of absence, lateness, demand fluctuations, etc. The team leader is responsible for maintaining both discipline and morale on the line, and is supported by (typically three or four) 'senior members'.

The day at K-Electric begins with the firm's Production Manager and the team leaders looking at their schedules and 'customer' requirements for the day. The labour that they have available is determined by a Labour Hours Analysis that – on the basis of production schedules (derived from the PSI; see above) and standard times – gives the number of labour hours required in each area on a month-by-month basis. A shopfloor micro-computer using internally developed software will tell team leaders and the Production Manager their precise labour needs for a given level of efficiency in the light of the day's schedule.

The Labour Hours Analysis takes account of operator efficiency, attendance ratios, 'non-productive work' ratios, learning curves on new models, etc., employing retrospective information. Production managers and team leaders are then expected, on a monthly basis, to agree to targets using a specified amount of labour. (Determining staffing levels is the primary purpose of the Labour Hours Analysis, but a by-product of the process is an ability to calculate accurately and in detail 'direct employment hours' versus 'other hours', and this information is fed back to head office in Japan. Improving the 'direct' versus 'other hours' ratio is a key management concern.) Standard times are produced in Japan with a simple work-factor method and are indicated in precise detail. Times are provided to K-Electric in the UK for a whole unit of finished goods, for the sections of the factory, for activities within each section, and right down to the level of components to be assembled or inserted in fractions of a second. Allowances are built in for factors such as inadequate production facilities and learning time on the first batches of a new product; and there is a 5 per cent allowance that applies to all overseas factories, to take account of problems with delays due to communications with Japan and, according to one manager, also because of 'the belief that foreigners can't work as fast' as the Japanese.

Assembly manuals, which include detailed standard times broken down to the level of individual component insertion and assembly, are regularly updated in Japan in the light of improvements in methods. Whenever an overseas factory makes an improvement, this fact, and details of the new method, are relayed back to Japan and information on the improvement is passed on to all group factories the next time that the manual is revised. Some improvements come from the improvement programme and some from management.

When workers arrive at the start of a shift they are briefed by their team leaders on targets for the day and any special problems that might arise. The team leaders then immediately check for absences and consider how best to 'balance' the line. There is no slack labour, so, if necessary, decisions have to be made on how to redistribute tasks on the assembly line to cover for those operators missing from their work stations. Often this means increasing the number of components that some operators have to insert or assemble as the panels move past on the line. Occasionally, team leaders cope by coming to an agreement among themselves and with their production managers on a redistribution of available labour between work teams, and in exceptional circumstances absences may mean that overtime becomes necessary to meet targets.

Because of the problems that absences cause in the context of tight manning, the matter is taken very seriously. An absent member, on return to work, is automatically interviewed by the team leader, and the reasons for the absence and any action taken against the absentee are recorded on the employee's personal file. The employee is invited to sign the statement indicating that she or he agrees that it is accurate. Frequent absence, even if due for instance to chronic illness, will lead to a 'separation' of employer and employee. The names of absentees, together with the dates and reasons for their absence, are publicly displayed adjacent to each production line.

To the casual observer, the pace of work on the lines is intense, and during working hours the lines rarely seem to stop. Work cycle times are typically around 30 seconds in the labour-intensive section. One operator commented that 'you get used to it; it's when the line stops – you think it's going backwards.' There is a ten-minute break in each of the morning and afternoon working periods, and operators must not leave the line before a buzzer sounds to indicate the start of the break. After nine minutes the buzzer goes again and the operator must be back at his or her work station at the sound of the next buzzer exactly one minute later. (Until 1990, the operators could remain in the canteen for the full ten minutes. One minute was forfeited as part of a 9 per cent pay deal.) Within these ten minutes there is a frantic scurrying to and from the canteen. It takes another 30 minutes for the pall of cigarette smoke to clear from the area. (Smoking, eating and drinking are strictly prohibited on the line.)

K-Electric seeks to achieve between 96 and 98 per cent efficiency (as measured against the Labour Hours Analysis). Efficiency ratings are displayed at the end of each assembly line and these are regularly updated by the team leader, using information from the shopfloor micro-computer. If any team is performing below expectation then the section production manager is expected to examine the situation in great detail and take appropriate corrective action. Team leaders are encouraged to compare their teams' performances with those of other teams, which leads to a degree of competition between them. This does not, however, necessarily lead to inter-team conflict over labour deployment, because the efficiency ratings take account of exactly who is working where at any particular time. The system depends, of course, on accurate information on labour deployment being fed into the labour calculation, the importance of which is constantly impressed on all team leaders and section managers. Each team leader is expected to keep an 'ins and outs' book (presently being computerized) to record all details of labour movements, any downtime, with the reasons for it, and so on. Management selectively uses information from these books to feed into the efficiency calculations and to examine possible solutions to problems identified.

If a team is performing *above* expectation, again management will look very closely at the reasons why. According to one manager, 'we keep them going at 110 per cent and get them to pass on the savings.' Sometimes this will involve a time study, which is conducted without warning. In this manner, continuous improvement is built into the system of production.

The impact of such detailed monitoring and control of production on the line is summed up by the following comments from operators:

They pay you well but you have to work for it.

You reach your targets and they just push you harder and harder.

They make you work every second in the day here . . . If they spot you doing something faster they put the targets up . . . they find out. Now and then they come with a watch, and if they catch you doing it faster you have to do it all the time – it's not fair.

Interviews with operators, however, revealed an overall acceptance of hard work and tight discipline in return for some of the best wages and working conditions in the locality. Team leaders also face heavy demands. One team leader, referring to a particularly hectic period, commented:

I used to think, Jesus Christ, I don't know whether I'm on my head or my feet . . . With [the previous British owners] we had two or three thousand people with far less output than we have today.

At the same time as 'waste' is ruthlessly eliminated and labour productivity pushed to its limits, quality has to be carefully maintained. In-process control is the responsibility of the manufacturing function, and sections are held accountable for any quality problems. Each team conducts its own visual and electronic inspections on the lines, and an attempt is made to take corrective action before products move on to the 'customer'. Any mistakes identified by line inspectors are attributed to the individual operator responsible, and charts at the end of each line display how many assembly defects were caused by each operator.

Some defects do, nonetheless, get through to the end of final assembly, to be discovered on the final electronic test. Here a probe is inserted into the completed good, and a screen flashes 'pass' or 'fail'. When it states 'fail' it then automatically gives information on the nature of the fault, and this allows the tracing of the fault immediately to the individual culprit. Senior team members collect defect information every hour, and this is used to update charts that indicate team and individual errors. As with efficiency ratings, quality ratings lead to a degree of competition between teams, which have reject targets. A notice board in the canteen displays daily and weekly rejects team-by-team, both numerically and graphically.

For individuals, quality performance is recorded on charts above their heads at the work station. A green A4-sized card that reads 'good' indicates zero defects the previous day. An amber card reading 'caution' indicates between one and four defects. And a red card that reads 'danger' indicates five or more defects. Also alongside each operator is a daisy chart that indicates quality performance for each day of the whole month. The in-section inspectors also have cards that indicate the number of faulty components that they were responsible for letting pass.

The Production Manager commented that the card system:

> ... makes people nervous a little bit. Nobody likes the red, I'll tell you that for a fact. I've only had one person feel as if she were back at school. I had to explain that we were only doing it to help her.

A team leader explained how the system was introduced with the help of engineers from Japan. She commented, 'the girls don't mind the cards, they think it's a good thing. When they see caution they go "Ooh, maybe I could do a bit better."' When someone is identified as having a quality problem, the first step is counselling.

The team leader takes the offender off the line to the canteen (the line is re-balanced meantime) and tries to get to the root of the problem. As one team leader said, 'I ask them "have you got a problem? Have you got a personal problem?" They could have something on their minds and it's best to find out why.' While discussing counselling sessions, another team leader said 'sometimes I don't feel like a manager. I feel like a social worker, a solicitor, a policeman.'

More than 20 defects in a month results in a verbal warning under disciplinary procedure, and repetitions ultimately lead to dismissal. Where individual operators are found to have made three or more mistakes on the same batch of panels (batches are typically of between 500 and 1,000 units) they are taken to their 'customer' areas and requested to do a manual check on the whole of the batch. This can cause disruption for an hour or two for fellow team members, who have to take on the absent operators' tasks.

Personnel policies

K-Electric's working practices are supported by a set of personnel and industrial relations policies that are not untypical of other Japanese manufacturers in Britain (see chapters 9 and 10). Selection is rigorous, and includes tests for dexterity (which is crucial to many of the assembly jobs) together with interviews that look for commitment, enthusiasm, willingness to work overtime, and an ability to work in a team. Previous attendance records (from school if the candidate is a school-leaver) are closely scrutinized. Recruits have a one-week induction period, which includes on-the-job instruction in a training facility, before being put on the line. All the time, the team leader, who is largely responsible for the selection and induction process for his or her own team, is 'getting a feel' for how and where the recruit would best fit into it. Before the end of the induction week, recruits are invited to give their impressions and to confirm that they will be happy with a job in which attendance, attention to detail and quality are strongly emphasized. Many recruits withdraw their applications at the end of the first week; those who remain are likely to stay with K-Electric for at least several years. As indicated in the section on working practices, team leaders also play a crucial role in human resource management more generally.

Pay levels at K-Electric are well above the average for comparable jobs in the consumer electronics industry in Britain and in the local economy. The company is among the top five in the pay leagues for both domains. According to one manager, this was the quid pro quo for being employed by 'pretty tough task masters . . . In [K-City] K-Electric is known for being strong on quality and on attendance and absenteeism.' Operators are paid by a straight time rate. There is no piecework and there are no bonuses except for a small attendance bonus paid twice a year. However, there is an appraisal system that applies to every worker. The appraisal is carried out annually by the worker's team leader or immediate supervisor, and attention is paid to 'cooperativeness', 'teamwork ability', and so on, as well as objective measures of performance and behaviour. The results of the appraisal directly affect the worker's pay level, and can feed into considerations of promotion or transfer.

The company has a single-union agreement, which is characterized by a strike-free clause, a flexibility provision that stipulates complete managerial prerogatives over the deployment of labour, and arrangements for the establishment of a Company Advisory Board, which makes recommendations on issues such as pay and working conditions that, in Britain, would normally be the preserve of collective bargaining (see chapter 10). The Company Advisory Board is also used to impart company information to the workforce, and is part of a comprehensive system of communications within the company that also includes company newsletters and team briefings at the start of every working day. K-Electric operates a single-status employment policy. Everyone is issued with the company jacket, and toilet, canteen and car parking facilities are shared in common.

Having looked in some detail at the cases of three Japanese companies, in the chapter that follows we move on to examine the data from both our 1987 and 1991 surveys concerning the activities of Japanese manufacturers in the UK.

9
Japanese Companies in Britain

This chapter explores the nature and extent of Japanese direct investment in the UK – 'direct Japanization', in the terms used by Ackroyd et al. (1988) – and examines the practices that the Japanese companies involved are employing. Like the chapters on the UK companies emulating Japanese practices, this chapter is based on two surveys, one undertaken in 1987, one in 1991, and is backed up by additional case study material. The 1987 survey was supplemented by work undertaken by colleagues of the authors at Cardiff Business School, notably Morris (1988b), Gleave (1987) and Pang (1987).

The Globalization of Japanese Business

During recent years, Japanese manufacturers have been moving overseas in increasing numbers. Morris (1988a) identifies three broad phases of Japanese overseas investment. The period 1945–71 saw steady but modest increases. In 1971–80 there was a surge of growth followed by later fluctuations, and from 1980 onwards there was a steep upward trend. A number of factors have been driving this development. One reason for overseas investment is the need to be close to local markets and in touch with local needs and demands. This is particularly significant in the light of a trend towards 'global localization' – a process in which, it is alleged, the world is evolving into a series of supranational trading blocs, such as Europe, North America and the Pacific Rim (Oliver, Morris and Wilkinson 1992). A second reason has been economic friction between Japan and its export-destination countries (Okumura 1989), friction which has recently been especially evident between Japan and the EC. For instance, with regard to automobile exports, the Japanese Ministry of

International Trade and Industry (MITI) was recently pushed into accepting a limit of 1.23 million units per year – roughly the 1991 level – until the end of 1999 (*Japan Times*, 2 August 1991). A third reason is a generally very tight labour market and relatively high wages, as discussed in chapter 1, and a fourth is the high-Yen crisis known as *endaka*. In 1985, Britain, France, West Germany, the US and Japan agreed to appreciate the Yen's value against the dollar. The result was a more than doubling in the value of the Yen against the dollar, from 265 Yen to the dollar in summer 1985 to 130 Yen to the dollar three years later (Fujita and Child-Hill 1988). Japanese corporations' response to falling profits on exports was to accelerate overseas production sharply, as shown in table 9.1.

In the late 1980s, within Japan there were fears of a 'hollowing out' of Japanese manufacturing, particularly in regional economies outside Tokyo and Osaka that were heavily dependent on manufacturing employment. However, by 1991 the worst fears had abated, for three reasons. First, strong domestic demand had softened Japan's dependency on exports (Steven 1991). Secondly, Japanese manufacturers within Japan put great efforts into cost-cutting and boosting local productivity, often successfully. For

Table 9.1   Japanese foreign direct investment 1951–1988

	1951–80		1980–4		1984–8	
	($m)	(%)	($m)	(%)	($m)	(%)
North America	8,202	25.8	9,724	32.8	57,165	45.8
Europe (total)	3,885	12.3	3,249	11.0	23,028	18.5
UK	1,824	5.8	624	2.2	8,106	6.4
W. Germany	387	1.2	538	1.8	1,439	1.2
France	301	0.9	331	1.1	1,130	0.9
Netherlands	257	0.8	365	1.2	4,903	3.9
Belgium	224	0.7	364	1.2	439	0.4
Other	892	2.8	1,027	3.5	7,011	5.6
Latin America	5,580	17.6	5,150	17.4	20,887	16.7
Middle East	2,101	6.6	553	1.8	684	0.5
Africa	1,306	4.1	1,565	5.3	1,733	1.3
Oceania	2,077	6.6	1,483	5.0	5,755	4.6
Asia	8,544	27.0	7,855	26.6	15,828	12.6
Total	31,695	100.0	29,581	100.0	125,080	100.0

Source: Adapted from Dunning 1986; Japanese Ministry of Finance 1990

instance, as the Yen rose to a level of 150 Yen to the dollar, workers at one Canon factory in Toride wore '150' badges to demonstrate commitment to achieving profitability at that exchange rate (*Financial Times*, 25 May 1989). Thirdly, the Japanese government, and especially MITI, in collaboration with industry leaders, has directed efforts towards restructuring the mismatch between manufacturing and service sector employment in the different Japanese regions (Fujita and Child-Hill 1988). By 1991, the latter initiatives had proved to be largely unnecessary. Indeed, manufacturing companies are, if anything, still expanding, and being forced to locate new facilities in the more rural areas.

The Extent of Japanese Direct Investment

The establishment of Japanese manufacturers in the UK has received a great deal of media attention since the mid-1980s. As well as frequent news items, TV documentaries on Nissan and Komatsu, respectively entitled 'Syonara Pet' and 'Chopsticks, Bulldozers and Newcastle Brown', were screened nationally in 1986 and 1987 and many others have followed since then. Although Japanese direct investment is still very much smaller than, say, American investment, the figures demonstrate that Japan has become a significant investor in the UK.

Morris (1988a) demonstrates that Japanese investment in the UK has lagged behind that in the US, and began on a significant scale only in the mid-1970s. The most recent figures show a sharp acceleration of investment from the mid-1980s. The rapid growth is part of a trend on the part of Japanese investors to increase overseas investment world-wide, reflecting the effects of trade frictions and the strong Yen. The Japanese Ministry of Finance calculated direct investment overseas (cumulative total since 1951) to have increased from US$4.7 billion at the end of 1973 to US$22.3 billion by 1979. By the end of 1986, the figure stood at almost US$106 billion, and two years later it had almost doubled to US$186 billion.

The Finance Ministry further calculated that, in the UK, direct investment from Japan reached a cumulative total (since 1951) of US$4.1 billion at the end of 1986, almost US$1 billion of which was committed in 1986 alone. Two years later the figure was US$10.7 billion, around 5.7 per cent of the total amount invested overseas by the Japanese. Meanwhile, the UK, up to 1988, was the recipient of over a third of the total Japanese investment commitment in the EC. The *Financial Times* (24 April 1987) reported that Japanese investment in the UK involved the direct employment of over 17,500 people. Since then, many further investment decisions have been made, and many Japanese companies previously established in the UK have expanded investment commitments and employment levels. Nissan alone announced a plan to add £250 million to its present commitment of £350 million, creating an additional 1,400 jobs by 1992.

Estimates of employment figures in Japanese companies in the UK sometimes contradict one another, but it is clear that the numbers of workers directly employed by Japanese organizations have grown rapidly during the 1980s. Examination of figures cited by Dunning (1986), Morris (1988a) and Hove et al. (1990) suggests a rise from 15,800 at the end of 1983 to 18,000 at the beginning of 1987, and to over 50,000 by 1990. Around 60 per cent of the last figure is estimated to be accounted for by manufacturing industry. George Bull, Director of the Anglo-Japanese Economic Institute, has claimed that Japanese companies in the UK could employ over 200,000 workers by the year 2000 (*The Observer*, 26 February 1989).

Investment commitment and employment figures both demonstrate significant growth in the 1980s, as does the number of Japanese manufacturing establishments in the UK. The number of Japanese manufacturers rose from around 20 companies in 1980, to around 50 in 1987, and up to around 160 by 1991 (Dunning 1986; Morris 1988a; Dillow 1989; Hove et al. 1990; Anglo-Japanese Economic Institute 1991).

There are at least two reasons to expect further increases in the significance of Japanese direct investment. One is the expected continued inflow of suppliers to the major Japanese corporations. A second is that (at least until Nissan arrived) manufacturing investment commitment was heavily concentrated in the electronics sector – it is likely that other sectors will continue to follow. Indeed, the big Japanese construction companies, already well established overseas in the Far East and Australia, are now looking further afield – including to Europe (*Financial Times*, 18 May 1987).

Japanese manufacturers in Britain have received some criticism on the grounds that their manufacturing investment commitments are largely in low-value-added assembly operations, that the jobs created have been low-paid, low-skilled ones and that R&D and the pro-

Table 9.2 UK manufacturing productivity by plant ownership

	Gross output		*Gross value-added*	
	Per operative	*Per employee*	*Per operative*	*Per employee*
UK	100	100	100	100
EC	150	136	140	128
German	157	138	153	134
Japanese	167	182	75	81
US	188	171	161	146
Total foreign	174	160	152	140

Source: 1986 Census of Production; cited in Dillow 1989

duction of high-value-added components remain in Japan (Morris 1988a; James 1989).

Census of Production figures that compare output and value-added and wage and salary levels per employee lend some support to this view, as tables 9.2 and 9.3 demonstrate. However, it should be noted that these figures are dated, and Japanese manufacturing investment has clearly progressed since they were compiled.

This is not to say that the Japanese are low-payers in terms of the industries in which they operate. Indeed, a 1989 survey suggests that Japanese companies in Britain tend, if anything, to pay above-average rates in relation to the industries in which they operate and in relation to their local labour markets (see table 9.4, with findings supported by a separate survey of 11 Japanese companies in Pang and Oliver 1988).

The apparent contrast between the wage figures in tables 9.3 and 9.4 is most likely due to the fact that investment commitments so far have tended to be in low-skilled assembly operations and in relatively low-labour-cost areas of Britain, such as Wales (which has the highest concentration of Japanese transplants in Europe) and the North East of England, a point discussed in more depth below. Further, it is to be expected that the quality of investment commitment will begin by being low and rise gradually. On this point, some commentators (such as James 1989) remain pessimistic, suggesting that Japanese overseas investments have more to do with finding ways around trade barriers than with genuine globalization. Others

Table 9.3 Annual wage and salary levels by nationality of enterprise

	Manual workers	Non-manual
Total foreign	£9,347	£12,685
Total domestic	£7,787	£10,862
US	£9,378	£13,216
EC	£8,566	£12,041
German	£8,391	£11,201
Japanese	£6,773	£9,286

Source: 1986 Census of Production; cited in Dillow 1989

Table 9.4 Relative pay levels of Japanese manufacturers in the UK

	Sectoral comparison		Regional comparison	
	N	(%)	N	(%)
Top 10%	2	5.0	2	5.0
Top 30%	9	22.5	10	25.0
30–50%	11	27.5	9	22.5
Average	16	40.0	16	40.0
Below average	1	2.5	1	2.5
Don't know	1	2.5	2	5.0
N (number in sample) = 40				

Source: Yu and Wilkinson 1989

(such as Dillow 1989) forecast increases in R&D commitments and high-value-added operations as Japanese companies gradually upgrade their presence.

Entry Strategies and Location Decisions

During the 1980s, the favoured entry strategy for Japanese companies setting up operations in Europe was the use of the greenfield site. In 1988, for instance, only 8.5 per cent of Japanese European investments comprised acquisitions (Dillow 1989). Hostile takeovers have been virtually ruled out, according to BIC (1989), because of the bad publicity that they would attract. Joint ventures, on the other hand, may be emerging as a favoured entry strategy for the smaller Japanese companies – for instance, sub-contractors to the vehicle assemblers – who are increasingly setting up in Europe (Oliver, Morris and Wilkinson 1992).

Within Europe, the UK is by far the favourite location. This is due to factors such as low costs, a positive political climate, the English language, and the existence of a 'soft' domestic market in which to start EC production (Morris 1988a). Moreover, by the mid-1980s a 'momentum' effect was occurring. In addition, Dillow (1989, p. 16) comments that:

> To the extent that the UK has reduced trade union power, and created a large pool of non-unionised workers, it has obviously fostered the conditions favourable to such investment.

Within Britain, Japanese manufacturers have tended to concentrate their investments in areas of relatively high unemployment and cheap labour, such as the North East and South Wales. One report states that by 1991 Wales alone accounted for 41 Japanese companies, employing 12,000 people (*Western Mail*, 19 September 1991). However, new towns, such as Livingston in Scotland, Milton Keynes and Telford, have also received significant investments. Most location decisions have been met with generous local and national government aid (Morris 1988b), though a recent survey puts government financial assistance at the bottom of a list of the most important business and logistical criteria behind Japanese companies' choices of location. At the top come factors such as the quality and supply of labour, and transport and communication links (Hove et al. 1990).

How long the factors, such as the strong Yen, political pressure and so on, that are leading to substantial Japanese commitments will continue is debatable. Nonetheless, the long-term commitment of those companies that have invested appears to be strong, as is indicated in the following quotation, which suggests an intent to increase both the quantity and the quality of investment. The quotation is part of a speech made by Takao Negishi, European Director of Japan's Electronic Industries Association, at the launch of a pamphlet promoting the Japanese contribution to Britain, which was sent to all 633 British MPs:

We are in a transition period, at the infant stage, and we need time and understanding . . . [I]n the second stage we will be picking up the best brains in the country.

The Research

The practices of Japanese companies with manufacturing operations in the UK were explored in both 1987 and 1991 using a similar survey questionnaire to that used to explore the practices of the 'emulators' described in previous chapters. Because most companies had set up within the last few years, there seemed little point in examining the dates of introduction of practices. In 1987, questionnaires were sent to all 49 Japanese manufacturing companies whose addresses were given in the 1986 Anglo-Japanese Economic Institute's Japanese company directory. Fourteen were returned completed, a response rate of 29 per cent. The companies' workforces varied in size from three employees up to 2,550. Two of the companies were established British businesses that had been taken over by Japanese firms in the two years prior to the survey. Although the sample size of this survey was small, three other studies into Japanese companies in the UK were carried out at the Cardiff Business School in 1987: Gleave (1987), Morris (1988b) and Pang (1987). In combination, the four studies covered a total of 31 companies (about 60 per cent of the total number of Japanese manufacturers in Britain in 1987).

The 1991 survey consisted of a similar, though somewhat extended questionnaire, which was mailed to the 155 or so Japanese manufacturing companies listed in the 1991 Anglo-Japanese Economic Institute's Japanese company directory. Of the forms sent out, 52 were returned completed, a response rate of 34 per cent.

The mean size of the companies in the 1987 survey was a workforce of 469, though many expected rapid growth over the next few years. The 1991 respondents varied in size from workforces of four to 2,600 employees, with a mean of 409. Most (75 per cent) were single-site concerns; 17 per cent operated on two sites and 8 per cent on three sites.

The rest of this chapter explores four aspects of the activities and experiences of Japanese manufacturers in the UK: location, operations and markets; manufacturing practices; personnel and industrial relations practices; and relations with suppliers.

Operations and Markets

The operations of the Japanese companies that responded to the 1987 survey are shown in table 9.5, and those of the ones that participated in the 1991 survey in table 9.6.

As tables 9.5 and 9.6 show, manufacturers of electrical and electronic products were dominant in both the 1987 and 1991 samples, as indeed they are in the total population of Japanese companies operating in Britain. The companies falling into the category of miscellaneous represent a diverse array of operations,

Table 9.5 Operations of Japanese companies in the UK (1987)

Operations	Number in sample	Percentage of sample
Vehicles and automotive	4	13
Electronics/electrical	16	52
Engineering	1	3
Food/drink/tobacco	1	3
Miscellaneous manufacturing	9	29
Petrochemicals	–	–
Pharmaceuticals	–	–
	(31)	(100)

Table 9.6 Operations of Japanese companies in the UK (1991)

Operations	Number in sample	Percentage of sample
Vehicles and components	6	12
Chemicals	0	0
Consumer goods	3	6
Electronics	19	35
Plastics and rubber	6	12
Capital goods	6	12
Textiles	1	2
Miscellaneous engineering	3	6
Metals and minerals processing	0	0
Miscellaneous manufacturing	8	15
Food	0	0
	(52)	(100)

from sports gear to PVC sheeting. The proportion of companies in the vehicle and automotive category is remarkably stable across the two surveys; this proportion is likely to increase as Japanese sub-contractors follow the major vehicle assemblers overseas. As might be expected, there was a greater diversity of operations apparent in 1991 compared with 1987.

The main markets served by the Japanese companies in 1987 and 1991 are shown in table 9.7, along with those of UK companies by way of comparison. As might be expected, the Japanese companies are somewhat more 'multinational' in their marketing outlook than the UK sample. Also interesting, is the shift in emphasis on the part of the Japanese companies between 1987 and 1991, the trend being towards a reduced reliance on UK markets and world markets, with a corresponding increase in their European focus. This seems to indicate that the UK arms of Japanese manufacturers are indeed being used to form a major part of their European base. This is also consistent with the 'global localization' thesis.

In the 1987 survey, Japanese companies were asked to indicate the nationalities of up to four of their major competitors. The responses to this question are given in table 9.8.

Interestingly, leaving aside the general 'European countries' category, other Japanese companies were most often seen as the major competitors of our sample firms, which calls into question the popular stereotype of 'Japan Inc.' Notable also is the presence of the Pacific Basin countries as competitors, a trend that is likely to continue as these countries become more highly developed.

Table 9.7 Main markets of UK manufacturers and Japanese manufacturers in the UK (1987, 1991)

	UK companies	*Japanese companies*	
Markets	*1991 (%)*	*1987 (%)*	*1991 (%)*
UK only	28	36	25
Europe	35	43	59
World	37	21	16

Manufacturing and Working Practices

Manufacturing practices are presented in descending order of usage in tables 9.9 and 9.10 for 1987 and 1991 respectively. Because of the recent establishment of the companies involved, the 'current usage' category was combined with the 'planned or being implemented' category, on the grounds that a number of companies had simply not had time to implement these practices by the date at which they completed the survey.

The first feature to note about table 9.9 is that all companies were either using or implementing total quality control (TQC), although a third reported that they were still only in the process of planning or implementing it. This implies that TQC is taking the Japanese

Table 9.8 Nationalities of main competitors of Japanese companies in the UK (1987)

Country	Number of citations
Japan	10
USA	7
Britain	5
Pacific Basin (Taiwan, Korea, etc.)	5
Other European countries	11

Table 9.9 Manufacturing practices in Japanese companies in the UK (1987)

Practice	Never used (%)	In use, planned or being implemented (%)	Number in sample
Total quality control	0	100	19
Flexible working	5	95	19
Group working	7	93	14
SPC	21	79	14
Quality circles	27	73	30
JIT production	36	64	22

Source: Authors' survey; Morris 1988a; Gleave 1987; Pang 1987

companies some time to develop in the UK environment (or that it is something that they themselves are still learning about). Flexibility and the use of work teams also showed extensive usage. The incidence of usage of other techniques is less marked: only two-thirds of companies reported using, planning or implementing JIT. Of these, 42 per cent reported that they were currently using it, while half of the non-users were planning or implementing it.

The 1991 survey shows some similarities to and some differences from the 1987 one. Of the items that were common to both surveys, the use of JIT production and quality circles shows an increase between the two; SPC remains the same and the use of TQC and cells – the nearest equivalent to team working – shows a fall. The drop in the case of cells or teams is probably due to the change in wording between the two surveys, as cells represent a 'purer' form of responsibility than do the ubiquitous 'work teams'. The drop in the use of total quality appears to be due to the fact that a number of the Japanese-owned companies in the 1991 survey represented recent takeovers of established UK businesses, and hence were still operating established systems. The pattern of the *relative* usage of Japanese practices in this survey largely mirrors that found in the 1991 sample of UK firms.

When we turn to examine how highly Japanese companies

Table 9.10 Manufacturing practices in Japanese companies in the UK (1991)

Practice	Never used (%)	In use (%)	Planned or being implemented (%)
Operator responsibility for quality	4	80	16
Continuous improvement	6	65	29
Quality circles	12	62	26
SPC	21	54	25
Design for manufacture	40	54	6
Set-up time reductions	30	50	20
JIT production	27	46	27
Total quality control	10	39	51
Cellular manufacture	60	33	7
Kanban materials control	55	30	15
N = 52			

evaluate their success with these practices, we are limited to our own survey findings; consequently some of the numbers are rather small. Nevertheless, this information (presented in table 9.11) gives some indication of the relative success rates in 1987.

The first point to note from table 9.11 is the success that, on the whole, Japanese companies reported with these practices (although variation between practices is apparent). Flexible working, total quality control and the use of work teams all stand out as particularly successful. This pattern broadly follows that of the evaluations made by the UK companies emulating Japanese practices in 1987, although the mean scores – and by implication degree of success – recorded by the Japanese companies is greater for every practice apart from JIT. However, statistically, the Japanese companies emerge as *significantly* more successful on only one of the above items, namely flexible working. In common with the experiences of the emulating companies, quality circles again come well down the league table in terms of their success. The comparable figures for the 1991 sample are shown in table 9.12.

The main point of general interest to note from table 9.12 is that the mean 'success' scores are on the whole *lower* than those in the 1987 survey, a pattern also found in the case of the emulators. The reported success of total quality shows a particular fall, as does that of SPC. The success of quality circles stays the same, and JIT production, the least successful practice in 1987, shows a slight increase in success, although it still comes towards the foot of the list.

Table 9.11 Evaluation of manufacturing practices by Japanese companies in the UK (1987)

Practice	Not successful (%)	Quite–very successful (%)	Highly successful (%)	Mean*
Flexible working	–	33	67	3.50
Total quality control	–	42	58	3.42
Work teams	8	33	59	3.33
SPC	–	67	33	2.89
Quality circles	10	80	10	2.50
JIT production	12	76	12	2.25
N = 14				

*1 = Not successful 4 = Highly successful

Table 9.12 Evaluation of manufacturing practices by Japanese companies in the UK (1991)

Practice	Not successful (%)	Quite–very successful (%)	Highly successful (%)	Mean
Continuous improvement	3	78	19	2.83
Operator responsibility for quality	5	74	21	2.81
Cellular manufacture	6	82	12	2.56
Total quality control	4	85	11	2.53
Design for manufacture	5	80	15	2.50
Quality circles	9	79	12	2.50
SPC	3	87	10	2.39
JIT production	14	75	11	2.39
Set-up time reductions	4	96	–	2.39
Kanban materials control	13	74	13	2.33
N = 52				

What explanations are there for these patterns, particularly the greater early success of the Japanese companies with flexible working?

Anecdotal evidence points to a shopfloor regime markedly different from that in typical British firms. Takamiya (1981) noted much greater attention paid to minor details in the production process. In particular, he contrasted British and Japanese practice in printed circuit board assembly: the British strategy to safeguard quality was to buy an extremely sophisticated and expensive testing machine; the Japanese approach was to organize assembly into three-worker teams, with two workers inserting components and one visually checking and correcting. He recounts:

> Every movement of the operators is closely watched and constantly improved upon. Every mistake they make is constantly and individually fed back to them verbally by supervisors, formally by tables and graphs displayed in front of them and visually by supervisors taking them to the other production section where their mistake is causing trouble. (Takamiya 1981, p. 8)

Many accounts (including our own case study of K-Electric)

suggest that discipline on the shopfloor is much tighter, and this manifests itself in a variety of ways. In comparing Japanese TV manufacturers in Britain with equivalent British and American companies, Reitsperger (1986) found that they exacted much stricter work discipline, discouraged social interaction of semi-skilled workers on the assembly line, and meticulously enforced work standards and procedures. Similarly, Takamiya (1981, p. 9), also comparing Japanese firms with British and American ones, noted:

> While both British and American companies allow eating, drinking and smoking on the shopfloor, the Japanese strictly prohibit such activities even during breaks. Sometimes chatting can be cause for a warning.

Another characteristic of Japanese companies that is frequently commented upon is an insistence on 'bell-to-bell' working. As a senior official from the EETPU, who had negotiated a number of agreements with Japanese firms, remarked to the authors during an interview:

> The Japanese believe in bell-to-bell working. They cannot understand the mentality of the British people where they have to go to the toilet at times other than their natural break because they have conditioned themselves to do that. They can't understand why they are not prepared to cooperate with the company and give back to the company the two-and-a-half-minute washing time before the end of the bell because the Japanese say 'Well it's our company and that two-and-a-half minutes, if added up throughout the week is 70 television sets.' Whichever way you look at it they are absolutely right.

In some cases, bell-to-bell working is written into union agreements. The Nissan–AEU agreement, for example, states 'Employees will be prepared for work at the start and end of their normal working day/shift' (Wickens 1985). The supervisor from Komatsu, quoted in chapter 8, also felt that such discipline was important in Japanese companies' success, when he commented that all that the British worker had to do to work to the Japanese system was to work during the time for which he was paid.

At one Japanese electronics company studied by the authors, assembly line workers occasionally voiced complaints about the demands of the production system. One worker commented that:

> ... when you're interviewed they ask you what's the most important –
> quality or quantity. They want you to say quality, but when you get
> on the line you see they want both. You can't have both.

Another operator commented that:

> Sometimes you just slide them [the components] in the wrong way
> round or whatever without knowing, and suddenly somebody shouts
> it up the line. You don't know how you did it ... 20 rejects [within a
> month] mean you get ... a warning. We do 8,000 components a day,
> sometimes 10,000. Twenty rejects isn't many.

Anecdotal evidence concerning quality circles in Japanese companies provides instances of both successes and relative failures. The
industrial relations executive of a Japanese colour TV manufacturer
described the company's success with quality circles as 'patchy'.
Most of their 'quality activity groups' were supervisor-led in order
to provide a focus; people were generally reluctant to take the
initiative themselves. On the other hand, there have been reports
from Komatsu of workers forming quality circles and meeting after
work to discuss quality problems, which indicates a high level of
success – from the company's point of view at least (BBC 1987).
Mitsubishi, located in Livingston new town, also reports success,
with a version of quality circles that involves splitting operators into
teams that seek to achieve performance targets for attendance,
housekeeping and 'zero defects'.

A shopfloor control technique used at Mitsubishi, and also reported in Nissan and K-Electric (chapter 8), is to display performance
details publicly. At Mitsubishi the weekly performance ratings of
operators are displayed on charts above their heads, and charts at the
ends of assembly lines show the performance of the quality circle
(*Financial Times*, 18 January 1988). Views on this practice are
mixed. In one company, a supervisor who was responsible for
updating individual performance charts commented to the authors:

> I don't like the cards ... putting them up over their heads is like
> you're putting them [the operators] down morally.

In general, however, public displays of performance, absenteeism
and the like, are more or less accepted, and there is little indication
of serious resistance to such devices. Saso (1990) similarly documents

an acceptance of tight shopfloor discipline among women workers in Japanese transplants in both Britain and Ireland.

Flexible working stands out as an area in which the Japanese companies have been particularly successful in comparison with their British counterparts, both in the 1987 survey and according to other published accounts. An IRS survey (*IRS Employment Trends* 470, 21 August 1990) of 25 Japanese manufacturers found that all but one used multi-skilling, while all but three claimed flexibility across skilled and unskilled grades. Takamiya (1981) reports the case of a Japanese colour TV manufacturer in Britain in which secretaries and clerical workers helped out on the shopfloor with insertion and packing when adverse weather conditions led to a shortage of operators. At the same company there were also instances of supervisors, operators and technicians installing a conveyer because of delays with a sub-contractor. Where there have been problems with flexible working these have tended to be limited by ability rather than motivation.

Reward systems in Japanese companies in Britain are often clearly designed to encourage such flexibility. For instance, Toshiba has a reward system that pays workers to be flexible; there are 18 recognized production skills, and increments are paid for each one mastered. More generally, as described below, the systems of appraisal used by most Japanese manufacturers mean that a willingness to work flexibly has a favourable impact on pay grades.

A number of conditions present in the Japanese companies appear to facilitate the flexibility, discipline and bell-to-bell working that characterize them. These relate to their personnel practices, and it is to these that we now turn attention.

Personnel and Industrial Relations Practices

The usage of six Japanese personnel and industrial relations practices is explored in this section: the provision of single-status facilities; the establishment of systems of communication and involvement; the granting of 'staff' benefits to all; the offer of job security; the setting-up of representative bodies; and the employment of temporary workers. The results are shown in table 9.13.

In 1987, single status was practised in all but two companies. Of the two that did not have single-status conditions, one was very small, employing only three people, and the other a long-established

Table 9.13 Personnel practices in Japanese companies in the UK (1987)

Practice	Never used (%)	In use, planned or being implemented (%)	Number in sample
Single-status facilities	12	88	24
In-company communications	17	83	18
'Staff' benefits for all	25	75	16
High job-security	27	73	22
Company representative bodies	45	55	20
Use of temporary workers	67	33	21

Source: Authors' survey; Gleave 1987; Pang 1987

British company taken into Japanese ownership only the year before the survey was conducted. In all the other companies, single status was in use. Almost as high a proportion of companies used some form of direct communication with workers, although this clearly took a variety of forms. One prevalent form was the regular team briefing, which also functioned as a forum for discussion.

A majority of the companies reported that they offered high job-security for their core workers, although, as in Japan, this was never offered contractually, but rather as a matter of general policy. Gleave and Oliver (1990) suggest that this policy is largely attributable to influence by the Japanese parent companies.

Company representative bodies exist in just over half the firms in the combined sample. Since these carry implications for industrial relations they will be discussed in some detail below.

As we saw in chapter 2, in Japan the major corporations segment their labour markets and make extensive use of temporary and other peripheral workers. In the UK in 1987, a significant minority of Japanese companies (33 per cent) routinely used temporary workers. They still represented a smaller proportion of the total sample than in the case of the UK companies emulating Japanese practices. However, some had deployed temporary workers in positions traditionally the prerogative of permanent employees. As already mentioned, Nissan was the first company to employ temporary workers on a car assembly line in Britain since the Second World

Table 9.14 Personnel practices in Japanese companies in the UK (1991)

Practice	Never used (%)	In use (%)	Planned or being implemented (%)
Team briefings	8	88	4
Performance appraisal	15	66	19
Single-status facilities	29	65	6
Company council	35	54	11
Use of temporary workers	43	50	7
Performance-related pay	48	50	2
Profit sharing	78	15	7
N = 52			

War (*Financial Times*, 16 February 1987). Table 9.14 shows the status of a comparable range of personnel practices in Japanese companies in the UK in 1991.

Notable shifts over the four years include a reduction in the proportion of companies reporting single-status facilities, probably as a consequence of the acquisition of traditional firms. In addition, there are increases in the use of employee involvement via team briefings, and in company councils and the use of temporary workers. The use of performance appraisal also figures quite highly amongst the companies in the 1991 survey, an issue discussed at some length below.

Turning to how the Japanese companies evaluated their success with personnel practices, a generally favourable picture emerged in 1987, with a majority of companies considering these practices 'highly successful'. Two qualifications should, however, be made. First, and self-evidently, the number of companies reporting in 1987 was small – only three in the case of temporary workers, for example. Secondly, 'success' was defined by the companies themselves, and therefore may have meant different things to different organizations, according to what their objectives were in using such practices in the first place.

In common with the pattern for manufacturing practices, the picture from the 1991 survey of the evaluation of personnel practices, in table 9.16, is of much lower levels of success than in 1987. Indeed,

Table 9.15 Evaluation of personnel practices by Japanese companies in the UK (1987)

Practice	Not successful (%)	Quite–very successful (%)	Highly successful (%)	Mean
Temporary workers	–	33	67	3.67
In-company communications	–	27	73	3.64
Single-status facilities	–	40	60	3.60
'Staff' benefits for all	–	38	62	3.50
High job-security	–	38	62	3.50
Employee involvement	9	36	55	3.27
N = 14				

Table 9.16 Evaluation of personnel practices by Japanese companies in the UK (1991)

Practice	Not successful (%)	Quite–very successful (%)	Highly successful (%)	Mean
Single-status facilities	7	60	33	3.11
Use of temporary workers	5	80	15	2.65
Company council	8	80	12	2.50
Team briefings	7	78	15	2.49
Performance appraisal	7	83	10	2.48
Performance-related pay	14	86	–	2.19
Profit sharing	33	56	11	1.89
N = 52				

so pronounced is this that the worst-rated practice in 1987 (employee involvement) still received a higher score than the best-rated practice in 1991 (single-status facilities). The use of temporary workers still came near the top of the list in performance terms; while the use of financial incentives likely to create 'a community of interests' in the firm (profit sharing, performance-related pay and so on) came lowest down it.

The sections that follow discuss Japanese companies' experiences in the light of the survey findings, using case study material.

Other aspects of personnel practices, such as recruitment, appraisal and reward, are also considered.

Direct communication and single status

In-company communications, single-status facilities and the provision of 'staff' benefits for blue-collar workers take a variety of forms. From the companies' perspectives, these practices were regarded quite favourably in both surveys, although other evidence suggests that the picture is a little more mixed at lower levels in the organizations. Single status appears to have been generally welcomed by direct employees and by trade unions, although some of its trappings – for example the wearing of uniforms – have not always been wholeheartedly appreciated. At Matsushita in Cardiff, for example, some of the female administrative workers were reluctant to wear uniforms as they considered them unflattering; at Hoya, the Managing Director had a problem convincing a delivery driver that he was in fact the Managing Director, on account of the uniform that he was wearing (Gleave 1987).

Single status is usually appreciated by those who would otherwise be well down the status hierarchy, but what about those who would traditionally be at an advantage in terms of status distinctions? In general it does not appear to have caused many problems, although there are signs from some of the longer-established companies that the homogeneity created by single status tends to degenerate over time, partly due to the existence of status differentials in the wider industrial environment. Commenting on the situation at a TV manufacturing company, a trade union official remarked to us:

> When senior management are taken on they ask 'What's the pension scheme? Is there a special incentive scheme?' They are told that it's the same as the guy on the shopfloor. So there is a little bit of change and resentment about the old British type of understanding about perks creeping back into the company.

The case of the newly appointed supervisor at Komatsu, ruefully reflecting on how he used to dream about the day when he would come to work in a suit and tie (reported in chapter 8), provides another example of this sentiment, and at Mitsubishi managers have 'quietly' ceased wearing uniforms (*Financial Times*, 18 January 1988). There is some evidence that managerial turnover in the

Japanese companies is relatively high, but one might expect this to be so unless the lack of status-related rewards is compensated for by more pronounced salary differentials. As yet, the experience of managers in Japanese companies in the UK has received scant attention. Given the predominance of single status, and the often-heard complaint that there exists a 'ceiling' above which UK managers cannot rise, this may be an area worthy of further research.

Selection

Another notable aspect of Japanese companies' personnel practices lies in their selection and recruitment criteria, and some explanation of their success with flexible working and the apparent willingness to accept bell-to-bell discipline may plausibly be ascribed to this. Morris (1988b) noted that 15 out of the 20 companies that he approached recruited young, unskilled workers – generally school-leavers – to perform production jobs. The Commercial Director of Livingston Development Corporation refers to a preference on the part of newly investing companies for 'uncontaminated' labour (*Financial Times*, 18 January 1988). Pang (1987) found a similar emphasis in seven of the 11 companies that she studied, although there was a marked tendency for managerial talent to be 'bought in'.

This pattern may be partly explained by the generally low skill levels required in many of these companies, but also by a desire to have a disciplined and flexible workforce. For instance, NEC's Personnel Manager, responsible for the employment of 280 operators whose average age is eighteen-and-a-half, argued that the company needed a young workforce willing to undergo frequent training. As he put it, 'We cannot offer them a long-term job. But we are guaranteeing them long-term employment.'

It is possible that the emphasis on raw recruits at all levels may increase as Japanese companies establish themselves and have to rely less heavily on externally acquired professionals and skilled workers. One exception to the 'raw recruit' policy is presented by Takiron, a Japanese company established in Wales, with a single-union agreement with the TGWU. Its policy is to recruit young married men because of their perceived dependability as well as their ability to work shifts (Gleave 1987). Some regional variation is also apparent; due to the tight labour market in its area, the Personnel Manager of a company in the South East of England remarked to one of the authors that all that his firm required of would-be recruits was that they should be 'warm and walking'.

Whether or not Japanese companies intend this, the effect of their policy, in many cases, is to provide them with a workforce untainted by established working habits. Nor is such a workforce likely to have any previous experience of, or involvement in, trade union activity of any kind. Hence recruits are more easily socialized into the ways of the company, and if the company does have a trade union, more easily socialized into cooperative union-management relations. Some companies, of which Komatsu is an example, make use of a variety of attitude tests in their selection procedures.

Following recruitment, new members of many Japanese companies in Britain typically undergo a company-organized induction programme (Gleave 1987), the length of which varies from company to company. At Matsushita's Panasonic plant in Cardiff, for instance, the formal induction lasts only one day, whereas at Komatsu in Birtley there are ten full-day sessions spread over the first ten weeks at work, including Japan-familiarization courses. Further induction is typically given with immediate on-the-job training in a variety of tasks or jobs. At Mazak, the Japanese machine-tool plant in Worcester, this involves trainees submitting weekly reports on progress, and serves to impress on them the importance of flexible working.

Pay and appraisal

As discussed earlier in this chapter, levels of pay relative to industry and local labour markets tend to be average or above average in Japanese firms. Pay structures tend to be very simple, with relatively small numbers of job classifications, and while various forms of bonus scheme exist in many Japanese companies, they tend to account for a small proportion of total pay – typically less than 5 per cent (Yu and Wilkinson 1989).

It is in the area of appraisals – and their use with regard to pay and promotion – that Japanese companies stand out as exceptional. The following account summarizes the findings of a survey of their practices. Of the 40 companies that responded, 27 used appraisal schemes, including *all* those employing over 200 workers and 11 out of the 12 manufacturing companies contained in the sample. In 25 of the 27 companies that used appraisals, the system was applied to *all* workers, rather than being restricted, as has been typical in Britain, to white-collar and managerial staffs. Even more remarkable was the use to which appraisals were put. Appraisal results were widely used in the context of determining wage levels, promotion prospects and task allocation (table 9.17).

Twenty-one of the 40 companies said that seniority had some influence on individual salary levels, and 15 that it affected promotion. Asked to weight the relative importance of appraisal results and seniority, most companies ascribed them equal importance or showed a bias towards appraisal.

Analysis of 13 sets of appraisal documentation that were received demonstrated a mix of task performance indicators and subjectively assessed personal characteristics, as is found in the *satei* system in Japanese companies in Japan (see chapter 2). Table 9.18 lists appraisal criteria in order of frequency of use.

Very striking is the emphasis on factors such as teamwork, communications and attitudes, an emphasis that would appear to fit with Japanese companies' flexible deployment of labour and use of work teams.

Although revealing similarities between the personnel practices of different Japanese companies in the UK, detailed case study work also highlights the variations in practice that one finds. In analysing the personnel practices of five such firms, Gleave and Oliver (1990) noted not only similarities but also important differences. All five of these businesses had an underlying ethos of long-term employment, though none specified lifetime employment contractually. In contrast, the nature of the employee–organization relationship varied considerably from company to company; two offered long-term career development with the company, while the other three, though possessing informal 'no-redundancies' policies, placed less emphasis on this aspect of employment prospects. The nature of the pro-

Table 9.17   Use of appraisal systems in Japanese companies in the UK

Influenced by appraisal	Job grade/ wage level	Job class/ promotion	Task allocation/ transfers
Yes	26 (96.3%)	24 (88.9%)	19 (70.4%)
No	1 (3.7%)	3 (11.1%)	8 (29.6%)
N = 27			

Source: Yu and Wilkinson 1989

duction processes of the first two companies placed shopfloor employees in a more strategic position, and personnel practices seemed to reflect this. Put simply, those companies in which the employees could make the most impact on product quality and levels of output appeared to be the ones where the most sophisticated human resource practices were employed.

The reward systems of the five companies also varied considerably. Some paid their shopfloor workers wages, others salaries. Only one paid a Japanese-style annual bonus linked to company profitability. Three had an element of pay linked to an individual's performance; one paid an attendance bonus (a reflection of problems with absenteeism). The very variety in reward systems in Gleave and Oliver's cases illustrates the danger of viewing Japanese-style management as a homogeneous phenomenon. The companies studied faced different contingencies, different issues and different problems. Their reward systems reflected the various strategies that they had adopted to meet these demands.

Table 9.18 Appraisal criteria at 13 Japanese companies in the UK

Criteria	No. of companies using criteria
Team working ability, cooperation	11
Self-organization, problem-solving skills	10
Leadership, persuasiveness	9
Attendance, punctuality	8
Quantity of work, efficiency, productivity	8
Communication skills	7
Job knowledge	7
Accuracy, attention to detail	7
Attitude, motivation, loyalty	7
Creativity, initiative	6
Flexibility, adaptability	5
Quality of work	5
Ability to work under pressure	4
Enthusiasm, willingness to work	4
Safety, housekeeping	4
Reasoning, analytical skills	4
Persistence, determination	3
Work skills	3

Source: Yu and Wilkinson 1989

Management–union relations

Given the extensive use of company-based representative bodies, what role do such bodies play, and how does their role relate to that of the trade unions in these Japanese companies?

At Toshiba, the Company Advisory Board consists of 14 elected representatives from all areas of the company, plus the senior union representative, with the Managing Director in the chair. Representatives need not be union members. The Company Advisory Board can discuss 'any subject from the size of the Managing Director's car to the annual salary review' (Trevor 1988). Management–union bargaining is available as a 'backstop' if agreement cannot be reached in the Advisory Board context. Gleave reports a similar backstop role for the AEU at Komatsu, and suggests that there is a feeling within the company that management and workers sitting on its Advisory Council have 'failed' if they have to resort to official company–union bargaining.

Some elements of (implicit if not explicit) bargaining are inevitable between the agents who sit on these bodies, but in general they are rarely construed, by management at least, as bargaining or decision-making agencies. The emphasis is on consultation, an ambiguity that can lead to cynicism about the role of such bodies, as the case of the Komatsu Advisory Council reported in chapter 8 illustrates. At Toshiba, whose arrangements constitute the model on which many other company representative bodies are based, there was some initial confusion about the role of shop stewards on the Company Advisory Board. The traditional view that shop stewards should not sit on such bodies meant that it was primarily non-union members who were sitting on the Board – something that alarmed the EETPU, as it implied a short-circuiting of the trade union structure. Subsequently, EETPU policy has been that stewards should seek election to the Company Advisory Board, and EETPU official Wyn Bevan (during an interview with the authors) pointed out that this was one of the reasons why the EETPU had retained a credible role in the eyes of its membership and hence kept relatively high membership levels.

According to Hove et al. (1990) over half of the Japanese companies with manufacturing facilities in the UK recognize one or more trade unions. Of the 31 Japanese companies in our 1987 sample, 21 (68 per cent) recognized trade unions and, of these 21, all but one had single-union agreements. One of the major motivations behind this was clearly a concern for labour force flexibility. The sole multi-union company had seven trade unions, though this was originally a British company that had been taken into Japanese ownership in 1984. In 1987, the single-union deals were concentrated in the hands of a relatively small set of unions, as is shown in table 9.19.

Unsurprisingly, those unions with 'progressive' reputations, such as the EETPU and the AEU, had been accepted as single unions in rather more Japanese companies than those with a more traditional image, such as the TGWU. Because of the membership crisis in the trade union movement, competition between unions for single-union deals with inwardly investing companies has led to conflict. For example, in a 1987 television interview one trade unionist described some of his colleagues in other trade unions as 'pigs at the trough of Thatcherism' on account of their behaviour towards inwardly investing companies in South Wales. The TGWU has been one of the most bitter critics of single-union deals, particularly those that contain so-called no-strike clauses. Indeed, in January 1988 the regional secretary of the TGWU in Wales appealed to the Japanese government to urge companies setting up in the UK to do so without reaching strike-free agreements with British unions. This move was intended to prevent companies from signing agreements with the EETPU in preference to other unions on the grounds that the former would offer a 'strike-free' package (*Financial Times*, 20 January 1988). Partly as a consequence of a row over a 'beauty contest' for recognition rights at a Japanese company the EETPU was expelled from the TUC.

Contrary to the impression given by some reports in the press at the time about very low levels of union membership in Japanese companies, the 1987 results indicated a wide range of variation in

Table 9.19 Trade unions in Japanese companies in the UK (1987)

Union	Number of companies	Average membership density
EETPU	8	64%
AEU	5	58%
GMB	3	65%
TGWU	2	60%
N	(18)	(62%)

Source: Authors' survey; Pang and Oliver 1988

membership levels, from a low of 25 per cent up to a claimed 100 per cent. Average union membership reported by the 16 Japanese companies on which data were available was 59 per cent. A more recent IRS survey (*IRS Employment Trends* 470, 21 August 1990) found an average membership density of 68 per cent among a sample of 14 companies.

The data from our 1991 survey show something of a shift compared with those from 1987. A much lower percentage of firms recognize trade unions – 47 per cent in 1991 (table 9.20), against 68 per cent in 1987. This may in part be a function of the stage reached in a firm's life cycle, with many new starts being captured by the second survey, but the average number of employees of the companies in the 1991 survey, at 409, was only slightly down from the 1987 level of 469.

A slight increase in multi-union firms is also apparent, this being the legacy of a handful of acquisitions. Table 9.21 shows the identity of the main unions in the unionized Japanese firms, along with their membership levels.

It is interesting to note that although the proportion of Japanese companies that are unionized has declined, the (claimed) member-

Table 9.20 Union status in Japanese companies in the UK (1991)

Status	Number	Percentage
Non-union	27	53
Single-union	19	37
One staff union, one blue-collar union	4	8
Multiple unions	1	2
	(51)	(100)

Table 9.21 Trade unions in Japanese companies in the UK (1991)

Union	Number of companies	Average membership density
EETPU	7	64.6%
AEU	6	92.6%
GMB	4	78.5%
TGWU	5	69.0%
	(22)	(75.8%)

ship levels of those that are unionized actually appear to have risen to an average of 75 per cent. Some variations between unions are also apparent.

Given the extensive use of company-based representative bodies, there is potential for confusion between the role of these bodies and the role of trade unions. It has been suggested that company-based bodies serve to marginalize trade unions, or prevent their penetration in the first place. At Mitsubishi, for instance, approaches for recognition by the EETPU were rebutted by the company on the grounds that its elected staff consultative committee eliminated the need for union recognition (*Financial Times*, 18 January 1988). However, if company-based bodies are generally being used successfully to keep trade unions out, we would expect unionized companies to have a lower proportion of company representative bodies than non-union companies. As table 9.22 shows, such a pattern did not exist among the 1987 sample of companies.

Of the four configurations of company representative bodies and unions, the one most frequently found is the combination of a union presence plus a company representative body. This effectively refutes the idea that there is an either/or situation between company representative bodies and trade unions. If that were the case, we would expect companies to be clustered in categories two and three in table 9.22; that is unionized companies would be less likely to possess a company representative body than non-unionized ones.

In the 1991 survey, this issue was further explored by examining the degree of usage of the company council, where one existed, in the context of whether the company was unionized. These findings are shown in table 9.23.

As table 9.23 demonstrates, the picture is clearly not one of company councils *or* a union representing the workforce. Indeed, the

Table 9.22 Trade unions and company representative bodies in Japanese companies in the UK (1987)

Unionized with company representative body	8	(40%)
Unionized, no company representative body	4	(20%)
Not unionized with company representative body	3	(15%)
Not unionized, no company representative body	5	(25%)
	(20)	(100%)

Source: Authors' survey; Gleave 1987; Pang and Oliver 1988

biggest single grouping of companies consists of those that have *neither* a company council nor a trade union. Among those that are unionized, it is those that have little-used company councils that are most prone to unionization, suggesting that people turn to unionization where there *is* a company council, but where the council is perceived to be ineffective.

It could be argued that the recognition of a trade union is, in itself, a poor index of the effect of company-based representation, and that trade union membership levels are a more meaningful indicator of union status. In 1987, the average union membership in firms with company-based representation was 62 per cent (eight firms), compared with 87 per cent in firms without such representative apparatus (three firms). With such small numbers, there are obviously limits to how far one can extrapolate from these results, but they do suggest a link between trade union membership and the presence of company-based representative bodies. The equivalent results from the 1991 survey are shown in table 9.24.

These figures broadly confirm those of 1987, but they also show the same curvilinear relationship between company councils and unionization that occurs in table 9.23, revealing that union activity is

Table 9.23 Trade unions and company representative bodies in Japanese companies in the UK (1991)

	No union	*Unionized*
No company council	11 (65%)	6 (35%)
Company council – used a little	2 (22%)	7 (78%)
Company council – used widely	9 (53%)	8 (47%)
	(22)	(21)

Table 9.24 Union density and company councils in Japanese companies in the UK (1991)

	Union density
No company council	65.7%
Company council – used a little	82.5%
Company council – used widely	65.6%
N = 52	

moderate in companies without any company council at all *and* in those that have a widely used council, but *high* in companies that have councils that are deemed to be relatively inactive.

In 1987, it was clear that Japanese companies were not conforming to the standard British multi-union model of industrial relations. With the exception of a recent multi-union acquisition, all 31 companies pursued either single-union or non-union policies. Reitsperger (1986, p. 75) has suggested that:

> Multi-union representation, and a resultant difficulty in flexibility and labour utilization, problems of demarcation and the complexity of multi-union bargaining are deeply worrying and seen by Japanese management as impediments to productive performance improvement.

He goes on to argue that Japanese companies essentially face three industrial relations options: to accept unionization in its usual (multi-union) form; to avoid it altogether; or to accept unionization but to utilize strategies to neutralize its negative (from a managerial perspective) consequences. On the 1987 evidence, it appeared that most Japanese companies were selecting either the second or, particularly, the third of these options. The 1991 data indicate something of a convergence between UK companies and their Japanese counterparts, perhaps under the influence of four years of the rhetoric of HRM and continuing hostility to unions on the part of the UK government. In chapter 10, the relationship between company advisory boards and trade unions is explored further.

Buyer–Supplier Relations

This section provides an overview of Japanese companies and their buyer–supplier practices, and examines how successful they consider these practices to be. The status of four aspects of supplier relations as of 1987 is shown in table 9.25.

All the companies surveyed considered themselves to be collaborating very closely with their suppliers; the other three aspects of supplier relations – quality assured supplies, the sub-contracting of non-core activities and JIT – were used with decreasing degrees of frequency. Moreover, the proportion of companies planning or implementing these practices (as distinct from already using them) increased as one moved down the table; the 62 per cent of companies using, planning or implementing the sub-contracting of non-core activities were virtually evenly divided between those already doing so and those planning to so do.

By 1991, there was evidence of increased usage of a number of the practices under consideration (table 9.26). For example, by this date 94 per cent of companies were claiming QA supply, compared with 79 per cent four years previously, perhaps indicating increased confidence in their UK supply bases. JIT supply had also gone up, from about 50 per cent usage to 64 per cent.

For the 1991 survey, the general item of 'close supplier collaboration' was broken down into a series of more focused items, all of which were used on a significant scale by the Japanese companies. We now turn to the evaluation of these practices.

Table 9.25 Buyer–supplier practices in Japanese companies in the UK (1987)

Practice	Never used (%)	In use, planned or being implemented (%)	Number in sample
Close supplier collaboration	0	100	17
Quality assured supplies	21	79	14
Sub-contracting (non-core)	38	62	14
JIT supply	50	50	26

Source: Authors' survey; Morris 1988b

Table 9.26 Buyer–supplier practices in Japanese companies in the UK (1991)

Practice	Never used (%)	In use (%)	Planned or being implemented (%)
Single sourcing	17	79	4
QA supplies	6	75	19
Supplier development	23	62	15
Supplier involvement in design	33	55	12
JIT supplies	36	48	16
N = 52			

In 1987, supplier relations practices all received less favourable evaluation ratings than did the personnel practices discussed earlier, with the 'mechanics' of buyer–supplier relations, such as quality and JIT delivery of purchased supplies, coming in the lower half of the list (table 9.27).

The equivalent information for 1991 is shown in table 9.28. Consistent with in-house manufacturing practices and personnel practices, supplier practices generally received lower ratings in the 1991 survey than they did in 1987. In 1991, JIT supply had moved to the bottom of the list in terms of success, and, interestingly, QA supplies had moved from bottom position to top. The implication of this is that UK suppliers are starting to improve their performance with respect to quality, with JIT delivery now being the greater problem area.

Certainly, in the late 1980s there was evidence that local suppliers

Table 9.27 Evaluation of buyer–supplier practices by Japanese companies in the UK (1987)

Practice	Not successful (%)	Quite–very successful (%)	Highly successful (%)	Mean
Close collaboration with suppliers	–	58	42	3.00
Sub-contracting	12	63	25	2.75
JIT supply	11	67	22	2.56
Quality assured supplies	10	45	45	2.00

Table 9.28 Evaluation of buyer–supplier practices by Japanese companies in the UK (1991)

Practice	Not successful (%)	Quite–very successful (%)	Highly successful (%)	Mean
QA supplies	5	84	11	2.45
Single sourcing	6	88	6	2.32
Supplier development	10	83	7	2.24
Supplier involvement in design	15	81	4	2.15
JIT supplies	10	87	3	2.10

were improving their capabilities (Morris and Imrie 1991), although Japanese manufacturers continued to be uncomplimentary about local components with regard to price, quality and delivery. Critics argue that these sentiments represent a smokescreen that hides a pro-Japanese bias.

In the mid-1980s, reported problems with locally produced components centred around 'a casual management style – particularly with respect to quality control – inadequate capacity and relaxed attitudes to deliveries' (Dunning 1986, pp. 116f.). A report conducted in 1987–8 by Coopers and Lybrand into the automotive component purchasing patterns of Japanese manufacturers in the UK reached broadly similar conclusions. Issues included:

- The *quality* of components, which was generally lower than in Japan. Quality improvement programmes 'tended to be somewhat superficial and not effectively implemented down to shopfloor level'.
- *Prices*, which were considered high; for consumer products 10–20 per cent more than in Japan.
- *Delivery*. British suppliers often failed to meet delivery dates, which were quoted in weeks. Japanese suppliers kept to their delivery dates, which were cited in days (and sometimes hours).

The report found simple pressed metal components, such as small brackets, to be up to 50 per cent more expensive than in Japan with variable (but poor) quality from batch to batch. Precision machined components were of high quality, but expensive – 100 per cent more expensive than in Japan. UK suppliers of plastic parts were accused of inefficient management, resulting in high prices and poor quality. The report concludes:

> There was considerable criticism and very little praise of UK suppliers'
> performance in general, which suggests that legislative pressure
> currently is very significant in 'forcing' the levels of local sourcing
> achieved (*Financial Times*, 5 April 1988).

Other more recent reports reinforce the view that British suppliers have not been meeting the needs of Japanese manufacturers in the UK, and predict that Japanese component suppliers will take advantage of these shortcomings to set up factories in Europe, thereby displacing indigenous suppliers (Morris and Imrie 1991; Trevor and Christie 1988; Dillow 1989). Certainly, throughout the 1980s, accounts of Japanese companies' concern about the quality of locally sourced parts were frequent. In the words of a Japanese colour TV manufacturer,

> In deciding where to buy our components from, quality availability is the key factor, together with continuity of supply. The fact that we do not buy more components from the EEC reflects our inability to persuade suppliers to provide us with components at the right quality and competitive price (Dunning 1986, p. 107)

Sony, the colour television manufacturer, has about 80 to 85 per cent local content in its sets, but this is because it makes many of its own parts on-site – primarily to safeguard quality and permit the use of JIT production. Its TV plant at Bridgend was described to the authors as 'probably the most vertically integrated TV plant in Europe, if not the world', with a very high proportion of components made on-site. Sony aspires to long-term relationships with its suppliers, with an emphasis on mutual trust and understanding, but in the past this has not always worked out. A Sony executive recounted to us:

> In some cases Sony have ended up managing the supplier's business as well as our own. They have absolutely no idea of how to produce a consistently good quality product.

Dunning (1986, p. 113) recounts similar sentiments, also from a Japanese colour TV manufacturer:

> It's not so much that suppliers do not know what they have to do to satisfy our standards; but they do not pay enough attention to ensuring that these standards are met.

Sony's Bridgend plant is now, nonetheless, moving towards a just-in-time supply system (Morris and Imrie 1991). Some Sony managers have been encouraged to set up their own businesses, which now supply Sony with parts; suppliers' employees are invited to work for spells on Sony's assembly lines so that they better understand Sony's processes. Sony also has an intention of ensuring that 90 per cent of its suppliers are located within one hour's drive of the factory, and by now 90 per cent of Sony suppliers' goods are not inward-inspected.

Instructive examples of the possible shape of things to come are worth mentioning. The purchasing activities of Komatsu, which were examined in chapter 8, illustrate a pattern of buyer–supplier relations that appears to be emerging generally within the British vehicle and automotive industry. The Komatsu engineers looked hard at the manufacturing operations of their potential suppliers, and suggested improvements that the suppliers could make in order to meet the efficiency levels considered appropriate by Komatsu itself – hence enabling price reductions. The UK suppliers obviously found this 'hands-on' approach unfamiliar and unsettling. Even once the orders had been landed, the closeness of the buyer–supplier relationship expected by the Japanese was startling to the British suppliers.

This degree of contact is likely to be more intense in the early days of production, so in the case of Komatsu the 'Japanese' effect is being confounded with the 'start-up' effect; nonetheless, a clear divide is apparent in the way in which buyer–supplier relations are conducted.

A final example worthy of mention involves Toyota, whose £700-million car plant in Derbyshire will come on stream in December 1992. Here, selection of suppliers began back in early 1989, data being compiled on 2,000 potential supply companies. Checks on reputations, customer bases, and so on were used to reduce the number to 400, and then over a period of 10 months several multi-disciplinary teams assessed would-be supplier capabilities in great detail. The number was then reduced to 250, which were asked to submit costs. Only then were orders placed for prototype production. Before production parts contracts are awarded, suppliers will have to attend a further series of presentations and meetings. Brian Jackson, a manager responsible for parts procurement at Toyota, contrasted his previous work experience in Europe with that at Toyota as follows:

> [In Europe] it was ten minutes to make the decision, ten to implement it, and three months to correct it. In Toyota there's three months discussions, ten minutes to approve it and no time correcting it. (*Financial Times*, 10 April 1991)

Pressure in the area of supplier relations is already high and could increase: to escape tariff barriers, a high proportion of the input to a product has to be of local (that is EC) origin. As more Japanese companies set up manufacturing operations overseas, more of their sub-contractors are likely to follow them; some already have, such as Ikeda–Hoover, which makes seats for Nissan. The number of Japanese sub-contractors entering Britain could rise to a higher level than would otherwise be the case, we would suggest, because of the lack of confidence on the part of the Japanese in the quality of locally sourced materials.

Conclusions

The most important point arising from the evidence presented in this chapter is that Japanese direct investors *are* bringing with them to the UK many of the manufacturing and personnel practices that they use in Japan. That is, 'adaptation' to the local environment does not necessarily entail the abandonment of the essential elements of the Japanese approach to manufacturing. The survey data indicate that some problems have been encountered, and continue to be encountered; for example, in the case of just-in-time supplies. In the early days of a Japanese company's presence in the UK quality circles and just-in-time production have not always been overwhelmingly successful.

A second point is that many of the personnel practices for which the Japanese are renowned – consultation, direct communication, highly selective recruitment, long-term employment for core workers and so on – are being introduced in tandem with the new Japanese-style manufacturing methods and working practices. Indeed, in 1987 it appeared that the personnel practices were being put in place more rapidly than the manufacturing practices, hence laying the ground for total quality manufacturing methods. In comparison, the UK companies emulating Japanese practices often faced problems because their personnel practices were 'out of sync.' with their manufacturing ones. This may explain why, as table 9.29 demonstrates, the Japanese reported greater success with *all* practices in 1987 (excepting JIT) than did the emulators.

Statistical tests revealed *significant* differences in the 1987 data only with regard to four practices: flexible working, in-company communications, single status, and high job-security for core workers. Nonetheless the consistency of perceived relative success by the Japanese, as compared with the emulators, pointed very strongly to a better overall performance by the Japanese.

Table 9.29   Relative success of Japanese practices: Japanese companies in the UK vs emulating companies (1987)

Practice	UK emulators	Japanese companies
Flexible working	2.91	3.50
Total quality control	2.98	3.42
Group working/work teams	2.78	3.33
Statistical process control	2.60	2.89
Quality circles	2.12	2.50
Just-in-time production	2.50	2.25
Temporary workers	2.69	3.67
In-company communications	2.66	3.64
Single-status facilities	3.15	3.60
'Staff' benefits for all	3.09	3.50
High job-security	2.97	3.50
Employee involvement	2.76	3.27

1 = Not successful   4 = Highly successful

This relative success – a success most marked with regard to personnel and working practices – appeared at the time to be explicable by the advantages that the Japanese companies had in terms of greenfield sites and by implication (selected) 'green' labour. Under such conditions, with no history of adversarial industrial relations and the restrictive practices that typically accompany them, a greater success with Japanese-style practices was to be expected.

A remark made to the authors by an executive of a Japanese TV manufacturer operating in the UK struck us as particularly pertinent to the question of the relationship between manufacturing and personnel strategies in Japanese companies at that time:

I don't think it is very profitable for [British] companies to come along to Japanese companies and pinch their techniques. They have got to get to the fundamental point and say 'What are we trying to do here?' In our case it is to create a very high-quality product and sell it at a relatively high price . . . It is all a question of deciding what the end object of the organization is. Once you've done that it is very easy to begin to see what techniques you should use. If you are producing cheap, nasty products that are disposable, where it does not really matter what the appearance is, then why devote an enormous amount of time to the welfare of your employees, because it is not going to produce any benefits to you?

What was so significant about this comment was the way in which personnel strategy was unquestionably an integrated part, indeed a necessary element, of a total business strategy for this company. Considered thus, the real issue is not simply one of whether or not particular elements of Japanese business strategy (such as production methods, personnel practices and so on) can be transferred to a different socio-cultural environment. Equally significant, is the extent to which these personnel practices fit in with other elements of a company's total strategy, such as its manufacturing strategy, which in turn must fit in with its marketing strategy. What appears noteworthy about the major Japanese companies (in general) is the goodness of fit between the strategies employed by their various constituent parts, particularly the fit between their manufacturing strategy and their human resource strategy.

In 1987 it appeared that Japanese manufacturers in the UK were more aware than UK companies of the importance of carefully managing the dependency relationships characteristic of Japanese-style manufacturing systems. Selection and induction procedures ensured a degree of homogeneity amongst recruits, and practices such as long-term employment, relatively good pay for core workers, single-status provisions, and frequent and direct consultation and communication helped to foster the 'community of interests' to support work systems that demanded willing cooperation and not mere compliance.

Clearly, newly investing companies are in a better position to introduce personnel practices of their choice than are established organizations. Interestingly, whilst indicating 'never used' and 'not planned' in relation to single-union deals, some respondents to the 1987 emulator survey wrote comments in the questionnaire margin to the effect that they would like such a deal 'if only it were feasible'.

By 1991, the picture looked rather different, as table 9.30 demonstrates. Of the 22 management practices examined in the survey that year, there were 14 in which UK companies reported greater success than the Japanese, though few of the differences approached statistical significance. The differences are fairly evenly matched as far as manufacturing and personnel practices are concerned. However, it is striking that the UK companies reported higher success with *all* their supplier practices.

Table 9.30   Relative success of Japanese practices: Japanese companies in the UK vs emulating companies (1991)

Practice	UK emulators	Japanese companies
Continuous improvement	2.55	*2.83
Operator responsibility for quality	2.72	*2.81
Cellular manufacture	*2.97	2.56
Total quality control	2.48	*2.53
Design for manufacture	*2.56	2.50
Quality circles	2.37	*2.50
SPC	*2.40	2.39
JIT production	*2.44	2.39
Set-up time reductions	*2.53	2.39
Kanban materials control	*2.54	2.33
Single-status facilities	2.74	*3.11
Use of temporary workers	2.60	*2.65
Company council	2.34	*2.50
Team briefings	*2.80	2.49
Performance appraisal	2.35	*2.48
Performance-related pay	*2.33	2.19
Profit sharing	*2.44	1.89
QA supplies	*2.55	2.45
Single sourcing	*2.35	2.32
Supplier development	*2.52	2.24
Supplier involvement in design	*2.49	2.15
JIT supplies	*2.30	2.10

*indicates the greater value

Some care is needed in interpreting this information. First, many of the disparities are *very* small. Secondly, a report of degree of success is influenced as much by expectations as it is by actual outcomes – perhaps the expectations of the Japanese companies with respect to, say, supplier relations are different from those of the emulators. Finally, Japanese companies – and their employees – may be in less of a 'honeymoon' period in the early 1990s than they were in the mid-1980s, further depressing their scores. The fact that it is perhaps the smaller, less internationalized Japanese companies that are now coming over to the UK may well be affecting the results, while the adoption of acquisition as an entry strategy is also likely to involve a fresh crop of problems for the inward investors. The findings here suggest that these avenues merit further investigation.

10
Industrial Relations and Trade Unions

Previous chapters have described how the adoption and introduction of new production systems, employment practices and human resource management strategies by Japanese and Japanizing companies have significant implications for the structure and distribution of power and control in the workplace, and therefore for industrial relations. In our opinion, the new manufacturing systems, and in particular just-in-time methods, serve to increase the dependency of employer on employee. However, the *visibility* characteristic of just-in-time systems and module-based production, together with employment and human resource management practices that facilitate tighter control, is likely to counterbalance this effect in favour of the employer.

In practice, the relative success or failure of these initiatives will be affected by, and may be contingent upon, wider changes in the British political and economic system – that is, on a set of supportive or 'facilitative' conditions – and these will be discussed in the final chapter. Success (in management terms) is also dependent, at least in most large companies, on employee responses, for employees and the trade unions that represent them are clearly in a position to thwart attempts to apply the techniques in question. For example, the circulation of bad publicity about quality circles or continuous improvement activities could easily breed cynicism among company members. The fragility of a just-in-time production system similarly provides a potential advantage to labour. Success with the techniques thus appears to be dependent on a form of trade unionism that is sympathetic towards, or at least accepting of, their use.

We suggested in chapter 2 that Japanese unions tend to have relationships with employers that make for relatively stable industrial relations. At least since the 1950s, unions have been enterprise-based and company-oriented to the extent that the union is sometimes a career route into senior management. This situation, which in large part accounts for the low level of industrial action in Japan, emerged in the context of state initiatives (with the blessing of the US in the 1950s) that curbed the rise of a budding independent trade union movement.

While Japan enjoys a relatively stable industrial relations environment, British trade unions historically have been less inclined to facilitate the introduction of manufacturing systems that are inherently vulnerable. Britain experiences more industrial disputes, and British unions enjoy more independence and influence at both local and national levels, than is the case in Japan, while occupation-based and industry-wide unions are the norm. However, during the 1980s British trade unions underwent changes that, while perhaps not actually making them more akin to their Japanese counterparts, at least made them more receptive (in some cases) and less able to provide resistance (in others) to the new managerial initiatives.

This chapter summarizes the position of trade unions in Britain in the late 1980s and early 1990s and argues that the current industrial relations climate is facilitating changes in management strategies and working practices. It then examines the manifest implications of Japanization – that is the form of trade unionism implied by, indeed often demanded by, Japanese and Japanizing companies – before ending with a discussion of the latent implications for trade unions, which, we would argue, could have equally profound consequences.

Contemporary Trade Unionism in Context

The ascendancy of a new movement in British trade unionism is captured by the term 'new realism'. 'New realism' is described by Bassett (1986) as an:

> explicit rejection of class-based industrial enmity in favour of mu-
> tually beneficial co-operation, pragmatically embracing social and
> technological change, resting [its] market based vanguardism on the
> aggregated assent of the individual. (Bassett 1986, pp. 1f.)

The adoption of new realism has not taken place 'across the board'. Many of the leaders of some of Britain's largest unions – the TGWU and NUM, for instance – have provided vociferous resistance. But new realism does enjoy significant popular support, having been presented as a pragmatic and logical response to political, social and economic change. The context of the emergence of new realism is one of a decline in trade union membership and power. Beaumont (1987) identifies a drop in union membership in Britain of over 10 per cent between 1979 and 1984, and a decline of around 5 per cent in union density, *excluding* the unemployed, over the same period. This decline continued into the late 1980s, though there is debate over its extent and significance (Stirling and Rainie 1989; Marchington 1990; Wood 1989).

Beaumont identifies the problems underlying the decline in membership and power as many and varied, but, worryingly for the unions, most are related to deep-seated changes in the UK's industrial and economic structure. Perhaps most important has been the trend in employment in the private sector away from manufacturing towards the service industries, which are more difficult (and costly) for unions to organize because of the relatively small size of establishments and the high labour turnover. In 1987, the level of trade union membership in the private services sector was around 15 per cent, compared with 60 per cent in manufacturing (*Financial Times*, 2 October 1987). Private services have been particularly important in new job generation in recent years. Other changes that are contributing to the declining membership and power of trade unions include: (1) increased corporate divisionalization and further subdivisions into wholly owned limited liability companies – union recognition in one legal entity does not necessarily mean unionization of a division, let alone the whole corporation, as the GMB recently discovered in its dealings with Matsushita (see below); (2) a trend towards manufacturing employment growth in small towns, new towns and rural areas rather than the old conurbations – workers in these areas are less likely to have traditions of trade union organization; (3) privatization – the private sector is much less densely organized than the public; and (4) a trend towards more sub-contracting of non-core operations, more fixed-term contracts and increasing use of part-time, mostly female, workers – all leading to the growth of 'peripheral' categories of employee that are more difficult for trade unions to organize.

In addition to these structural changes, the 1980s have seen government attempts to limit trade union power through legislation, which represents a break from the tradition of active governmental encouragement of union membership in the public sector (perhaps thereby providing a lead for the private sector); while the general political climate has also become hostile to militant trade unionism

(Beaumont 1987; Stirling and Rainie 1989). Though the precise impact of these political changes on union membership and power is unclear, one might safely assume some detrimental effect.

Finally, there are the new human resource management and industrial relations strategies of companies, which are the focus of this chapter. These can be seen both as a factor contributing towards a decline in union membership (though so far their effect has probably been small, according to Beaumont), and as an attempt to take advantage of the weakened position of unions caused by their declining membership. Besides anything else, management might identify a cost incentive in moving away from a philosophy of 'union acceptance' – one study suggests that the union 'mark-up' (the extra amount that the average worker receives when represented in pay bargaining by a trade union) increased from 4.7 per cent in the 1960s, to 7.5 per cent in the 1970s and 11.1 per cent in the early 1980s (Beaumont 1987). (This is notwithstanding the fact that *some* companies pay premium wages as part of a non-union strategy.)

Trade union responses to these changes in economic structure, political climate and management strategies have so far not significantly slowed or diverted the trends. Perhaps most importantly, the industrial restructuring of Britain's traditional heavy industries – steel, shipbuilding and coal, in particular – has been largely achieved despite bitter disputes. Workers from these sectors, traditionally well organized in strong unions, have either joined the ranks of the unemployed or have been scattered across new occupations where union density is often lower and union power normally weaker. As regards the problems posed to trade unions by the new political climate, four successive general election victories for the Conservatives have forced the labour movement in general and trade unions in particular to rethink their position. This situation was summed up in the following typical comment made to the authors by one trade union official:

> I use Merthyr Tydfil as the barometer. From coming here until four years ago, about four times a year I had to go there and persuade the refuse men to go back to work. The last time I went I was trying to persuade them to come out. They wouldn't.

Given that part-time and temporary workers are today an important segment of the workforce, that the private services sector is rapidly rising in importance, that manufacturing employment growth is more likely to be on greenfield rather than established sites, and that militant union activity is less likely to receive popular or practical support in the current political climate, unions have looked closely at their recruitment and organizing strategies, at the services that they provide to their members, and even at the image that they present to potential recruits and the public in general.

The increasing use of part-time and temporary workers is generally blamed by the unions on employers' attempts to cut costs. For example, in the late 1980s the TUC General Council calculated that an hourly-paid part-time female manual worker earned only 63 per cent of the wage of a male manual worker. The TUC further argued that the position of part-timers – accounting for almost one in five of the labour force – had been further undermined by government measures reducing their legal protection (*The Guardian*, 8 September 1987). However, there is little that the unions can do to halt or change legislation, and many unions have publicly acknowledged that increasing numbers of people work part-time out of choice – for instance, women with child-rearing responsibilities or people pursuing higher education.

Several unions have therefore turned their recruiters' attention to part-timers, the TGWU through the launch of its 'Link Up' campaign and the GMB through its 'Flair' campaign. Unions have similarly turned their attention to temporary or fixed-term contract workers, offering to attempt to gain them better terms and conditions. So far, these initiatives have had little success, though the GMB has won acceptance of its model agreement on temporary labour at British Cable Services. This agreement lays down the circumstances under which temporary workers may be employed and the terms and conditions under which such employees will operate (*Incomes Data Services*, Report 502, August 1987). Temporary workers will be eligible for union membership on the first day of their employment.

The TUC has been taking an increasing interest in recruitment, traditionally a responsibility and prerogative of individual unions. Amongst other things it has announced campaigns in non-union areas such as Milton Keynes, the new town that Bassett describes as a 'foreshadow of the future . . . almost a paradigm of how government ministers would like the UK economy, labour market and industrial relations to be', with two-thirds of all jobs in services, 27 per cent in production, many small employers and only three employing over 1,000 workers, a large number of foreign-owned companies, and increasing numbers of women in the labour force (*Financial Times*, 9 May 1987).

Compared with these sorts of problem, explicit de-unionization moves have not so far been of enormous import. They are in any case rare (McLoughlin and Beardwell 1989), and most employers appear satisfied that their flexibility initiatives are being embraced, or at least not overtly impeded, by trade unions.

Estimating that union membership could decline from its level of 9.2 million in the late 1980s to 7 million by the year 2000, GMB General Secretary John Edmunds, among others, called for a radical change in union strategy to halt a potential 'terminal decline' (*Financial Times*, 8 May 1987). Recruitment, rather than bargaining, is to be the crucial issue. As well as aiming at temporary and part-time workers, and at the 'non-union' new town areas, some unions, notably the EETPU, have increasingly offered extended services to their members, such as discount cards and special deals on life assurance. For instance, the EETPU has bought a £6-million Georgian mansion in Sussex to serve as a holiday centre for its members, and has begun offering a free legal advice service – extensions of what Bassett refers to as 'market unionism' (*Financial Times*, 30 July 1987). Others are cynical of these initiatives, Ron Todd, then TGWU General Secretary, stating that 'we are not going down the road of gimmicks and treating our members as customers' (*Financial Times*, 23 February 1987). Nonetheless, some unions have gone to great lengths to change how they are perceived, the GMB for instance dropping its 'unity is strength' slogan in favour of a 'welcoming, lively and friendly' image (*Financial Times*, 23 June 1987).

Perhaps predictably, as membership levels have declined, so the number of inter-union disputes over recognition rights has risen, the problem being worsened as traditional demarcations are broken down and previously craft-based or occupation-based unions become 'general' unions (the latter, of course, being a long-term trend).

A related factor in the rise in inter-union competition in the 1980s, described at length below, is the increasing number of single-union deals sought by inward-investing companies. Rivalry over these deals accounted for the majority of the 23 inter-union disputes being examined by the TUC's Inter-union Disputes Committee in June 1987 (*Financial Times*, 25 June 1987). It is in this context that the TUC attempted to become involved in recruitment, suggesting the establishment of specially designated organizing areas to give individual unions a 'clear run' at non-union companies, and proposing an agreement that if a union could not achieve an acceptable membership level in its sector within a specified period, other unions should be allowed to attempt recruitment and organization in that area. At the end of 1987, however, inter-union disputes continued, and following the EETPU's refusal to withdraw from agreements with Orion Electric and Christian Salvesen, it was suspended, finally being expelled from the TUC in September 1988. The EETPU has not been allowed back into the TUC since that date. At the 1991 TUC conference, Norman Willis said:

> The EETPU's recent conduct is a breach of working class morality. The hand of welcome is held out to the EETPU, but it has to be by the rule book of the TUC. (*Financial Times*, 6 September 1991)

Finally, there is the offer by some unions – notably the EETPU – of agreements that make strikes or other industrial action extremely unlikely. Often referred to as 'no-strike agreements', they have become a prerequisite for union recognition in many newly establishing companies. The offer of so-called no-strike deals is possibly the most radical response by trade unions to the problem of declining membership, and though it is still difficult to say to what extent they are a pointer for the future, the EETPU, at least, is determined to continue signing such agreements.

It is in the context of declining union membership and power, inter-union rivalry, and uncertainty and disagreement as to the strategies that unions should adopt, that Japanese and Japanizing companies have introduced radically different production, management and industrial relations practices from those traditionally found in the UK. As we shall see, change is not unproblematic, but certainly the current defensive position of *all* unions, and the 'new realism' of some, make it significantly easier.

The implications of Japanization for patterns of industrial relations and trade union arrangements will be considered in two parts. First, it will be viewed in terms of the types of agreements that unions are currently making with companies, particularly with inwardly investing companies. Such agreements have been the subject of popular debate and have caught the attention of national and local newspapers – the signing of single-union deals and flexibility agreements being particularly widely discussed. Secondly, we shall consider the *latent* implications of the new management practices, which, we shall argue, may have equally serious consequences for traditional union organization, if managements can achieve their objectives of reorienting the attitudes and allegiances of workers on a significant scale.

New Style Company–Union Agreements

No-strike deals and binding arbitration

Partly because of a search by employers for flexibility and industrial relations stability, the 1980s saw the establishment of many single-union deals by newly investing companies. The Japanese were seen, somewhat inaccurately, as providing the lead in this, but the reality is that nearly all recent new investors, foreign or otherwise, have sought single-union or non-union arrangements on greenfield sites. In themselves, single-union deals are not new, but their increased rate of adoption in the 1980s is of note; more significantly, the typical contents of recent deals – which provide for virtually complete flexibility of the labour force and often for binding arbitration in the case of failure to reach agreement during bargaining – represent a break from traditional British employer–union relations. Bassett (1986) describes EETPU National Engineering Officer Roy Sanderson as the 'principal architect' of the 1980s 'strike-free package', and the 1981 agreement between Plymouth-based Toshiba and the EETPU as its 'testbed'. Sanderson has been reported to be an admirer of Japanese employee relations practices, though he has insisted that strike-free deals are a British solution to British industrial relations problems.

Since the signing of the first 'no-strike deal' by Toshiba, other companies have followed the Japanese lead. By the end of 1987, some 28 companies in Britain were known to have strike-free agreements. These included nine Japanese, three American and 12 British companies. The EETPU was involved in 21 of these deals, and the GMB in three. AEU shop stewards were involved in another deal, though in this case without the sanction of the local district committee (Gregory 1986). Bassett (1986) estimated that a total of 9,000 workers were covered by strike-free deals, and Gregory (1986) that around 5,000 trade union members were subject to them. Another 2,000 or so workers were encompassed by deals negotiated in 1987. Hence, at this date, the numbers involved were still small. However, with some trade unions advertising their model agreements, encompassing binding arbitration, to prospective employers, the numbers could well increase rapidly.

Further, these figures relate only to those deals that do include binding arbitration – many other deals are similar in content in all but this respect. For instance, one 1989 survey covered 52 companies (19 of them Japanese) with single-union deals including most of the features that we describe (*IRS Employment Trends* 442, 27 June 1989).

Before describing the typical contents of the deals, it is worth commenting on exactly what is meant by binding arbitration and making a clear distinction between this and another recently emerging practice – pendulum arbitration. When employer and union agree on binding arbitration, they agree that if a dispute is not resolved after exhausting other procedures (the last normally being conciliation), it will be referred to an independent arbitrator (normally ACAS) whose findings will be binding on both parties. In contrast, pendulum arbitration simply means that the arbitrator is obliged to find wholly in favour of one side or the other when asked to adjudicate in a dispute. Hence an agreement that incorporates pendulum arbitration does not necessarily imply binding arbitration, or vice versa.

Pendulum arbitration has been adopted recently in a number of agreements in Britain, copying a practice widely used in the public sector (interestingly, rarely in the private) in the United States (Bassett 1986). The EETPU tends to favour pendulum arbitration in its strike-free agreements – the advantage claimed being that it makes industrial action improbable because each side is more likely to make 'realistic' opening bids in any negotiation lest it lose the dispute altogether. For example, the EETPU's agreement with Toshiba reads:

> Both the company and the trade union shall represent their case to an agreed independent arbitrator. The terms of reference to the arbitrator will be to find in favour of either the company or the trade union. A compromise solution shall not be recommended. Both parties agree to abide by the decision of the arbitrator.

MATSA, the GMB's white-collar section, on the other hand, prefers binding, but not pendulum, arbitration. In its glossy draft agreement offered to employers, it suggests simply:

If conciliation fails then the difference may be referred by either side to arbitration. If arbitration is used then both parties are considered bound by the findings of the arbitrator.

In both cases, and as far as we know in all cases to date, binding arbitration is invoked only after other lengthy procedures have been exhausted, the penultimate one being conciliation by ACAS.

Binding arbitration may not be enforceable under present legislation, but it is difficult to imagine a party to such a deal taking industrial action in other than exceptional circumstances. Hence the term 'strike-free' deal is for most intents and purposes appropriate. It may be going too far, on the other hand, to extend the term to include the large number of other deals that make strike action unlikely. These deals, including the one signed by Nissan and the AEU, rule out industrial action while disputes procedures are in progress, and spell out union respect for managerial prerogatives and the commitment of the union to company goals. However, although industrial action is unlikely it is still in principle possible. For instance, after describing elaborate procedures involving the Advisory Council, the deal between Komatsu and the AEU states:

> The company and the union are totally committed to resolving negotiations as above within the domestic procedure. However, exceptionally, in the case of non-resolution by domestic procedure, both parties agree to refer the matter for conciliation to the Advisory Conciliation and Arbitration Service.
>
> If the matter is still unresolved, both parties may agree to refer the dispute to an independent arbitrator who will determine positively in favour of one side or the other. The arbitrator will take into account the common ground achieved between the parties. Both parties agree to accept the decision of the arbitrator.
>
> There will be no industrial action of any kind while an issue is in procedure or the subject of conciliation and arbitration. In the unlikely event of total exhaustion of the above procedure without resolution, no industrial action will be taken without a full, secret, audited ballot of all affected employees.

Given that deals such as Nissan–AEU and Komatsu–AEU are similar in most respects to the strike-free deals described by Gregory (1986), we shall consider them together. These 'new realist' deals, we shall argue, facilitate Japanization. Indeed they are frequently sought by newly investing firms, and sometimes established firms too, as recent developments at Rover testify; and this is no accident, since they make up a crucial part of the package of industrial changes currently being sought in the UK.

Such deals are characterized by the inclusion of *most or all* of the following elements: an emphasis on cooperation and common purpose, and the denial of a conflict of interests between employer and employee; binding arbitration; an agreement for extensive labour flexibility; the harmonization of terms and conditions of employment; the establishment of company advisory boards independent of the trade union; and sole recognition of the signing union. Each element in itself is not new, but, taken together, these features characterize a type of deal that emerged only in the 1980s; and, binding arbitration apart, their adoption has been increasingly wide (*IRS Employment Trends* 442, 27 June 1989). We shall now examine each element of the new realist deal in detail.

Trade union roles

The ethos that typifies the agreements under discussion is remarkable in that it defines the role of the trade union as being that of a *partner in commercial success* rather than a *company adversary*. Toshiba's agreement with the EETPU, for instance, reads:

> The company . . , and the trade union . . . in reaching this agreement wish to establish and operate policies and procedures which will ensure that the company and its employees enjoy a harmonious relationship to their mutual benefit. Both parties recognize, in this joint approach, that the security of employment and advancement of all employees can only be through the company's commercial success and through the common purpose and involvement of all employees in the company's activities.

'Harmony', 'mutual benefit' and a 'commitment to company success' feature prominently in other new realist deals. At Nissan in Sunderland, the AEU signed an agreement with the company, the stated objectives of which are:

> to develop and maintain the prosperity of the company and its employees . . . to promote and maintain mutual trust and co-operation between the company, its employees and the union [and] to establish an enterprise committed to the highest levels of quality, productivity and competitiveness using modern technology and working practices

and to make such changes to this technology and working practices as will maintain this position. (Crowther and Garrahan 1988)

Another illustration of a union accepting a role as partner rather than adversary comes from a deal between a British company, INMOS, and the EETPU. This agreement states that, to meet their objectives, the union and the company agree on the need to:

Keep open and direct communication with all employees on matters of mutual interest and concern. Avoid any action which interrupts the continuity of production.
Respond flexibly and quickly to changes in the pattern of demand for the company's products and to technological innovation.

This ethos of common purpose is all the more remarkable as the initiative is frequently taken by the trade unions themselves, whose rationale for existence is based on relations that are at root adversarial. The GMB's MATSA, for instance, which recently signed a single-union no-strike deal with a Pirelli subsidiary in South Wales, offers employers a draft agreement intended to:

form the basis of a progressive, responsible and stable relationship between the company and its employees . . . an agreement based on *realism* and *mutuality* [MATSA's emphasis].

Likewise, the Wales TUC's General Secretary David Jenkins, responsible for overseeing many no-strike agreements, claims in a public statement targeted at potential inward investors in Wales to start:

from the basis that industrial disruption is contrary to the interests of management, the workforce, the company as a whole . . . I would ask you to consider myself and my trade union colleagues as potential allies should you be considering investment in Wales, a country within the UK where industrial relations are making a positive contribution towards securing economic success. (ACAS/WINvest 1986)

The emergence of non-adversarial trade unions identifying mutual benefit in collaborating with the companies in which their members work is clearly in line with the shift to the new manufacturing and management methods that we have described above.
Strike-free deals have virtually all been signed with single unions

on greenfield sites or in the context of an enterprise being re-established out of the collapse of a previous business (Gregory 1986). The latter include the Toshiba–EETPU deal at Plymouth and the deal between Hitachi and the EETPU at Hirwaun (Pegge 1986). As a consequence, the argument that the alternative was probably no union at all could hold some weight. GMB General Secretary John Edmunds, for instance, characterized his union's willingness to sign single-union deals on new sites as 'not a very noble policy, but a pragmatic one' (*Financial Times*, 29 December 1986). However, new realist unions have increasingly sought to justify strike-free deals as politically and morally desirable. For instance, Roy Sanderson of the EETPU describes his union's strike-free package as 'designed to enhance the collective and individual rights of workers' (Bassett 1986, p. 111). We shall return to the arguments for and against these agreements later in the chapter.

While agreements encompassing binding arbitration have (so far) been limited to new sites or takeovers (an exception being the AEU stewards' agreement with Eaton, a US vehicle components manu-facturer with a history of union militancy; Gregory 1986), other aspects of the new realist deal have not.

Flexibility agreements

Worker flexibility, in particular, has been demanded by many companies and has been accepted by trade unions, often in return for the harmonization of terms and conditions. Companies requiring it include recent Japanese investors such as Nissan and Komatsu, and, most significantly, many British companies and companies long established in Britain. Typically, the new realist agreement stipulates complete labour flexibility (within skill constraints), traditional job demarcations being broken down and managerial prerogatives over labour deployment being unambiguously established. The Komatsu–AEU agreement, for instance, provides for the following work practices:

> Complete flexibility and mobility of employees; Changes in processes and practices will be introduced to increase competitiveness and . . . these will improve productivity and affect manning levels; To achieve such change employees will work as required by the company and participate in the training of themselves or other employees as

required; Manning levels will be determined by the company using appropriate industrial engineering and manpower planning techniques.

Ironically, British trade unionists have for many years sought the single-status arrangements that often accompany flexibility agreements, with common provisions for staff and manual workers regarding items such as the working week, sick pay, holidays, pensions, and toilet and canteen facilities. Hence the EETPU has been able to claim a contribution to the breakdown of the British system of 'industrial apartheid' (Gregory 1986), and to argue that the single-status provisions in no-strike packages are one of the real benefits to workers that justify the signing of such deals (Bevan 1987). This is not only because discrimination against blue-collar workers is removed, but also because single-status and flexible working arrangements encourage a commitment by the company to the provision of training in a variety of skills that could enhance a worker's personal development. The EETPU's agreement with Hitachi, for instance, states that:

> All company members will agree the complete flexibility of jobs and duties within and between the various company functions and departments. The main flexibility principle will be that when necessary to fit the needs of the business, all company members may be required to perform whatever jobs and duties are within their capability.
>
> The company accepts its responsibility to train, retrain and develop company members to broaden their skills, grow their potential and meet the needs of rapid technological change. The company also accepts that in the instances where more competitive manning levels can be achieved by agreed flexibility, any directly related manning reductions will be achieved without compulsory redundancy.

Established companies with established unions and established agreements obviously have more difficulty in introducing such industrial relations contracts and practices, and, indeed, while the UK motor industry has, as we have shown in previous chapters, made substantial progress in terms of adopting Japanese manufacturing techniques, it has been slower in changing its industrial relations.

This was demonstrated most clearly in 1987 at General Motors' Vauxhall and Bedford plants. In 1986, John Bagshaw, the Chairman of Vauxhall, had claimed that poor industrial relations and restrictive practices were preventing the company from winning more investment from its US parent, and had declared a need for no-strike agreements and new work practices (*The Guardian*, 16 December 1986). His justification for these remarks involved a comparison with Nissan's new plant in the UK which, he declared, had cost-advantages of between £250 and £500 per car over Vauxhall. Following this, the first major move by GM in the UK was to establish a Nissan-style flexibility agreement at its Bedford van plant in Luton, though the unions signed only after considerable demur, when GM threatened that the Japanese company Isuzu, which was to take a 40 per cent stake in a new company to run the plant, might withdraw from the project, causing the plant be closed altogether (*Financial Times*, 26 June 1987). GM was forced to give way on its initial demand for binding arbitration, but gained agreement from the several major unions representing the workforce for total shopfloor flexibility, as well as on most of its other requirements, such as a simplified pay structure, the establishment of a Works Council, and the right to use temporary workers and sub-contractors where considered appropriate by management (*Financial Times*, 25 July 1987). By way of concessions, GM agreed to make a one-off cash payment of £500 per employee and to enlarge the Works Council to include five full-time union officials.

At a workshop on Japanization held in Oxford in early 1991, a TGWU convenor at the renamed IBC van plant described the developments there in the late 1980s:

> The company was in a crisis. Closure seemed assured. But as they say 'Out of the rising sun came our saviour' – Isuzu Motors of Japan, who were prepared to enter into a partnership with General Motors and form a new joint venture company. This saving act, however, was conditional. It was conditional on all the trade unions agreeing to a new employee agreement which was to include the Japanization of working practices – total flexibility, team working, just-in-time, continuous improvement – through the Isuzu production system, and a totally new system of industrial relations based on a company joint council with strict controls on union activity. (Oxford Motor Industry Research Project 1991)

The TGWU convenor reported that the unions won some concessions mitigating these original demands, particularly a change from compulsory arbitration to voluntary arbitration, thereby protecting their right to strike, and other entitlements that gave them considerable influence on the company council. Despite these successes, however, he made some bitter comments:

> The new joint venture was formed on 1 October 1987 and was called IBC Vehicles. We called it 'I've been conned'. With the start of IBC the Japanization of the company – I have to use that word, it's either Japanization or just capitalism – came into full swing. Team leaders were created, all employees were formed into teams, team discussions began, total flexibility came into effect. (Oxford Motor Industry Research Project 1991)

Having secured an agreement at the van plant, GM indicated its intention to seek similar changes at its Vauxhall car plants. Here its declared flexibility requirements related to production worker responsibility for quality control, the breakdown of demarcations between trades, and the obligation of production workers to take responsibility for cleaning and routine maintenance (*Financial Times*, 21 August 1987). In April 1990, GM announced its intention to extend its Ellesmere Port operations by building a £200-million engine plant (*The Guardian*, 7 April 1990). Shop stewards at Ellesmere Port were reported as seeing the investment as a bargaining tool being used by the company to win reduced demarcations, a Works Council and 'right-first-time' production practices. Under the perceived threat of loss of investment, which might have implied a problematic future for the whole of the Ellesmere Port operation, GM's unions accepted the changes (Kirkpatrick et al. 1991).

Finally, it is worth repeating here that flexible working arrangements are important to a just-in-time system of production – without stocks to absorb fluctuations in production, adjustments must, of necessity, be made through flexibility in the system itself.

Company advisory boards

The next element of the new realist deal is the company advisory board. These boards are frequently sought by both Japanese companies and their emulators as an additional means of gaining the stability and predictability in industrial relations so crucial to their manufacturing systems. Company advisory boards appear under a variety of names such as Company Council (Nissan), Company

Members Board (Hitachi), Advisory Committee (Orion), Staff Council (Kyushu Matsushita), Advisory Council (Komatsu and Norsk-Hydro) or Works Council (GM). What they share in common, however, is that first, unlike in the case of the joint consultative committees, their employee representatives (who are elected, normally by secret ballot) are not necessarily shop stewards, nor necessarily trade union members, and are chosen by non-union employees as well as union members. Occasionally, a few places on the board may be reserved for shop stewards, as at GM, and the local district official of the recognized union sometimes has the right to attend board meetings, but the principle and the practice that the board is independent of the union remain. Secondly, also unlike Britain's traditional joint consultative committees, which normally limit themselves to non-collective bargaining issues (Marchington and Armstrong 1986), company advisory boards typically go beyond 'tea and toilets', providing a forum for negotiations on pay and conditions. Hence they break down the traditional distinction between consultation and bargaining. For instance, the EETPU's agreements with Control Data (now Xidex), Hitachi, Inmos, Yuasa Battery, Orion and Kyushu Matsushita, all place responsibility for the first stage in collective bargaining on the company advisory board. If agreement is achieved there, the union and the company consider the advisory board's recommendations, and union involvement in negotiation begins only if either party does not accept the board's findings. Provision for secret ballots is typically made towards the later stages of the negotiating procedure, and, as described, the procedure often ends with binding arbitration.

In these circumstances, the role of the trade union representative is called into question. The Toshiba agreement with the EETPU makes this clear in stating that:

> The function of the [union] representative will be *to represent trade union members on those issues which cannot be resolved through the Company Advisory Board* and to represent individual members of the trade union in cases of individual grievances, discipline or other related matters. [Emphasis added.]

Toshiba also requests new union representatives to sign a form, together with the trade union official and personnel manager, stating that:

It is recognized that the Company Advisory Board is the best and first means of resolving all collective issues between the company and its employees, and *the representative fully supports and encourages the role of the Company Advisory Board* in the conduct of relationships between the company and its employees. [Emphasis added]

The shift of responsibilities from shop stewards to company advisory boards that is typical of the new realist deal has been the subject of criticism. Crowther and Garrahan (1988), in describing Nissan's deal with the AEU, claim that:

it allows virtually no independent role for shop stewards, and whilst it appears that the company does not intend to actively obstruct union activities, the mechanisms for representation are highly supportive of non-union participation.

This is one explanation, they suggest, for the low union membership density at Nissan, which in 1991 stood at 30 per cent, much lower than the average for Japanese plants in the UK organized by the AEU, despite the encouragement that Nissan management gives to new recruits to join the union.

In signing single-union deals with various companies, the EETPU has often persuaded managements to encourage union membership. This has been achieved largely through managements offering union membership forms and displaying positive attitudes towards the union to new recruits, and also through the provision of 'check-off' arrangements. (A check-off scheme means that union subscriptions are automatically deducted from union members' pay until the individual member gives written notice that this should cease – this makes loss of union membership due simply to allowing subscriptions to lapse impossible, and eases the burden of the shop steward as money collector.) Company commitment to the encouragement of union membership is actually written into the deals with Yuasa, Hitachi and Orion, while Kyushu Matsushita states that it will provide check-off facilities.

Linn (1986, p. 28), in a detailed study of the new realist agreement between the TGWU and Norsk-Hydro in Humberside, concisely summarizes the problems for trade union organization:

should the TGWU change its stewards' constituencies to correspond with those of the advisory council? Should it persist in putting up candidates for the advisory council or should it play a very low profile in that arena, to effectively allow the 'supervisory types' that the ex-TGWU convenors believe will dominate the employee constituencies to do so, and thereby discredit it in the eyes of the workforce? Is the union organization equipped to counter the arguments of those who will start to question why they should join the union when they can have a say in collective issues through their representative on the advisory council?

In a follow-up study, Heaton and Linn (1989) reported that the TGWU was putting pro-union sympathizers forward as candidates for the Advisory Council, and noted some successes in elections and in achieving union influence on the Council.

A further defence of the company advisory board that is often posited is that it is a consultative mechanism that makes available company information on important matters that companies in the UK have tended to keep secret. Kyushu Matsushita states in its agreement that its Staff Council is to be used for the provision of information and consultation on 'company investment and business plans' and 'company operating efficiency and manpower plans', as well as on terms and conditions, pay and benefits, and health and safety. A high level of access to information normally the sole preserve of managements is, like single-status arrangements, considered quite a coup by EETPU leaders, and cited as further justification for the new realist deal. (Critics claim that the seriousness and extent of information provision remain dependent on the goodwill of management.)

Single-union status

The final element of the new realist agreements favoured by Japanese companies and their emulators to be dealt with here is single-union status. Of course, established companies with established multi-union deals generally have to manage without this part of the package. The advantages of a single union are that bargaining and consultation are made far simpler, that 'spillover' disputes are made less likely, and, perhaps most importantly, that introducing flexible working arrangements is made easier. As Bevan (1987, p. 9) put it:

Obviously, the fact the agreements are single union, at a stroke, removes many of the potential obstacles to flexibility. Inter-union demarcation lines are a thing of the past and flexibility depends on nothing more than receiving the necessary training to carry out the task required.

As with other aspects of the new realist deal, single-union recognition is hardly new – indeed in the late 1980s Eric Hammond, the EETPU leader, pointed out that the TGWU (at that time a vociferous opponent of new realism) held 76 such deals, the AEU 65, and the GMB 25. On this basis, he claimed that other unions were 'hypocritical' and 'envious' of the EETPU's recent activities (*Financial Times*, 3 June 1987). The single-union deal simply entails that the signing company recognizes only one union, which has sole bargaining rights. Employees are free to join any other union that they wish, or not to join any union at all, but collective representation is only allowed via the union with which the agreement was signed.

The case of Matsushita is particularly interesting, in that the GMB already had a single-union deal at the company's first UK plant, in Cardiff. A new deal with the EETPU for a second plant, in nearby Newport, took many by surprise, including the GMB itself, though a separate deal fits the logic of a manufacturing system vulnerable to disruption – a separate deal with a separate union ensures that bargaining does not become centralized for all Matsushita subsidiaries in the UK and makes less likely the possibility of plant-to-plant comparisons and the spill over of any dispute from one plant to the other.

Previous chapters have described the new Japanese-style business strategies and manufacturing practices now being adopted, and it has been made clear that these are dependent on high degrees of industrial relations stability and workforce flexibility. These appear to be exactly what the new realist agreements provide. The ethos of the agreements stresses the obligation of the parties to the deal to work together in a 'spirit of cooperation'. Binding arbitration and other procedures rendering industrial action less likely – at least in the short term – make for greater industrial relations stability and predictability. Harmonization, flexibility and single-union agreements facilitate the degree of workforce flexibility necessary for a system of production based on low stocks and inventories. Company advisory boards provide management with the opportunity for direct consultation and communication with the workforce, circumventing the shop steward organization and thereby ensuring every opportunity to identify problems and grievances directly and immediately.

Given these developments in the area of company–union agreements, how have unions responded thus far? It is this question that is the focus of the section that follows.

Trade Union Responses

With the declining membership and influence of trade unions in the 1980s and the unions' resultant scramble to recruit new members, newly investing companies of all nationalities have found themselves in the enviable position of being able to play off one union against the other in their search for stability and control. Describing Nissan, Crowther and Garrahan (1988) remark that it:

> was in a position to offer a non-negotiable agreement, and watch regional union officials struggle with their consciences as to whether they should accept.

In an interview with the authors, a GMB officer further confirmed the strength of the employers' position. Explaining the difference between Matsushita management's approach to trade unions in the 1970s, when it set up its plant in Cardiff, and in the 1980s when it set up its plant in Newport, as a separate company, he said of the first plant:

> They plumped for us before we started negotiating an agreement. The talks and discussions were long and drawn out, but there was never any question that they might go elsewhere. Today companies won't indicate which union they will recognize until they've got the agreement tied up . . . Panasonic [the Matsushita Cardiff company] were looking for single-union status. But we talked initially about a section of the plant which involved skilled electronics workers which might need to be organized by the EETPU or AEU. Now it's not just a preference for a single union – it's there at the top . . . At Panasonic we said we'd do everything we could to avoid industrial action. In agreements of late that's become written in bright colours.

Regarding the second, Newport, plant, he commented:

> At Newport they deliberately chose another union [the EETPU] to prevent cross-pollenization. What the Japanese were saying was that policy would not let the management of the Newport project go to

the GMB – they were worried about sympathetic disputes, cross-fertilization, comparisons of pay and conditions and therefore parity demands . . . they wanted to compartmentalize it.

The Newport agreement, unlike the Cardiff agreement, contains a no-strike provision. The same officer's comments on a no-strike deal made in 1987 between Pirelli and the GMB's white-collar section MATSA are perhaps even more telling:

The negotiations were of the new type. They'd got to the third draft of an agreement before the company said 'Well we've been talking to the three of you, we're not certain, but we're approaching a decision.' I thought f***ing hell, is it worth it – a couple of hundred members?

He went on:

This [membership problem] is what leads trade unions to sign these sorts of agreements – the chase, the desperate need for membership – but then the Nissans and Hitachis make them a waste of time altogether.

Waste of time or not, inter-union competition was the most dramatic response of the trade union movement to the new industrial relations strategies of newly investing companies. In June 1987, before its expulsion from the TUC, the EETPU was involved in 11 of the 23 disputes then under examination by the TUC's Inter-union Disputes Committee (*Financial Times*, 25 June 1987), and indeed the EETPU has been in the firing line more than any other union in attacks against new realism by the left wing of the union movement.

Critics of new realist deals have been damning in their comments. Ken Gill, General Secretary of what was then TASS, stated that:

The difference between a slave and a worker is the right to withdraw his labour. So while the pendulum arbitration agreement does not specifically forbid strikes, it obliges both sides to accept the arbitrator's verdict, thereby denying the workers the ultimate expression of rejection. (Bassett 1986, p. 2)

On another occasion, Gill was quoted as claiming that strike-free deals are

the most right wing development since the birth of corporatism under fascism. (*The Guardian*, 7 September 1987)

And Rodney Bickerstaffe, NUPE's General Secretary, claimed:

> What such organizations are saying is 'we will be less militant, we will
> be more accommodating, we will crawl lower and further, if you will
> give us the membership.' (Bassett 1986, p. 2)

The competition – involving 'beauty parades' between rival unions
seeking sole recognition rights – has been characterized by the
TGWU North Eastern Region Secretary, Joe Mills, as follows:

> Because of high unemployment and in desperation to co-operate with
> inward investment some unions are ignoring their traditional role . . .
> they are standing back and allowing companies to choose which union
> they want, similar to choosing washing powder from a super-market.
> (*Financial Times*, 30 December 1986)

One of the most dramatic outbursts from a trade union leader
came at the height of recognition disputes at two Japanese companies
in South Wales. George Wright of the TGWU attacked the companies
as well as the EETPU at a Wales TUC conference, accusing some
Japanese firms of using 'samurai management' and expecting to
operate in a 'coolie economy' (*South Wales Echo*, 1 May 1987). The
EETPU, he implied, was encouraging them with 'sweetheart deals'.
Complaining of a change in industrial relations strategy by inward-
investing Japanese companies since 1980, he declared:

> Enough is enough. They had better change their ways. If you operate
> in this country you live by our standards and observe the rights of
> democratic people.

After protracted disputes and TUC investigation, the deals between the EETPU and Orion and Yuasa went through, though other
disputes have continued to surface, including the one involving the
proposed new Ford plant in Dundee described in chapter 4.

The TUC has regularly been called upon to offer more detailed
policy guidelines regarding single-union deals: since 1985 there has
been a TUC ban on such agreements except on greenfield sites or
where the consent of other unions involved is gained (Linn 1986),
but this has been insufficient to prevent disputes. What counts
as a 'greenfield site', for instance, is highly debatable, as in the
Ford Dundee case. Leaders of the GMB and TGWU called for a
'minimum standards code' that would rule out binding arbitration
(*Financial Times*, 1 June 1987) and for occasional audits of companies

with single-union deals so that if membership fell below a designated level in the one recognized union, other unions would have the right to recruit and attempt recognition in its place (*Financial Times*, 30 December 1986). The 1987 TUC conference, however, resulted only in General Secretary Norman Willis 'winning time' for further investigation, and in October it was announced that a TUC review body would report by March 1988 on the related issues of inter-union disputes, single-union deals and no-strike agreements (*The Guardian*, 24 October 1987).

The resulting report, which was accepted in full by the TUC, laid down the following principles: a union should notify the TUC when it intended to sign a single-union agreement; the TUC would issue guidance regarding whether other unions had significant membership on that site or with the same employer on different sites; unions should not sign any clause that removed the right of a union to take industrial action. The TUC appears reluctant to make stronger rulings, partly because TUC interference in union recruitment strategy and tactics has traditionally been minimal, and partly because unions have on the whole, until the late 1980s, managed to sort out their own disputes without reference to it. Norman Willis therefore suggested that, rather than rely on the intervention of the TUC's Inter-union Disputes Committee after deals have been signed, unions should come to an informal agreement with regard to recruit-ment and organizing 'territories' in the context of newly investing companies (*Financial Times*, 5 June 1987).

In the early 1990s, squabbling over single-union deals has con-tinued within the TUC, exacerbated by Toyota's invitation to unions to consider their responses to a draft agreement for its new plant in Derbyshire, due to come on stream in 1992. The 50-page document alarmed some of the unions competing for sole recognition rights. In it the company said that it wanted: a 39-hour working week; the ability to roster workers for up to two hours extra per day and alternate Saturdays if required; the first pay talks after the initial settlement to be delayed until April 1994 (which would delay the introduction of a 37-hour working week until at least 1995); and a 'no-disruption' deal whereby pay and work-practice disputes would be resolved by binding arbitration at ACAS if negotiations failed. Having taken a firm stance against no-strike deals, the MSF and TGWU (which were competing alongside the EETPU, AEU and GMB) were worried about being ruled out from the beginning. However, Bryan Jackson, Head of Human Resources at Toyota, emphasized that the proposals were only initial ideas, and stated:

Some people think we want to hold a gun to the unions' heads, but that is not our approach at all. (*Financial Times*, 6 September 1991)

Toyota's thoroughness was demonstrated by the fact that it scheduled three meetings with each union, and asked for each union's attitudes to 21 questions on the proposed deal. At the 1991 TUC conference, a resolution put forward by the MSF condemning several Japanese projects that, it was claimed, had 'brought an alien approach to trade union organization' was given overwhelming support. Criticism was especially levelled against no-strike, compulsory arbitration clauses. Only the AEU and GMB voted against the motion, with Gavin Laird, AEU General Secretary, condemning it as 'racist' (*Financial Times*, 7 September 1991).

There is thus a clear split in views on new realist agreements in the union movement, and this has continued into the 1990s. Perhaps the most obvious and immediate defence of new realist agreements is that the alternative might be no unions at all. As Eric Hammond put it,

> in some cases, it has been clear that the alternative to an employer's package deal with us has been a closure or a non-union plant. Rival unions prefer that to seeing us make an agreement. Some principle! (Bevan 1987)

Others have talked of the need for trade unions to 'rise to the challenge' to prevent 'the spread of the IBM approach to industrial relations across the hi-tech sector' (Bevan 1987). It is impossible to test the 'non-union alternative' thesis, but it does appear plausible, as Hammond suggests, in many cases. An example can be claimed at Orion; before the agreement with the EETPU the Osake corporation, of which Orion is a part, had never signed a collective bargaining agreement with any union anywhere in the world (*Financial Times*, 3 June 1987). Similarly, the Personnel Director of Ford's Electrical and Electronics Division told unions, in the light of debate over the proposed Dundee plant, that the company would not reconsider its single-union agreement with the AEU, and that Ford would actually have preferred a non-union factory (*The Guardian*, 31 October 1987). Finally, the threat of an 'investment strike' by Isuzu was held over the heads of workers at General Motors' Bedford van plant when negotiations involving a flexibility package there were at a stalemate, while a similar threat with respect to a new engine plant was used to put pressure on Vauxhall's Ellesmere Port workers in 1990.

Many new realists go beyond simple pragmatism in defence of the new realist deal and the no-strike agreement. Positive benefits are claimed for workers in the form of open and extensive consultation, single-status terms and conditions, training in a range of skills, and greater union democracy. Bevan (1987), in a speech to the CBI, made it clear that the EETPU would not compromise its defence of its members' interests:

> One . . . possibility that we are determined will not happen is that the agreements could be used, no doubt by more unscrupulous employers, as a front for what is, in effect, an anti-union policy. In other words, as a paper agreement, to wave in the faces of other unions who attempt to recruit on site.

Referring to Nissan, he went on:

> the reason they decided to sign the agreement . . . was the fact that it was the lesser of two evils. That is, the soft option between traditional trade unionism and anti-unionism as was desired by the parent company and as is operated at its American plant. Since the agreement was signed, the union has struggled to maintain membership above 25 per cent. Moreover, the company remains adamant that it will not and cannot recommend union membership to its employees. One wonders why they signed the agreement if they are prepared to operate it with a density of membership that renders the agreement virtually impotent.

Union membership densities in companies that have new realist deals with the EETPU have been far higher, and, as already mentioned, some EETPU agreements specifically state that the company will encourage employees to join the trade union.

One may or may not support the new realist position with regard to these deals. However, it is clear, and certainly agreed among trade unionists, that the challenge posed in the 1980s and 1990s by the new industrial relations strategies of many companies is a radical one. What is less well known is the latent implications of this process for trade unions and worker organization, implications that, we would suggest, could be equally important in the long term.

Latent Implications of Japanization

As we have argued in previous chapters, just-in-time and total quality systems of production create a dependency on employee flexibility and cooperation and render a company – indeed the whole supply–manufacturing chain – vulnerable to any disruption, including industrial disputes. Industrial disputes are made less likely with new realist deals – indeed this is one of their declared objectives when they are sold by unions to prospective employers. Kelly (1987) nonetheless believes that flexibility agreements will not necessarily weaken shopfloor union power:

> New systems of labour flexibility often require extensive co-operation from workers in moving from job to job, and if conditions permit, this co-operation can be withheld, as a power resource in bargaining.

He predicts that strike activity may increase again, as and when the economy recovers. A similar argument is offered in a joint report by the TGWU and Northern College (1987). They argue that, in the long term, flexible work practices and just-in-time production could place workers in a stronger bargaining position than that traditionally enjoyed.

However, other interrelated developments in Japanizing companies, we would argue, are likely to weaken further the collective motivation of workers to utilize this power capacity. These include: production modules and group working; flexible work practices and job rotation; individual performance appraisal systems; the promotion of images of the firm as a 'community' or 'family' with a common destiny for employee and employer; selective recruitment, induction and socialization; and direct communications between company and workers. Such practices, which were discussed in detail in earlier chapters, could potentially change the identification and orientation of employees away from the occupational group and trade union and towards the work team and employing organization. Here we shall briefly summarize the implications of these factors for union organization at shopfloor level.

Appraisals

The seniority component of wages in Japan may work against individual competitiveness, though, as described in an earlier chapter,

Japanese companies are attempting gradually to reduce this element and increase the importance of individual performance considerations in determining wage packages. Japanese companies in the UK have not generally brought with them seniority-based pay systems, and individual merit appraisals are typically used instead (Pang and Oliver 1988; Gleave and Oliver 1990; Yu and Wilkinson 1989). Emulators, such as Lucas and Bedford, are also seeking to introduce individual merit appraisals for shopfloor workers. We suggest that such appraisal schemes encourage an individual rather than a collective orientation towards a company, with potentially damaging effects on the solidarity of shopfloor union organization.

Individual appraisals do not necessarily mean that cooperation and loyalty to company are lost. On the contrary, the appraisal is based not just on performance per se, but also on a demonstration of cooperative ability and a commitment to the team and company (Robbins 1983). As Clegg (1986, p. 36) remarks in the context of a Canon factory in Japan:

> the worst failing for an employee is to fail to share the overall goals [of the company]: this is much worse than failing to achieve certain tasks. Attitude and commitment are highly significant aspects of performance.

In the British subsidiaries of Japanese companies, the emphasis on what Townley (1989) calls 'regulatory and extra-functional norms' also appears strong. Such norms (for example an 'ability to work without supervision') encourage attitudes and behaviour supportive of cooperative and flexible work, and support the authority structure of the firm.

Clearly, all this goes against the logic of collective representation by an independent trade union – both individual competition and a requirement to display company loyalty are anathema to union solidarity. As Turnbull (1988) points out, the appraisals, being 'based on company procedures that deliberately exclude existing forms of union regulation and channels of union representation', mean that the whole rationale of unionism is brought into question.

Team spirit

Often written into the new realist agreements is a clause on competitiveness and high productivity. Womack et al. (1990) describe

how lean production systems, by their very nature, force performance improvement. Critics, such as Domingo (1985) and Slaughter
(1987), refer to the same system as 'management-by-stress'. One
trade union official interviewed by the authors was struck more than
anything else in the Japanese companies that he had visited in Britain
by the practice of bell-to-bell working. With little slack in the
system to make up for fluctuations in work rate (or to compensate
for absenteeism), pressure to maintain output and meet targets is
increased, and absenteeism and lateness are frowned upon as much
by an employee's peers (who have to bear the burden of the re-
calcitrant employee's actions) as by his or her manager. The working
atmosphere is, then, rather different from that in traditional organizations, and so long as management can capture peer pressure and
competitive team spirit and use them to the benefit of the employer,
unions may find difficulty in resisting an intensification of work.
Indeed, any limits to work intensification could arguably come
from labour turnover and low morale, rather than from organized
resistance.

The disputed issue of turnover and low morale reported at Nissan
in 1987 would make sense in this context – most complaints related
to work overload (*The Daily Telegraph*, 6 May 1987; *The Guardian*,
8 May 1987). Later in the same year, Nissan claimed that by June
it had reduced its absentee rate to 3 per cent (lower than the British
average for the car industry) and publicly defended its working
methods (*The Guardian*, 8 September 1987) At the Nissan factory,
the names of absentees and their dates of absence are publicly
displayed for all to see, an idea that, according to Personnel Director
Peter Wickens, came from the workforce itself (*Financial Times*,
19 August 1987). The AEU line on this action is not recorded.

Selection and induction

Both Japanese companies and British companies attempting the
adoption of methods from Japan have introduced formal induction
and new selection criteria – Rover, for instance, has adopted
a one-week induction foundation programme that is preceded by
successful applicants and their families being taken around the
Longbridge plant. A senior Rover manager was quoted as follows:
'We are not just looking for manual skills and dexterity. We want
to know whether their aspirations are the same as the company's'
(Smith 1988). Similarly, in chapter 5 we recounted the comment of a

team leader regarding his selection criteria for his work team – 'You could almost forget the job spec. and write attitude.' Within the context of a slack labour market, such philosophies are most unlikely to assist union recruitment unless the unions themselves change their image and rationale. As we saw, some unions have already taken steps in this regard.

Harmonization

Workers' identification with their companies is further encouraged by single-status terms and facilities, which, in Japanese companies in Britain as well as in Japan, are normally symbolized by company uniforms, common car parks and canteen facilities, and clocking on for *all* staff, followed by exercises at the start of each shift. Pang and Oliver (1988) found extensive provision of single-status facilities in Japanese companies in Britain. A more recent survey of 25 Japanese companies (*IRS Employment Trends* 470, 21 August 1990) found that four out of five firms had single-status terms and conditions, findings that mirror those of our own surveys. As we have seen, most Japanese companies and their British emulators seek harmonization, often with the support of the union. Add to this the typical long-term employment policies for the core workforce, and one can begin to understand some of the difficulties that trade unions may face – the reality may still be 'them and us', but the 'them-and-us' symbols are less readily apparent, and core workers may feel privileged and perhaps even 'cared for'.

Discussing a Japanizing company that had introduced single status and harmonization extensively, Rawlinson et al. (1991, pp. 16f.) comment that:

> the upgrading of terms and conditions for manual workers to levels enjoyed by the staff has pre-empted any claims that the unions may have had for enhanced benefits. As one worker commented, employees no longer feel the need to be in a union because they have been awarded improvements in sick pay and in holidays, etc., through the harmonization programme.

Ironically, the single-status conditions and staff benefits so much sought by trade unions, and suddenly being granted in exchange for flexible working practices and the like, perhaps pose one of the greatest threats to union organization as it currently exists. By removing many of the trappings of the divisions that lead people to join trade unions in the first place, harmonization may be undermining one of the premises on which membership is based. Wickens (1985) points out that, in Japan, subtle differences are still evident. For instance, the uniform wearer's rank may be distinguished by the number and width of bands around his cap, and only managers wear a collar and tie underneath the jacket of their uniform. Similarly, we recorded instances in the UK of subtle status distinctions creeping back in to 'single-status' companies. Nonetheless, single-status provisions are more prevalent than in the traditional British company, and may serve to reinforce the new orientations of workers under a harmonized system of conditions and benefits.

Direct communication

Japanese companies and their emulators use a host of means for communicating directly with their workforces. Alastair Graham, Director of the Industrial Society, has claimed that team briefings are now so widespread that every month 250,000 managers are communicating directly with 4 million workers without using trade unions (Heaton and Linn 1989). The clear problem for trade unions is that shop stewards, traditionally the go-betweens for employers and employees, are bypassed. As Rawlinson et al. (1991, pp. 15–17) argue:

> employers can circumvent unions by introducing techniques such as team briefings, videos and information-sharing, which communicate directly with the workforce . . . As the head of [a case study company] put it: 'our aim . . . is not to communicate with the unions, but to communicate with all 600 people, so that all 600 people understand the key result areas and the needs of the factory' . . . Among the shopfloor workers, the distance that these measures had created between the union and its members was apparent. Some employees, although they were union members, could not remember the last time they were in contact with their union representative and, in some cases, were not sure to which union they belonged.

Another important channel for direct communication that circumvents the union was described earlier in this chapter – namely the company advisory board. As we saw, the company advisory board is typically involved in the resolution of issues that are traditionally the preserve of collective bargaining between union and company.

Trade unions, in such a situation, have the choice of using the company advisory board as their primary avenue for representing workers in the company, by seeking election of union representatives to the board. If they do not, the danger is that they could be 'frozen out' – found irrelevant – as seems to have happened at Nissan. If they do, they may come to have more in common with Japanese enterprise unions than with traditional British unions. It seems clear that the successful use of systems of direct communication between management and workforce, and especially of the company advisory board, could pose a challenge to British unions in the 1990s equal to that posed by the new realist deals themselves.

Work organization

Group working, sometimes in the form of production modules, as at Lucas, entails 'semi-autonomy' and heightened responsibility for the foreman or team leader. Each 'manufacturing cell' is responsible and accountable for a definable 'product', and inputs and outputs come from and go to other cells, which are viewed as 'clients' and 'customers'. Each cell consists of a team of workers including crafts-men as well as semi-skilled staff, and flexible work practices mean that distinctions between occupations are blurred – as described in the cases of Lucas and Rover in chapter 4. Identification with the work group in the cell, rather than with colleagues of the same occupation or craft, poses a challenge to the logic of traditional trade union representation. The implications are as follows. First, the representation of members, regarding grievances and perhaps even pay, is no longer appropriately handled by a trade-specific union. Secondly, to the extent that a form of team spirit does emerge, management has a natural direct communication channel with the workforce via the team leader, and hence the potential to bypass the shop steward. A steward from Rover's Cowley plant, describing the introduction of team leaders, put it thus:

> Bringing in team leaders does create a big counter pressure [to the trade union] . . . They're the ones who get a source of information, they're the ones who will then be countering a trade union organ-ization. We saw this as being what it's all about. In fact that *is* what it's all about. It isn't just about taking other people's jobs and being

cheap foremen. It is crucially about being in a counter position with the workforce, with quality circles so that people get a feeling of 'jointness' about their activity, plus a team leader who you go to for your gloves and your information. (*Oxford Motor Industry Project* 1991)

Thirdly, with buffer stocks held to a minimum, any lapses in production or quality will be identified immediately – because the next cell down the line will have problems – meaning that cells are likely to be held accountable not just by management but by other cells as well. In some companies, this is reinforced with public displays of cell productivity performance, as in K-Electric. The potentially divisive effect on workforce solidarity is obvious, particularly if a strong 'customer-driven' ethos pervades the organization.

Temporary workers

Significantly, Nissan was the first company in Britain to employ auto-assembly workers on temporary contracts since the 1940s (*Financial Times*, 16 February 1987), and its precedent was quickly followed by the GM–Isuzu joint venture in which the company demanded complete freedom to contract out work, and to use temporary labour to meet seasonal variations in demand (*Financial Times*, 26 June 1987). Similarly, the agreement between Control Data and the EETPU actually stated the policy of creating 'a buffer of approximately 100 jobs to protect the full-time jobs from shortfalls in the business'. The buffer here is the granting to new recruits of short-term contracts that may be confirmed later. Most agreements do not contain such statements, but it is clear that any increased use of sub-contracting and temporary labour poses difficulties for trade unions, in that union membership densities are typically far lower for those categories of worker. Furthermore, it could be argued that the emergence of core–periphery distinctions among workforces could defeat the object of harmonization in the new realist deal, from the point of view of the trade union. Unions at Lucas resisted attempts to increase the use of part-time employees to gain greater flexibility of production (Turnbull 1988), and in January 1988 so did unions at Ford, using the threat of industrial action. However, such resistance has become increasingly difficult in the climate of the late 1980s and early 1990s.

Buyer–supplier relations and unions

As pointed out previously, the dependencies endemic in a Japanese-style production system extend beyond the single enterprise to suppliers as well. This raises the question of whether Japanese and Japanese-emulating companies in the UK will extend their influence to cover their suppliers' industrial relations policies, as they have done in the context of quality control, pricing, and product development. The high dependency of a company with a just-in-time system on its suppliers suggests that they will, and McFadden and Towler (1987) claim that Nissan, with the largest investment commitment of any Japanese company in the UK to date, lists in its criteria for the selection of primary suppliers items including industrial relations, trade union structure, working practices and strike record. Turnbull (1988) argues that established motor manufacturers:

> Will experience far greater difficulty in their attempts to influence the employment practices of their suppliers and to use those suppliers as a device for cutting wages/costs.

However, he indicates that such attempts are already being made. Certainly, trade union leaders have expressed fears that some large companies have recently been attempting to extend their influence to the labour relations practices of suppliers, one instance that is cited being the controversial no-strike agreement between the EETPU and Christian Salvesen, a supplier to the non-union company Marks and Spencer. Marks and Spencer denied forcing the deal (*Financial Times*, 22 June 1987).

Conclusion

Japanization has important implications for trade unions. Some of these are overt and have manifested themselves in the form of new realist deals, sometimes single union, sometimes strike-free, and more often enshrining clauses on managerial prerogatives over labour deployment, harmonization of terms and conditions, and the establishment of company-based representative bodies. Equally important for the future of trade unionism, we have argued, are the new workplace cultures implied by teamwork, and the new systems of selection, payment, appraisal, and so on. The initiatives of Japanese companies and their emulators thus pose serious threats to British trade unionism as it has historically existed.

However, as well as posing problems to organized labour, the managerial initiatives that we have collectively referred to as 'Japanization' could also provide certain opportunities (Kirkpatrick et al. 1991). For instance, the system vulnerability and reduced capital mobility characteristic of JIT production may give a degree of bargaining power to labour, and it is not completely unthinkable that local shop steward organizations could regroup and come to have some influence at the work team level. True, the current political and legal framework supports management: Legge (1989) has argued that the new management strategies are a reflection of the rise of a 'new Right'. But this framework conceivably could change during the 1990s if worker participation programmes, proposed as part of the Social Charter, come to be enforced in Britain. The CBI, recognizing the threat to managerial prerogatives, has commented that the Charter would:

> potentially disrupt industrial relations, requiring companies to decide a wide range of issues through collective bargaining rather than individually with employees. (House of Lords 1990)

In the light of these fears, it is unsurprising that these proposals have met with substantial (and expensive) lobbying by US, Japanese and European employers' associations (De Vos 1989).

Having reviewed the evidence on developments in the area of unions and industrial relations, we now move on to explore the policy implications of the Japanization of British industry.

11
Policy Implications and Conclusions

In chapter 3 we argued the importance of the broad social, economic and political environment for the successful functioning of a system of production characterized by – and indeed based on – a set of high-dependency relationships. In chapters 4 to 9 we presented evidence in support of the thesis of a 'Japanization' of British industry, and in chapter 10 we explored trade union responses to the new initiatives. In this final chapter we seek to consider the policy implications that arise out of this evidence. After commenting on what the recent evidence for a widespread Japanization process suggests, we shall examine these implications in relation to four areas: employer–employee relations; organization–environment relations; trade unions; and finally public policy. We shall then conclude with some final comments on the usefulness of the Japanization concept.

The Japanization Process

As chapters 4 to 9 demonstrate, there is strong evidence of the Japanization process at the level of individual companies, evidence that has previously led some commentators to claim that 'the Japanization of British industry is now unequivocal' (Turnbull 1987). Our impression in 1987 was of a strong determination among engineers and managers to advance the process by the emulation of Japanese manufacturing practices. The logic and simplicity of the Japanese methods were certainly remarkable, and the wave of attempts to implement JIT and total quality principles was indicative of a belief that they held the promise of improving the performance of British manufacturing industry, the international reputation of which had become progressively tarnished during the twentieth century.

Certainly, some commentators suggested – and are continuing to suggest – that for British manufacturing industry the alternative to the adoption of these manufacturing techniques was to lose out in international competition, so furthering the process of apparent decline. Given the unavailability of other models of manufacturing organization that promised the same performance levels, the key question seemed not one of whether or not a process of Japanization would occur, but *to what extent* it would occur.

So, on the basis of the available material, what is the evidence in support of a widespread 'Japanization' of British industry by the early 1990s? First, the survey data from both the 1987 and 1991 surveys reported here demonstrate a clear *wish* to move towards Japanese production methods on the part of UK companies as well as Japanese investors, and of themselves would suggest very substantial use of these methods. However, some cautionary notes are in order. The 1991 survey did not show as fast an advance in use of these methods as the 1987 study would have predicted, and actually indicated a *decline* in the usage of some of them. Moreover, the implementation dates reported in the second survey were much more recent than in the first, suggesting that companies are either redefining what Japanese methods really are, or revising their perceptions of when they 'really' started their programmes of change, or most probably a combination of both. Although some variation between the results of the two surveys may be due to the fact that they did not cover exactly the same companies, the clear implication of these results is a gap between rhetoric and reality. Such a gap clearly needs to be borne in mind when assessing the spread of the methods concerned.

A second and related point concerns the success of these methods. In 1991 both Western and Japanese companies reported lower success rates with the practices almost across the board than had been recorded in 1987. This concords with anecdotal impressions picked up by the authors during company visits that the evangelism of the mid-1980s was subsiding as the recognition of the difficulties in putting these practices into place dawned. For example, in 1986 an article about manufacturing reform at Lucas carried the title 'Where Lucas Sees the Light', and Lucas's Manufacturing Director, describing just-in-time production, wrote:

It is not the latest gimmick, *it is fundamental and when completed there can be no other improvement* since it completely tailors a manufacturing strategy to the needs of a market and produces mixed products in exactly the order required. (Parnaby 1987a; emphasis added)

Two years later, comments by Parnaby carried a different tone:

It's a balls-aching job. It cannot be anything other than that. You just have to grind your way through it. (*Financial Times*, 12 April 1989)

A third point concerns the picture provided by aggregate data on company performance, which, if the programmes of manufacturing reform that companies allege they have in place are working, should start to show indications of this. Clearly one would expect variations in this respect between sectors, but some changes should be detectable. However, studies on this subject are rare; to date we know of only two. Williams, Williams and Haslam (1989) used sector-level data to compare stock levels between sectors in Japan and the UK and over time, on the assumption that the extensive use of techniques such as JIT should be reflected at sector level in lower levels of stockholding. Their analysis indicated lower stocks in Japan than in the UK; moreover, they detected little evidence of a significant drop in stock levels in the West in recent years, despite all the claims by UK companies to be pursuing JIT programmes. More recently, Delbridge and Oliver (1991b) conducted a longitudinal analysis of stock turns in the Japanese and Western car industries and drew similar conclusions. As the vehicle industry is the sector in which Japanese ideas find their purest expression, it provides an interesting test case for the Japanization thesis. We shall therefore describe the Delbridge and Oliver study in some detail.

Delbridge and Oliver examined the stock turnover ratio (STR) figures of Japanese, North American and European vehicle assemblers and component suppliers. The stock turnover ratio represents the ratio of the value of total stocks (at the time when the annual accounts were compiled) to annual sales. This figure can also be expressed in terms of the number of days of stock held (by dividing 365 by the stock turnover ratio). The case for using the stock turnover ratio as a performance measure to assess the spread of Japanese manufacturing methods is threefold. First, STR is inherently sensitive to the impact of JIT practices. Secondly, stock turns are one of the few measures pertinent to manufacturing performance that are readily accessible in publicly available sources.

Thirdly, the data on stock turns are reasonably (though not totally) comparable across companies and regions.

Delbridge and Oliver compared the average STR figures for all eight Japanese vehicle assemblers (weighted according to their total turnovers) with the same figures for European and North American producers between 1975 and 1989. The results are shown in figure 11.1.

Due to Toyota's dominant position (its output represented some 45 per cent of total Japanese output in 1987) the overall average STR for the Japanese assemblers strongly reflects Toyota's performance. To allow for this 'Toyota effect' the average for all Japanese assemblers excluding Toyota is also given. The first point to note from figure 11.1 is the variation in performance between the Japanese assemblers, with the stock turnover ratios of the best and worst performers differing by a factor of four in 1988. Toyota stands out as exceptional, recording STRs approximately double the average of the other Japanese assemblers from 1983 onwards. When Toyota is excluded from the average of the Japanese assemblers, a stable picture emerges. Between 1975 and 1988, stock turns rose slowly but steadily, from approximately 11 to 21, apart from a dip in the period 1981–2. This dip aside, the relentless, albeit modest, improvement on a year-by-year basis is particularly striking.

Comparison of the Japanese STR figures with Western ones reveals that in this context the Japanese, even excluding Toyota, are outperforming Western producers by about 65–70 per cent. When Toyota is added to the picture, the differential jumps to around 150 per cent in favour of the Japanese producers. Looking at trends over time, the stock turn data presented here show little evidence that the programmes of manufacturing reform claimed by the Western producers are (as yet) making a significant impact on stock turns. Although Western assemblers show some improvement in stock turn performance during the 1980s, so too do the Japanese. Indeed, when Western stock turn figures are viewed alongside Japanese ones (with or without Toyota) it is clear that the gap between them shows no signs of narrowing and may even be widening. European assemblers show lower stock turns than US producers, and within Europe, the UK volume producers show some of the lowest stock turns.

One explanation put forward by some observers is that the performance of the Japanese vehicle assemblers is achieved at the cost of reduced performance on the part of their suppliers, because stock-

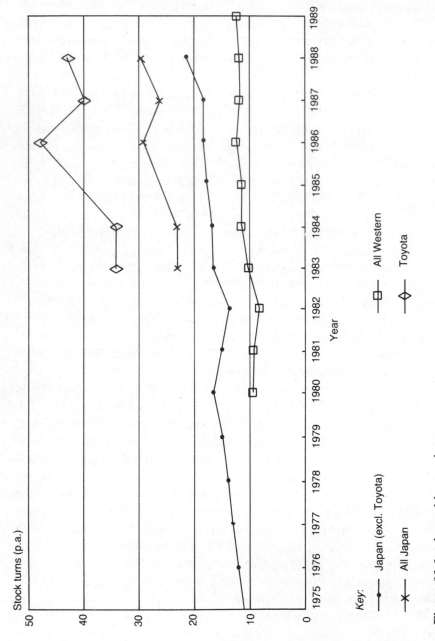

Figure 11.1 Assembler stock turns

holding costs are simply transferred from assembler to supplier. To explore this, data on the comparative performances of Japanese and UK components suppliers from the Delbridge and Oliver study are shown in figure 11.2.

One problem with comparing UK and Japanese 'supplier' performance is that in Japan some vehicle assembly work is contracted out to suppliers. For that reason, the Japanese data are shown with the 'assembler-suppliers' separated out.

The stock turn figures for the Japanese suppliers (excluding those engaged in assembly operations) show a steady rise throughout the period covered, from 9.7 in 1975 to 21.6 in 1988. This pattern is virtually identical to that of the Japanese vehicle assemblers (excluding Toyota), in terms both of trend and of the absolute magnitude of average stock turns. This implies that the relatively high stock turns of the Japanese vehicle assemblers are not achieved at the price of their (larger) suppliers. When the UK averages are compared with those of the Japanese, a significant gap is apparent. Moreover, this gap clearly *widened* during the 1980s. In 1980–1 the sample of Japanese components suppliers showed a stock turn performance some 230 per cent above that of the UK group. By 1987–8 this differential had risen to nearly 280 per cent, despite the fact that the UK components suppliers were also claiming vigorous programmes of manufacturing reform. By all accounts, the motor industry is the sector where these reforms are likely to be *most* advanced, which bodes ill for other sectors in terms of their progress towards the Japanese model.

In sum, the extent of change in British industry appears not to be so great as we would have expected, given the enthusiasm – and the perceived imperative – for Japanese-style manufacturing reform being expressed during the mid-to-late 1980s. It may be that the 'obstacles to Japanization', which we have described in detail throughout the book, are more deep-seated, perhaps more 'culturally embedded', than we originally believed. Nonetheless, the imperative to change is still fixed in the minds of British managers and engineers, albeit often now along with the realization that the changes required are not so easy to implement as to conceptualize, and the 'balls-aching job' described by Parnaby continues.

We shall now turn attention to the implications of Japanese methods.

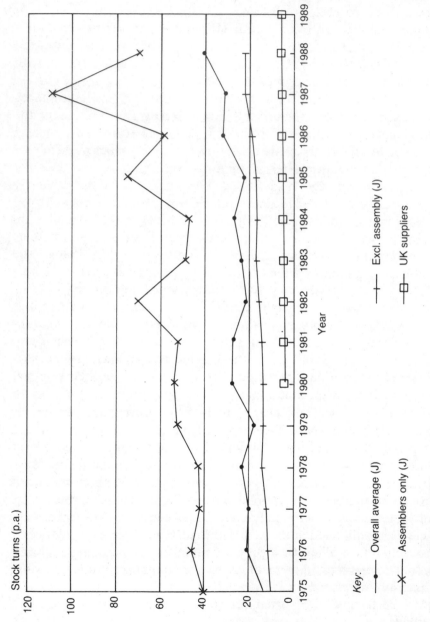

Stock turns (p.a.)

Key:
— Overall average (J)
—✕— Assemblers only (J)
—†— Excl. assembly (J)
—☐— UK suppliers

Figure 11.2 Japan/UK supplier stock turns

Implications of Japanese methods

Japanese or lean manufacturing systems have captured the imagination of British industry because of their promise of leaps in productivity and quality. As described in chapter 1, people with radical political views see the transformation involved in their introduction as greatly intensifying the rate of exploitation of workers, with the aim of enhancing the financial return to those who supply capital. Hence Graham (1988) suggests that the term 'Japanization' may be preferred to alternatives because of its ideological appeal – the implication is that 'we all have to pull together to beat the Japanese at their own game', and divisions due to differences of interest within (and outside) companies are obscured.

Leaving aside the ideological connotations of the term for the moment, the evidence does suggest that Japanization, from either of the two perspectives mentioned above, implies a fundamental change. Japanese methods of production organization are *high-dependency strategies*. Consequently they demand a set of social (and technical) relations to support the fragile production system. Under this system, strategies for living with uncertainty are swept away, leaving management no choice but to confront uncertainty at source. This implies a high degree of organizational influence over the behaviour of a company's constituents – most obviously over labour and suppliers, but arguably extending to markets and key political and economic agencies outside the organization as well.

The theoretical analysis in chapter 3 suggests that this may be achieved by avoiding resource scarcity and by the creation and maintenance of a homogeneous social system around the production process. Traditional mass production on the other hand functions as a relatively *low-dependency* system. This is reflected, for instance, in the quest for substitutability of labour by the simplification and standardization of work roles (Braverman 1974), by lodging authority and responsibility with the upper echelons of an organization's hierarchy, and by the extensive use of indirect labour in 'safety net' functions, such as quality control inspection of outgoing products and extensive inspection of materials coming in. Multiple sourcing, thereby making suppliers substitutable, is a further expression of this philosophy.

Since we wrote the 1988 version of this book, more systematic evidence has accumulated of the importance of a functional fit between production methods and the social relations within which they are embedded, a central tenet behind our use of the term Japanization. Some of the most rigorous work on this subject has come from researchers on the International Motor Vehicle Programme, who set out to test the idea of functional fit empirically. Krafcik and MacDuffie (1989) examined the relationship between what they described as factory practice, work systems and human resource management. In common with our own observations, they argued that the Japanese production system 'is highly dependent on the contributions of a skilled, flexible and motivated workforce' and characterized the system as 'fragile because of its dependence on human resource capabilities'.

In accordance with their empirical approach, the variable of 'factory practice' was measured by examining how 'buffered' or 'lean' a production system was, using indices such as how much factory space was allocated to repairs and how much inventory was held between stages in the production process. 'Work systems' were gauged by the extent to which team working and quality circles were used, the extent to which responsibility for quality lay with production workers, and so on. 'HRM policy' was judged by the sophistication of selection and training procedures, the extent of single-status conditions and the presence of 'contingent compensation' – performance-related pay.

When these three variables were combined into a single index, Krafcik and MacDuffie found that they were strongly related to both quality and productivity. Each of the three variables seemed to play an equally important part in explaining productivity, but HRM practice was particularly important in determining quality. Krafcik and MacDuffie (p. 13) conclude:

> This analysis . . . supports our argument that all three of these components of production system management are important determinants of world-class manufacturing performance.

MacDuffie later argues (1991) that lean production methods need to be embedded in both an appropriate 'organizational logic' (structures and systems) *and* an appropriate 'cultural logic' (covering factors such as attitudes to production problems). The appropriate cultural logic, he suggests, is one in which production problems are seen as opportunities for innovation rather than occasions for apportioning blame. Such a finding fits our own conclusions regarding obstacles to Japanization – an entrenched culture antagonistic towards the new production methods was the most frequently cited obstacle identified by our own research (see chapter 5).

Having indicated just how fundamental we regard the changes entailed by Japanization as being, let us now turn our attention to specific implications, beginning with organization–employee relations.

Organization–Employee Relations

The experience of working in organizations operating Japanese-style methods is likely to be different from that to which many British workers, and indeed managers, are used. On the one hand, work is likely to be more varied, and involvement in and 'ownership' of the work that one is doing, higher. On the other, accountability and responsibility are increased, performance is more closely monitored, and the visibility of failings (and successes) is heightened. This mix of outcomes explains the split of opinion between the critics and the advocates of these methods. Advocates claim that Japanese-style work organization is humanistic; critics see it as manipulative and coercive. Certainly, many contemporary changes, such as cellular or group working and employee involvement, resemble the practices promoted by the quality of working life movement in the late 1960s and early 1970s; however, the driving forces behind contemporary developments are quite different. For example, the Ingersoll Engineers study of cellular manufacture found that 'increased job satisfaction' ranked eleventh out of a list of 12 objectives cited by companies as reasons for the introduction of cellular manufacture (Ingersoll Engineers 1990).

The European and American quality of working life initiatives of the 1960s and 1970s – of which the Volvo plant at Kalmar in Sweden is the most frequently cited example – emerged in the context of rapid economic growth and tight labour markets, associated with acute problems of absenteeism and labour turnover, growing trade union strength, and, in some countries (particularly Norway, Sweden and West Germany), employment legislation that *enforced* a degree of worker participation (Friedman 1977; Ramsey 1983). 'Humanistic' forms of work organization – semi-autonomous work groups and the like – were invariably *responses* by employers to their own lack of control over labour (Lupton et al. 1979). The 'humanism', no doubt genuine on the part of some employers, was an attempt to win labour's commitment and loyalty through meeting workers' increased expectations, associated with the greater affluence and improved educational arrangements that followed the Second World War. 'If we are humanistic and respect the demands and rights of workers', the logic went, 'then our employees are more likely to turn up for work, stay with the company for more than a few weeks, and pay more attention to quality.'

Japanization, on the other hand, at least in Britain, is an initiative taken by employers in response not so much to problems of labour turnover and absenteeism as to problems of manufacturing performance. The results, we would argue, are in some respects similar to those of quality of working life initiatives, but in other respects very different.

In this context, improved manufacturing performance is achieved by introducing flexible work practices and by pushing responsibilities that were previously the preserve of specialist indirect staffs onto production workers, thereby assisting in the elimination of waste – where waste is defined as any activity that adds cost, but not value, to a product. This distinction between quality of working life initiatives and contemporary industrial reforms may improve our understanding of developments at British Leyland/Rover, for example. There, as Smith (1988) relates, the 1970s saw the introduction of the Ryder 'participation scheme', which was abandoned when Sir Michael Edwardes took over and reasserted managerial prerogatives in the context of recession and the decline of trade union power. The programme of introducing teamwork and related institutions and practices, such as zone circles and zone briefings, which has followed in the 1980s, is primarily an exercise in efficiency, not a defensive human relations response to problems of worker recruitment and retention.

Japanese practices, then, seem to hold out the opportunity for improved quality of working life. Giving workers responsibility for quality, routine maintenance and so on, in addition to machine operation, implies broader tasks and the delegation of authority – including authority to stop the line: *jidoka*. But it also implies accountability and heightened pressure to produce the right quantity of the right quality products exactly on time. As illustrated elsewhere in this book, a JIT production process heightens the visibility of behaviour and performance, and increases the pressure (from operators' peers, as well as managers) to meet performance targets.

Some Japanese companies and other total quality organizations reinforce this visibility through various devices, such as public displays of group or individual output and quality levels. In sum, more job interest and responsibility are necessarily accompanied by more job demands.

An additional aspect of the Japanization process concerns employment contracts and career management. Because of the lifetime employment and internal promotion policies associated with a high-dependency system, recruitment and selection procedures are rigorous and place significant emphasis on a candidate's personal characteristics, company training and socialization are extensive, and job rotation is desired as a way of gaining promotion to the ranks of management. Each of these elements serves to contribute towards a homogeneity of goals and a willingness to work flexibly. The effects are twofold. First, employees are being asked in a sense to become more intimately related to their organizations – the contract of employment goes beyond 'a fair day's work for a fair day's pay' towards mutual commitment and identification. This point alone bitterly divides the critics and the advocates of Japanization, as we shall see in the concluding section. Secondly, task flexibility and job rotation serve to reduce the salience of occupational specialities – craft and professional identifications are difficult to sustain, and allegiance to a particular department is prevented from dominating allegiance to the organization as a whole. The employee's primary point of reference thus becomes the organization, as other bonds are discouraged. Enterprise-based unions working closely with the company and representing all occupational groups are best suited to this type of employer–employee relationship, while the provision of relatively good wages and working conditions, and single-status facilities also serves to ensure that organization–employee dependency is mutual. There is, however, some evidence of British cynicism towards attempts to create 'strong-culture' organizations in the Japanese style. Smith (1988), for instance, recounts that:

> during the induction course [at Rover] a number of references to Japan . . . recalled the last war and, implicitly, the British way of life being defended. It was generally acknowledged that the home came before the company; that you worked for money and not out of slavish devotion; and that when holiday time came round you took your full entitlement. One participant remarked to murmurs of assent that his mortgage was with the Halifax, not the Rover group.

The benefits that Japanese-style arrangements afford to workers include: relative security of well-paid employment; the opportunity to upgrade and broaden skills and abilities; and the opportunity to pursue a career in line with one's capacity. On the other hand, there are costs of being tied to the company, because of the dilution of occupation-specific expertise and the salience of internal promotion. Relatedly, the paternalism of these personnel practices may be difficult for many to swallow: speaking to one of the authors, the Personnel Manager of a long-established Japanese company described its ethos as 'Victorian'. Critics may thus argue that employer paternalism was a nineteenth century British phenomenon that disappeared in the face of advances in democracy and the extension of individual rights, and that a reversion to it would be a morally and politically backward step. These, then, are some of the pros and cons of working in companies operating Japanese-style techniques. There is, however, one final point of crucial importance. The Japanese model includes the building of 'rings of defence' for the protection of core workers and activities. Employees who find themselves in the outer rings – peripheral workers employed on temporary contracts, or employees of firms sub-contracted to the main sub-contractors – are likely to have a rather different experience of work. Paternalistic provision for them is less likely, meaning job insecurity, relatively low wages, harsher working conditions, and so on. To the extent that the privileges of the core workforces are provided at the expense of the periphery, as they clearly are, the Japanization process may further contribute to the already significant divisions in British society.

Organization–Environment Relations

In the context of relations with suppliers, the use of Japanese practices implies a high degree of dependency, since the supplier must be trusted to deliver goods of the right quality, in the right quantity, and 'just in time'. It is thus essential for buyers to nurture long-term relations with their suppliers and to exert influence over their operations.

Whilst significant moves are afoot aimed at changing buyer–supplier relations in British industry, and particularly in the automotive industry, our 1987 study showed that significant problems had been encountered, especially with regard to JIT supply. Nonetheless, many organizations do seem to be evolving strategies to enable them to cope with their increased dependency on their suppliers. Examples are the pursuit of preferred supplier status policies and the establishment of longer-term relationships. Such policies, of course, carry a price for suppliers. A long-term relationship is liable to involve interference in their internal arrangements, such as cost structures, quality control methods, purchasing policy, and sometimes even personnel policies, as in the case of Marks and Spencer and its suppliers (Paton 1983). The advantages to the supplier are equally obvious: a long-term relationship, a predictable market, help and advice, financial security, and so on. On the other hand, the fact that the supplier has the buyer constantly 'on its doorstep', relies on it heavily as a long-term major customer and, in many Japanese cases, depends on it financially, means that the supplier is under intense pressure to 'deliver the goods'.

In theory, establishing influence and control over supplier operations should be unproblematic compared with the problem of controlling constituents within the organization. This is because suppliers do not enjoy the same sort of collective representation as workers. Suppliers have on occasion voiced their concerns about their futures with organizations that were making radical changes to their supplies policies, but, for most suppliers, taking action is out of the question – they would simply be struck off the list of candidates for preferred supplier status. However, there are two reasons why the achievement of Japanese-style supplier relations can be difficult. The first reason relates to the obvious temptation of large corporations to use JIT production as nothing more than an excuse to pass on the costs of holding inventories to their suppliers. In 1987 this seemed to be occurring in some cases. In these instances, UK companies were really abandoning, or at least subverting, the philosophy of total quality, and the nature of the whole exercise, aimed, in theory, at improving the relationship of trust and dependability between the two parties, was brought into question. By 1991, there were signs that UK companies were getting better at managing this aspect of their operations, although adjustment problems were still apparent.

The second difficulty may be still more serious, since it relates to the fact that Japanese-style supplier relations, and JIT supplies in particular, require buyers to exert control not only over suppliers, but also over those agencies that can influence supplier performance – for example trade unions inside the suppliers themselves. We have

already pointed out that reducing inventories increases workers'
capacity to disrupt the production process, and that this can be used
as a bargaining tool if workers perceive the need for one. Just-in-time
supply provides a choke point that can be the target of industrial
action. Hence, the introduction of JIT supplies proper implies the
necessity to guard against disruption not just from sources within
one's own organization, but from within one's suppliers too. We
might expect, then, that in the scramble by suppliers to gain preferred
supplier status with British firms emulating Japanese practices, those
suppliers identified as having poor industrial relations will be the
least likely to have a long-term future.

Management of the environment?

There is one final issue on which we should touch before we leave
the question of the management of dependency relationships. It
concerns the attempts of companies operating lean systems of production to eliminate uncertainty, from whatever source, in order
to minimize the resources invested in 'insurance' policies, such as
buffer stocks and the like. If, as we have suggested, the elimination
of uncertainty is important, then it seems logical that such organizations should attempt to influence their environments so as to make
them less uncertain. Japanese strategic marketing, with an emphasis
on market share, may represent one way of doing this. Similarly,
market dominance, by reducing the number of competitors, also cuts
down uncertainty. In addition, market dominance typically allows a
company higher margins (by increasing the entry barriers to that
market), giving the company the 'elbow room' to pay premium
salaries, provide staff benefits and high job security for core workers,
and so on. Once it is in this position, a company may be in a self-
sustaining cycle. Comments such as 'the Japanese have "market
share" tattooed across their hearts' (made to one of the authors by a
director of an inward investment agency) make sense in this context.

Relatedly, Japanese companies seek to reduce uncertainty by
closely linking production activities to retailing and distribution. It is
such close links that help to explain Toyota's ability to build to
order.

This leads to a 'Catch-22' situation as far as change is concerned.
Companies that face so much uncertainty, from whatever source,
that they are constantly 'fire-fighting' may lack the stability to begin
to put these techniques in place. On the other hand, because of the

scale of the change involved, those that do not experience a sense of crisis may face insurmountable problems in implementing it, from their existing cultures. Womack, Jones and Roos (1990) refer to the need for a 'creative crisis' and quote the example of Ford US; in 1982 'the company keeled over so far that the senior executives on the bridge were practically catapulted into the raging torrent' (p. 258). For companies without such a crisis (real or engineered), getting into the virtuous circle outlined above may not be possible.

The same may apply in the context of the corporation and the local economy. Crowther and Garrahan (1988) suggest that Nissan took advantage of its ability to influence the local authority in the North East and thereby secure, at low cost, the land necessary for the creation of a 'spatially concentrated' production arrangement suited to just-in-time supplies. They claim that there was:

> . . . a concerted effort by local 'power brokers' (regional government officials, elected local councillors, the Washington New Town Development Corporation, private sector firms, regional trade unionists and the media) to conform with the pattern *determined by* Nissan. (Crowther and Garrahan 1988, p. 52; authors' emphasis)

The extension of mutual dependencies to a company's external constituents may be welcomed by many, due to its implications of cooperation and common purpose. However, critics such as Bonis view this situation less favourably:

> A kind of disguised Imperialism results when the organization seeks to control the external elements: customers, suppliers, subcontractors, members of other organizations, politicians and political organizations, the press, public opinion, pressure groups . . . (Bonis 1980, p. 163)

Trade Unions

As the previous chapter was devoted to trade unions and industrial relations, we shall just briefly summarize the key points regarding the implications of Japanese practices in this context. Our argument is that lean production systems demand a workforce that is dependable, hard-working, flexible and unlikely to disrupt production. An antagonistic or adversarial form of industrial relations is undesirable because of the fragility of the production system, which provides workers with too great a power base for a company to be able to risk them having goals that differ radically from its own. The typical tactics developed for coping with the uncertainty generated by having to rely on parties upon whom one cannot depend – such as the use of slack resources – go against the lean philosophy on which Japanese-style production systems are based.

As Reitsperger (1986) has suggested, the options open to Japanese (and, by implication, emulating) organizations in this situation are stark: they can either avoid unions altogether, or accept them but develop strategies to neutralize potential problems. As we have seen, about a third of the Japanese organizations in our 1987 sample opted for a union avoidance strategy, a proportion that had risen to over half by 1991. Where Japanese companies have recognized unions, they have almost invariably opted for single-union deals, often accompanied by agreements that reduce the likelihood of industrial disruption (sometimes with a binding arbitration clause) and that explicitly give the union a *collaborative* rather than an *adversarial* role. In 1987, in nearly half of our cases unions co-existed with company advisory boards, the members of which were elected independently of the trade union and subject to company-determined rules. These boards functioned as the first line of communication between company and worker and handled many issues typically handled by unions via collective bargaining. The 1991 survey showed a similar picture.

The existence of company advisory boards is particularly problematic for unions, because ignoring them could lead to marginalization, whilst attempting to use company representative bodies to increase union influence (by seeking the election of union representatives to the boards) implies incorporation. From the point of view of a company avoiding adversarial relations, this situation is ideal, for the union in effect becomes *voluntarily* incorporated.

The extent to which the predominance of enterprise unions in Japan in itself represents a form of trade union incorporation is a debatable point, particularly in the light of the unions' historical origins. In any case, Japanese industrial relations serve to support a high degree of stability and workforce involvement. In Britain, incorporation appears to be achieved, or at least attempted, by means of the single-union deal, with the company advisory board as the most important mechanism for resolution of collective issues. Any occupation-wide or industry-wide allegiances that trade unions may have (and, as we saw in chapter 10, these had already significantly declined before the advent of Japanization) are effectively dissolved, leaving the corporation as the union's only point of reference.

This is not to say that Japanese companies have been unwilling to adapt themselves to local cultural and political realities in the UK. When one considers the geography of union recognition among Japanese companies, the tendency has been for companies setting up operations in areas without traditions of collective worker organization – such as new towns – to avoid trade unions, and for those setting up operations in the older industrial centres to accept trade unions. For instance, at least nine out of the 11 Japanese companies that had established factories in Wales by the end of 1987 had recognized trade unions, whereas those Japanese companies located in Livingston, Telford, Worcester and Northampton had not. According to the evidence available, there appear to be few exceptions to this tendency. The important point is, however, that, where trade unions *are* accepted, a non-adversarial role is sought and, at least judging by the contents of the deals signed, gained. Either option – union avoidance or incorporation – satisfies the requirements of a production system based on high-dependency relations, because both allow for frequent and direct communication with the workforce and both serve to increase goal homogeneity by appealing to principles of cooperation and a sense of common purpose. The obvious problem that this poses for trade unions is that they draw the rationale for their very existence from the presence of differences of interest, and hence goal heterogeneity.

The position of unions in traditional long-established British companies is rather different. Many of these companies have sought new realist agreements with unions, often as part of a whole pro-gramme of Japanization. Obviously the acceptance of such agree-ments is more difficult to achieve in such firms, given established traditions and vested interests, but the threat of plant closures, redundancies and investment strikes has been used successfully to gain acceptance of, for instance, flexible work practices and new pay structures. On the whole, in these cases unions do appear to have retained a degree of independence from the companies in which they operate; and although the present economic and political climate may militate against industrial action, and despite a trade union membership crisis in the 1980s, British unions are still capable of posing a challenge to the introduction and operation of just-in-time systems and total quality methods. This was demonstrated, for instance, by union resistance to zone briefings and circles at Rover, and to quality circles and the other elements of the 'After Japan' campaign at Ford.

Many employers in Britain would clearly prefer to have the sorts of single-union agreement that have been signed with newly investing companies. However, even putting aside the political ramifications of such a shift, the same context of declining trade union membership and power and increased inter-union competition that leads unions to scramble to sign single-union deals with newly investing companies at the same time reduces the likelihood of any union surrendering membership to a rival union. With membership on the decline even in the 'new realist' unions, and in the absence of clearer direction and policy from the TUC, the picture of inter-union rivalry looks unlikely to change in the near future. If one adds to this the latent implications of Japanese-style management practices, union organization surely cannot survive in a significant way in its existing form.

Public Policy

The dual economy

As explained in chapter 2, in Japan the large numbers of temporary workers, part-time workers and workers employed by smaller organizations enjoy relatively poor pay and conditions in comparison with their counterparts in the large corporations. The army of peripheral workers serves to bear the brunt of economic misfortune by providing numerical flexibility. Hence these workers could be construed as supporting the lifetime employment policies, generous benefits and so on enjoyed in the large corporations, by enabling potential problems to be 'exported' outside these organizations. For example, if a company has temporary workers or sub-contractors that it can shed in the event of a downturn, potentially divisive redundancies within the core organization can be avoided, because the potential losers are kept outside the organization's boundaries.

In Britain also, there is a substantial peripheral labour force, and this rose in importance during the 1980s. In 1985, 8.1 million workers, or 34 per cent of those in employment, were either part-timers, temporary workers, or self-employed – a 16 per cent increase since 1981. Over the same period, the number of full-time permanent employees fell by 1.02 million to 15.62 million. The majority (60 per cent) of workers in the peripheral categories were female. According to Rajan (1987), the main factor in the rise in the use of peripheral workers is constituted by employers' attempts – particularly in the services sector – to gain the flexibility necessary to adapt to fluctuating demand and to save on non-wage costs, such as sick pay, pensions and holidays. Reports by the white-collar union APEX (1987) and the GMB (*Financial Times*, 5 May 1987) confirm this finding. APEX adds that there is a real and significant demand by women for part-time work. In 1987, this situation looked as if it would facilitate, and itself be fostered by, the Japanization process. As things turned out, this impression seems to have been flawed. Perhaps because of the enhanced demands on labour made by Japanese-style systems, *functional* rather than *numerical* flexibility seems to be the route that most employers have chosen to follow, so that the use of temporary workers shows only a marginal increase between 1987 and 1991.

Government strategy and support to industry

In chapter 2 we recounted how some commentators have related Japanese success in penetrating (and in some cases dominating) world markets to a history of government intervention in manufacturing industry and selective support for those sectors considered to be of strategic importance. If this *is* a key aspect of Japanese success, then there is as yet little sign of it being replicated in Britain. The industrial and economic policies of the Conservative governments of the 1980s and early 1990s have been driven by a laissez-faire philosophy of minimal government intervention. Looser restrictions on capital movements, deregulation, decreased employment protection, and privatization are all examples of this philosophy. (Intervention in trade union activities and industrial relations is the significant exception to it.) Despite some successes with regard to inward investment, the overall consequence has been a net outflow of capital from the UK (*British Business*, 22 May 1987). Further, the increases in profit margins of manufacturing industry, for which the government may or may not be given credit, have not yet been accompanied by the desired rise in levels of investment.

Despite the productivity gains made in the early 1980s, British manufacturing productivity is low, as are British wages, when compared with the international competition. A report made in 1987 by the National Institute (*Economic Review*, no. 20, summarized in *Financial Times*, 28 May 1987) stated that Britain's recent 'moderately favourable' productivity performance still left a 'formidable' gap between it and its rivals. Measured in terms of output per hour, American productivity was two-and-a-half times greater, and that of Japan, West Germany and France around 80 per cent higher. In contrast, Britain came a clear second-from-bottom (to Ireland) in a league table of 12 industrial nations covering unit hourly labour costs, when taking employers' social charges into account. America's costs were 61 per cent higher and Japan's 29 per cent. The report's conclusion was that the British competitive advantage of very cheap labour was 'more than offset' by its very low level of productivity. Whilst attempting to extend the cheap labour advantage may have been the government's strategy for improving competitiveness, outside government circles, and especially in industry, Japanization, as a means of tackling deficiencies in *productivity*, is increasingly identified as the solution to the competitiveness problem.

Import barriers, such as local EC content requirements, may be serving to slow the impact of international competition, but their design is not to halt foreign competition per se, only to prevent 'unfair' competition. The main effect of the establishment of the single European market in 1992 has been to bring competition, particularly Japanese competition, onto British soil, and in doing so to expose the relative inadequacies of British manufacturing in an alarming fashion.

Economic structures

Closely related to the problem of government support for manufacturing industry (or the lack of it), is the general problem of finance for manufacturing industry. In the late 1980s investment expenditure remained subdued, despite the fact that manufacturing productivity rose by 30 per cent between 1979 and 1986 – an average of around 5 per cent per year – and that manufacturers' profit margins rose in every single year over the same period. In 1986, margins were at their highest since the early 1970s (*Financial Times*, 13 August 1987). Yet, again over the same 1979 to 1986 period, the top 40 British manufacturers increased their overseas investments and foreign-based workforces, the latter going up from 34 per cent of the total in 1979 to 44 per cent in 1986 (*Financial Times*, 5 May 1987).

Manufacturers, then, continue to be dependent on 'the City', a situation that Ackroyd et al. (1988) argue has existed throughout this century, but the City continues to be reluctant to commit itself to manufacturing, at least to British manufacturing. As we pointed out in chapter 2, British banks, unlike their Japanese counterparts, are not in business to provide low-interest, long-term loans, and a short-term profit mentality is reinforced by British companies' typically high dependency on the stock market. The fact that, as a nation, Britain lacks the 'savings' culture of Japan clearly aggravates this problem, by restricting the funds available for investment in the first place. The problem for UK manufacturers is that their dependency on the City is not reciprocal, and, in the absence of measures by the government, reciprocal dependency seems unlikely to emerge.

The continued scarcity of long-term investment commitments in British manufacturing industry clearly limits its developmental possibilities. Without this commitment, production reorganization is made difficult, training and development programmes are less likely to be seen as a wise investment, and getting manufacturers onto a trajectory of long-term growth and development is made problematic. In our 1991 survey, it was striking how most of the answers to a question on the reasons for undertaking manufacturing reform referred to short-term 'defensive' considerations rather than active, forward-looking ones. Whilst conducting research for the 1988 edition of this book, we came across many examples of 'short-termism' having detrimental effects on companies attempting to implement new Japanese-style methods. The same issue arose in many guises – the 'debasement' of total quality principles by their use as a smokescreen to push through redundancies, the questioning and blocking of factory reorganization plans by finance functions and the short payback times demanded of projects. Engineers at one of Rolls-Royce's aero-engine plants, currently subject to a Japanese-style reorganization, related their scepticism to one of the authors. It was due, they said, to the 'accountant mentality' that they saw as dominating the company at the top level. Japanese-style ideas, they said, were sound, but they had been presented with similar ideas and reorganization proposals in the past: 'we've heard it all before.' Previous attempts to introduce new ideas had floundered on the lack of long-term financial commitment, and unless someone had determined a way to provide the resources necessary for the massive commitment required, they figured that there was no reason why present attempts at reorganization should be a complete success. The ideas would be either diluted in the face of the practical realities of resource constraints, or dropped altogether in the face of failure.

Whilst we do not wish to suggest that things have changed significantly in this regard, resource constraints were not particularly frequently reported impediments to change in our 1991 survey, suggesting that although short-term financial horizons are part of the problem, they do not represent the whole picture.

This is consistent with the results of a survey contrasting British companies' marketing strategies with those of Japanese companies in the UK. The study found that 80 per cent of the sample of British companies had a strategy described as 'prevent decline', 'defensive', or 'maintain position'. In contrast, *all* the Japanese companies described their strategy as either 'steady growth', 'aggressive growth', or 'dominate market' (Wong, Saunders and Doyle 1987). Wong, Saunders and Doyle (p. 62) argue that too many British companies:

> are dominated by short-term profit considerations or over-emphasis on internal production capabilities. To improve competitiveness, there is need for re-orientation at the top. The chief executive should take the lead in demonstrating his commitment to marketing and stimulate continuous, informal monitoring and anticipation of developments in the market.

They go on to suggest that better professional education in marketing for British managers is required. This may be so, but unless short-term business horizons can somehow be changed to long-term ones, it seems unlikely that growth strategies can be pursued aggressively, regardless of marketing philosophy and skills.

A report by the Manpower Services Commission (1987) confirms the notion that Japanese companies' business horizons are of a longer-term nature than those of British firms. As well as paying more attention to employee training and education than their British counterparts, Japanese organizations were found to have higher proportions of technologists at board level. Interestingly, the MSC characterized Japanese companies as 'technology-driven', as opposed to 'finance-driven' like those of the UK. The fact that some British companies are manifestly worse than others in this respect suggests that not all the blame can be laid at the door of the City, but its modus operandi is obviously not assisting long-term manufacturing development, and this raises the serious question of the feasibility of stimulating world-class manufacturing in a non-world-class economy.

Thus there is a danger that the cost-cutting elements of just-in-time and total quality principles are being embraced in the UK without the development work essential for their long-term success. Given the extent of the shake-out in British manufacturing in the early 1980s, it seems likely that the cost-cutting knife is beginning to shave the bone. Indeed, the figure of 5 per cent annual productivity growth in the 1980s cited above contrasts with a 'real' productivity growth rate – that is, growth in output per person employed – of 1.9 per cent per year between 1979 and 1985 (Matthews and Minford 1987). This is not an insignificant figure, but it does imply that the gains made during that period were due more to cutting away the 'fat' than to genuine advances in technology and efficiency. The use of JIT supplies simply to pass on the costs of inventories to suppliers is a good illustration of this danger; failure to provide adequate compensation and promises of long-term employment to workers who accept the flexible working practices and greater demands characteristic of a JIT system would be another.

Being financed from Japan, Japanese companies investing in the UK appear to be willing to forgo short-term gains in their quest for market share in Europe. This is indicated by the extremely slow (and expensive) planning process that they go through before choosing a location, and was confirmed in comments to the authors by representatives of an inward investment agency and by representatives of various Japanese companies in the UK. The findings of the survey by Wong, Saunders and Doyle (1987) into Japanese marketing strategies in Britain also support this argument – such aggressive market share strategies would simply not be possible if short-term profitability were of primary importance. The growth in the importance of 'direct' Japanization that appeared likely in 1987 has subsequently materialized, as those Japanese companies with an early presence in Britain have expanded and suppliers have followed them over.

The evidence presented here suggests that the spread of the Japanese model through British manufacturing industry will continue. However, comparison between the situations in 1987 and 1991 reveals that care is needed to distinguish between actual progress down this route and corporate 'wish-statements'. The fact that the implementation dates of the Japanese-style practices picked up by the 1991 survey were much later than would have been predicted using the 1987 survey suggests that there is something of a gap between rhetoric and reality, and that there is probably more of the former than the latter. Analyses of aggregate manufacturing performance data, such as those of Williams, Williams and Haslam

(1989) and Delbridge and Oliver (1991b) that were reported earlier in this chapter, cast some doubt on the extent of real progress.

As we argued in chapter 2, the comments on the key factors in Japan's success offered by various authors have mostly been one-dimensional formulas. For instance, Pascale and Athos (1982) suggest that the secret is their human asset management; and Schonberger (1982) and Parnaby (1987a) argue for their skills in manufacturing organization; while Wong, Saunders and Doyle (1987) argue that production issues have been over-stressed to the neglect of aggressive marketing strategies. Our own very clear conclusion on the basis of the extensive evidence presented here is that the high interdependencies characteristic of the flagship Japanese corporations mean that *all* these factors are crucial, and that *none* of them is likely to be achieved in the absence of the potential for long-term strategic planning provided by long-term financial guarantees.

Japanization: Taking the Debate Forward

At a number of points in the 1988 edition of this book we noted a marked divergence in perspective between the various commentators on Japanese practice, both here and in Japan. Examples of this included descriptions of Toyota's production system as 'a respect-for-human' system by one set of commentators and as 'inhuman' by another. It is reflected in the description of a Japanese production system as one over which, when implemented, 'there can be no other improvement', and in the less enthusiastic comment:

> Faced with the choice of going on the dole or working like the Japanese, the men so far would prefer the dole. It's as simple as that. (Turnbull 1988, p. 44)

In the four years that have passed since the book was originally written, the diversity of opinions about the Japanization process has increased, as the overview of positions in chapter 1 has indicated. Moreover, at the extremes, the differences between the advocates and the critics seem wider than ever. For example, Womack, Jones and Roos (1990) comment:

> It took more than fifty years for mass production to spread across the world. Can lean production spread faster? Clearly we think it is in

everyone's interest to introduce lean production everywhere as soon as possible . . . Lean production can quickly triple the productivity of the motor vehicle industry while providing more fulfilling jobs for factory workers, engineers and middle managers. (Womack, Jones and Roos 1990, p. 256)

Yet, commenting on Nissan UK, widely regarded as one of the best examples of lean production in Britain, Garrahan and Stewart (1992) write:

The uniqueness of the 'Nissan Way' lies in its combination of external political control and careful regulation of internal conflict, institutionalized in the company's image. As part of this new regime of subordination, the 'Nissan Way' rests upon control through quality; exploitation via flexibility and surveillance via teamworking. (Garrahan and Stewart 1992, p. 145)

In 1991, as in 1987, the criticisms of Japanese practices centre on claims that it entails work intensification and heightened control by companies over their constituent agencies – their workers, their suppliers and so on. On the other hand, the advocates of Japanese methods continue to point to their benefits in terms of manufacturing performance, and hence to the competitiveness of British companies in world markets, arguing that British industry must either become more competitive internationally or cease to exist in a significant form. Both critics and advocates would probably agree that these production systems mean 'working harder', though they may disagree as to whether this also involves 'working smarter'; Nissan's statements on its application forms (quoted in chapter 8) indicate this, along with other evidence that we have presented. The advocates argue that the benefits of Japanese-style practices compensate for the intensified workload; the critics are unconvinced of this.

Where the two sides appear to be separated by an *unbridgeable* gap is in their perspectives on control. In chapter 2, we argued that low-waste, high-dependency systems require that uncertainty from whatever source should be minimized, if not eliminated, if they are to operate successfully. This implies *control* over the resources involved in the production process, both mechanical and human. It is on this issue that opinions most sharply divide. The critics view Japanese-style practices as insidious control devices, the worst of which are represented by strategies to elicit loyalty and commitment to the company. The advocates see loyalty and commitment as desirable and morally acceptable on the grounds that everyone benefits in the long run:

> It is the concept of loyalty to the company which so rankles left wing opponents of these new initiatives. Failing to realize that the intention is that all shall benefit, they attack what they believe are companies' attempts to usurp the traditional loyalty of workers to union . . . Companies *do* seek employee loyalty and they *do* want to develop an environment where industrial action is inconceivable! (Wickens 1987)

Ironically, it is the very conditions most applauded by the advocates, such as single status, long-term employment and identification with one's work team, that create the conditions most scorned by the critics: 'The Japanese corporation [operates] as a culturally homogeneous social system that . . . can withstand no internal cultural diversity' (Ouchi 1981). While one side applauds the Japanese corporations for their unity and apparent ability to create a homogeneous culture and a sense of common purpose, the other castigates them for it. Advocates claim the removal of 'artificial' barriers through the harmonization of employment conditions and the removal of tangible divisions of status within the organization; critics point to a false consensus and the obscuring of 'real' interests.

Of course, the Japanization debate – or whatever label one wishes to put upon it – says as much about the politics and philosophies of those who are engaging in it as about the 'facts' over which they are allegedly arguing. We have used the expression 'Japanization' as a short-hand term to describe a package of changes that appear to be taking place in British manufacturing industry. In doing so, we are really using Japanization as a metaphor, to try to describe and better understand one phenomenon (what is going on in UK industry) in terms of another (what is going on in Japanese industry). Japanese industry carries different associations for different people: for some, efficiency, quality, value for money; for others, work intensification, conformity, subordination, oppression – to name but a few. Thus Japanization evokes powerful images, and, in using such images, there are undoubtedly problems. Quoting Nisbet on the use of metaphors and images to understand contemporary industrial change in the UK, Dunn (1990) points out that:

> The larger, the more general, abstract and distant in experience the object of our interest the greater the utility of the metaphor. The

problem is that 'becoming' metaphors . . . tend to be . . . given literal relevance not just to abstractions and wholes but to the highly empirical problems of change which are the substance of contemporary social science. (Dunn 1990, pp. 22 f.)

Doubtless it is for reasons such as these that commentators such as Dickens and Savage (1988) have labelled Japanization a 'bad abstraction' and a 'chaotic conception'. Perhaps it is. But it provides a powerful image with which to think about contemporary change in industrial Britain and, in so doing, it has stimulated, and is continuing to stimulate, a rich debate at many levels – about shopfloor organization, about management systems, about relations between organizations, about economic structures. This debate has led us and, it would appear, many others as well to refine and sometimes question our perspectives on these changes. That, to us, must be the ultimate criterion of the past and future usefulness of the concept of Japanization.

References

Abraham, Y., Holt, T. and Kathawala, Y. (1990), 'Just-in-time: Supplier-side Strategic Implications', *Industrial Management and Data Systems*, no. 3, pp. 12–17.

Abrahams, P. (1989), 'When Just-in-Time is Not Good Enough', *Financial Times*, 4 May.

ACAS/WINvest (1986), *Successful Industrial Relations: The Experience of Overseas Companies in Wales*, Cardiff, ACAS Wales.

Ackroyd, S., Burrell, G., Hughes, M. and Whitaker, A. (1988), 'The Japanization of British Industry?' *Industrial Relations Journal*, vol. 19, no. 1, pp. 11–23.

Aggarwal, S. C. (1985), 'MRP, JIT, OPT, FMS? Making sense of production operations systems', *Harvard Business Review*, September–October, pp. 8–16.

Anglo-Japanese Economic Institute (1991), *Japanese Addresses in the UK*, London, Anglo-Japanese Economic Institute.

Aoki, M. (1987), *A New Paradigm in Work Organization: The Japanese Experience*, Helsinki, World Institute for Development Economics Research.

APEX (1987), *Less than Full-time Working*, London, APEX.

Atkinson, J. (1987), 'Flexibility or Fragmentation? The United Kingdom Labour Market in the Eighties', *Labour and Society*, vol. 12, no. 1, pp. 87–105.

Azumi, K. (1969), *Higher Education and Business Recruitment in Japan*, New York, Columbia University Press.

Bassett, P. (1986), *Strike-free: New Industrial Relations in Britain*, London, Macmillan.

Batstone, E. (1988), *The Reform of Workplace Industrial Relations: Theory, Myth and Evidence*, Oxford, Oxford University Press.

BBC (1987), 'Chopsticks, Bulldozers and Newcastle Brown', BBC Productions [Film].

BBC (1988), 'Working with Pride', *Ideas Unlimited*, BBC Productions [Film in series].

BBC/OU (1986a), 'Strategies for Change: The Task Force', *PT 611: The*

Structure and Design of Manufacturing Systems, Open University/BBC Productions [Film].

BBC/OU (1986b), 'Process Capability and Control', *PT 619: Quality Techniques*, Open University/BBC Productions [Film].

Beasley, M. (1984), 'Participation in Jaguar Cars', *Industrial Participation*, no. 586, pp. 18–21.

Beaumont, P. (1987), *The Decline of Trade Union Organization*, London, Croom Helm.

Bertodo, R. (1989), 'Japonification: the Automotive Determinant of the 1990s'. Paper presented to the Business International Conference on Japan and Europe, Claridges Hotel, London, November 1989.

Bevan, W. (1987), 'Creating a "No Strike" Environment: The Trade Union View'. Text of a speech given to the CBI Conference on Strike-Free Deals, London, 24 June 1987.

BIC (1989), *Gaining a Competitive Edge in Europe: Strategic Responses of non-European Companies to 1992*, New York, Business International Corporation.

Bicheno, J. (1987), 'A Framework for JIT Implementation', in Voss, C. (ed.), *Just-in-Time Manufacture*, London, IFS, pp. 191–204.

Black, J. and Ackers, P. (1988), 'The Japanisation of British Industry? A Case Study of Quality Circles in the Carpet Industry', *Employee Relations*, vol. 10, no. 6, pp. 9–16.

Blauner, R. (1964), *Alienation and Freedom*, Chicago, University of Chicago Press.

Bonis, J. (1980), 'Organization and Environment', in Lockett, M. and Spear, R. (eds), *Organizations as Systems*, Milton Keynes, Open University Press.

Boyer, E. (1983), 'How Japan Manages Declining Industries', *Fortune*, 10 January, pp. 58–63.

Braverman, H. (1974), *Labour and Monopoly Capital: the Degradation of Work in the Twentieth Century*, New York, Monthly Review Press.

Briggs, P. (1988), 'The Japanese at Work. Illusions of the Ideal', *Industrial Relations Journal*, vol. 19, no. 1, pp. 24–30.

Buchanan, D. and Bessant, J. (1985), 'Failure, Uncertainty and Control: The Role of Operators in a Computer Integrated Production System', *Journal of Management Studies*, vol. 22, no. 3, pp. 292–308.

Burbidge, J. (1979), *Group Technology in the Mechanical Engineering Industry*, London, Mechanical Engineering Publications.

Burbidge, J. (1982), 'Japanese Kanban System', *International Journal of Production Control*, January/February, pp. 1–5.

Clegg, C. (1986), 'Trip to Japan: A Synergistic Approach to Managing Human Resources', *Personnel Management*, August, pp. 35–9.

Clutterbuck, D. (ed.) (1985), *New Patterns of Work*, Aldershot, Gower.

Cooper, C. (1987), 'Executive Stress Around the World', *University of Wales Business Review*, no. 2, Winter, pp. 3–8.

Crowther, S. and Garrahan, P. (1988), 'Invitation to Sunderland: Corporate Power and the Local Economy', *Industrial Relations Journal*, vol. 19, no. 1, pp. 51–9.

Cusumano, M. (1986), *The Japanese Automobile Industry: Technology and Management at Nissan and Toyota*, Harvard, Harvard University Press.

Dace, R. (1987), 'Japanese Strategic Marketing: An Insight into Product and Market Plans of Japanese Companies'. Paper presented to the Conference on the Japanization of British Industry, Cardiff Business School, 17–18 September.

Dale, B. and Hayward, S. (1984), *A Study of Quality Circle Failures*, Manchester, UMIST.

Dale, B. and Barlow, E. (1984), 'Facilitator Viewpoints on Specific Aspects of Quality Circle Programmes', *Personnel Review*, vol. 13, no. 4, pp. 22–9.

Dawson, P. and Webb, J. (1990), 'New Production Arrangements: The Totally Flexible Cage?' *Work, Employment and Society*, vol. 3, no. 2, pp. 221–38.

De Vos, T. (1989), *Multinational Corporations in Democratic Host Countries*, Aldershot, Gower.

Delbridge, R. and Oliver, N. (1991a), 'Just-in-time or Just the Same? Developments in the Auto Industry – the Retailers' View', *International Journal of Retailing and Distribution Management*, vol. 19, no. 2, pp. 20–6.

Delbridge, R. and Oliver, N. (1991b), 'Narrowing the Gap? Stock Turns in the Japanese and Western Car Industries', *International Journal of Production Research*, vol. 29, no. 10, pp. 2083–95.

Dickens, P. and Savage, M. (1988), 'The Japanization of British Industry? Instances from a High Growth Area', *Industrial Relations Journal*, vol. 19, no. 1, pp. 60–8.

Dillow, C. (1989), *A Return to Trade Surplus? The Impact of Japanese Investment on the UK*, London, Nomura Research Institute.

Dohse, K., Ulrich, J. and Malsch, T. (1986), 'From Fordism to Toyotism? The Social Organization of the Labour Process in the Japanese Automobile Industry', *Politics and Society*, vol. 14, no. 2, pp. 115–46.

Domingo, R. (1985), ' "Kanban": Crisis Management Japanese Style', *Euro-Asia Business Review*, vol. 4, no. 3, pp. 22–4.

Dore, R. (1973a), *British Factory – Japanese Factory*, London, Allen and Unwin.

Dore, R. (1973b), *Origins of the Japanese Employment System*, London, Allen and Unwin.

Dore, R. (1983), 'Goodwill and the Spirit of Market Capitalism', *British Journal of Psychology*, vol. 34, no. 4, pp. 459–82.

Dore, R. (1986), *Flexible Rigidities*, London, Athlone.

Dunn, S. (1990), 'Root Metaphor in the Old and New Industrial Relations', *British Journal of Industrial Relations*, vol. 28, March, p. 1080.

Dunning, J. (1986), *Japanese Participation in British Industry*, London, Croom Helm.

Economist Intelligence Unit (1990), 'The Rover Group: Where to Now?' *European Motor Business*, February, pp. 35–57.

Edwards, G. A. B. (1974), 'Group Technology', *Personnel Management*, March.

Edwards, J. N. (1988), 'Integrating MRP II with JIT', *BPICS Control*, October/November, pp. 45–53.

Egan, J. (1985), 'Quality: The Jaguar Obsession', *EOQC Quality*, vol. 1, pp. 3–4.

Elger, T. (1990), 'Technical Innovation and Work Reorganisation in British Manufacturing in the 1980s: Continuity, Intensification or Transformation?' *Work, Employment and Society*, Special Issue, pp. 67–101.

Endo, K. (1991), *Satei (Personal Assessment) and Inter-Worker Competition in Japanese Firms*. Unpublished paper for the Department of Economics, Yamagata University, Japan.

Feigenbaum, A. (1983), *Total Quality Control*, New York, McGraw-Hill.

Fletcher, D. (1984), 'Quality Circles at Wedgwood', in Sasaki, N. and Hutchins, D. (eds), *The Japanese Approach to Product Quality*, Oxford, Pergamon, pp. 79–82.

Ford Motor Company (1984), 'Durability, Quality and Reliability'.

Fortune, J. (1986), *Quality of Purchased Supplies*, unit 2, PT 619, Milton Keynes, Open University Press.

Fortune, J. and Oliver, N. (1986), *Human Aspects of Quality*, unit 4, PT 622, Milton Keynes, Open University Press.

Franko, L. (1983), *The Threat of Japanese Multinationals*, New York, Wiley.

Friedman, A. (1977), *Industry and Labour*, London, Macmillan.

Fucini, J. J. and Fucini, S. (1990), *Working for the Japanese*, New York, Free Press.

Fujita, K. and Child-Hill, R. (1988), 'Global Production and Regional "Hollowing Out" in Japan'. Revised version of a paper originally prepared for the 40th Annual Meeting of the Association for Asian Studies, San Francisco, 25–7 March.

Galbraith, J. (1974), 'Organization Design: An Information Processing View', *Interfaces*, vol. 4, no. 3, pp. 28–36.

Garrahan, P. and Stewart, P. (1989), 'Working for Nissan'. Paper presented to the Conference of Socialist Economists, Sheffield Polytechnic, 7–9 July.

Garrahan, P. and Stewart, P. (1992), *The Nissan Enigma: Flexibility at Work in a Local Economy*, London, Mansell.

Gleave, S. (1987), *How Japanese are Japanese Factories in Britain? A Study of Japanese Personnel Management in Japan and Britain*. MBA dissertation for Cardiff Business School.

Gleave, S. and Oliver, N. (1990), 'Human Resources Management in Japanese Manufacturing Companies in the UK: Five Case Studies', *Journal of General Management*, vol. 16, no. 1, pp. 54–68.

Goldratt, E. M. (1983), 'Cost Accounting: the Number One Enemy Of Productivity', *Proceedings of the 1983 American Production and Inventory Control Society Conference*, pp. 433–35.

Goldratt, E. M. (1990), 'Theory of Constraints'. Seminar at the Excelsior Hotel, London, 16 March.

Goldratt, E. M. and Cox, J. (1984), *The Goal*, Hounslow, Creative Output Books.

Gordon, A. (1985), *The Evolution of Labour Relations in Japan: Heavy Industry, 1853–1945*, Cambridge, MA, Harvard University Press.

Gow, I. (1989), 'Japanese Technological Advance: Problems of Evaluation', *European Management Journal*, vol. 16, no. 2, pp. 127–33.

Graham, I. (1988), 'Japanization as Mythology', *Industrial Relations Journal*, vol. 19, no. 1, pp. 69–75.

Gregory, M. (1986), 'The No-strike Deal in Action', *Personnel Management*, vol. 18, December, pp. 30–4.

Guest, D. (1987), 'Human Resource Management and Industrial Relations', *Journal of Management Studies*, vol. 24, no. 5, pp. 503–21.

Guthrie, G. (1987), 'After Japan and Beyond', *Production Engineer*, May, pp. 29–31.

Hague, R. (1989), 'Japanising Geordie Land?' *Employee Relations*, vol. 11, no. 2, pp. 3–16.

Halliday, J. and McCormack, G. (1973), *Japanese Imperialism Today*, Harmondsworth, Penguin.

Harrington, H. (1982), *Quality Education Rides the Crest of the Third Wave*. IBM Internal Document, July.

Heard, E. (1983), 'Why MRP II Won't Get Japanese Level Inventory Turns', *Proceedings of the 1983 American Production and Inventory Control Society Conference*, pp. 581–5.

Heaton, N. and Linn, I. (1989), *Fighting Back: A Report on the Shop Steward Response to New Management Techniques in TGWU Region 10*, Barnsley, Northern College and TGWU Region 10.

Heller, R. (1986), 'Growth, Profitability and Earnings', *Management Today*, June, pp. 46–63.

Hill, F. (1986), 'Quality Circles in the UK: A Longitudinal Case Study', *Personnel Review*, vol. 15, no. 3, pp. 25–34.

Hiromoto, T. (1988), 'Another Hidden Edge – Japanese Management Accounting', *Harvard Business Review*, July–August, pp. 22–6.

Hirschmeier, J. and Yui, T. (1981), *The Development of Japanese Business*, London, Allen and Unwin.

Hofstede, G. (1980), *Culture's Consequences*, Beverly Hills, CA, Sage.

Holloway, J. (1987), 'The Red Rose of Nissan', *Capital and Class*, no. 32, Summer, pp. 142–64.

House of Lords (1990), *EC Select Committee Report: A Community Social Charter*, London, HMSO.

Hove, T., Cunningham, G., Tucker, T. and Liddle, D. (1990), *The Japanese Business and Investment Survey*, London, Economic Development Briefing.

Ingersoll Engineers (1986), 'Just-in-time' – the People Implications'. Paper presented to the Association of Teachers and Managers, Manchester Business School, March.

Ingersoll Engineers (1990), 'The Quiet Revolution', Rugby, Ingersoll Engineers.

International Labour Organization (1989), *Working Time Issues in Industrialized Countries*, Geneva, ILO.

Isaac, D. (1984), 'How Jaguar Lost its Spots', *Management Today*, April, pp. 38–42.

Ishida, H. (1977), *Exportability of the Japanese Employment System*, Tokyo, Japan Institute of Labour.

Ishikawa, K. (1984), 'Quality Control in Japan', in Sasaki, N. and Hutchins, D. (eds), *The Japanese Approach to Product Quality*, Oxford, Pergamon.

Ishizuna, Y. (1990), 'The Transformation of Nissan – The Reform of Corporate Culture', *Long Range Planning*, vol. 23, no. 3, pp. 9–15.

James, B. (1989), *Trojan Horse: The Ultimate Japanese Challenge*, London, Mercury.

Japan Institute of Labour (1984), *Wages and Hours of Work*, Japanese Industrial Relations Series, no. 3.

Johnson, T. H. and Kaplan, R. S. (1987), *Relevance Cost: The Rise and Fall of Management Accounting*, Boston, MA, Harvard University Press.

Kamata, S. (1983), *Japan in the Passing Lane: An Insider's Account of Life in a Japanese Auto Factory*, London, Allen and Unwin.

Kanter, R. (1985), *The Change Masters*, London, Unwin.

Kaplan, R. S. (1984), 'Yesterday's Accounting Undermines Production', *Harvard Business Review*, August, pp. 95–101.

Kawahito, H. (1991), 'Death and the Corporate Warrior', *Japan Quarterly*, April–June, pp. 149–57.

Kelly, J. (1987), *Labour and the Union*, London, Verso.

Kendall, W. (1984), 'Why Japanese Workers Work', *Management Today*, January, pp. 72–5.

Kenney, M. and Florida, R. (1988), 'Beyond Mass Production: Production and the Labour Process in Japan', *Politics and Society*, vol. 16, no. 1, pp. 121–58.

Kirkpatrick, I., Lowe, J., Morris, J., Oliver, N., Salmon, J. and Weston, S. (1991), *Japanization: Issues and Opportunities for Trade Unions*. Unpublished paper for Cardiff Business School, UWCC.

Klein, J. A. (1984), 'Why Supervisors Resist Employee Involvement', *Harvard Business Review*, September–October, pp. 87–95.

Klein, J. A. (1989), 'The Human Costs of Manufacturing Reform', *Harvard Business Review*, March–April, pp. 60–6.

Kolm, S. C. (1985), 'Must One Be Buddhist to Grow? An Analysis of the Cultural Basis of Japanese Productivity', in Koslowski, P. (ed.), *Economics and Philosophy*, Tübingen, J. C. B. Mohr, pp. 221–42.

Krafcik, J. F. and MacDuffie, J. P. (1989), 'Explaining High Performance Manufacturing: The International Automotive Assembly Plant Study'. Paper presented to the IMVP International Policy Forum, Pierre Marques, Acapulco, 7–10 May.

Labour Research (1987), vol. 76, no. 8, August.

Lamming, R. (1989), 'The International Automotive Components Industry: The Next "Best Practice" For Suppliers'. Paper presented to the IMVP International Policy Forum, Pierre Marques, Acapulco, 7–10 May.

Lee, D. (1986), 'Set-up Time Reduction: Making JIT Work', *Management Services*, May, pp. 8–13.

Legge, K. (1988), 'Personnel Management in Recession and Recovery: A Comparative Analysis of What the Surveys Say', *Personnel Review*, vol. 17, no. 2, pp. 1–72.

Legge, K. (1989), 'Human Resource Management: A Critical Perspective', in Storey, J. (ed.), *New Perspectives on Human Resource Management*, London, Routledge.

Lincoln, J. R. and Kalleburg, A. L. (1990), *Culture, Control, and Commitment*, Cambridge, Cambridge University Press.

Linn, I. (1986), *Single Union Deals: A Case Study of the Norsk-Hydro Plant at Immingham, Humberside*, Barnsley, Northern College and TGWU Region 10.

Littler, C. R. (1982), *The Development of the Labour Process in Capitalist Societies*, London, Heinemann.

Lupton, T. et al. (1979), 'Manufacturing System Design in Europe', in Cooper, C. and Mumford, E. (eds), *The Quality of Working Life in Western and Eastern Europe*, London, Associated Business Press, pp. 44–75.

Macbeth, D. K. (1987), 'Supplier Management in Support of JIT Activity: A Research Agenda', *International Journal of Operations and Production*

Management, vol. 7, no. 4, pp. 53–63.

MacDuffie, J. P. (1991), *Beyond Mass Production: Flexible Production Systems and Manufacturing Performance in the World Auto Industry*. Unpublished PhD thesis for the University of Michigan.

MacInnes, J. (1987), *Economic Restructuring Relevant to Industrial Relations in Scotland*, Centre for Urban and Regional Research, University of Glasgow, Discussion Paper no. 26.

MacInnes, J. (1988), 'The Question of Flexibility', *Personnel Review*, vol. 17, no. 3, pp. 12–15.

Main, J. (1984), 'The Trouble with Managing Japanese-Style', *Fortune*, 2 April, pp. 10–14.

Manpower Services Commission (1987), *Management Development and Technological Innovation in Japan*, London, MSC.

Marchington, M. (1979), 'Shopfloor Control and Industrial Relations', in Purcell, M. and Smith, R. (eds), *The Control of Work*, London, Macmillan.

Marchington, M. (1990), 'Unions on the Margin?' *Employee Relations*, vol. 12, no. 5, pp. 1–24.

Marchington, M. and Armstrong, R. (1986), 'The Nature of the New Joint Consultation', *Industrial Relations Journal*, vol. 17, no. 2, pp. 158–70.

Marchington, M. and Parker, P. (1988), 'Japanisation: A Lack Of Chemical Reaction', *Industrial Relations Journal*, vol. 19, no. 4, pp. 272–85.

Marginson, P. (1989), 'Employment Flexibility in Large Companies: Change and Continuity', *Industrial Relations Journal*, vol. 20, no. 2, pp. 101–9.

Marsden, D., Morris, T., Willman, P. and Wood, S. (1985), *The Car Industry: Labour Relations and Industrial Adjustment*, London, Tavistock.

Maskell, B. M. (1989), 'Performance Measurement for World Class Manufacturing', *Management Accounting*, vol. 67, no. 5, pp. 32–3.

Matthews, K. and Minford, P. (1987), 'Mrs Thatcher's Economic Policies 1979–87', *Economic Policy*, vol. 2, no. 5, pp. 57–102.

McFadden, A. and Towler, D. (1987), *Nissan – the Challenge to the Trade Union Movement*. Report to the Northern Regional TUC, April.

McKenna, S. (1988), 'Japanisation and Recent Developments in Britain', *Employee Relations*, vol. 10, no. 4, pp. 6–12.

McLoughlin, I. and Beardwell, I. (1989), *Non-Unionism and the Non-Union Firm in British Industrial Relations*, Kingston Business School of Industrial Relations and Personnel Management, Occasional Paper no. 7.

Mercer, D. (1987), *IBM: How the World's Most Successful Corporation is Managed*, London, Kogan Page.

Merrette, E. (1987), 'Industrial Change: A Practical Experience'. Paper presented to the ACAS Wales Conference on Industrial Change, Swansea, 11 November.

Mitchell, T. and Larson, J. (1987), *People in Organizations* (3rd edn), London, McGraw-Hill.

Miyano, S. (1990), 'The Labour Unions', in National Defense Counsel for Victims of *Karoshi, Karoshi: When the Corporate Warrior Dies*, Tokyo, Mado-Sha, pp. 77–83.

Monden, Y. (1981a), 'What Makes the Toyota Production System Really Tick?' *Industrial Engineering Magazine*, January, pp. 36–46.

Monden, Y. (1981b), 'Adaptable Kanban System Helps Toyota Maintain Just-in-Time Production', *Industrial Engineering Magazine*, May, pp. 29–46.

Monden, Y. (1983), *Toyota Production System*, Georgia, US, Industrial Engineering and Management Press.

Moore, J. B. (1987), 'Japanese Industrial Relations', *Labour and Industry*, vol. 1, no. 1, pp. 140–55.

Morioka, K. (1990), 'The Life Style of Japanese Workers', in National Defense Counsel for Victims of *Karoshi, Karoshi: When the Corporate Warrior Dies*, Tokyo, Mado-Sha, pp. 64–76.

Morishima, M. (1982), *Why has Japan 'Succeeded'? Western Technology and the Japanese Ethos*, Cambridge, Cambridge University Press.

Morris, J. (1988a), 'The Who, Why and Where of Japanese Manufacturing Investment in the UK', *Industrial Relations Journal*, vol. 19, no. 1, pp. 31–40.

Morris, J. (1988b), *Japanese Companies in Britain*. Unpublished survey results, Cardiff Business School.

Morris, J. (1988c), 'The Japanese Are Here: For Better or Worse?' *Welsh Economic Review*, vol. 1, no. 1, pp. 45–7.

Morris, J. and Imrie, R. (1991), *The End of Adversarialism? The Adaptation of Japanese-Style Buyer–Supplier Relations in a Western Context*, London, Macmillan.

Nakane, C. (1973), *Japanese Society*, Harmondsworth, Penguin.

Naylor, L. (1984), 'Bringing Home the Lessons', *Personnel Management*, vol. 16, no. 3, pp. 34–7.

NEDO (1986), *Changing Work Patterns – How Companies Achieve Flexibility to Meet the New Needs*, London, NEDO.

Nishiguchi, T. (1989), 'Is JIT really JIT?' Paper presented to the IMVP International Policy Forum, Pierre Marques, Acapulco, 7–10 May.

Ohmae, K. (1983), 'Japan's Admiration for US Business', *Asian Wall Street Journal*, 11 October.

Ohno, T. (1988), *Just-in-Time for Today and Tomorrow*, Cambridge, MA, Productivity Press.

Okumura, A. (1989), 'The Globalization of Japanese Companies', in Shibagaki, K., Trevor, M. and Abo, T. (eds), *Japanese and European Management: Their International Adaptability*, Tokyo, University of Tokyo Press, pp. 31–40.

Okumura, A. (1990), 'Keiretsu Flaws and Merits', *Japan Times*, 30 July.

Okumura, A. (1991), 'Enterprise Groups in Japan', *Financial Digest*, no. 4, Japan Credit Rating Agency, pp. 1–4.

Oliver, N. (1986), *Computers and Quality*, PT 622, unit 3, Milton Keynes, Open University Press.

Oliver, N. (1987), 'The Evolution of Recycles Ltd', *CRU Case Study* no. 9, Milton Keynes, Open University Press.

Oliver, N. (1990), 'Human Factors and the Implementation of JIT', *International Journal of Operations and Production Management*, vol. 10, no. 4, pp. 33–41.

Oliver, N. (1991), 'The Dynamics of Just-in-time', *New Technology, Work and Employment*, vol. 6, no. 1, pp. 19–27.

Oliver, N. and Davies, A. (1990), 'Implementing Japanese Manufacturing Techniques: A Tale Of Two (UK) Factories', *Journal of Management Studies*, vol. 27, no. 5, September, pp. 555–70.

Oliver, N. and Wilkinson, B. (1988), *The Japanization of British Industry*, Oxford, Basil Blackwell.

Oliver, N. and Wilkinson, B. (1992), 'Japanization: The Experience from the Car Industry', in Legge, K., Clegg, C. and Gowler, D. (eds), *Cases in Organizational Behaviour*, forthcoming.

Oliver, N., Morris, J. and Wilkinson, B. (1992), 'The Impact of Japanese Direct Investment on European Industry', in Young, S. and Hamill, J. (eds), *Europe and the Multinationals: Issues and Responses for the 1990s*, Oxford, Edward Elgar.

Orru, M. (1990), *Institutional Cooperation in Japanese and German Capitalism*, Programme in East Asian Business and Development, Working Paper Series, no. 35, Institute of Governmental Affairs, University of California, Davis.

Ouchi, W. (1981), *Theory Z: How American Business Can Meet the Japanese Challenge*, Boston, Addison Wesley.

Oxford Motor Industry Research Project and Oxford Polytechnic (1991), Workshop on New Management Techniques.

Palmer, G. and Allen, C. (1989), 'The Sociology of Quality Management and its Interface with Employment Relations'. Paper presented to the Third International APROS Colloquium on 'Organizations, Technologies and Cultures in Comparative Perspective', Australian National University, Canberra, 13–15 December.

Pang, K. K. (1987), *Japanese Management Practices in Overseas Subsidiaries: A Case Approach*. MBA dissertation for Cardiff Business School.

Pang, K. K. and Oliver, N. (1988), 'Personnel Strategy in Eleven Japanese Manufacturing Companies in the UK', *Personnel Review*, vol. 17, no. 3, pp. 16–21.

Parnaby, J. (1986), 'The Japanese Systems Engineering Approach', Lucas Industries Internal Document.

Parnaby, J. (1987a), 'Competitiveness via Total Quality of Performance', *Progress in Rubber and Plastics Technology*, vol. 3, no. 1, pp. 42–50.

Parnaby, J. (1987b), 'A Systems Engineering Approach to Fundamental Change in Manufacturing'. Paper presented to the 9th Industrial Engineering Managers' Conference, New Orleans, 9–11 March.

Parnaby, J. (1987c), 'Practical Just-in-time – Inside and Outside the Factory'. Paper presented to the Fifth *Financial Times* Manufacturing Forum, London, 6–7 May.

Parnaby, J. and Bignell, V. (1986), 'Manufacturing Systems: Concept Design', in PT 611, *The Structure and Design of Manufacturing Systems*, unit 6, Milton Keynes, Open University Press.

Pascale, R. (1984), 'Fitting New Employees into the Company Culture', *Fortune International*, vol. 109, no. 11, pp. 62–9.

Pascale, R. and Athos, A. (1982), *The Art of Japanese Management*, Harmondsworth, Penguin.

Paton, R. (1983), *Coping with Uncertainty*, PT 244, unit 12, Milton Keynes, Open University Press.

Peach, L. H. (1983), 'Employee Relations in IBM', *Employee Relations*, vol. 5, no. 3, pp. 17–20.

Pegge, T. (1986), 'Hitachi Two Years On', *Personnel Management*, October, pp. 42–7.

Peters, T. and Waterman, R. (1982), *In Search of Excellence*, New York, Harper and Row.

Pfeffer, J. (1981), *Power in Organizations*, Boston MA, Pitman Publishing.

Piore, M. and Sabel, C. (1984), *The Second Industrial Divide*, New York, Basic Books.

Pollert, A. (1988), 'Dismantling Flexibility', *Capital and Class*, no. 34, Spring, pp. 42–75.

Potts, D. (1986), 'Just-in-time Improves the Bottom Line', *Engineering Computers*, September, pp. 55–60.

Pucik, V. (1985), 'Managing Japan's White-collar Workers', *Euro-Asia Business Review*, vol. 4, no. 3, pp. 16–21.

Pugh, D. S. and Hickson, D. J. (1976), *Organizational Structure in its Context: The Aston Programme I*, Farnborough, Saxon House.

Radford, G. D. (1989), 'How Sumitomo Transformed Dunlop Tyres', *Long Range Planning*, vol. 22, no. 3, pp. 28–33.

Rajan, A. (1987), *Services: The Second Industrial Revolution*. Report by the Institute of Manpower Studies to the Occupational Services Group, London, Butterworths.

Ramsey, H. (1983), 'An International Participation Cycle: Variations on a Recurring Theme', in Clegg, S. et al. (eds), *The State, Class and the Recession*, New York, St Martins Press, pp. 257–317.

Ramsey, J. (1985), 'Just Too Late?' *Purchasing and Supply Management*, January, pp. 22f.

Rawlinson, M., McArdle, L., Hassard, J., Procter, S. and Forrester, P. (1991), 'The Changing Face of Industrial Democracy: Evidence from the UK Electronics Industry'. Paper presented to the Annual Conference of the Employment Research Unit, Cardiff Business School, UWCC, 17–18 September.

Regional Trends 22 (1987), London, HMSO.

Rehder, R. (1990), 'Japanese Transplants: After the Honeymoon', *Business Horizons*, January–February, pp. 87–98.

Reitsperger, W. (1986), 'Japanese Management: Coping with British Industrial Relations', *Journal of Management Studies*, vol. 23, no. 1, pp. 72–88.

Robbins, S. (1983), 'Theory Z from a Power–Control Perspective', *California Management Review*, vol. 25, no. 2, pp. 67–75.

Rover Group Purchasing (1991), 'Supplier's Guide to Total Customer Satisfaction'.

Sako, M. (1987), 'Buyer–Supplier Relationships in Britain: A Case of Japanization?' Paper presented to the Conference on the Japanization of British Industry, Cardiff Business School, 17–18 September.

Salmon, J. (1991), 'The Future of Trade Unionism in the Japanese Electronics Industry'. Paper presented to the Annual Conference of the Employment Research Unit, Cardiff Business School, UWCC, 17–18 September.

Saso, M. (1990), *Women in the Japanese Workplace*, London, Hilary Shipman.

Sayer, A. (1984), *Method in Social Science: A Realist Perspective*, London, Hutchinson.

Sayer, A. (1986), 'New Developments in Manufacturing: The Just-in-Time System', *Capital and Class*, 30, Winter, pp. 43–72.

Schonberger, R. (1982), *Japanese Manufacturing Techniques*, New York, The Free Press.

Schonberger, R. (1986), *World Class Manufacturing*, New York, The Free Press.

Sethi, S., Namiki, N. and Swanson, C. (1984), *The False Promise of the Japanese Miracle*, London, Pitman.

Slaughter, J. (1987), 'The Team Concept in the US Auto Industry'. Paper presented to the Conference on the Japanization of British Industry, Cardiff Business School, 17–18 September.

Smith, D. (1988), 'The Japanese Example in South West Birmingham', *Industrial Relations Journal*, vol. 19, no. 1, pp. 41–50.

Smith, R. (1990), 'Good Thinking, Good Product', *Purchasing and Supply Management*, June, pp. 17–21.

Sonnenburg, R. D. (1983), 'The MRP and Just-in-Time Marriage', *Proceedings of the 1983 American Production and Inventory Control Society Conference*, pp. 683–7.

Spiridion, R. H. (1987), *Personnel Management at IBM: Theory and*

Practice. MBA dissertation for Cardiff Business School, UWIST.

Starkey, K. and McKinlay, A. (1989), 'Beyond Fordism? Strategic Choice and Labour Relations in Ford UK', *Industrial Relations Journal*, vol. 20, pp. 93–100.

Steven, R. (1991), 'Structural Origins of Japan's Direct Foreign Investment', in Morris, J. (ed.), *Japan and the Global Economy*, London, Routledge, pp. 45–60.

Stirling, J. and Rainie, A. (1989), 'All is Changed but Nothing is Different'. Paper presented to the Conference of Socialist Economists, Sheffield Polytechnic, 7–9 July.

Sugimoro, Y., Kusonoki, F. C. and Uchikawa, S. (1977), 'Toyota Production System and Kanban System: Materialization of Just-in-Time and Respect-for-Human System', *International Journal of Production Research*, vol. 15, no. 6, pp. 553–64.

Swyngedouw, E. (1991), Presentation to the Oxford Motor Industry Research Project, Workshop on New Management Techniques, 19 January.

Tabata, H. (1989), *Changes in Plant Level Trade Union Organizations: A Case Study of the Automobile Industry*, University of Tokyo Institute of Social Science, Occasional Papers in Labour Problems and Social Policy, no. 3.

Takamiya, M. (1981), 'Japanese Multinationals in Europe: International Operations and their Public Policy Implications', *Columbia Journal of World Business*, Summer, pp. 5–17.

TGWU Region 10 and Northern College Research Unit (1987), *Change at Work*.

Thomas, R. and Oliver, N. (1991), 'Components Supplier Patterns in the UK Motor Industry', *International Journal of Management Science*, vol. 19, no. 6, pp. 609–16.

Townley, B. (1989), 'Selection and Appraisal: Reconstituting Social Relations?' in Storey, J. (ed.), *New Perspectives on Human Resource Management*, London, Routledge.

Trevor, M. (1988), *Toshiba's New British Company: Competitiveness Through Innovation*. Unpublished paper.

Trevor, M. and Christie, I. (1988), *Manufacturers and Suppliers in Britain and Japan*, London, Policy Studies Institute.

Turnbull, P. (1986), 'The "Japanization" of Production and Industrial Relations at Lucas Electrical', *Industrial Relations Journal*, vol. 17, no. 3, pp. 193–206.

Turnbull, P. (1987), 'The Limits to Japanization – Just-in-Time, Labour Relations and the UK Automotive Industry'. Paper presented to the Conference on the Japanization of British Industry, Cardiff Business School, 17–18 September.

Turnbull, P. (1988), 'The Limits to Japanization – Just-in-Time, Labour Relations and the UK Automotive Industry', *New Technology, Work and Employment*, vol. 3, no. 1, pp. 7–20.

Turpin, D. V. (1991), 'Gambare: "Never Say Die!" Why Japanese Companies Won't Give Up', *Perspectives for Managers*, International Institute for Management Development, no. 3, pp. 1–4.

Vehata, T. (1991), '*Karoshi* Due to Occupational Stress-Related Cardiovascular Injuries Among Middle-Aged Workers in Japan', *Journal of the Science of Labour*, vol. 67, no. 1, pp. 20–8.

Vliet, A. (1986), 'Where Lucas Sees the Light', *Management Today*, June.

Vogel, E. (1980), *Japan as Number One: Lessons for America*, Harvard, Harvard University Press.

Voss, C. (ed.) (1987), *Just-in-Time Manufacture*, London, IFS.

Voss, C. and Robinson, S. (1987), 'The Application of Just-in-Time Techniques', *International Journal of Operations and Production Management*, vol. 7, no. 4, pp. 46–52.

Waldron, D. (1989a), 'Factory Economics that Liberate your Idle Assets', *Works Management*, vol. 42, no. 3, pp. 42–5.

Waldron, D. (1989b), 'Material Free Flow Beats the Bottlenecks', *Works Management*, vol. 42, no. 5, pp. 48–53.

Ward, J. (1987), 'IBM', in Voss, C. (ed.) *Just-in-Time Manufacture*, London, IFS, pp. 365–73.

White, M. and Trevor, M. (1983), *Under Japanese Management: The Experience of British Workers*, London, Heinemann.

Whitehill, A. and Takezawa, S. (1986), *The Other Worker*, Honolulu, East–West Centre Press.

Wickens, P. (1985), 'Nissan: the Thinking Behind the Union Agreement', *Personnel Management*, August, pp. 18–21.

Wickens, P. (1987), *The Road to Nissan*, London, Macmillan.

Wilkinson, B. and Smith, S. (1983), 'Management Strategies for Technical Change', *Science and Public Policy*, vol. 10, no. 2, pp. 56–61.

Wilkinson, B. and Leggett, C. (1985), 'Human and Industrial Relations in Singapore: the Management of Compliance', *Euro-Asia Business Review*, vol. 4, no. 3, pp. 9–15.

Wilkinson, B. and Oliver, N. (1989), 'Power, Control and the Kanban', *Journal of Management Studies*, vol. 26, no. 1, pp. 47–58.

Wilkinson, B. and Oliver, N. (1990), 'Obstacles to Japanization: the Case of Ford UK', *Employee Relations*, vol. 12, no. 1, pp. 17–21.

Williams, K., Williams, K. and Haslam, C. (1989), 'Why Take the Stocks Out? Britain vs Japan', *International Journal of Operations and Production Management*, vol. 9, no. 8, pp. 91–105.

Wolf, M. (1985), *The Japanese Conspiracy*, Sevenoaks, New English Library.

Womack, J. P., Jones, D. T. and Roos, D. (1990), *The Machine that Changed the World: The Triumph of Lean Production*, New York, Rawson Macmillan.

Wong, V., Saunders, J. and Doyle, P. (1987), 'Japanese Marketing Strategies in the United Kingdom', *Long Range Planning*, vol. 20, no. 6, pp. 54–63.

Wood, S. (1989), 'The Transformation of Work', in Wood, S. (ed.), *The Transformation of Work*, London, Unwin Hyman, pp. 1–43.

Wood, S. J. (1992), 'Japanization and/or Toyotaism?' *Work, Employment and Society*, vol. 5, no. 4, pp. 567–600.

Woodward, J. (1965), *Industrial Organization: Theory and Practice*, London, Oxford University Press.

Yamamoto, K. (1990), *The 'Japanese-Style Industrial Relations' and an 'Informal' Employee Organization: A Case Study of the Ohgi-Kai at T-Electric*, University of Tokyo Institute of Social Science, Occasional Papers in Labour Problems and Social Policy, no. 8.

Yap, F. (1984), *A Guide to Quality Control Circles and Work Improvement Teams*, Singapore, Aequitas Management Consultants.

Yu, C. and Wilkinson, B. (1989), *Pay and Appraisal in Japanese Companies in Britain*, Japanese Management Research Unit Working Paper no. 8, Cardiff Business School, UWCC.

Index